Flash™ MX ActionScript™ For Designers

Doug Sahlin

Wiley Publishing, Inc.

Best-Selling Books • Digital Downloads • e-Books • Answer Networks • e-Newsletters • Branded Web Sites • e-Learning

Flash™ MX ActionScript™ For Designers

Published by
Wiley Publishing, Inc.
909 Third Avenue
New York, NY 10022
www.wiley.com

Copyright © 2002 by Wiley Publishing, Inc., Indianapolis, Indiana

Library of Congress Control Number: 2002106038

ISBN: 0-7645-3687-7

Manufactured in the United States of America

10 9 8 7 6 5 4 3 2 1

1O/QR/QX/QS/IN

Published by Wiley Publishing, Inc., Indianapolis, Indiana
Published simultaneously in Canada

For general information on our other products and services or to obtain technical support, please contact our Customer Care Department within the U.S. at 800-762-2974, outside the U.S. at 317-572-3993 or fax 317-572-4002.

Wiley also publishes its books in a variety of electronic formats. Some content that appears in print may not be available in electronic books.

Library of Congress Cataloging-in-Publication Data

Ⓦ**Wiley Publishing, Inc.** is a trademark of Wiley Publishing, Inc.

About the Author

Doug Sahlin is an author, graphic designer, and Web site designer living in Central Florida. He is the author of *Carrara 1 Bible, Carrara 1 For Dummies, Fireworks For Dummies, Macromedia Flash MX ActionScript For Dummies,* and several other books about graphics and Web design. His articles and tutorials have appeared in national publications and have been featured at Web sites devoted to graphics and Web design. Doug developed and authored an online Flash 4 course. When he's busy writing, his steadfast companion Niki the cat occupies a sliver of sunlight within arm's reach of the author. When he's not writing books, he designs Web sites for his clients. When he manages to find a spare moment or two, Doug enjoys photography, playing his guitar, or curling up with a good mystery novel.

For Emily, I know you're out there somewhere.

Credits

Preface

Flash MX is the predominant choice for Web designers who want to create interactive designs for their clients. With more features than ever before, Flash is a total Web publishing solution. With Flash MX, you can now include video in your designs. The total number of available actions has more than doubled with this major Flash upgrade.

The Flash Player is included with every computer operating system and the most popular Web browsers. With a user base of 442,692,972 installed Flash Players as of May 2, 2002, it's no wonder Web designers and developers using Flash practice the fine art of one-upmanship for their clients. With such a large a user-base, all Web designers need to know how to use Flash if they are to get their fair share of this immense pie.

Flash MX ActionScript For Designers will show you how to harness the power of ActionScript. If you've wanted to come up to speed with ActionScript but the sheer volume of available actions caused you to stick with the tried-and-true Flash animation methods, you'll find the answers to many of your questions in this book. I show you how to use the basic actions to control the flow of your design. Even though ActionScript can be daunting, the basics of ActionScript's Object Oriented Programming are presented in easy-to-understand layman's terms.

The primary focus of this book is to show you how to use ActionScript to add excitement and diversity to your designs. If you've wanted to take the next step and push the envelope with ActionScript, you have the right book in your hands. Throughout this book you'll find concise examples of ActionScript at work — examples that you can put to use in your daily work. In addition, many chapters feature a project that shows you how to use the material to create a finished object with ActionScript.

Who Should Read This Book

This book was written with the designer in mind. Even if you already know a bit of basic ActionScript, the techniques and material presented in this book will help you take your work to the next level.

As a rule, designers are right-brained people who shy away from the cold hard logic of programming and code. If you fall into that category, you'll be pleased to know that ActionScript is approachable, even for the code-challenged. In this book you'll be exposed to concepts and theory that give you a firm background of what you can and cannot do with ActionScript. And as you will find out, the cannots are limited largely by your imagination.

If you're ready to combine your artistic talent and imagination with the power of ActionScript, you'll find many things to whet your appetite in this book. If you've ever wondered how the hotshot designers make their magic with Flash, you'll find some of the answers in this book.

How This Book Is Organized

This book is organized into four parts, plus three appendixes.

Part I: Comprehending the Mechanics of ActionScript

This first part of the book discusses the theory behind ActionScript. When you started out designing Web pages, you had to learn all about pixels and resolution. This part of the book is no different than your basic graphic design information. It shows you the ActionScript equivalent of pixels and resolution, the actions themselves, and the tools you use to turn them into a little bit of magic. In this section, you'll get a formal introduction to the main tool you use to create ActionScript: the Actions panel. You'll also get a brief tour of the Actions panel and learn some techniques for planning an ActionScript design.

Part II: Using Basic ActionScript in Your Movie

In this part of the book, you walk down the steps into the shallow end of the pool. You'll take your first foray into ActionScript by learning to use the basic actions to control the flow of your designs. You'll also learn how to divide a potential bandwidth breaking design into byte-sized pieces.

Part III: Creating ActionScript Elements for Your Movie

The third part of this book focuses on creating the elements you can use to make the objects in your designs jump through the virtual hoop, so to speak. If you've ever wondered how to create a button that's animated, yet the animation is not predictable, you'll learn how in this section. If you've seen pop-up menus and thought they were okay but not the bee's knees, wait until you see the flyout menu project in this section. And if you need more, there's part four.

Part IV: Building Additional Design Elements for Your Movie

In this fourth part, you'll start using some of the theory and logic from the earlier sections to create elements you can use in your own work. You'll learn how to create a background full of sparkling stars that won't break the bandwidth barrier of your user's connection. You'll also learn to create eye candy such as a moving slide show that stops when the users move their cursors over the moving images and motion trails that fade off into the background. You'll also learn how to integrate Flash with your HTML work.

Appendixes

The final section of the book is devoted to three appendixes:

✦ **Appendix A: What's on the CD-ROM** details the contents of the CD, from the author-created materials to the applications and software available for your use as you work your way through the book.

✦ **Appendix B: Flash Resources** is a roadmap to sources of Flash information on the Internet. In this section you'll find the URLs to sites where you can find additional tutorials and examples of ActionScript at work.

✦ **Appendix C: Flash Inspiration** is a list of Web sites designed by ActionScript gurus. If you've ever been at a loss for a new idea, a quick trip to one of the sites in this section will get your creative juices flowing.

How to Approach This Book

If you're completely new to ActionScript, read this book from cover to cover. The theory parts of the book may not be awe inspiring, but in order to create awe-inspiring designs with ActionScript, it is often necessary to crawl before you walk.

If you've got some experience with ActionScript, but need to hone your skills, feel free to jump to the sections that interest you the most. If you're interested in learning new concepts, try out some of the chapter projects. Here you'll find full-fledged projects that guide you from start to finish. Much of the work has already been done for you, but the ActionScript has been left in your creative hands, with a little help from the author.

If you want cookbook recipes you can use immediately in your work, check out the various chapter projects. The projects presented are clear-cut examples of ActionScript at work. Modify them with your own artistic touch and make them your own.

Conventions Used in This Book

Each chapter in this book begins with a heads-up of the topics covered in the chapter and ends with a section called Designer Notes that summarizes the information you should have learned by reading the chapter and gives you an idea of what to expect next.

Throughout this book, you will find icons in the margins that highlight special or important information. Keep an eye out for the following:

 Cross-Reference icons point to additional information about a topic, which you can find in other sections of the book.

 A Note icon contains additional information about the topic of discussion. In fact, you can use notes and tips to locate sections of interest if you're in a hurry.

 The On the CD-ROM icon is your signpost to the raw materials for a chapter project. When you see this icon, you'll be directed to a folder and a file that contains the raw material for the project you'll finish.

 When you see a Tip icon, you'll find information that will streamline your work with ActionScript, as well as handy shortcuts to speed up your production.

In addition to the icons listed previously, the following typographical conventions are used throughout the book:

+ Code examples appear in a courier font.

+ Actions are designated as follows: `goto`.

+ When you are required to enter code in an ActionScript text box, the required entry will be designated as **bold text**.

+ You'll see many examples of ActionScript code shown in a listing.

+ The Actions panel's got lots of books. And some of these books have books within a book. To add some actions to your scripts, you have to click this book icon, then click that book icon, then click another book icon, and so on. Rather than bore you with a lot of words, I'm going to show the path to each action as shown in the following example: Click Actions➪Movie Control and then double-click `goto`.

Acknowledgments

Even though one person's name appears on the cover of this book, a project of this magnitude would not be possible without the concerted effort of many. Thanks to the fine folks at Wiley Publishing for giving me the opportunity to bring this project to fruition. Special thanks to Acquisitions Editor Tom Heine for working out the fine points of the concept and content.

As always, thanks to the lovely and talented Margot Maley Hutchinson for ironing out the fine print in the contract. You're a gem, Margot. Speaking of gems, another young lady played a large part in this production. Kudos to the effervescent and ebullient Andrea Boucher, Project Editor extraordinaire, and just another example of why blonde-haired people will soon rule the universe. Thank you for your steadfast, guiding hand and kind words of encouragement when the going got tough. Thanks to Marisa Pearman, Wiley Media Development Specialist, for employing her magic on the creation of this book's CD-ROM. Many thanks to the vendors who contributed software for this CD-ROM.

Special thanks to the Macromedia Flash MX development team and all of the creative people at Macromedia. Thank you for your continued support of authors and for producing the best Web design software on the planet. Special thanks to the wild and wacky members of the Flash community, people who survive on but a few hours sleep and offer support beyond measure to fellow Flash users and authors. You people are truly amazing.

As always, thanks to my mentors, friends, and family, especially you, Ted and Karen. Congratulations to Karen and Shel on their recent marriage. And thank you Karen and Shel for the wonderful memories of St. John. Special thanks to a lovely lady who will live on always in my memory: my dear mother Inez. She provided the wind in my sails when I was a young boy and used her gentle wisdom to guide me, and yet at the same time allowed me to become the individual that I am. I wish you were here to share this with me.

Contents at a Glance

Preface v
Acknowledgments ix

Part I: Comprehending the Mechanics of ActionScript 1
CHAPTER 1: Introducing ActionScript for Designers 3
CHAPTER 2: Delving into Your ActionScript Toolkit 19
CHAPTER 3: Planning Your ActionScript Movie 51

Part II: Using Basic ActionScript in Your Movie 63
CHAPTER 4: Charting the Timeline of Your Movie 65
CHAPTER 5: Creating Basic Interactivity 81
CHAPTER 6: Creating Elements for Your Movie 97
CHAPTER 7: Taking Control of Your Movie 119
CHAPTER 8: Creating Variables to Store and Dispense Information 141

Part III: Creating ActionScript Elements for Your Movie 165
CHAPTER 9: Generating ActionScript to Modify Objects 167
CHAPTER 10: Designing Interactive Navigation 189
CHAPTER 11: Composing Dynamic Text 209
CHAPTER 12: Building Interactive Interfaces 231
CHAPTER 13: Creating ActionScript Sound Objects 257
CHAPTER 14: Debugging an ActionScript 283

Part IV: Building Additional Design Elements for Your Movie 295
CHAPTER 15: Building Web Site Elements with ActionScript 297
CHAPTER 16: Creating Flash Eye Candy 315
CHAPTER 17: Integrating Flash with HTML 339
Appendix A: What's on the CD-ROM 357
Appendix B: Flash Resources 363
Appendix C: Flash Inspiration 369

Index 375
End-User License Agreement 389

Contents

● ●

Preface v

Acknowledgments ix

Part I: Comprehending the Mechanics of ActionScript   1

Chapter 1: Introducing ActionScript for Designers 3

Why Designers Need ActionScript 4
   Managing movie content with ActionScript 4
   Storing and dispensing information with variables 5
   Creating visual effects with ActionScript 6
   Modifying design elements with ActionScript 6
   Other uses for ActionScript 7
Decoding Object-Oriented Scripting 7
Understanding How ActionScript Works 8
Using ActionScript as a Design Element 12
When to Use ActionScript 16

Chapter 2: Delving into Your ActionScript Toolkit 19

Surveying the Actions Panel 20
Essential Actions for Designers 21
   Exploring the Actions book 21
   Exploring the Operators book 24
   Delving into the Functions book 25
   Exploring the Constants book 25
   Modifying objects with the Properties book 25
   Exploring the Objects book 25
   Dealing with Deprecated actions 26
   Using actions from the Flash UI Components book 26
   Using actions from the Index book 26
Adding Actions to Your Documents 27
   Working in modes 28
   Adding an action to your script 29
   Using the parameter text boxes 30
   Deleting an action from your script 31
   Changing the hierarchy of actions 31
   Navigating to scripts with the Script window 31
   Pinning a script 32
   Finding and replacing text in a script 32
   Using the ActionScript Reference panel 33

Changing your viewing options 35
Using the Actions panel Options menu 35
Creating ActionScript in expert mode 36
Using the Actions panel context menu 37
Understanding ActionScript conventions 37
Understanding Symbol Types 42
About the button symbol 42
About the graphics symbol 42
About the movie clip symbol 43
About the component symbol 43
About the Document Library 43
Chapter Project: Creating Your First ActionScript 44

Chapter 3: Planning Your ActionScript Movie **51**
The Evolution of an ActionScript 52
Planning Your Design 55
Getting inspired 55
Drafting your design 56
Mapping your ActionScript 57
Fleshing Out Your Idea 58
Gathering your assets 58
Saving time with extensions 59
Chapter Project: Drawing Outside the Lines 60

Part II: Using Basic ActionScript in Your Movie   **63**

Chapter 4: Charting the Timeline of Your Movie **65**
Controlling the Timeline 66
Working with frames 66
Creating an Actions layer 69
Adding comments to keyframes 70
Allocating Actions to a Frame 70
Creating Buttons 72
Adding a button to your document 72
About button states 73
Creating an invisible button 74
Assigning actions to a button 74
Navigating with ActionScript 76
Using the stop action 76
Using the play action 76
Using the goto action 77
Using the getURL action 77
Using JavaScript to open an HTML page in a
different size window 79

Chapter 5: Creating Basic Interactivity 81

Creating Movie Clips 81
   Using movie clips for interactive content 82
   Importing a video file into a movie clip 84
   Creating instances of movie clips 86
   Labeling the movie clip with the Property inspector 86
Assigning Actions to an Object 87
   About clip events 87
   Using the with action 89
Assigning Actions to a Button 91
   About mouse events 92
   Using the Key Press mouse event 93
   Using the on action 94
   Using buttons for navigation 95
   Using buttons for interactivity 95

Chapter 6: Creating Elements for Your Movie 97

Working with Symbols 98
   Converting a graphic to a symbol 98
   Converting a timeline animation to a movie clip 98
   Nesting symbols 99
   Swapping symbols 101
   Swapping bitmaps 101
Creating Loops 102
   Looping frames 103
   Creating ActionScript loops 103
Generating Random Numbers 107
   Using the random method of the Math object 107
   Rounding numbers 109
Saving Time with Functions 110
   Creating a function 110
   Calling a function 112
Creating Modular ActionScript 113
Chapter Project: Navigating to a Random Frame 114
   Creating a function to generate a random frame number 114
   Putting the function to work 116

Chapter 7: Taking Control of Your Movie 119

Breaking Movies into Segments 119
   Dividing a Flash site into individual movies 120
   Understanding levels 121
   Creating movies for site sections 121
Using the loadMovie and unloadMovie Actions 123
   Loading a movie 123
   Unloading a movie 124

Loading a Different-Sized Movie into a Target 125
  Creating a target movie clip 125
  Loading a movie into a target 127
Communicating between Timelines 129
Demystifying Targets and Paths 130
  Using Absolute mode 131
  Using Relative mode 131
Introducing the User-Defined Component 132
Chapter Project: Creating an Organizational Chart 135
  Beginning the design 136
  Creating the ActionScript 137

**Chapter 8: Creating Variables to Store and
Dispense Information 141**
Understanding Variable Types 142
  About string data 143
  About expressions 144
  Creating mathematical expressions 145
  About operator precedence 146
Creating a Variable 147
  Naming a variable 147
  Declaring a variable 148
  Creating a local variable 149
  Passing a variable's value to other objects 150
Storing Data with an Array 151
  Creating an array 152
  Creating elements for an array 153
  Creating an associative array 154
Working with Conditional Statements 155
  Creating conditional statements 156
  Working with conditional statements that have
    multiple outcomes 156
Using Logical Operators 158
Working with Boolean Expressions 159
Chapter Project: Generating Random Quotes 160
  Generating the random number 161
  Adding a timer and accessing the array 161
  Finishing the project 163

**Part III: Creating ActionScript Elements
          for Your Movie   165**

Chapter 9: Generating ActionScript to Modify Objects 167
Modifying an Object's Properties 168
  Setting an object's properties 168
  Using the setProperty action 170

Modifying an object by addressing its target path 171
Getting an object's properties 173
Using the Color Object 175
Creating a Color object 175
Modifying an object's color 175
Using the Key Object 180
Duplicating an Object Using the duplicateMovieClip Action 182
Chapter Project: Creating an Interactive Animation 183

Chapter 10: Designing Interactive Navigation 189

Navigating to Scenes 189
Adding a scene 190
Naming a scene 190
Navigating to a scene 191
Deleting a scene 191
Duplicating a scene 192
Rearranging scene order 192
Using Named Anchors 193
Creating a named anchor 193
Publishing a document with named anchors 193
Creating an On When Pressed Button 194
Creating a Navigation Bar 196
Creating a label template 197
Creating a button template 197
Building the navigation bar 199
Creating an Animated Button 199
Creating the movie clip 200
Creating the ActionScript to animate the label 200
Nesting the movie clip in a button symbol 203
Chapter Project: Creating a Flyout Menu 204

Chapter 11: Composing Dynamic Text 209

Creating Flashy Text with the Property Inspector 209
Creating input text boxes 210
Creating dynamic text boxes 211
Setting character options 212
Creating rich formatted text 213
Loading Text from External Sources 215
Creating text data 216
Using the loadVariables action 216
Creating an E-Mail Link 216
Chapter Project: Creating a Scrolling Text Box 217
Programming the down arrow 218
Deciphering the rest of the code 221
Creating a Text Hyperlink 223
Populating Dynamic Text with Array Elements 224
Chapter Project: Creating a Ticker Text Marquee 225

Chapter 12: Building Interactive Interfaces 231

Building Tooltips 231
Creating the tooltips 232
Creating the tooltip functions 235
Programming the buttons 237
Creating Drag-and-Drop Elements 238
Creating a drag-and-drop window 239
Closing a window 240
Creating a User Customizable Interface 241
Telling Time with ActionScript 245
Creating a Date object 245
Displaying the current date 246
Displaying the current time 247
Using the ScrollBar Component 249
Chapter Project: Creating a Moving Navigation Bar 251

Chapter 13: Creating ActionScript Sound Objects 257

Creating a Soundtrack 257
Importing a sound 258
Creating a custom effect 260
Modifying export settings 263
Creating a Movie with Interactive Sound 266
Creating a soundtrack movie 266
Loading the soundtrack into your design 267
Using the Sound Object 268
Creating an instance of the Sound object 268
Working with sound from the document Library 268
Attaching a sound 269
Starting a sound 270
Stopping a sound 271
Changing a sound's volume 272
Panning a sound 273
Triggering an event with the onSoundComplete event 273
Chapter Project: Creating a Sound Controller 274
Adding the sliders 275
Programming the movie clip 277

Chapter 14: Debugging an ActionScript 283

Testing Your Design 284
Using the Debugger 285
Watching a variable 286
Displaying a list of movie objects 287
Displaying a list of variables in the movie 288

Using the Trace Action 288
Stopping the Movie with Breakpoints 290
    Setting a breakpoint 290
    Debugging a movie with breakpoints 290
Tracking ActionScript with Comments 292
Using the Movie Explorer 293

Part IV: Building Additional Design Elements for Your Movie   295

Chapter 15: Building Web Site Elements with ActionScript 297

Creating an Animated Preloader 298
    Analyzing your movie 299
    Creating the preloader 302
Creating a Flash Form 306
    Creating the form elements 306
    Creating ActionScript for the Reset button 308
    Creating ActionScript for the Submit button 308
Creating a Printable Frame 310
Chapter Project: Create an E-Commerce Catalog 312

Chapter 16: Creating Flash Eye Candy 315

Creating a Mouse Chaser 315
Creating an ActionScript Mouse Chaser 318
Creating a Mask with ActionScript 321
Using the Mouse Object 324
Creating a Custom Cursor 325
Creating Motion Trails 326
Creating a Starburst Backdrop 330
Chapter Project: Creating a Flash Slide Show 334

Chapter 17: Integrating Flash with HTML 339

Creating a Pop-Up Window with JavaScript 339
Creating Banner Ads 341
Detecting the Flash Player 345
Creating a Flash Introduction 346
Integrating Flash with Dreamweaver 348
Chapter Project: Creating an Animated Flash Banner 352
Where to Go from Here 355

Appendix A: What's on the CD-ROM **357**

Appendix B: Flash Resources **363**

Appendix C: Flash Inspiration **369**

Index 375

End-User License Agreement 389

Comprehending the Mechanics of ActionScript

◆ ◆ ◆ ◆

In This Part

Chapter 1
Introducing
ActionScript for
Designers

Chapter 2
Delving into Your
ActionScript Toolkit

Chapter 3
Planning Your
ActionScript Movie

◆ ◆ ◆ ◆

Introducing ActionScript for Designers

✦ ✦ ✦ ✦

In This Chapter

Understanding why designers need ActionScript

Decoding object-oriented scripting

Understanding how ActionScript works

Using ActionScript as a design element

Figuring out when to use ActionScript

✦ ✦ ✦ ✦

Web site designers tend to avoid like the plague anything resembling programming code. Web site developers, on the other hand, like the cold, hard logic of code with names like JavaScript, PERL, and CGI. When Web site designers use Flash as a tool for animation, they also have a tendency to shy away from Flash's programming language, ActionScript, using only the most basic actions to add minimum interactivity to their designs. Designers using Flash tend to populate their designs with pretty graphics, a text effect or two, and tweened animations. However, by not stretching the ActionScript envelope, many designers are missing the gusto and impact that can be part of a Flash Web design.

Web designers tend to be visually oriented, right-brained folks. They can visualize a tastefully designed page and execute it quickly within a graphics program like Macromedia Fireworks that supports HTML export. Designers are also able to integrate JavaScript automatically with many Web authoring programs. Using programs that automatically generate JavaScript, Web designers can also add sophisticated effects like image swapping and button rollovers without having to learn complicated code.

With Flash ActionScript, you can choose to have code generated automatically. However, the designer can't just point and click to create the compelling effects you see at premier Web sites created by designers like Hillman Curtis or Juxt Interactive. In order to create the effects, you have to know which actions to include in your script and how to implement them. This is where many Web designers give up on all but the simplest actions. The programmers who designed Flash did an excellent job of creating an easy-to-use tool for scripting (the Actions panel), but let's face it, even a quick tour of this tool, with its dozens of books brimming with Actions, is enough to strike fear into the heart of a right-brained creative.

In this chapter, you learn the benefits of using ActionScript and when you should use ActionScript, as well as how ActionScript works both as a scripting language and a design element.

Note In Flash MX, there is an additional Actions book called Index. Instead of blindly plodding through each book searching for the right action, the Index book organizes every action alphabetically. In addition, there is also a Reference panel within the Actions panel that tells you what each action does and shows you the correct syntax for every action.

Why Designers Need ActionScript

The Internet is in a constant state of flux. What was new and exciting three months ago quickly becomes blasé as new tools and techniques are introduced. Pioneering Web developers — and some adventurous designers — embrace these new tools and techniques, learning and then applying them to their latest designs. These are the designers who get the high-paying assignments from prestigious clients such as major car manufacturers, fashion designers, and movie production companies. It's no secret that Flash is featured on most of the top Internet sites.

When a Flash movie is designed correctly, the file loads quickly into the user's browser and provides more entertainment than a static HTML Web page. In addition, a Flash movie is often a seamless experience for the user, flowing from one scene to the next without having to wait for another HTML page to download. Another advantage of a well-designed Flash movie is that it's a dynamic experience for the user. HTML pages can have embedded movies and animated graphics (but pages like these are not for the faint of bandwidth).

Managing movie content with ActionScript

If you've dabbled at all in Flash, you know that you can create a fair amount of action without taxing the bandwidth bank. Your Flash designs can entertain Web surfers with background music, sounds that play when buttons are clicked, and compelling animations. The extension for a published Flash movie is *SWF*, which stands for **S**mall **W**eb **F**ile. Indeed, a properly designed Flash production, when published, produces a small file that downloads quickly into the user's browser. However, many Flash designers go overboard and add so many bells and whistles that the published file — while impressively smaller than conventional HTML pages attempting to add the same bells and whistles — can become so large, most users are clicking the browser's Back button before the file fully loads.

This is where ActionScript can help you. You can break a large Flash production into multiple movies that the user can download on demand. This is a technique often used by prominent Web developers and designers to create a primo site for their client that keeps Web visitors coming back time and again.

You learn to take advantage of the multiple-movies technique in Chapter 7.

If any of your clients have a need for a Flash movie that needs frequent updating, you can use ActionScript to load text, images, and movies externally. When the site needs updating, you don't need to create a new movie — just refresh the text, image, or movies, upload the new content to the Web site, and your client is good to go. Your client need not know you used ActionScript to take the drudgery out of this task. Your client will appreciate the quick turnaround and pay you what you're worth.

You can write your ActionScript in a manner that makes it possible for you to reuse your best effects in another Flash movie. You create a movie clip with the effects you want to replicate in another movie. Then all you need to do is use the Flash Open As Library command, drag the movie clip into the current document, and you're ready to go.

I show you how to create modular ActionScript in Chapter 6.

Flash ActionScript also has an item you can use to create programmable objects. If you're familiar with Flash 5, you may recall the smart clip, which in essence is a movie clip with programmable parameters. In Flash MX, you have more versatility with the next generation of the smart clip known as a *user-defined component*. User-defined components are another item you can use to streamline your work. If you work with other designers, all they need to do is modify the parameters of your component to use it. You can also use this little gem for a movie that needs frequent updating. If, for example, you create an e-commerce site, you can create a component to store variables that change often, such as the price of an object. When it comes time to update the product, you merely modify the parameters in your component and republish the document.

See Chapter 7 for more on the powerful user-defined component.

Storing and dispensing information with variables

Another advantage of ActionScript is that you can design a movie to interact with the user. Through the use of *variables*, Flash ActionScript can store information from the user and dispense information on demand. You can use variables to create a personalized experience for the user by asking the user to enter a name and then displaying the user's name with a welcome message or with a congratulatory message upon achieving a high score after taking a quiz designed with Flash. You can also use variables to score games, keep track of an object's position on Stage, and send information.

You learn how to make the most of ActionScript variables in Chapter 8.

ActionScript also has an object called an *array*. An array is like a file cabinet filled with information. You can think of an array as a super-charged variable; instead of creating 20 variables to store product names, you create one array with 20 elements that stores this information. Then instead of having to remember the names of twenty variables, you remember the name of one array and the element number that houses the information. You can use arrays to store items like product names, prices, and descriptions to name a few.

Creating visual effects with ActionScript

In addition to managing large productions and storing and dispensing information, you can also use ActionScript to create exciting visual effects. If you've ever been to a Flash site and watched a small constellation of stars follow your mouse's every move, you've seen ActionScript at work. Special effects can be used to good effect when creating *preloaders*.

 Find out more about preloaders in Chapter 15.

Modifying design elements with ActionScript

When you add ActionScript to your designs, you have the ability to modify certain elements used in your design and add others. For example, you can use ActionScript to modify the color of an object in your design, alter a sound used in your design, or add the time and date to your productions.

 For information on working with the Color object, refer to Chapter 9. To learn how to work with the Date object, see Chapter 12.

One ActionScript element designers find invaluable is the TextField object. If you've ever designed a static HTML document with lots of text, you have two choices: a standard page where the menu disappears as user scrolls through the text, or a frames site where the menu stays in place as the text is scrolled, but when the user clicks another menu button, a new page must load, disrupting the flow of information. Using the TextField object, you can create a seamless experience for the user by constraining the text to a small box and providing buttons for the user to scroll forwards or backwards while all of the navigation elements stay in place.

 You learn how to create scrolling text in Chapter 11.

One of Flash's strong suits has always been the ability to add sound to a production. With ActionScript, you can take sound to the next level. You can design a movie that gives the user the ability to choose which sound plays while viewing your production. Add the ActionScript Sound object to the mix, and you give the user the ability to control the volume of the sound and control the balance of the sound between speakers.

Cross-Reference   Chapter 13 offers more information on using the Sound object.

Other uses for ActionScript

Multimedia is another area where Flash shines. In Flash MX, you can import video clips and export them as Flash movies. Add a bit of ActionScript to the equation and you give the movie viewer the option to load a video clip on demand.

Cross-Reference   You learn how to create movie clips and import video files in Chapter 5.

When you put your mind to it, the uses of ActionScript are potentially limitless. Instead of worrying about the lines and lines of code used to create some effects, follow the various tutorials in this book and use them in your own productions. As you become more conversant with ActionScript, let your right brain ramble, daydream, and come up with ideas you'd like to incorporate in your designs. After your inspiration strikes, use ActionScript to bring it to life on the Word Wide Web or within a CD-ROM production. By stretching the ActionScript envelope, you can expand your creativity in ways you never thought possible.

Decoding Object-Oriented Scripting

ActionScript is a programming language, make no mistake about it. As with most programming languages you have certain procedures you must follow in order for your scripts to execute properly. The types of scripts you create with ActionScript are object oriented, meaning that in ActionScript, you can apply your code only to these objects: a keyframe, a button, a movie clip, or a user-defined component.

✦ When you assign an action to a keyframe, the Flash Player executes the action when the frame is reached.

✦ When you assign an action to a button, you can choose to have the action execute based on the user's interaction with the button. For example, you may want the button to play a sound when the user's mouse rolls over the button and advance to a keyframe after the user clicks and releases the mouse button. Each of these actions occurs based on a different event, one being a rollover, the other being the release of a button.

✦ When you create an ActionScript for a movie clip, you also have control over when the code executes. You can also create your ActionScript in such a manner that different actions execute based on the event that occurs. You can have one set of actions occur when the movie clip loads and another set occur when the user clicks the mouse button within the movie clip's target area. The button and movie clip triggers for actions are known as *events*. For example, when you program code to occur when a user rolls a mouse over a button, the event is rollover. If you program an action with a movie clip and want it to execute when the user clicks a mouse over the clip's target area, the event is mouseDown.

You apply ActionScript to the aforementioned objects, and you also use ActionScript objects to get the job done. This may sound redundant, but it isn't. The ActionScript objects you use and the ensuing code you create make certain things happen. For example, if you want to modify a sound, you use the Sound object. If you want to retrieve the date and time from the host computer playing the published Flash movie, you use the Date object. Each object has methods that achieve certain results. For example, the Sound object has a method called *setVolume*, which, as the title suggests, is used to control the volume of a sound. Some objects also have properties. The Sound object has a property called *duration* that returns the amount of milliseconds the sound has been playing. You also find objects that have events, which you can use as a trigger for another action. The Sound object has an event called `onSoundComplete`. An example of a use for this property would be advancing to another frame once a descriptive narration has finished playing.

Understanding How ActionScript Works

If you've ever looked at a bit of JavaScript, you know that it often takes many lines of linear code to create an effect such as an image swap. With Flash ActionScript, you don't create a long linear script. Instead, you apply bits of code to each object you want to modify. For example, if you want to program a button to load external text, you apply a few lines of code to the button.

Listing 1-1 shows the JavaScript necessary to create an image swap. Fortunately, this code was generated automatically by a HTML authoring program. Complicated code like this is more than most designers are willing to learn. Compare the JavaScript code with the ActionScript in Listing 1-2. This script loads variables from an external text file when the user's mouse button interacts with the button; in this case, when the mouse button is released. You can quickly create ActionScript like this in the Actions panel.

Listing 1-1: **JavaScript Used to Create an Image Swap**

```
<script language="JavaScript">
<!--
function MM_findObj(n, d) { //v3.0
  var p,i,x; if(!d) d=document;
  if((p=n.indexOf("?"))>0&&parent.frames.length) {
  d=parent.frames[n.substring(p+1)].document;
  n=n.substring(0,p);}
  if(!(x=d[n])&&d.all) x=d.all[n];
  for (i=0;!x&&i<d.forms.length;i++) x=d.forms[i][n];
  for(i=0;!x&&d.layers&&i<d.layers.length;i++)
  x=MM_findObj(n,d.layers[i].document); return x;
```

```
}
   function MM_swapImage() { //v3.0
   var i,j=0,x,a=MM_swapImage.arguments; document.MM_sr=new Array;
   for(i=0;i<(a.length-2);i+=3)
   if ((x=MM_findObj(a[i]))!=null){document.MM_sr[j++]=x;
   if(!x.oSrc) x.oSrc=x.src; x.src=a[i+2];}
}
   function MM_preloadImages() { //v3.0
   var d=document; if(d.images){ if(!d.MM_p) d.MM_p=new Array();
   var i,j=d.MM_p.length,a=MM_preloadImages.arguments; for(i=0;
   i<a.length; i++)
   if (a[i].indexOf("#")!=0){ d.MM_p[j]=new Image;
   d.MM_p[j++].src=a[i];}}
}
//-->
</script>
```

Listing 1-2: **ActionScript Used to Load Variables**

```
on (release) {
    loadVariablesNum("intro.txt", 0);
}
```

If you examine the ActionScript in Listing 1-2, you see another important ActionScript element: the event. The first line of code in Listing 1-2 reads on(Release). The code following the Release event occurs when the user releases the mouse button. Events for buttons are known as mouse events; events for movie clips are called clip events. An event is known as a *code handler*. In other words, the code is handled (executed) when the event occurs. For example, the code on(Release) gotoAndPlay (2) instructs Flash to go to frame 2 and play the frame when the user releases the mouse button.

When you create a movie clip, you are creating an object that has its own timeline. A movie clip is a symbol stored in the document Library. When you create an instance of a symbol on Stage, you are creating an entity with its own timeline. When you create an action from the base timeline to transform the movie clip instance, you need to specify a path so that Flash knows where to find the movie clip. A path is similar to a URL address that instructs a Web browser where a linked page is located. An ActionScript path references the timeline, the *instance* name of the movie clip, and the individual part of the movie clip you want Flash to access when an event occurs, for example, an individual frame in the movie clip. In essence, you are supplying Flash with a path to the target, which is the named instance of a movie clip.

Cross-Reference   You learn how to assign paths to an action in Chapter 7.

You also need to reference the path to a variable you want Flash to read when an event occurs. For example, you may have a variable stored in a movie clip or perhaps in a user-defined component. Again, you must supply the proper path in order for Flash to know where the variable you want read is stored. You can also think of a path as the Flash equivalent of a Zip code. Fortunately, you don't have to type in each and every path when creating ActionScript. Flash stores the path to every named instance of a movie clip in a document within the Insert Target Path dialog box shown in Figure 1-1.

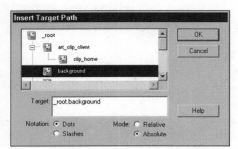

Figure 1-1: You insert target paths in your ActionScript from this dialog box.

With the most basic actions, you can control the flow of a movie, telling Flash which frame to go to when a user interacts with the movie. You can also use basic actions to load content upon demand. You can specify to load a movie, load variables, or load a JPEG image with ActionScript. You structure your ActionScript in a manner that Flash executes the desired action when the event triggered by the user occurs.

You can use other actions to change the properties of an object. For example, you can change the color of an object, move an object to a different position, change an object's opacity, and much more depending upon the actions you add to your script. Figure 1-2 shows an example of ActionScript at work. The figure in the left pane is the movie clip as originally created; the figure in the right pane has undergone a makeover through the magic of ActionScript.

Figure 1-2: You can modify the physical characteristics of an object with ActionScript.

Cross-Reference You learn how to change the properties of an object in Chapter 9.

Another powerful feature of ActionScript you can use is decision making. That's right, you can create ActionScript that determines what happens next based on user input or a change in one or more of an object's properties. A line of ActionScript that makes a decision based on an outcome is known in programmer speak as a *conditional statement*. The crux of a conditional statement can be summed up as follows: If these conditions are present, then this event happens. You can use a conditional statement to determine what happens next in your movie. Listing 1-3 shows an ActionScript that adds a zero in front of a variable named seconds if the variable's value is less than 10.

Listing 1-3: **An ActionScript Conditional Statement**

```
if (seconds<10) {
    seconds = "0"+seconds;
}
```

Another powerful element you can use in your ActionScript designs is the *loop*. With a loop, you can repeat an action a given number of times. Instead of rewriting the code you want to occur over and over, you simply create a loop that tells Flash how many times you want to code within the loop to execute. You can use loops to duplicate and move a movie clip. You can also use a loop to display the elements in an array. Figure 1-3 shows the result of a loop used to create a background of a moving starfields.

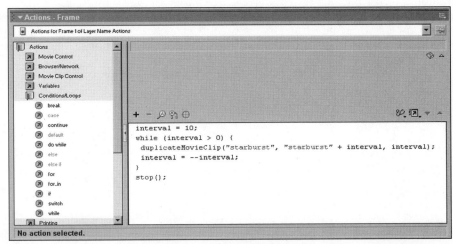

Figure 1-3: You use an ActionScript loop to repeat code a given number of times.

You learn how to create loops in Chapter 6.

Using ActionScript as a Design Element

When you have a spare moment, log on to the Internet, go to Macromedia's Web site (www.macromedia.com) and click the Showcase button. Click the Site of the Day link, and if the site was created with Flash, you'll probably see an example of ActionScript used as a design element.

You can use ActionScript to create a pop-up menu similar to the one shown in Figure 1-4. When you create a pop-up menu, you use tweening to create the motion and ActionScript to expand and contract the menu. You also use ActionScript to program the buttons within the menu. With a bit of additional code, you can create a menu that users can drag to a different part of the Stage.

Figure 1-4: You can use ActionScript to create a pop-up menu.

Another great use for ActionScript is creating interactive buttons. You've probably created rollover buttons for your HTML designs. However, with ActionScript, you can take a rollover button to the next level. You can create ActionScript that makes a tooltip appear when a user lingers over a button, as shown in Figure 1-5. You can create ActionScript to play a small movie when the user rolls a mouse over the button.

 In Chapter 12, I show you how to write ActionScript code for tooltips.

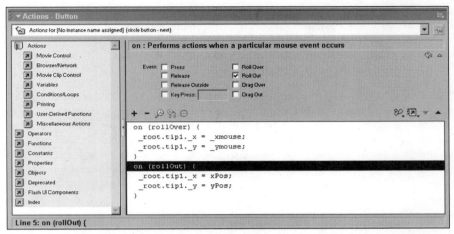

Figure 1-5: With a bit of ActionScript code, you can create useful elements for your designs.

You can also use ActionScript to create a modular interface. By creating a base movie with a few navigation buttons and a pop-up menu, you have the basis for many Flash productions. Using ActionScript components such as the user-defined component, you can change the button text when using the menu for a different production.

If you're really adventurous, you can use ActionScript to add eye candy to your designs. With a few lines of code, you can achieve stunning effects like mouse trails, motion trails, and animated backgrounds. If your design calls for an animated background, it's fairly easy to achieve with ActionScript. Figure 1-6 shows a motion trail effect you learn to create in Chapter 16.

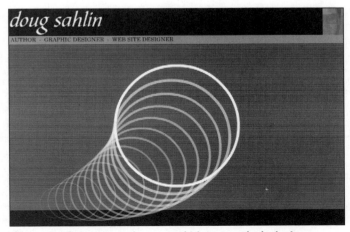

Figure 1-6: If you need eye candy for your Flash design, ActionScript is the answer.

ActionScript is also useful when you want to add bells and whistles to your design. Using the Date object, it's possible to incorporate the date and time to any movie you design. If you create all the code for your online clock in an individual movie clip, your Flash timepiece is modular; you can use it in other movies. You learn how to create modular ActionScript in Chapter 6.

If you design Flash movies for online merchants, you can use ActionScript to change the properties of the objects they sell. For example, you can use the Color object to modify the color of a ball cap, giving the user the ability to preview the product in available colors before purchase. You can also use ActionScript to create online forms and transmit the results of the form to the merchant. Figure 1-7 shows an example of an online Flash form. By combining Flash design elements with ActionScript and your own creativity, you can escape the humdrum forms that permeate HTML pages.

Cross-Reference   You learn how to create a Flash form in Chapter 15.

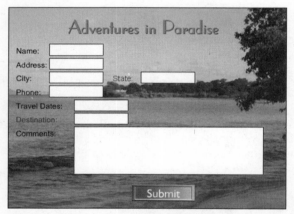

Figure 1-7: A form created with Flash can be a thing of beauty.

You can also integrate Flash movies with your HTML designs. If you have a client who wants a bit of Flash magic but isn't willing to cough up the coin for a full-fledged Flash design, you can create a compelling Flash intro that links to the site's home page. You can also create animated banners with Flash. A banner animated with Flash packs more punch than a traditional Animated GIF. With Flash you can create realistic motion instead of frame based animation, and you can add ActionScript elements such as programmable buttons to link the banner to another URL, or another part of the site. Figure 1-8 shows an animated Flash banner integrated with a static HTML page.

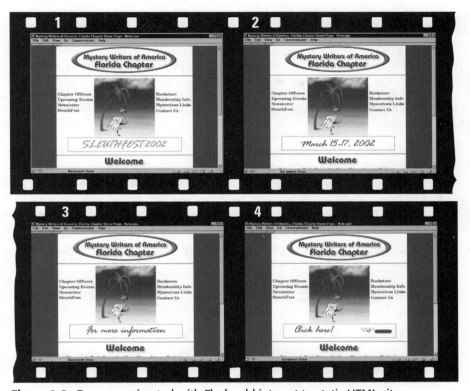

Figure 1-8: Banners animated with Flash add interest to static HTML sites.

Surfing for inspiration

Designers are creative people by nature, but sometimes the well runs dry. If you ever find yourself at a loss for a fresh idea, log on to the Internet and start surfing. You can make a first stop at the Macromedia Showcase (www.macromedia.com/showcase). If the site of the day is done in Flash, check it out. As a rule, these sites represent the latest effects possible with Flash. If the designer's site is also listed, take a look at it for further inspiration. If something catches your eye, do a thumbnail sketch of the effect and then try to figure out how it was done. If you don't find inspiration there, visit the Web sites of major manufacturers such as Nike Shoes, Ford, or Porsche, and you're sure to find some parts of the site were created with Flash. Remember that a Flash movie can be embedded with other HTML elements. Right-click (Windows) or Ctrl+click (Macintosh) while your cursor is over an effect. If you see the words "About Macromedia Flash Player . . ." the effect was done in Flash. After you finish surfing for inspiration, put your own creative twist on an effect you like and you've got something unique you can add to your own designs.

When to Use ActionScript

After you make the decision to create a Web site using Flash, you must then decide which Flash elements you are going to use when designing the site. As you are already aware, you can create an intriguing Flash site by using the standard timeline animation features. Whether or not you need to include ActionScript depends on a number of factors. Before you create the first graphic object for your design, provide the answers for the following questions:

✦ Do the elements in your design frequently change one or more properties, such as size, color, and opacity?

If the answer to this question is yes, you need ActionScript to modify the object's properties. You have limited control over properties such as an object's tint and opacity without using ActionScript; however, using these non-ActionScript techniques may bloat the file size of the finished movie.

✦ Does your client require that you frequently update text elements such as product descriptions?

If you answer yes to this question, you can create all of your text in an external .txt file and use the `loadVariables` action to enter the text data in a dynamic text box, a technique you learn in Chapter 11.

✦ Does your client require images used in the design to be updated frequently?

If so, you can use the `loadMovie` action to load a jpeg file into the movie. When the content needs to be updated, you merely replace the JPEG file with a different image but use the same file name, a technique you learn in Chapter 7.

✦ Does the movie you're creating contain a lot of bitmap images or embedded videos?

Flash movies with a lot of bitmap images and embedded videos can become very large. If the content needed for your movie prevents it from loading quickly, you'll need to break the movie down into sections. You learn how to use the `loadMovie` action to load additional content into the base movie in Chapter 7.

✦ Does your client require input from a user?

If the answer to this question is yes, you need to create variables as placeholders for the data that will be dispensed, and then use input text boxes to receive the data from the user. If the data is a form, you need to send the variables from the form to your client's site administrator.

✦ Does your client require a choice of background music for viewers of the finished movie?

If you answered yes, you need the `loadMovie` action. Without ActionScript, you can add looping background music to any Flash design. However, when you need to change selection based on user input, you need to create the necessary ActionScript to load a different background sound into the movie.

✦ Does your design involve a spoken narrative that must be coordinated with other content?

If the answer to this question is yes, you need the `onSoundComplete` method of the Sound object to trigger the next event upon termination of the narrative.

✦ After you decide to create an ActionScript movie, which items or keyframes will you need to create code for?

After you've answered these questions (and any you may have come up with on your own), you're ready to begin planning your ActionScript movie. Every designer has a different way of planning. In Chapter 3, I offer a few suggestions that have worked for me.

Note This list of questions is not all inclusive. You need to consider your specific situation, the actual content for your movie, and your client's requirements. After you've worked with ActionScript for a while, you know what other questions you need answered before beginning a new design project.

After you answer these questions, you may find that you don't know each and every action required to create the design. That's one of the beauties of ActionScript—you don't need to know it all, just enough to get the job done. When you run across an action you don't know or understand, refer to this book for the answer. Unfortunately, a detailed treatise and tutorial for each and every action in the Actions panel (there are approximately 800 actions in all, but who's counting) is beyond the scope of this book. If you need an action not covered in this book, refer to the Flash MX ActionScript Reference Guide that was shipped with your software.

Tip If you need to use an action you're not familiar with, you can also refer to the Reference panel from within Flash. Open the Actions panel and then click the icon that looks like a book with a question mark on its cover. After clicking the icon, Flash opens the Reference panel, which is a duplicate of every book in the Actions panel. Open a book, click the action you need to know about and Flash displays a description of the action along with required formatting syntax.

Designer Notes

In this chapter, you received your first taste of what ActionScript is and the power it can add to your designs. You also learned why designers need to know how to create ActionScript. In addition, you got a preview of the type of effects you can create with ActionScript as well as when you need to add ActionScript to your design. You also obtained an understanding of how ActionScript works. In the next chapter, you get your first look at the building blocks of ActionScript and also create your first ActionScript.

✦   ✦   ✦

Delving into Your ActionScript Toolkit

✦   ✦   ✦   ✦

In This Chapter

Exploring the
Actions panel

Essential actions
for designers

Adding actions to
your documents

Deciphering
symbol types

Adding symbols to
the document Library

Chapter project:
Creating your first
ActionScript

✦   ✦   ✦   ✦

The painter has canvas and palette; the poet has a quill pen and parchment; the guitarist has six or twelve strings and a sculpted wooden sound box. Every artist must have tools with which to ply their trade. It's no different for the designer who uses ActionScript. In order to create the underlying code that brings your Flash vision to life, you must adhere to certain rules, using the tools provided by the Flash programmers to flesh out your idea and bring it to your viewing audience.

Fortunately, the process of creating code is forgiving, not at all what you may expect. Instead of having to write line after line of laborious code with symbols that look like something from a foreign alphabet, you simply choose the item to which you want to apply the script, open the Actions panel, choose the action, and Flash does the rest. Well, almost.

In this chapter, you learn how to use the Actions panel. You'll learn how to navigate through the many books of actions and then add actions to your documents. You explore creating code through Flash's automated normal mode, and are introduced to creating your own code in expert mode. You also learn how to finish Flash's automation by adding instructions in the parameter text boxes. In latter parts of the chapter, you learn how the different Flash symbol types work with ActionScript and how to add them to the document library.

Note   The Actions panel's got lots of books. And some of these books have books within a book. To add some actions to your scripts, you have to click this book icon, then click that book icon, then click another book icon, and so on. Rather than bore you with a lot of words, I'm going to show the path to each action as shown in the following example: Click Actions⇨Movie Control and then double-click `goto`.

Surveying the Actions Panel

When you create a document and decide to add interactivity with ActionScript, you assign actions to keyframes, buttons, movie clips, and user-defined components. The tool through which you add interactivity is the Actions panel shown in Figure 2-1. Please note the panel has been expanded in order to give you a detailed view of the Actions books.

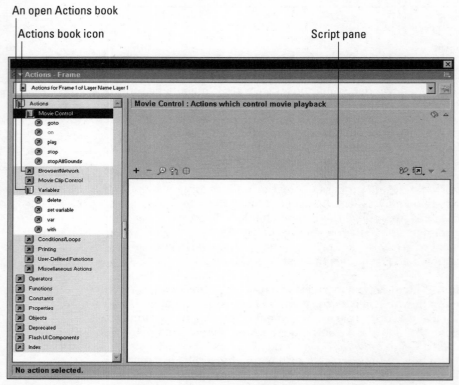

Figure 2-1: You add actions to a document with the Actions panel.

The Actions panel is divided into two panes. The pane on the left houses all the action books. Each book is a group of similar actions that perform like tasks. For example, the Movie Control book contains actions you use to control the flow of a movie: stopping on a frame when desired, going to a frame, playing a frame, and so on. As the title so aptly describes, the actions in this book control the flow of a movie.

The right pane of the Actions panel is called the Script pane. When you add an action to a keyframe or object, the code appears in this pane. As you push the ActionScript envelope, you often end up with several lines of code in the Script pane, more than can be viewed within the window. When this happens, you can use the up and down arrows to navigate to a specific line of code.

You also have several icons scattered about the perimeter of the Actions panel. You use these to access various features of the Actions panel. In upcoming sections you learn what each of these icons is used for and how they'll simplify your life as an ActionScript designer.

Essential Actions for Designers

The sheer volume of actions in the Actions panel may seem daunting to you at first. Many designers feel similar emotions upon opening the panel for the first time. The Actions panel is like a superstore. When you visit the store for the first time, you walk down aisles and aisles of merchandise until you find the item you're looking for. As you walk down the aisle, you notice other items you'd like but don't need right now, other items you'd love to own but can't afford, and still other items that you have absolutely no need for. And you end up going back to the store for some of these items you spotted on your first trip, just as you'll go back to the Actions panel for actions you spotted along the way.

If you've been dabbling in Flash for any amount of time, no doubt you've already had a visit to the Actions panel. Perhaps you needed a single action to navigate from one frame to the next, one scene to the next, or to stop the movie. After you assigned the action to your document, you quickly closed the panel and went back to what you like to do best: design.

In the sections to follow, you learn about various actions that you can use to control the flow of your movie, to change the properties of objects, add variables to your scripts, create conditional statements, and much more.

The beauty of ActionScript is that you don't have to know each and every action in order to add some interesting effects to your design. What I say next may sound very Zen, but here goes: All you need to know is what you need to know. In other words, learn the actions that apply to the particular effect you need; don't clutter your mind with the rest.

Exploring the Actions book

The first action book is named Actions, which in a way is vague, especially considering that the entire panel is named Actions. Upon exploration, however, you find that indeed this is an apt name for this book because within this book are other books that add action to your published documents. The expanded Actions book is shown in Figure 2-2.

You begin learning to use the Actions book's actions in Chapter 4.

Actions book

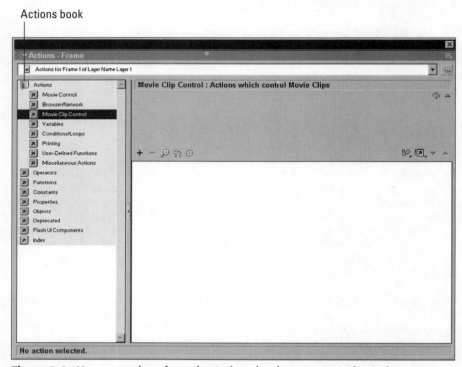

Figure 2-2: You use actions from the Actions book to create ActionScript.

When you open an individual book, each action in the book is designated by a circular icon with an angled arrow and the action's title. Shown in Figure 2-3 are all the actions in the Movie Control book.

The following sections details the individual books within the Actions book.

Using actions from the Movie Control book

Within the Movie Control book, you find the most elementary Flash Actions. Use the actions from this book to navigate to frames, play frames, stop action when a frame is reached, and stop sounds. By mastering these rudimentary actions, you can add a lot of interest to your designs.

In Chapter 4 you find detailed coverage of actions from this book.

Movie Control book

Movie Control actions

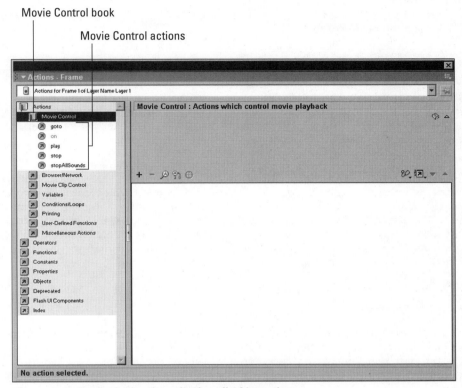

Figure 2-3: Expand a book to display all of its actions.

Using actions from the Browser/Network book

As you explore the depths of the Actions panel, each book contains actions that can add more interactivity to your movie; however, they're not quite as easy to use. In the Browser/Network book, you find actions you can add to your script that transport your viewer to other URLs, load other movies, and control the Flash Player.

Cross-Reference

In Chapter 7 you learn to use actions from this book to break large productions into manageable pieces that load quickly into the user's browser.

Using actions from the Movie Clip Control book

If your design calls for control of individual movie clips, the actions in this book are what you need. You can add actions that make it possible for you to modify one or more properties of a movie clip, enable you to clone a movie clip, allow the user to drag a movie clip, and more.

In Chapter 12 you learn how to use actions from this book to create interactive elements for interfaces.

Using actions from the Variables book

When you add variables to your documents, you give the Flash Player the capability to store and dispense information. Variables are an important building block for interactive movies. You can use variables to store information from the viewer and store information within the movie that is displayed upon user demand. Variables are discussed as needed throughout the course of this book.

Using actions from the Conditions/Loops book

When you add a conditional statement to your document, you create a fork in the road. What happens next depends upon the outcome of the statement. The main part of a conditional statement starts with the `if` action. If the statement is true, the next action in your script is executed. In other words, if this happens, do this. For example, you can create a conditional statement that evaluates a user ID and loads additional content based on the information received.

You learn to work with conditional statements in Chapter 8.

You use other actions from this book to repeat selected lines of code, or as programmers would say, *loop* them. Depending on the effect you want to achieve, or the task you're asking Flash to accomplish, you can create loops that last for a predetermined number of cycles or loops that continue while a certain condition is true.

You find detailed coverage of loops in Chapter 6.

Using other actions from the Actions book

There are three other books within the Actions book: Printing, User Defined Functions, and Miscellaneous. As a designer, you won't find yourself dipping into these books very often; however, it's a good idea to do a bit of exploring so you know what's there. Selected actions from these books are covered in later chapters.

Exploring the Operators book

The Operators book is also divided into other books. The operators most frequently used by designers are found in the Arithmetic Operators book, the Comparison Operators book, and the Logical Operators book. As a designer, you may wonder why you have to use the cold hard logic of math in your designs. Arithmetic operators make it possible for you to create mathematical expressions that modify the position and size of an object as well as other object properties. The comparison operators make it possible for you to compare two sides of an equation to see if a condition is true or false. For example, if you want to keep a moving object within the boundaries of the Stage, you compare the current position of the object with the boundaries of the Stage. You can use the logical operators to compare text objects, affectionately known to programmers as *strings*. You can use logical operators to in a quiz to compare a user's answer with the correct answer.

 You find information about the Logical, Comparison, and Arithmetic Operators in Chapter 8.

Delving into the Functions book

The items found in the Functions book contain various functions that you can use when creating expressions. You can make good use of all the functions, but the functions you'll find yourself using most are those that evaluate the contents of a variable, get the property of an object (for example, its position on Stage), and determine the version of the Flash Player the person viewing your production is using.

 For more information on selected actions from the Functions book, see Chapter 8.

Exploring the Constants book

Constants are values that are the same all the time. You can use a constant to define whether an expression is true or false or to define a new variable that has yet to be filled. The actions in this book are used infrequently. You will be using constants from this book while writing a Boolean expression, but you will manually enter the constant into the ActionScript.

Modifying objects with the Properties book

As a designer, the ability to change the properties of an object is invaluable. Using the actions from the Properties book, you can make objects appear or disappear, change the opacity of objects, change the height and width of an object, and much more. With actions from this book, you can change a static presentation into something visually exciting. Actions from the Properties book are covered throughout the course of this book. You'll find yourself frequently opening the Properties book.

Exploring the Objects book

The Objects book is a treasure trove of objects. But they're not the type of Flash objects you're already familiar with — buttons and movie clips. You use the objects in this book to accomplish other tasks, such as modifying the color of an object, changing the characteristics of a sound, or retrieving the current date and time from the computer playing your Flash movie. An ActionScript object has methods.

For example, the Color object has a method for changing the color of an object; the Sound object has a method for controlling the volume of a sound. Other objects have properties; the Sound object has properties for measuring the length of a sound clip and for how long a sound clip has been playing. Other objects have events that can be used in your ActionScript. The Sound object has an event called `onSoundComplete` that you use to trigger other actions in your movie when a sound stops playing. The different objects in this book are referred to in various projects and tutorials throughout the course of this book.

Dealing with Deprecated actions

Macromedia has created several different versions of Flash, each one more power-ful than the previous. As Flash grew in capabilities, new actions were added that have greater functionality than some of the actions introduced in earlier versions of Flash. The older actions are still available, but Flash programmers refer to these actions as *deprecated;* avoid using them when creating movies for the Flash 6 Player. These deprecated actions are all nestled within the Deprecated book.

Tip   The Internet sometimes lags behind designers and programmers; therefore, you may find that many potential viewers don't have the latest Flash Player. If you pub-lish a movie with the latest actions from Flash MX, it may not play properly on ear-lier Flash Players. To avoid this problem, publish the movie for the version of the Flash Player that you anticipate is in use by the majority of your intended audi-ence. Before you create the movie, adjust the publish settings for the desired ver-sion of Flash. After you do this, any actions that will not work with your publish settings are highlighted in yellow and should not be used.

Using actions from the Flash UI Components book

Flash MX has a Components panel with preset components such as checkboxes, scroll bars, and scroll panes you can add to your documents. The actions in the Flash UI Components book are used to create UI components with ActionScript or to modify existing UI components added to your document from the Components panel.

Cross-Reference   You'll learn to use the Scroll Bar UI component in Chapter 12.

Using actions from the Index book

Since the release of Flash 4, the available actions have increased exponentially. In Flash MX, there are so many actions, it's easy to forget which book or sub-book of a book a particular action is in. Fortunately, the Index book is comprised of every Flash action, conveniently arranged in alphabetical order. As you gain more famil-iarity with ActionScript, using the Index book is the quickest way to find the action you need.

Adding Actions to Your Documents

When you decide to add interactivity to your movies with ActionScript, you use the Actions panel. As I state earlier in the chapter, the Actions panel is divided into sections — actions on one side and a Script pane on the other side that displays your code as you create it. Figure 2-4 shows the Actions panel with several lines of code in it.

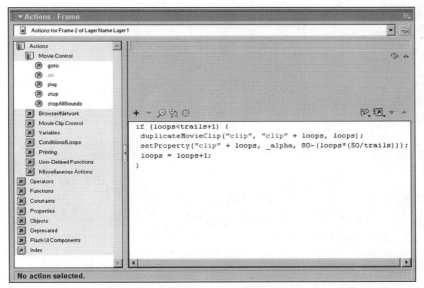

Figure 2-4: As you create ActionScript it is displayed in the Script pane.

The first step in creating any ActionScript is to open the Actions panel. The default position of the Actions panel is directly below the Stage. You open the panel by clicking the right pointing arrow or by clicking the panel's title.

If, as a designer, you decided to use the Designer panel layout as supplied by Macromedia, you can do so by choosing Window➪Panel Sets and then choosing the set for your desktop size. However, when you use one of the Designer panel sets, the Actions panel is hidden. Choose Window➪Actions, and Flash opens the panel, displaying it as a floating window (see Figure 2-5).

Why the Flash programmers decided to hide the Actions panel for designers is a mystery. Perhaps they realize what a powerful combination a creative designer and the Actions panel is and decided to protect their left-brained developer brethren by hiding the panel.

Actions panel

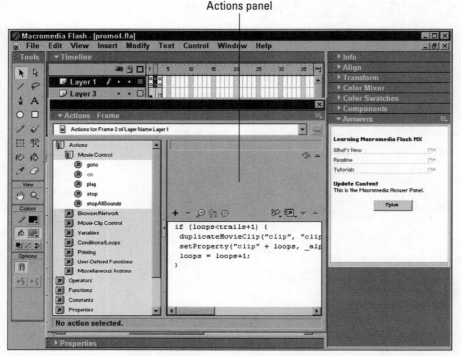

Figure 2-5: The Actions panel is displayed in a floating window with the Designer panel layout.

Tip

If you use ActionScript a lot, it's convenient to have the Actions panel available at all times. You may find that there are other panels you use frequently in conjunction with the Actions panel. You can begin with the default panel set or one of the Developer panel sets if you prefer to have the Actions panel docked at the bottom of the workspace with the Property inspector and Reference panel. You can then open and dock the panels you use frequently to create a panel layout that suits your working preference. When you have the workspace just the way you want it, choose Window⇨Save Panel Layout to open the Save Panel Layout dialog box. Enter a name for your layout, click OK, and your panel layout is added to the Panel Sets menu.

Working in modes

You have two methods of working in the Actions panel: normal mode and expert mode. In normal mode, Flash takes care of all of your formatting—you can be assured that the code you create will be formatted correctly and in the right syntax.

When you work in expert mode, Flash turns off all the warning messages and you can enter code by typing in the Script pane, just like you'd enter text into a word processing program. (More on syntax and expert mode in the upcoming section "Creating ActionScript in expert mode.")

Adding an action to your script

When you decide to add interactivity to your design by applying code to a keyframe or an object, you must first select the object, or keyframe, and then open the Actions panel as discussed previously. After opening the Actions panel, the type of object you have selected is displayed after the panel's title. For example, if you are assigning an action to a button, the panel reads: Actions – Button. Before proceeding any further, make sure you have the right object selected. The next step is to navigate to the book that contains the desired action and open it. After opening a book, you add an action to your script by doing one of the following:

✦ Double-click an action's title.

✦ Select an action and then drag and drop it into the Script pane.

✦ Click the plus sign (+) icon above the Script pane to reveal a drop-down menu of all action groups, as shown in Figure 2-6. Navigate to the desired action and click it.

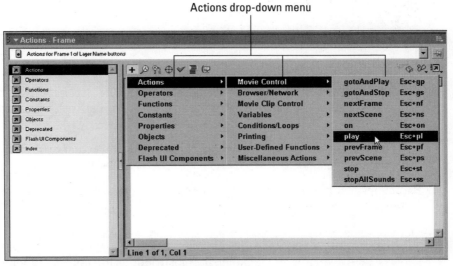

Figure 2-6: The drop-down menu of actions.

Using the parameter text boxes

Some of the actions you add to your script have parameters. *Parameters* are additional information needed by Flash to properly execute an action. For example, if you need to navigate to a different part of your movie when a button is clicked, you choose the `goto` action. When you choose this action, you must tell the Flash Player which frame in which scene to advance to, as well as whether to play the movie from that frame or stop. Each action has different parameters, which determines the number of parameter text boxes Flash displays in the Script pane after an action is added to a script. Figure 2-7 shows the parameter text boxes you need to when you add the `goto` action to a script.

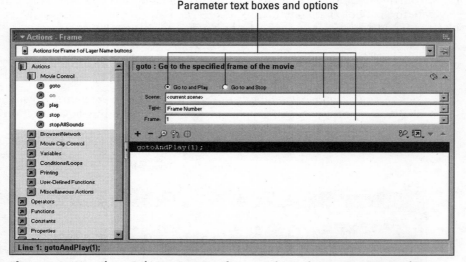

Figure 2-7: You choose the parameters for an action using parameter text boxes.

As you can see, you can choose the parameters for this action by clicking radio boxes or making choices from drop-down menus. Other actions require you to add information to a parameter text box, such as the contents of a variable or array. Parameter text boxes are discussed in detail as they relate to specific actions throughout this book.

Many of the actions you use are simple instructions to the Flash Player, such as `stop` or `play`. When you add an action like this to your script, the Flash Player knows exactly what to do and no further instructions are needed. When you add an action of this type to your script, parameter text boxes are not needed or displayed.

Deleting an action from your script

After you add a few lines of code to a script and test it, you may find that you need to delete a line of code or two. You can delete a single line of code, or contiguous lines of code, by doing the following:

1. Select the object or keyframe that contains the code you want to delete.

2. Open the Actions panel.

3. Within the Script pane, select the line of code you want to delete. When you click a line of code in normal mode, Flash selects the entire line of code for you. To select contiguous lines of code, Shift+click additional code.

4. Click the Delete Selected Lines of Code button that looks like a minus sign (–) to complete the operation. Or you can simply press Delete.

Changing the hierarchy of actions

When you create an ActionScript, the lines of code execute in numerical order. After you add several lines of code to a keyframe or an object, you may find the actions don't execute in the order you want. For example, if you create a script that instructs the Flash Player to play a sound, and the action appears after another instruction that advances the movie to a different frame, the sound will never play. You can easily rearrange the hierarchy (order) of actions in a script by doing the following:

1. Select the keyframe or object the code is applied to.

2. Open the Actions panel.

3. Select the line of code you need to move up or down in the order. Shift+click to select additional lines of contiguous code.

4. To move the selected line(s) of code up, click the Move the Selected Actions Up button; to move the selected code down the order, click the Move the Selected Actions Down button. Each click moves the selected code up or down one line.

Navigating to scripts with the Script window

At the top of the Actions panel is a narrow window called the Script window. The Script window shows the currently selected object. Click the button to the right of the window to reveal a drop-down menu of all objects in the selected keyframe that have ActionScript applied to them. Click a selection and Flash displays the ActionScript for the selected object in the Script pane (see Figure 2-8).

Script drop-down menu

Script window

Pin Current Script button

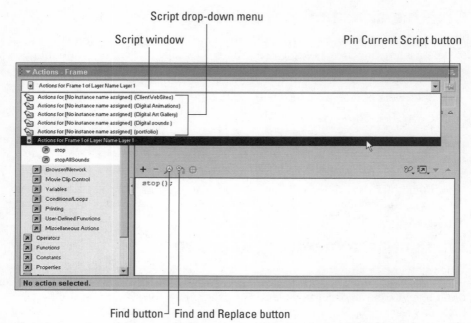

Find button ⌐ Find and Replace button

Figure 2-8: You use the Script window to navigate to other scripts in the same keyframe.

Pinning a script

When you fine-tune and work the bugs out of your ActionScript, it's often necessary to view the properties of other objects while using an ActionScript in a different keyframe for reference. Click the Pin Current Script button, and Flash locks the current script in the Script window while you navigate to other frames or view different objects. Click the Pin Current Script button again to unlock the script.

Finding and replacing text in a script

Your ActionScript is displayed in the Script pane, which is also used to edit your scripts. After you create a script, you often need to find certain text and replace it with something else. You cannot find text that is part of an action; however, you can find any text used to describe a variable, a variable's value, or an object. The Find and Find and Replace commands work like the similar commands in a word processing program.

To find text in a script:

1. Select the keyframe or object the containing the script that contains the text you want to find and open the Actions panel.

2. Click the Find button to open the Find dialog box. Alternately, choose Options⇨Find.

3. In the Find What field, enter the text you want to locate. To match the case you enter, click the Match Case checkbox.

4. Click the Find Next button, and Flash locates the first instance of the text and highlights the line of code it appears in.

5. To find the next instance of your query, click Find Next; otherwise, click Close to exit the dialog box.

 The Actions panel has another useful tool that allows you to find and replace text. This feature comes in handy when you copy code from another object, keyframe, or movie and just need to make minor modifications, such as changing the name of a variable.

To find and replace text in a script:

1. Select the keyframe or object containing the script with the text you want to replace and open the Actions panel.

2. Click the Find and Replace button to open the Replace dialog box. Alternately, choose Options⇨Find and Replace.

3. In the Find What field, enter the text you want to replace.

4. In the Replace field, enter the new text and do one of the following:

   • To review each instance of your query, click the Find Next button. If you want to replace the text Flash locates, click Replace.

   • To replace all instances of your query without review, click Replace All.

5. Click Close to exit the dialog box.

Using the ActionScript Reference panel

 ActionScript can be complicated and at times downright quirky. Sometimes the action you have in mind is the right answer; other times it is not. When you think you have the right action in mind but aren't sure, use the built-in dictionary supplied with Flash MX. This online dictionary known as the Reference panel gives you a description of every action along with examples of proper usage and syntax.

To look up an action in the Reference panel, do the following:

1. To open the Reference panel, click the Reference icon in that looks like a book with a question mark on it located in the right corner above the Script pane.

   The left pane of the Reference panel is a carbon copy of the left pane of the Actions panel.

2. Navigate to the action you want to know more about.

   As you click the title of each book, a description of the type of actions found in that book is displayed in the right pane.

3. Click an action to display information about it in the right pane of the Reference panel, as shown in Figure 2-9.

Opens ActionScript description window

Reference panel icon

Figure 2-9: To find out more about any action, open the Reference panel.

Tip   To the right of the Reference icon is an inverted triangle. Click the triangle to open another window that displays a brief description of a selected action. This window also displays information about the action used to create a selected line of code in the Script pane.

Changing your viewing options

    The ability to change from normal mode to expert mode comes in handy when you're working with script that references different timelines. When you need to add an identifier for the path, it's convenient to switch to expert mode and manually enter the identifier where needed rather than navigating through the different lines of code and then modifying the parameter text boxes. To switch from normal to expert mode, click the Viewing options icon and choose the desired option from the drop-down menu shown in Figure 2-10. Notice you can also use this menu to view line numbers in your scripts.

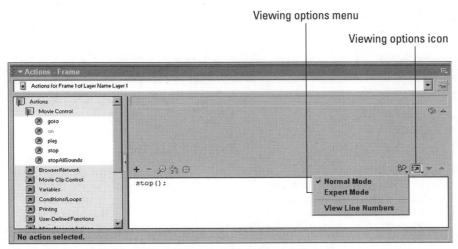

Figure 2-10: Click this icon to change your viewing options.

Using the Actions panel Options menu

    At the upper-right corner of the Actions panel, you find an icon that looks like three squares, three dashes, and an inverted triangle. Click the icon to reveal the Actions panel Options menu shown in Figure 2-11.

Many of the commands on this menu achieve the same results as commands discussed in previous section while other commands are self-explanatory. The remaining commands are covered in upcoming sections.

Actions panel Options menu   Options menu icon

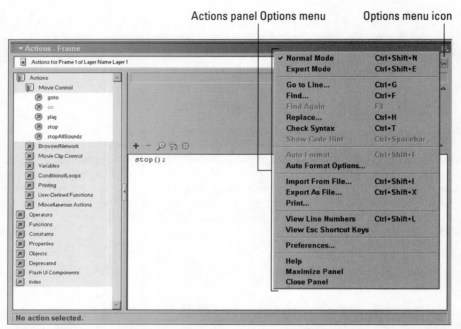

Figure 2-11: You use the commands in this menu to change ActionScript modes and much more.

Creating ActionScript in expert mode

When you switch to expert mode, the Script pane functions exactly like a text editor. You create ActionScript by placing your cursor inside the pane and typing. When you create a script in this mode, you no longer have the benefit of the parameter text boxes. When you switch to expert mode, Flash assumes you know ActionScript intimately, including the proper parameters for a chosen action.

Also when you switch to expert mode, the Delete Selected Actions button disappears. Instead of deleting an entire line of code with a button, you are now free to select desired parts of your code and drag and drop them to another part of your script in the same way you drag and drop text in your favorite word processor, or delete them entirely by pressing Delete. You can also cut, copy, and paste selected text within the Script pane.

In addition to losing the Delete Selected Actions button, you lose the buttons that move selected lines of code up or down within a script. After selecting an entire line of code, you can now drag it anywhere within the Script pane.

Using the Actions panel context menu

The Actions panel has its own context menu, a feature you can use to quickly access pertinent menu commands. You can use the context menu in Normal and Expert mode. To open the context menu shown in Figure 2-12, right-click (Windows) or Ctrl+click (Macintosh).

Actions panel Context menu

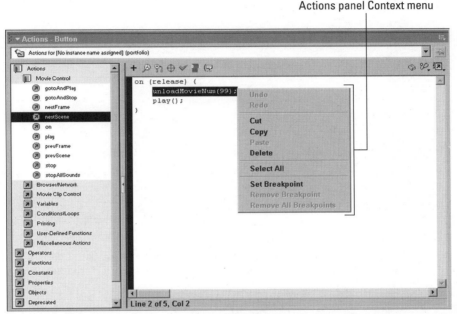

Figure 2-12: With the Action panel context menu, frequently used commands are just a mouse click away.

Understanding ActionScript conventions

Like any language, ActionScript has certain conventions you must follow. In ActionScript there is also a feature called *syntax coloring,* which highlights parts of your script so you can readily identify each element. This feature is handy when you try to decipher code created by other designers and will come in very handy when you're trying to unravel some particularly intense code created by a programmer or developer. Finally, there are certain words that Flash reserves for itself. In the sections that follow, you learn about the different ActionScript conventions. If you're like most designers, this may seem pretty droll — in fact, it may be borderline boredom. But these are essential facts you need to know in order for your design scripts to execute properly. After all, you had to learn about pixels, resolution, and resampling before you could manipulate photos in your image-editing software.

Formatting your code

Just as you add a period at the end of each sentence when creating documents in your word processor, you must also add an identifier to signify the end of a line of ActionScript code. You must also format the other elements in your scripts to separate them and tell Flash which group of actions work as a group. When you work in normal mode, Flash adds these identifiers automatically. When you work in expert mode, you must supply these identifiers (it may help to think of them as punctuation marks) manually. Table 2-1 shows the punctuation used with ActionScript.

	Table 2-1 ActionScript Formatting	
Identifier	**Description**	**Usage**
;	Semicolon	Used to end a line of code
( )	Parentheses	Used delineate or group parameters
{ }	Curly braces	Used to group a set of statements
.	Dot	Separates a property, variable name, or target path from a named instance
//	Forward slashes	Used to begin a comment

The formatting identifiers may seem a bit foreign until you see them used in context. Listing 2-1 shows some ActionScript code that uses all of the identifiers.

Listing 2-1: ActionScript Identifiers

```
on (Release) {
    // loads a jpeg image and defines the variables
    loadMovie("CEO.jpg", "_root.Target");
    _root.Name = "James Walker";
    _root.Title = "Chief Executive Officer";
}
```

The code in Listing 2-1 was assigned to a button that, when clicked, loads an image and defines two variables. The curly brace in line 1 instructs Flash that this is the beginning of the actions that will execute upon release of the mouse button. In the second line of code, the two forward slashes designate a comment. It may help if you think of comments as memory joggers. You can use comments to remind yourself, or another designer working on the project, what the lines of code following the comment actually do. In this case, they load a JPEG image and define the names of two variables. The parentheses in the second line group the image with the target the image will be loaded into. The semi-colons at the end of the lines 3 through 4 signify the end of a statement. Semi-colons are added automatically when you work in normal mode. If you forget to add one in expert mode, don't worry; the carriage return also lets Flash know you're ending a statement. The dot in _root.Target separates the path from the named instance of a movie clip. If the script was referencing a variable in the movie clip, an additional dot would appear before the variables name, for example _root.Target.xPos, where _root refers to the main timeline, Target is the instance name of a movie clip and xPos is the variable name. The dot in _root.Name is used to refer to a variable called Name on the root timeline. The solitary curly brace at the end of the code tells Flash to end the actions associated with the on (Release) event in the first line of code.

Using syntax coloring

By default, the objects in ActionScript are color coded, or as the Flash programmers call it, *syntax coloring*. You can use syntax coloring to debug your code. If a word is the wrong color, it's a dead giveaway the code will not execute as you planned. Table 2-2 shows the default syntax coloring.

Table 2-2
Syntax Coloring

Color	Used to identify
Blue	Identifies keywords, actions, paths, and object properties
Black	Identifies punctuation and other items as variable names
Light gray	Identifies comments
Green	Identifies strings (text objects used in variables)

After entering a line of code into the Script pane, examine the color Flash assigns to each word. For example, if you enter gotoandplay, the syntax is in error and Flash highlights the words with black. When you change the code to gotoAndPlay, the highlight changes to blue, indicating Flash recognizes it as an action.

Syntax coloring helps you construct correct code when working in expert mode, but you still have to be concerned with the parameters.

Tip   If you don't want syntax coloring, would like to change the colors currently used to highlight syntax, or would like to change any other part of the Actions panel, you can modify certain features and functions by choosing Actions⇨Options⇨ Preferences or by choosing Preferences from the Actions panel's Options menu. For more information on changing ActionScript preferences, refer to the manuals that shipped with the software.

Code hints

When you work in expert mode, Flash takes away the parameter text boxes, but fortunately provides you with a second line of defense: code hints. Code hints are enabled by default. When you enter code in the Script pane and Flash recognizes the code as the beginning of an Action, it posts a code hint. The code hint provides information you can use to properly format the line of code you are creating. The actual hint varies depending on the action you are using. For example, if you enter gotoAndPlay (, Flash displays the dialog box shown in Figure 2-13. In this case, you have two possible sets of parameters. The first parameter tells you the frame number (or label) you want the Flash Player to go to and play must be included between parentheses. The second parameter is accessed by clicking the arrow to the right of the number 2, which tells you that you can also supply the scene followed by the frame number separated by a comma, and the scene and frame must be surrounded by parentheses. Parameters are discussed in detail as they pertain to certain actions. For now it's helpful to know that you can get help when you need it with code hints.

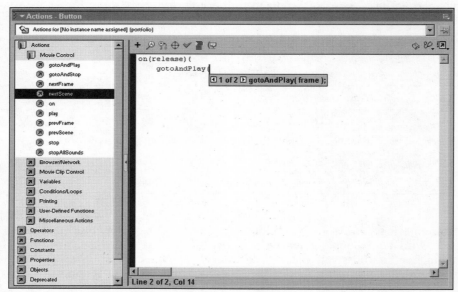

Figure 2-13: Code hints help you format script correctly.

About reserved keywords

Flash has certain keywords that are reserved for actions and functions. You cannot use these keywords when creating variables, functions, or label names. You can, however, use these words as part of a variable's contents. When you use a reserved keyword, Flash highlights the reserved word in red and displays this warning: The variable name you have entered contains an error. Table 2-3 is a list of all reserved keywords.

Table 2-3
Reserved Keywords

break	for	new	var
continue	function	return	void
delete	if	this	while
else	in	typeof	With
instance of	case	default	switch

Exporting a script

As you gain expertise in ActionScript, you find yourself creating some fairly lengthy scripts. The Script pane, while a good text editor, is not exceptionally large, and it doesn't have a spell check. If you prefer the luxury of editing your scripts in a word processor, you can do so by exporting a script and then opening it in a word processor. You can also export scripts to share with other designers or store in a folder for use with another project. To export a script:

1. Select the object or keyframe the script is assigned to.

2. Open the Actions panel.

3. Open the Action panel Options menu as discussed previously, and choose Export as File to open the Save As dialog box.

4. In the Save As dialog box, navigate to the folder where you want to store the script and enter a name in the File Name field, click Save, and Flash saves the file with the AS (ActionScript) extension.

Importing a script

You can export any script saved in the AS format. Importing a script is useful when you want to use a previously saved script in a new movie, use another designer's script, or used a saved script on another frame or object in the same document.

 Note   When you import a script, all other code assigned to the keyframe or object is overwritten.

To import a script:

1. Select the keyframe or object you want to use the imported script with.

2. Click the Actions panel and then open the Actions panel Options menu.

3. Choose Import from File, and the Open dialog box appears.

4. Navigate to the folder where you store your scripts, select the desired script, and click Open.

Tip   If you inadvertently overwrite or delete a desired bit of code, you can restore it by choosing Edit⇨Undo, choosing Undo from the ActionScript context menu, or by pressing Ctrl+Z (Windows) or ⌘ +C (Macintosh).

Understanding Symbol Types

Symbols are the building blocks of any Flash document. Most designers realize the value of the repetitive use of symbols. In addition to creating a movie with a smaller file size, it also makes it easier to edit a document. By editing one symbol, you update all instances of it used within the document. When it comes to ActionScript, you can only use ActionScript with certain objects. The sections offer a brief overview of each symbol.

About the button symbol

When you create a button symbol, you create an interactive object with four states: Up, Over, Down, and Hit, each state having a keyframe. You can choose to use one or all of the states, creating as many layers as you need to add sound, text, and other graphic elements to the symbol. Although the actual button itself has up to four keyframes, you cannot assign an action to any of these frames. You can assign an action only to an instance of the finished button symbol. A button symbol has an event handler known as the *mouse event*. When you add an action to a button symbol, it is preceded by the on(Release) event by default. The actions following the on(Release) event occur when the user releases the mouse button. You can choose a different mouse event or use multiple events for a button symbol.

Cross-Reference   Buttons and mouse events are covered in detail in Chapter 5.

About the graphics symbol

The graphic symbol is simply artwork or text that you designed as a symbol or have converted to a symbol. As with all symbols, you can use multiple instances of it within your documents. You can edit the graphics symbol and instantly update all instances of it used within your document. You cannot assign actions to a graphic symbol. If you need interactivity for a graphics symbol, you need to nest it in a movie clip.

About the movie clip symbol

The movie clip symbol is the heart of ActionScript interactivity. Movie clips have their own timeline. You can use them for reusable animations, or you can nest objects within them such as graphic symbols, sounds or video clips. After you add an instance of a movie clip symbol to a document and assign a name to it, you can then use ActionScript to play the contents of the movie clip on demand. If you've nested a graphic symbol in the movie clip, you can modify the object's properties, such as color, size, position or opacity with ActionScript. You can also use movie clips as containers for code. Movie clips are also the basis of user-defined components.

When you create ActionScript inside a movie clip, you use a clip event to determine when the ActionScript within the movie clip executes. By default, the ActionScript assigned to a movie clip executes when the movie clip loads. You can, however, choose a different clip event. For example, you can have the ActionScript execute when users move their mouse.

For more information on clip events, refer to Chapter 5.

About the component symbol

The component is a powerful new addition to Flash MX. Flash has preset components such as radio buttons, checkboxes, and push buttons. Each component has parameters that you can modify. For example, with the Push Button component, you can modify the label. When you create your own components from movie clips, you can assign your own parameters — in essence, program the component for what you need it to do.

User-defined components are covered in Chapter 7.

About the Document Library

If you've used Flash for some time, no doubt you're familiar with the document library. Whenever you create an object or import an object, it is added to the document. Whenever you need to use a symbol from the library choose Window⇨Library. Figure 2-14 shows a typical document library.

Notice that each symbol and imported object is represented by an icon. A selected symbol is displayed in the window at the top of the library. Symbols with timelines have a play and stop buttons you can use to preview the symbol. You can edit and update the symbols from within the library.

Library folders

Button symbol icon

Library preview window

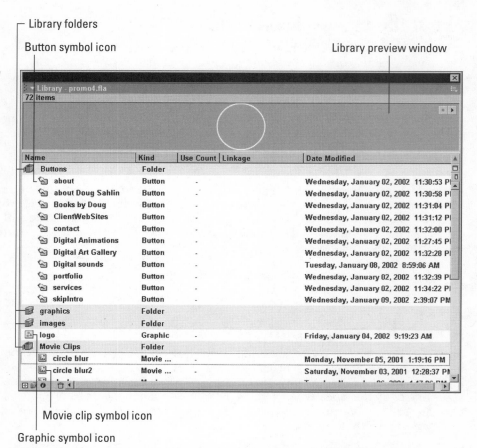

Movie clip symbol icon

Graphic symbol icon

Figure 2-14: Symbols you create are stored in the document library.

Chapter Project: Creating Your First ActionScript

Now that you've suffered through a bit of ActionScript theory, it's time for some hands-on experience. In this tutorial, you program a button to change the opacity and size of an image. The image is embedded in a movie clip symbol. In essence, what you're programming the button to do is change three properties of the object: alpha (the object's opacity), the scale of the object's x dimension, and the scale of the object's y dimension. Most of the ActionScript has already been created for you. Your mission is to program the button to apply the changes when clicked.

Navigate to this chapter's folder on the CD-ROM and copy the AS-02Start.fla file to your hard drive. Use your computer's operating system to disable the read-only attributes of the file.

To begin creating your first ActionScript, launch Flash and then choose File⇨Open, navigate to the AS_02Start.fla, and open it. Figure 2-15 shows the partially completed document.

Figure 2-15: All you need to do is program the button.

Before you get down to brass tacks and begin adding code to the button, take a look at the elements you already have in place. First and foremost is the image you'll be manipulating with ActionScript. The image is a JPEG file embedded in a movie clip. An instance of the movie clip has already been created on Stage and labeled myClip. Whenever you create a movie clip and want to manipulate it with ActionScript, you must give it a unique name.

I show you how to create movie clips and name them in Chapter 6.

Below the movie clip is text to instruct the user what to do and two input text boxes. The text boxes have been assigned variable names: opacity and scale. Variables are used to store and dispense information.

On the timeline are two keyframes. Notice the lower-case *a* in each frame. This designates that ActionScript has been applied to the frames. Listing 2-2 shows the code assigned to the first keyframe.

Listing 2-2: **ActionScript Assigned to the First Keyframe**

```
scale = " ";
opacity = " ";
_root.myClip._alpha = 100;
_root.myClip._yscale = 100;
_root.myClip._xscale = 100;
```

If you're fairly new to ActionScript, the last listing may seem a bit daunting. The first two lines of code define two new variables, the same variables used for the input text boxes. The initial value of the variables is nothing, or *null* in programmer speak. The last three lines of code are defining the initial state for the three properties that will be manipulated with ActionScript. The properties are set to make the movie clip fully visible at its original size.

The second keyframe contains a single action stop (). This is to keep the movie clip from looping between the two keyframes. When the movie initially starts, the first keyframe is used to initialize the variables, and then the movie advances to frame 2 where it stops, awaiting input from the user. When the user clicks the button, the values entered in the text boxes are what change the opacity and size of the image.

You may be wondering why it is necessary to set the initial state for each property. In spite of the instructions to enter a value between 1 and 100 to re-scale the image, the input text box will accept a value higher than 100. Every good designer knows that when you scale an image larger than it's original size, pixels must be redrawn, resulting in image degradation. If the user enters a value larger than 100, the movie will jump back to the first keyframe, no changes will be applied to the image, and the values for the variables will be reset to null. This is the interactivity that will occur in the published movie after you program the button by following these steps:

1. Select the button and then open the Actions panel. Notice that the title of the panel changes to Actions – Button.

2. Click Actions⇨Conditions/Loops. The first line of code you create checks to see if the user enters a value greater than 100.

3. Add the if action to the script.

   Remember you can add the action by dragging and dropping it into the Script pane or by double-clicking it. After you add the action to the script, Flash displays a warning, `<not set yet>`, in bright red. This is Flash's way of telling you it needs more information — in this case, the condition the statement will be evaluating.

4. Place your cursor inside the Condition parameter text box and type the following: `_root.scale>100`.

   This is the condition you want Flash to check for. The name of the variable is `scale`, but you need to add the path in order for Flash to find the variable. In this case the variable resides on the root timeline, which is designated by `_root` followed by a dot.

5. With the last line of code still selected, click the Movie Control book and then add the `goto` action to the script.

   Flash adds the action to the script, as shown in Figure 2-16. This is the action that occurs if the user enters a value greater than 100. Notice the number of parameter text boxes associated with this action.

Cross-Reference

You learn more about the `goto` action in Chapter 4.

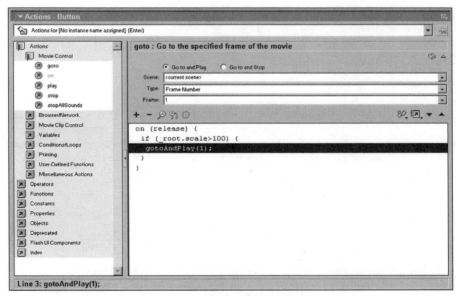

Figure 2-16: This action executes if the condition is true.

6. Add the `else` action from the Conditions/Loops book to your script. The information you supply with this action is what will occur if the conditional statement evaluates as false; in other words, if the user enters a valid value of 100 or less.

Tip   When you open an Actions book, it stays open. If you work with a lot of actions in a single script, it can become cumbersome to scroll past all of the actions in the open books. Close a book after adding an action to your script, or better yet, if you know all the actions you'll use in a script, open the Index book (an alphabetical listing of every action) and scroll directly the needed action.

7. Click Actions⇨Variables and then double-click `set variable` to add the action to the script.

8. Place your cursor inside the Variable parameter text box and then click the Insert a Target path icon the looks like a crosshair. After you click the icon, Flash opens the Insert Target Path dialog box shown in Figure 2-17.

Figure 2-17: In this dialog box, you find the path to every named instance of a movie clip.

9. Click the button that says `myClip` and then click OK to add the path to the script. After you click the button, the code `_root.myClip` appears in the Variable parameter text box followed by a flashing cursor that looks like an I-beam. This signifies that you can add text to the parameter box.

10. Type a dot (.) immediately following the word *Clip* and then click the Properties book.

11. Double-click the `_alpha` property to add it to the script.

12. In the Value Parameter text box, enter the word `opacity` and then click the Expression checkbox.

    Your finished line of code should read: `_root.myClip._alpha = opacity;`. Notice that Flash automatically added a semi-colon to designate the end of the statement. The code you just created sets the alpha property of the movie clip equal to the value the user enters in the Input Text box.

13. Now all you have to do is change the x and y dimensions of the movie clip to the value users will enter in the input text box with the variable name scale.

14. To change the y dimension, repeat Steps 7 through 12, substituting the _yscale property (found in the Properties book) for _alpha in Step 11, and the word *scale* for *opacity* in Step 12. To change the x dimension, follow Steps 7-12, using the _xscale property instead of _apha in Step 11 and the word *scale* in place of *opacity* in Step 12.

15. Scroll to the top of the top of the Actions panel and click the first line of code that reads: on (release) {. Flash created this line of code automatically when you added an action to the button. By default, Flash uses the release mouse event when you add an action to a button. Upon release of the button, the code following the statement is executed, which in this case is what you want. However, you can use more than one event handler with a button. For example, you can program the button so that it responds to the release of the mouse button, as well as a keyboard entry.

16. Click the Key Press checkbox, place your cursor in Key Press text field and then from your computer keyboard press Enter. Your finished code should be identical to Listing 2-3.

Listing 2-3: **ActionScript to Change an Object**

```
on (release, keyPress "<Enter>") {
if (_root.scale>100) {
  gotoAndPlay(1);
} else {
  _root.myClip._alpha = opacity;
  _root.myClip._yscale = scale;
  _root.myClip._xscale=scale;
  }
}
```

To test your handiwork, choose Control➪Test Movie to make Flash publish the movie and open it in another window. Enter a value in both text boxes and then press the button to scale the image and change its opacity. Press the Reset button and the movie goes to frame 1 and the initial values are restored. Enter a value greater than 100 in the right text field and then press the Enter button, or press Enter. If you followed the above steps exactly, the image didn't change size and the text fields were reset to null values.

Cross-Reference   Flash MX represents a considerable upgrade from Flash 5. If you're not familiar with how to use the new Flash tools to design and publish a movie, refer to *Flash MX Bible* by Robert Reinhardt and Snow Dowd (published by Wiley Publishing, Inc.).

Designer Notes

In this chapter you learned how to use the Actions panel to create ActionScript. You learned how to use the Actions panel in normal and expert mode. Now you should have a good idea of how to format your code and check the syntax of your code. You also received a brief overview of symbols as they relate to ActionScript. At the end of the chapter, you used the Actions panel to create your first ActionScript. In future chapters, you'll expand on this knowledge and use the building blocks from this chapter to create ActionScript elements for your designs. In the next chapter, you are introduced to some techniques for planning your ActionScript.

✦   ✦   ✦

Planning Your ActionScript Movie

✦ ✦ ✦ ✦

In This Chapter

The evolution of an ActionScript

Fleshing out your idea

Planning your Flash movie

Getting it down on paper

Creating new ideas

Chapter project: Drawing outside the lines

✦ ✦ ✦ ✦

When you are presented with a challenge from a client or yourself to create something special with Flash, you can use ActionScript to boldly go where you've never gone before. Making the decision to use ActionScript is the first step. Creating a scintillating design with ActionScript can be a long and arduous journey, and like any long journey, is doomed to fail without some careful thought and planning.

Even the most competent Flash ActionScript gurus don't take a new project lightly. There's so much that can go awry. If you put any credence in Murphy's Law, an ActionScript design that is not planned will fall flat on its face when the project is 90 percent completed. And then there's the client to consider. Clients never change their minds, do they?

In this chapter, you learn how an ActionScript can evolve from something very simple into something that takes your designs to the next level. As ActionScript flows, one action precipitates another. Some actions you create take the movie in a certain direction depending on if a condition or set of conditions is true. You also learn how ActionScript can be used to control the flow of a movie. In addition, you discover some techniques for planning your design and then fleshing it out. Finally, you see how to use your inner child and experiment to put your own unique spin on an existing ActionScript and make it your own. After all, if you do the same thing the same way every time, you'll get the same results, a trait you definitely don't want associated with a fine designer such as yourself.

Note The Actions panel's got lots of books. And some of these books have books within a book. To add some actions to your scripts, you have to click this book icon, then click that book icon, then click another book icon, and so on. Rather than bore you with a lot of words, I'm going to show the path to each action as shown in the following example: Click Actions⇨Movie Control and then double-click goto.

The Evolution of an ActionScript

When you are presented with a request from a client to design a Web site or come up with an idea of your own, the project starts out as a small thought, the genesis of creation, if you will. Your job as a designer is to flesh out the idea and bring it to the light of day. When you add ActionScript to the equation, your task becomes a bit more difficult. You need to figure out what actions you'll need to pull off the task and how you'll apply them. And of course there is more than one way to get from point A to B. It behooves you to find the path of least resistance and create the simplest ActionScript that gets the job done. This allows you more time to add the designerly touches to your creation and end up with something similar to Figure 3-1.

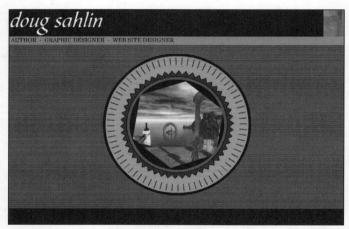

Figure 3-1: Use ActionScript to evolve your idea into a finished creation.

When you create a Flash movie and use ActionScript, you provide choices for your viewer. The choices you provide determine the ebb and flow of your movie. And you use ActionScript to direct this ebb and flow. For example, you can use ActionScript to control what type of background music the viewer hears when viewing your design or provide the user with the option of viewing your site in silence. A Flash design with ActionScript can be compared to the organization of a traditional HTML design. When the user makes a choice by clicking a button, another page loads. With a bit of JavaScript, you can add some interactivity to the HTML page — that is, if you're willing to learn the JavaScript necessary to accomplish the task.

While a traditional HTML design — even a JavaScript-enriched design — limits the amount of interactivity you can add to a design, ActionScript leaves you with a multitude of options. In Chapter 1, you learned some of the effects you can achieve with ActionScript. In Chapter 2, you popped the hood of the Actions panel and got a little grease under your fingernails and experienced a bit of the power you have at your disposal when you learn how to utilize ActionScript. But before you go any further and create your own designs from scratch, it's important to understand how a typical ActionScript gets the job done.

When you create a Flash movie, the Flash Player begins playing the first frame of the movie and plays each frame in succession; that is, it plays each frame in succession unless you use ActionScript to change the direction of your movie. For example, if you're creating a Flash design for a corporation and want to limit access to certain parts of the movie, use ActionScript to stop the movie while the user enters a password in an input text box, which is stored in a variable. You further direct the flow of the movie by using a conditional statement to evaluate the user name, and based on the result, determine whether a part of the movie will play or not.

You can create a similar scenario to create a password-protected site. This is also a conditional statement that evaluates whether a password is valid, in which case the condition is true, or invalid, in which case the condition is false. When you create a statement that evaluates as either true or false, you create a *Boolean* expression. The flow of an ActionScript that evaluates a Boolean expression is illustrated in Figure 3-2.

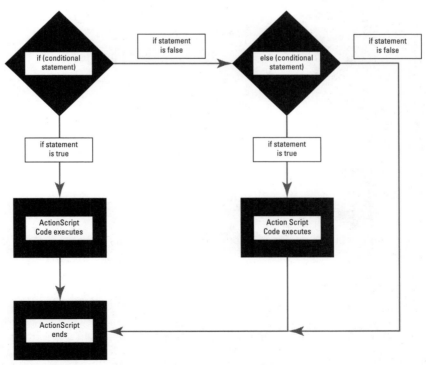

Figure 3-2: You use ActionScript to control the flow of a movie.

Another way to control the flow of a movie is with a loop. Certain loops repeat a given set of actions for a number of iterations before branching out to the next line of script or branching out to another part of the movie after the loop is completed. This type of control is useful when you have to duplicate an object in your production x number of times. Another type of loop repeats a certain action while a set of conditions evaluate as true. For example, if you use Flash to create a game, you can create a script that supplies a new question while the number of incorrect answers is less than the value you want to allow the player. When the player exceeds the number of incorrect choices, the movie branches out in another direction. GAME OVER! Figure 3-3 shows the flow of an ActionScript that loops while a condition is true.

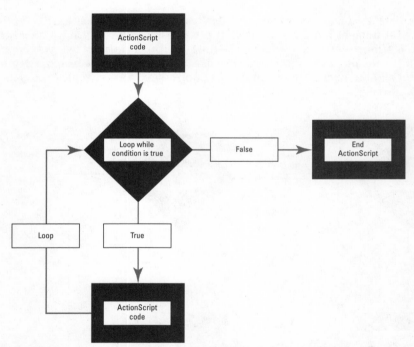

Figure 3-3: You can create an ActionScript where certain actions repeat while a given set of conditions is true.

You can use even the most mundane ActionScript to control the flow in certain parts of your production by instructing the Flash Player to go to a certain frame, play the movie, or stop the movie. But no matter how you decide to control your movie with ActionScript, your best ideas may all add up to naught without a bit of prior thought and pre-planning.

Planning Your Design

Before you create the first graphic for your design, it's imperative that you know where you're going. If you just begin recklessly splashing together graphics and tacking on bits of ActionScript here and there, it's like jumping in your car and going for a Sunday drive. The drive may be pleasurable, but you have no idea where you'll end up. If you don't know where you're going, any old road will do. If you take this "devil may care, forge ahead with reckless abandon" approach when attempting to create a design under deadline, you're usually doomed for failure. As some of the self-help gurus are fond of saying, "Fail to plan. Plan to fail."

Getting inspired

When a client entrusts you to take his or her corporate banner and display it on the Internet, getting your facts together is part of the planning process. Be sure that there is a good flow of communication between designer and client. Make sure you know all your client's expectations up front. That way neither your client nor yourself will be disappointed when you initially present your finished production for approval.

Tip   While you're gathering your facts, ask the client for his or her competitor's URLs.

Armed with your client's expectations and his or her competitor's URLs, you can begin doing some research. Visit the Web sites supplied by your client to get an idea of what your client is up against. Compare your client's ideas to what his competitors are doing and figure out what you need to do in order to build a better mousetrap. Without this information, you'll never be able to give you client a leg up on his competitors. At this stage, it's also import to ask yourself if your client's ideas are over the top or clash with the competitions. If this is the case, don't be afraid to diplomatically approach your client and seek the middle road between expectation and reality. Remember, your reputation as a designer will be at stake when you put the finished production out there for all the world to see.

In addition to the competitor URLs supplied by your client, you should also make it a point to visit Web sites of other companies offering the same product or service as your client. You can find these sites by typing a few keywords into your favorite search engine. Many of these sites will supply additional inspiration and add fuel to the creative fire your client first kindled when approaching you.

After you complete your research, you may begin to see a pattern for the type of industry you're creating the site for. Certain items may be staples for the industry you are creating the site for. Armed with this information, your client's expectation, and your own vision, you are now ready to begin planning the design.

Drafting your design

You may have the ability — as many creative people do — to visualize the finished production in your mind's eye. However, when you add the intricacy of ActionScript to the equation, you up the degree of difficulty. What looks so clear in your mind's eye may never see the light of day without putting your thoughts down on paper.

The first and most obvious weapon in your arsenal is the storyboard. Many designers use storyboards to help visualize their ideas. Your storyboard can be as primitive as a quick sketch on a notepad or as elaborate as a set of drawings. Use whichever method you're comfortable with, but by all means, create a concrete visual image of the keyframes in your production.

If you have a copy of Macromedia FreeHand installed on your machine, you can use this as a planning tool. With FreeHand, you have the capability to create a separate page for each keyframe in your production. You can also add animation to each page. As an added bonus, you can export the finished product as a Flash .SWF file and import the file into Flash. Figure 3-4 shows a storyboard created in FreeHand.

Document pages in FreeHand storyboard are used to show key events.

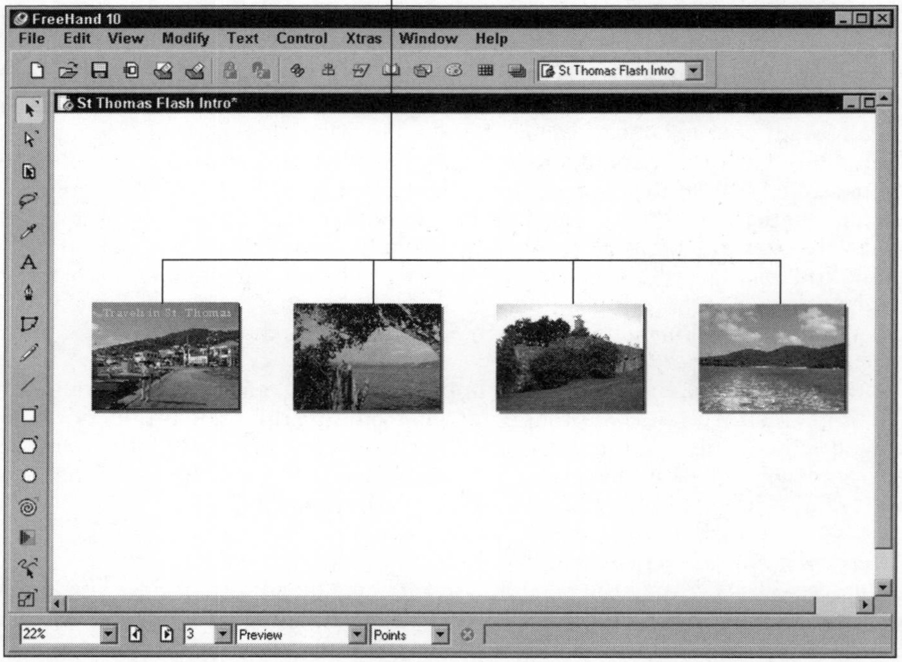

Figure 3-4: You can create a storyboard in FreeHand and export it for use in Flash.

Mapping your ActionScript

Armed with your storyboard, you can then begin to plan your ActionScript. Creating both a storyboard and planning your ActionScript may seem like a lot of work, but it's minimal compared to the frustration you'll experience when you hit a roadblock. For example, your idea may not be possible with ActionScript, or you may not have the necessary grasp of all the actions needed to pull off an effect in your design. It's better to see these things ahead of time than run up against them down the road.

You don't need to plan each and every ActionScript in your design. As you gain experience with ActionScript, you'll be able to script the simpler effects by rote. Concern yourself with the more difficult effects you or your client want to create for the production. For example, if your client wants you to create a Flash shopping cart that tallies the customer's final bill, your ActionScript not only has to calculate the number of products purchased and their price, it also needs to include a method for calculating tax based on the customer's locale.

One of the easiest ways to plan your ActionScript is to write it out in plain English. Create a single line for each event that will occur. For example, if you want the Flash Player to load a movie clip into a target when a button is clicked, your planning may look something like Listing 3-1.

Listing 3-1: Planning Your ActionScript

```
When the mouse button is released
Go to frame 2 of the target movie clip
Load the Web movie into the target
End of code
```

After you put the idea down on paper, you know what you need to get the job done. If you're not familiar with a needed action, you can learn how to use it by referencing a chapter in this book, the online Flash Reference panel, or figure out another way to achieve the same effect. If you create your plan line by line as you do ActionScript, you can transfer your idea directly from paper to the Actions panel. Listing 3-2 shows the ActionScript necessary to pull of the idea planned in Listing 3-1.

Listing 3-2: Translating Your Plan into ActionScript

```
on (release) {
  root.target.gotoAndStop(2);
  loadMovie("web.swf", "_root.target");
  }
```

Another tool many designers like to use is a *visual mind map*. If you're not familiar with this concept, you start with a clean sheet of paper, and as the ideas pop into your head, you create a circle and jot the idea inside it. Create additional circles for each idea and draw a line to connect related ideas. For example, if you know the effect you want to achieve with ActionScript, jot the effect down in one circle and create additional circles for each action you need to pull off the effect.

Creative planners who are visually oriented take this technique one step farther. They start with a clean sheet of paper and jot their ideas down on small sticky notes. With ActionScript, you can use a different colored sticky note for different elements of your script; for example, variables in pink, loops in yellow, and so on. The advantage of this technique is that as your ideas for a script change or evolve, you can reposition the sticky notes or add new ones. After you've done your mind mapping, you can create a written plan or launch Flash and begin fleshing out your idea.

Fleshing Out Your Idea

After completing the planning stage of your project, you are ready to do some serious design work. But wait — you won't want to jump straight into Flash until you've got everything in order. First and foremost, you need access to everything you need to complete the project. In other words, you need to have everything at the ready before creating your production. There's nothing more jarring than being in the middle of a project where your creative juices are flowing only to discover you're missing an important piece needed to complete the puzzle.

Tip   While you're creating your storyboard and planning your ActionScript, make a shopping list. On your shopping list, include the assets you'll need for the project: client artwork, clipart, code you need to learn, and so on. Collect everything on your shopping list before starting the project.

Gathering your assets

If you've created HTML pages with Dreamweaver, you've probably used the Assets folder. This folder is a collection of all the items used to create your design including JPEG images, buttons, scripts, and so forth. Flash doesn't have an Assets folder, but it does have a document Library.

After you know which items you need for your production, you can begin gathering them and storing them in folders. For example, if your production uses a lot of JPEG images, you can store them all in one folder as you gather the images from your client or from your clipart collection. After you launch Flash, choose File⇨Import and navigate to the folder where you've stored your JPEG images. Select all the images, click Open, and Flash imports all of the selected images at once. After Flash imports them, double-click the Eraser tool to clear the Stage. The imported images are all in the document Library for future use, and you can create an images folder to store all your bitmaps for the project in one place. You can use the same technique to import sounds and video files.

As you gather the assets for your project, remember that you can always use such as buttons and movie clips from your other Flash productions. Choose File⇨Open as Library and navigate to the *.FLA file that contains the assets you want to use. After choosing this command, Flash opens the other document Library. Drag the needed assets from one library and drop them into the current document Library. If you've been a fastidious designer and used graphic symbols as the basis for your buttons and clipart, you can modify the symbols to quickly update any instances of the symbol used in buttons or movie clips. Remember, if you create your ActionScript effects and store them in movie clips, you can use them in any production. For more information on creating modular ActionScript, refer to Chapter 6.

Tip

If you don't know how to create the needed ActionScript for a movie, you can often find out how to achieve the effect by visiting one of the many Flash tutorial Web sites. From many of these sites you can download a detailed tutorial, complete with a working example. Open the example in Flash and then open the Actions panel to see how the Flash author pieced together the ActionScript to pull off the effect.

Saving time with extensions

Macromedia has a tool called the Extensions Manager. *Extensions* are pieces of code or functions created for an application that take a lot of drudgery out of complex tasks. If you're familiar with Dreamweaver, you may have already used extensions to embed QuickTime movies. Extensions are available for free download from Macromedia's Web site at `www.macromedia.com/desdev/mx/flash/`. There's a boatload of good information on the home page. After you're done perusing that page, click the Exchange link. In order to download extensions, you must first register by clicking the Get a Macromedia ID link and following the prompts. The second step is to download the latest version of the Macromedia Extension Manager. This tool takes extensions and incorporates them with the proper program.

Before you go to the trouble of creating code for a complex effect, logon to Macromedia's site and check out the available extensions. When you find a useful extension (or extensions — there are over a hundred for Flash as of this writing), download it. After you download the extension, double-click it, and the Macromedia Extension Manager integrates it with the proper software. After installing an extension, you can use it by choosing Window⇨Common Libraries and then selecting it from the menu. Many of the extensions are user-defined components that come with instructions on how to use them.

Chapter Project: Drawing Outside the Lines

After you get a bit of experience with ActionScript and have several successful movies to your credit, you can let your inner child run amuck and experiment. One of the easiest ways to learn new techniques in ActionScript is to modify a successful effect you or another designer created. As long as you have access to the *.FLA file used to create the movie, you can modify it to your heart's content.

You can begin experimenting by opening an *.FLA file in Flash. Save the file under a different name so you don't accidentally destroy your original. You can begin by changing the parameters of ActionScript applied to movie clip objects. If you have graphic symbols embedded in the movie clip, create new graphic symbols and swap them with the symbols nested in movie clips you've assigned ActionScript to. The following tutorial gives you chance to see how you can fine-tune an effect by modifying an existing file.

On the CD-ROM   Locate the drawOutside.fla file, which you'll find in this chapter's folder on the CD-ROM that accompanies this book. Copy the file to your hard drive and use your computer's operating system to disable the file's read-only attribute.

1. Launch Flash and open the drawOutside.fla file. The file, as shown in Figure 3-5, consists of two layers: Background and Mask. If you've created masks in Flash before, you may notice that the mask layer doesn't look like a Flash mask layer. That's because the object doing the actual masking is the circle that looks like a compass. ActionScript has been used to convert this movie clip into a mask.

2. Choose Control⇨Test Movie. After Flash opens the file in another window, you notice the circle is rotating slowly and acts as a mask to an underlying image. You also notice that the background image is darker. Click the circle, and it increases in size so you can drag it to reveal other parts of the image. After you've finished experimenting with the movie, close the window to return to movie-editing mode.

3. Click the circle to select it and then open the Actions panel to view the code applied to the movie clip (see Figure 3-6).

   The code used to convert the movie clip to a mask may seem a bit foreign to you. You learn how to create a mask with ActionScript in Chapter 16. The third line of code modifies the movie clip's rotation property. This is what sets the mask spinning. Lines 7 and 8 change the size of the mask after the movie clip is clicked. If you haven't modified your Actions panel to view line numbers, doing so will help you follow the rest of this tutorial. Click the View Options button and select View Line Number from the menu.

Mask layer   Mask movie clip

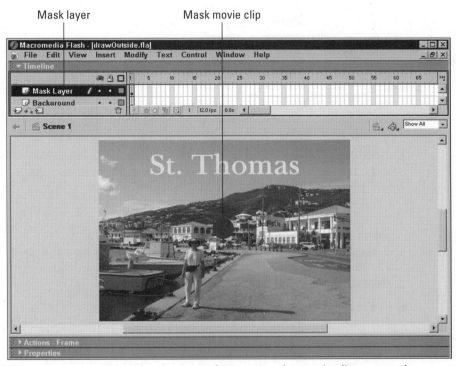

Figure 3-5: ActionScript has been used to convert the movie clip to a mask.

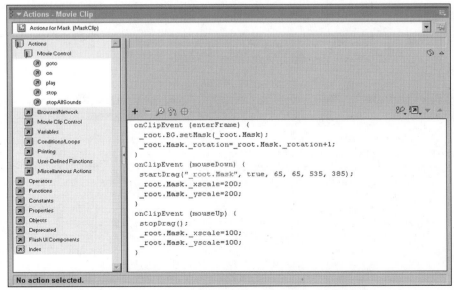

```
onClipEvent (enterFrame) {
  _root.BG.setMask(_root.Mask);
  _root.Mask._rotation=_root.Mask._rotation+1;
}
onClipEvent (mouseDown) {
  startDrag("_root.Mask", true, 65, 65, 535, 385);
  _root.Mask._xscale=200;
  _root.Mask._yscale=200;
}
onClipEvent (mouseUp) {
  stopDrag();
  _root.Mask._xscale=100;
  _root.Mask._yscale=100;
}
```

Figure 3-6: This ActionScript code converted the movie clip to a mask.

4. Click the third line of code to select it and in the Expression field, change +1 to –1. This sets the rotation of the circle in a counterclockwise direction. If you're feeling frivolous, change the value to a larger number. The rotation won't be as smooth, but it will give you an idea of the way ActionScript animation works.

5. Select the seventh line of code and in the Expression field, change the value from 200 to 150.

6. Select the eighth line of code and in the Expression field, change the value from 200 to 50.

7. Select the Mask layer and then select the background image.

8. Open the Actions panel and you should see the following code:

```
onClipEvent (load) {
  _root.MC2._alpha=25;
}
```

9. Select the second line of code and change the value from 25 to 50.

10. Choose Control⇨Test Movie. As a result of your changes, the background movie clip is now brighter and the mask is rotating counterclockwise. When you click the mask, it becomes an ellipse.

After you're done experimenting with the movie, examine the ActionScript used to code the mask. This will give you a taste of what you'll learn in upcoming chapters.

Designer Notes

In this chapter, you learned how an ActionScript flows and how a single idea evolves into a finished production. You also learned some techniques to chart your ActionScript course. I showed you time-saving techniques, and you learned a few ways to plan your work. In the next chapter, you'll learn how to use some basic actions to navigate within a movie.

Happy accidents

When you're between projects and have some time on your hands, launch Flash, create a new movie, and then create or import some objects. Embed the objects in movie clips and have some fun. Begin experimenting with different properties to create an effect. Try the exact opposite of something that's worked for you before. Replace one action with a different one or add additional actions to a script. There are no rules here—just try something, anything. If your script falls flat on its face, so what? No pixels were damaged and you don't have a client breathing down your neck. But if your script does work and you create something truly spectacular, or even moderately spectacular, jot down some notes (or add comments to your script) to remind yourself how you achieved the effect and save the file.

✦   ✦   ✦

Using Basic ActionScript in Your Movie

◆ ◆ ◆ ◆

In This Part

Chapter 4
Charting the Timeline
of Your Movie

Chapter 5
Creating Basic
Interactivity

Chapter 6
Creating Elements
for Your Movie

Chapter 7
Taking Control
of Your Movie

Chapter 8
Creating Variables to
Store and Dispense
Information

◆ ◆ ◆ ◆

Charting the Timeline of Your Movie

✦ ✦ ✦ ✦

In This Chapter

Controlling the
timeline

Adding actions to
keyframes

Adding actions to
objects

Working with buttons

Navigating with
ActionScript

✦ ✦ ✦ ✦

If you don't use ActionScript in your Flash documents, your published movies play in linear form, starting with frame 1. Each frame plays in succession until the movie ends. As you know, without ActionScript, when the movie reaches the last frame, it loops back to the first and continues playing over and over. This is fine if you're creating a Flash banner for use in an HTML document. However, if you want to give your standalone Flash designs the kind of interactivity that keeps viewers glued to their monitors, you need to take control of the timeline.

When you take control of the timeline, you choreograph the production, deciding what frame will play next when a keyframe is reached and what movie clip or scene will play when a button is clicked. When you use ActionScript to control the flow of a movie, you give your viewers a choice of what to view.

In this chapter, you learn how to use ActionScript to advance a movie to a specific frame or scene. You also learn how to assign actions to a button. In addition, you find out how to open up a Web page when a keyframe is reached or a button is clicked, a handy feature when you need to link to HTML content or launch an HTML page after a Flash intro has played.

Note   The Actions panel's got lots of books. And some of these books have books within a book. To add some actions to your scripts, you have to click this book icon, then click that book icon, then click another book icon, and so on. Rather than bore you with a lot of words, I'm going to show the path to each action as shown in the following example: Click Actions⇨Movie Control and then double-click goto.

Controlling the Timeline

The timeline of your movie is like a road map. A Flash movie without ActionScript is a stretch of interstate highway—it goes from Point A to Point B with no stop-offs. When you add ActionScript to the timeline, you give the viewer the choice of stopping and getting to know the lay of the land or moving on. You can also structure the timeline so the user can skip from Point A to Point D. You control the timeline by creating scripts on individual frames that determines what happens when the frame is reached. For example, if you have a large block of text displayed on a keyframe, you can add a `stop` action, which allows the viewer to read the text before moving on.

You can also use buttons to control the timeline. In the previous scenario, the viewer clicks a button with the play the action assigned to it and the movie resumes. You can also use buttons to set up a navigation menu and use the `goto` action to advance the movie to a specific keyframe when the button is clicked.

Working with frames

When you want action to occur when a frame on the timeline is reached, you create a script for the frame. The action can be as simple as stopping the movie or as complex as playing a movie clip that moves across the Stage. You can also add script to a keyframe that loops it back to a previous keyframe until a certain condition is met. A loop is an essential element in a preloader—it loops back to the first frame, continuing to play the preloader until the rest of the movie loads.

In Flash there are three types of frames:

   ✦ A standard frame that is designated by a white background and no boundaries

   ✦ A keyframe that is designated by a filled dot on the timeline

   ✦ A blank keyframe that is designated by an unfilled dot on the timeline

A frame is used to extend content from the previous frame. You use keyframes for significant event changes in your movie, such as an object changing size or position. You also use keyframes to create timeline-based ActionScript. A blank keyframe is used as a placeholder for content yet to be placed on Stage or ActionScript yet to be created. Keyframes are designated by a filled dot, blank keyframes by an unfilled dot. When you add ActionScript to a keyframe, it is still an unfilled dot; however, a small lower case *a* appears above the dot. If an object and ActionScript reside in the same keyframe, it is designated by a filled dot with a lower case *a* above it. Figure 4-1 shows a typical timeline.

Creating a frame

You create a frame when you need to copy content without making a change. This is used primarily for graphic objects. However, when you create a keyframe on one layer's timeline and need to display the content from another layer timeline without making a change, you also need to add a frame to carry the content forward.

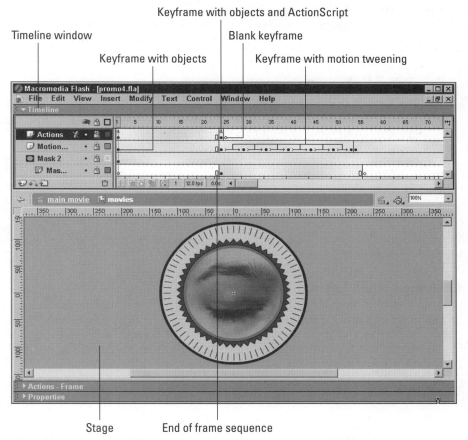

Figure 4-1: You use keyframes to create major event changes in a movie.

To create a frame:

1. Click the frame where you want the content to advance to.

2. Choose Insert⇨Frame. Alternately, you can press F5.

When you use this command, Flash adds a frame with a hollow rectangle to designate the end of the frame range and copies the graphic content from the previous keyframe to the frame you select when you invoke the command.

You can also add frames to a range of frames. This is often necessary to slow down a sequence of action. To add frames, click one or more frames, choose Insert⇨ Frame, and Flash inserts the number of frames you select when you invoke the command.

To speed up the action, you may need to delete one or more frames. To do so, select a frame or several frames, choose Insert⇨Remove Frames (or press Shift + F5), and Flash removes the number of frames you select when you invoke the command.

Creating a keyframe

You create a keyframe whenever you make a major change in your movie. The change can be replacing one object on Stage with another, manually changing a property of an object by moving it, changing the property of an object with ActionScript, or using ActionScript to alter the movie in another way.

To create a keyframe:

1. Click the frame where you want the change to occur.

2. Choose Insert⇨Keyframe. Alternately, you can press F6.

When you create a keyframe not adjacent to the previous keyframe, Flash fills in the blanks with standard frames.

Creating a blank keyframe

When you need to stop displaying content and create a placeholder for new content, or ActionScript yet to be written, you create a blank keyframe. If you plan the project out ahead of time and know where your major event changes will occur, you can create several blank keyframes and add graphic symbols or ActionScript as you progress with your design.

To create a blank keyframe:

1. Select the frame where you want to create a blank keyframe.

2. Choose Insert⇨Blank Keyframe or press F7.

After you choose this command, Flash adds a blank keyframe to the selected frame and fills the timeline with standard frames between the last keyframe and the new blank keyframe.

Tip   If you need to remove the content or ActionScript from a keyframe but still need the frame for timing purposes, choose Insert⇨Clear Keyframe. If you need to convert several standard frames to keyframes, select the frames and then choose Modify⇨Frames⇨Convert to Keyframes. To convert a selection of frames to blank keyframes, choose Modify⇨Frames⇨Convert to Blank Keyframes.

Labeling a keyframe

When you create ActionScript, it is often necessary to reference a particular frame in your code. Your ActionScript can refer to the frame by its number. However, when you fine-tune a movie by adding or deleting frames, the action that once occurred on frame 26 now occurs on a different frame, which causes a major problem with your script as it's still referring to frame 26. The solution is to label your keyframes. When you label a keyframe, the label appears on certain parameter text box drop-down menus. When you refer to a frame label in a script, the Flash Player always searches for the label, no matter how many frames you've added or subtracted from your design.

1. To label a keyframe:

2. Select the keyframe you want to label.

3. Open the Property inspector.

4. In the <frame label> field, enter a name for the frame and press Enter or Return.

When you enter a name for the keyframe, choose a label that reflects what happens. This makes it easier for you to decipher the reason you created the keyframe after working several hours on other parts of your production. It also makes it easier for other designers on your team to figure out exactly what you're doing. When you label a frame, a red flag appears in the frame on the timeline, followed by the frame's label. If you have several contiguous keyframes, or the frame label is long, it will be truncated. Hold your mouse over the labeled keyframe and a tooltip with the frame's name appears, as shown in Figure 4-2.

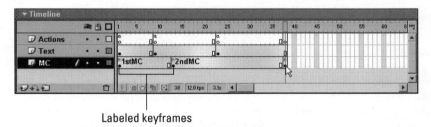

Labeled keyframes

Figure 4-2: You can use a labeled keyframe to help foolproof your ActionScript.

Creating an Actions layer

When you create a Flash movie, you can create as many frames as you need to get the job done. However, when you add ActionScript to several frames in a movie comprised of dozens or perhaps hundreds of frames, locating an individual keyframe with a specific script is downright difficult. When you create a movie with ActionScript, it's a good idea to set up a separate layer for your code. You use this layer for any action you assign to a frame. You'll still have to search for each individual object you assigned actions to, but on your Actions layer, you'll be able to easily spot the frames you added ActionScript to — they're the keyframes with a lowercase *a* at the top.

To create an actions layer:

1. Select the uppermost layer.

2. Choose Insert⇨Layer, or click the Insert Layer button that looks like a file folder preceded by a plus sign (+).

3. After Flash creates the layer, click the default layer name, type **Actions**, and then press Enter or Return.

After you create the Actions layer, remember to use this layer for any keyframes you create that will have ActionScript.

Adding comments to keyframes

Even when you're fastidious and create a layer for your keyframe actions, all you see on the layer is a lowercase *a* where actions have been added. If you're working with a limited number of actions, you can probably figure out the code you created on the keyframe. But when you're dealing with a large production or working on a project with other designers, you need a little more help in the form of a comment. When you add a comment to a keyframe, it's displayed on the timeline in the same manner as a label, yet it doesn't appear on any frame label drop-down menus.

To add a comment to a keyframe:

1. Select the keyframe to which you want to add the comment.

2. Open the Property inspector.

3. In the <frame label> field, enter two forward slashes (//) followed by the comment and then press Enter or Return.

The forward slashes tell Flash this is a comment and not a frame label. You can enter as much text as needed, however, it may be truncated if it encroaches on a neighboring keyframe. You can read the full comment by holding your cursor over the keyframe and a tooltip appears showing the full comment, as shown in Figure 4-3.

Keyframe with comment

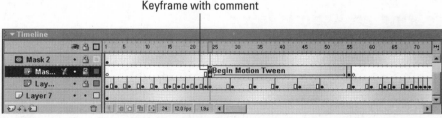

Figure 4-3: You use comments to keep tabs on your ActionScript.

Allocating Actions to a Frame

When you decide to add interactivity to your timeline, you first create a keyframe and then assign ActionScript to it. You can assign simple single line code to a keyframe that tells the Flash Player to stop playing the movie or direct the movie to another keyframe. You can also allocate multiple actions to a keyframe that define variables, evaluate expressions, or check to see whether a set of conditions exists.

To create ActionScript for a keyframe:

1. Select the keyframe you want to create ActionScript for.

2. Open the Actions panel. When you select a keyframe and open the Actions panel, the panel's title bar reads, Actions – Frame. If the title bar reads differently, you haven't selected the keyframe — try again.

3. Navigate to the action by either opening the book it is stored in, or open the Index book and select the appropriate action. Remember the Index book lists every Flash action in alphabetical order.

4. After selecting an action, use your favorite method to add it to a script. Remember you can double-click an action to add it to a script, or drag and drop it directly into the Script pane. You can also click the plus sign (+) above the Script pane and choose the desired action from a drop-down menu.

5. Continue adding actions as needed to complete your script. Figure 4-4 shows a script with several actions assigned to a keyframe. Notice the parameter text boxes above the Script pane. These boxes differ depending on the action and will be discussed as needed.

Parameter text boxes

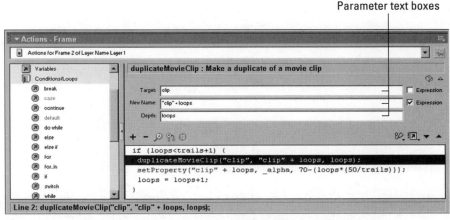

Figure 4-4: You use the Actions panel to write a script for a keyframe.

Caution   It is possible to select a standard frame and create an ActionScript. However, the code you create will be assigned to the previous keyframe on the timeline. Always make sure you have a keyframe selected when attempting to create a script on the timeline.

Creating Buttons

You also use buttons to add interactivity to your Flash productions. When you add buttons to a movie, you give the viewer a choice: to click or not to click. You can program a button to direct the viewer to another part of the movie when clicked, load additional content when clicked, and much more. Buttons can play a large part in any Flash movie you publish.

If you've worked with Flash for any length of time, you've probably already created a button or two. However, many designers don't take advantage of ActionScript and use Flash for simple animations that are incorporated with their HTML designs. If you fall into this category, this section will give you a brief overview on how to create a button. If you're an experienced pro at creating buttons, feel free to skip to the next section.

Adding a button to your document

A button is a symbol with four frames. You can create a button with a single frame or use all button frames. Each frame of the button can contain a different graphic that is displayed when the user's mouse interacts with the button's target area. When you create a button, you can add layers to segregate the various elements used to create the button. Remember you can use a symbol from the document Library to create your button. You should make it a point to use a symbol whenever possible. By using symbols instead of creating new objects, you help to create a smaller file.

To create a button, do the following:

1. Choose Insert⇨New Symbol to open the New Symbol dialog box.

2. Enter a name for the symbol, choose Button for the symbol behavior, and then click OK to enter symbol-editing mode.

3. Create the graphic needed for the Up state, or use an existing symbol from the document Library. If necessary, create additional layers for additional objects such as text or sound bytes. If your button only has one state, click the Back button to return to movie editing mode; otherwise, proceed to Step 4.

4. To use one of the other button states, select the appropriate frame and then press F6 to convert it to a keyframe. Create the graphic for the state or choose a symbol from the document Library. Remember, you can have an animated button. For example, you can have a small animation play when the user's mouse rolls over the button by adding a small movie clip to the Over state. If you're not familiar with individual button states, they're covered in detail in the next section.

5. Click the Back or current scene button to return to movie editing mode. To use the button, drag it from the document Library to the desired position on Stage. Figure 4-5 shows a multi-state button being created.

Button state frames

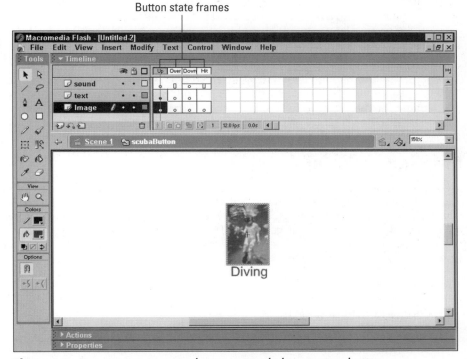

Figure 4-5: You can use as many layers as needed to create a button.

Tip

You can use any graphic for a button. However, if your design calls for a JPEG image for a button face, it may increase the file size of the published movie. If the image is being used exclusively for the button, you can use the Trace Bitmap command with fairly high settings to convert the image into Flash vector objects.

About button states

When you create a new button symbol, you have four available states: Up, Over, Down, and Hit. When you create a new button, by default you have a keyframe only in the Up state. In order to use the other states, you need to select the frame and then press F6 to convert it to a keyframe. Each state determines what the viewers see when their mouse interacts with the button.

✦ **Up:** This is the default button state. The graphic you include in this state is visible when the user's mouse is not in the button target area.

✦ **Over:** The content in this button frame is visible when the user's mouse rolls over the button target area.

✦ **Down:** The content in this keyframe is activated when the user's mouse clicks the button. This is the most logical state to add a sound. If you add a sound to the down state, remember that it will continue playing until conclusion. Use a sound less than a second in length, such as a single musical note or a mechanical noise like a camera shutter button being clicked.

✦ **Hit:** The graphic you use in this keyframe defines the target area of the button and is not visible. If you have a small button icon in the Up state, create a shape for this frame that is slightly bigger than the icon, thus giving the viewer a bigger target area.

Creating an invisible button

Invisible buttons may not be seen, but they can play a prominent role in your Flash designs. You can use an invisible button to trigger drag and drop elements such as interface pieces, dialog boxes, and elements in a game. You can also place an invisible button behind a large block of text. The button isn't seen, which makes the text visible. After the viewers read the text block, a button click advances them to the next part of your design.

To create an invisible button:

1. Choose Insert⇨New Symbol.
2. Name the button, choose the Button behavior and click OK to enter symbol-editing mode.
3. Select the Hit frame and press F6 to create a new keyframe.
4. Using one of the drawing tools, create a shape the desired size of the target area. You can use any shape, or you can import a shape created in a drawing program.
5. Click the Back button to exit symbol-editing mode. Your invisible button is in the document Library, ready for use.

As a rule, you nest an invisible button with another symbol such as a movie clip with a text block. You can also place an invisible object directly behind an object. Using an invisible button in this manner, you don't need to concern yourself with a target path if you're using it to navigate to a frame on the main timeline. Remember that an invisible button is a symbol. When you use an instance of it in a movie clip, or in any other part of your design, you can resize it to suit your needs and the original symbol remains unaltered. Figure 4-6 shows an invisible button nested in a movie clip. You can identify the button by its light aqua color. However, when the movie is published, viewers are never aware of the button until the hand icon appears when the mouse passes over the button.

Assigning actions to a button

After you create a button symbol and place an instance of it on Stage, you program the button to achieve the desired effect when a viewer clicks it. You can use a button to trigger a myriad of events. As previously mentioned, you can use a button for interactive elements in your movie and navigation. You can also use a button to modify objects on Stage. For example, you can program a button to change the size or opacity of an object. You can also assign multiple actions to a button.

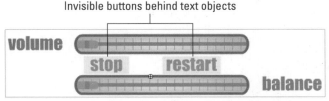

Figure 4-6: You use invisible buttons to add interactivity to movie clips.

To program a button:

1. Select the button you want to program.

2. Open the Actions panel. When you open the Actions panel after selecting a button, the title reads: Actions – Button. If you see anything else, reselect the button.

3. In the left pane of the Actions panel, navigate to the desired action and add the action to your script by double-clicking it or dragging and dropping it into the Script pane. If you work in normal mode, Flash automatically adds `on(Release)` to your code. This is the event that triggers the action you selected. `Release`, the default mouse event, executes the action when users release their mouse after clicking the button. (You learn how to use all the mouse events in Chapter 5.) Figure 4-7 shows a button with the `goto` action assigned to it.

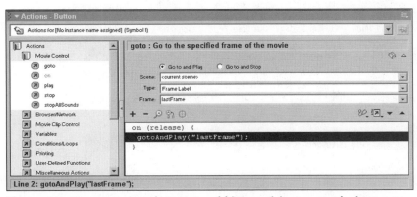

Figure 4-7: You program a button to add interactivity to your designs.

Navigating with ActionScript

You can use ActionScript to create a plethora of effects. However, in the beginning, you use ActionScript to navigate from one part of a movie to another or to go to another Web page. You can also use basic ActionScript to stop a movie and then resume it. If you've used Flash for a while, this may seem like old hat to you. However, if you're patient and read on, perhaps you'll learn a new trick or two that you can incorporate with your next Flash design.

Using the stop action

When you need to halt the action in a movie, the stop action will do it for you. The stop action has no parameters. When the Flash Player sees this action in one of your scripts, it stops the movie. As mentioned previously, you can use this action to stop the movie while viewers read a large block of text. You also use this action as part of a drop-down menu. You can use the stop action on a keyframe or button.

You find the stop action in the Movie Control book. To use the stop, navigate to the action and use your favorite method to add it to your script. Listing 4-1 shows the stop action assigned to a keyframe.

Listing 4-1: **Using the Stop Action**

```
stop ()
```

Using the play action

After you use the stop action to halt a movie, you use the play action to resume play. In the aforementioned scenario of stopping the movie to display a large block of text, you assign the stop action to a keyframe and assign the play action to an invisible button behind the text. You also use the play action when creating a pop-up menu.

You find the play action in the Movie Control book or listed alphabetically in the Index book. To use the play action, navigate to it and use your favorite method to add it to a script. Listing 4-2 shows the play action assigned to a button. In this case, the action occurs when the user releases the mouse button.

Listing 4-2: **Using the Play Action**

```
on (release) {
  play();
}
```

Using the goto action

You use the `goto` action to navigate to a specific frame or scene. You can refer to the frame or scene by number or by name. When you use this action, you can go to a frame and play the movie or go to a frame and stop the movie pending further interaction from the viewer.

You find the `goto` action in the Movie Control book. To add the `goto` action to your script:

1. Select the button or keyframe to which you want to assign the action.

2. Navigate to the action and add it to your script. After you add the action to your script, the parameter text boxes shown in Figure 4-8 appear above the Script pane.

3. Choose the Go to and Play or Go to and Stop option.

4. In the Scene field, accept the default current scene parameter or click the button to the right of the field and choose a scene from the drop-down menu. If you add a scene to a movie and give it a unique name, the name appears on this menu.

5. In the Type field, accept the default of frame number or click the button to the right of the field and choose one of the following:

   • **Frame Label:** Choose this option if you've labeled keyframes in your document.

   • **Expression:** Choose this option to use an expression that, when evaluated, directs the movie to another frame. If you choose this option, you create the expression in the Frame field.

   • **Next Frame:** Choose this option to advance the movie to the next frame when the action executes. Choose this option and the Frame parameter box is no longer available.

   • **Previous Frame:** Choose this option to rewind the movie to the prior frame when the action executes. Choose this option and the Frame parameter box is no longer available.

6. In the Frame field, enter the number of the frame you want the movie to advance to when the action executes. If you have labeled your keyframe and choose the Frame Label parameter, click the button to the right of the field and choose the desired frame label from the drop-down menu.

Using the getURL action

Like most designers, you probably shy away from opening another Web page from one of your designs. And when you do, you probably open it up in another window to keep your design open. With the `getURL` action, you can open another Web page from your Flash design. You can assign the action to a button or keyframe. You assign the `getURL` action to the final frame of a Flash intro to open a site's home page.

Parameter text boxes

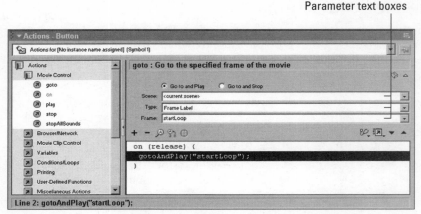

Figure 4-8: You supply the parameters that direct the movie to the desired frame.

You find the `getURL` action in the Browser/Network Control book and also in the Index book. To direct your movie to another Web page:

1. Select the button or keyframe you want to assign the action to.

2. Open the Actions panel.

3. Add the `getURL` action to your script. After you add the action to your script, the parameter text boxes shown in Figure 4-9 appear above the Script pane.

4. In the URL field, enter the URL of the page you want to open when the action executes. Enter the full path for the URL, for example: `http://www.dasdesigns.net/index.htm`. Alternately, you can check the Expression checkbox and enter an expression that, when evaluated, directs the movie to the desired Web site.

5. Click the button to the right of the Window field and choose one of the following:

   • **Self:** Opens the URL in the same window as the link.

   • **Blank:** Opens the specified URL in a new browser window. Choose this option, and your Flash movie plays in the background.

   • **Parent:** Loads the URL in the window of the frame that called the link. If the frame isn't nested, the URL opens in the full browser window.

   • **Top:** Loads the URL in the full browser window, removing all frames.

6. In the Variables field, accept the default Do Not Send or click the button to the right of the field and choose Send Using Get or Send Using Post. You use the Send Using Get option to send variables to another Web page; Send Using Post to send the variables to a CGI script at the URL's server. Figure 4-9 shows the `getURL` action as assigned to a button.

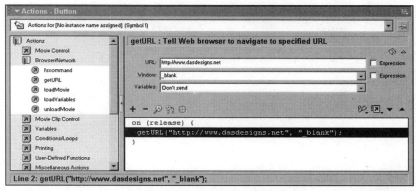

Figure 4-9: You use the getURL action to direct the movie to a specified URL.

Using JavaScript to open an HTML page in a different size window

When you use the `getURL` action to open a Web page from your Flash design, you can open it in another window by choosing the blank option. However, by default, most browser windows maximize when opened. You can use the `getURL` action and a bit of JavaScript in your HTML page to open the link in a different size browser window by doing the following:

1. Assign the `getURL` action to a button or keyframe as outlined in the preceding section.

2. In the URL field, enter the following: **Javascript:newwin1 ()**. This code tells the Flash Player to use JavaScript from the HTML document the Flash movie is embedded in. The URL for the site that opens when the action executes is within the HTML JavaScript.

That's all you need to do within Flash. When you publish the document, choose the Flash and HTML tabs. If you have more than one Web page to open, follow the above steps on another button or keyframe and in the URL field, enter Javscript:newwin2 (), Javscript:newwin3 (), and so on.

After the document is published, you'll have two files: the .SWF movie and the HTML page the movie is embedded in. Open the HTML document in your HTML editor or a word processor and enter the script in Listing 4-3 between the <head> </head> tags.

Listing 4-3: **JavaScript to Open a URL in a Different Size Window**

```
<script language="Javascript">
function newwin1() {
     window.open('http://www.dasdesigns.net.contact.htm', 'links'
,'scrollbars=yes,width=640,height=480')
}
</script>
```

The JavaScript in line 4 of the above code specifies whether scrollbars should be included and specifies the width and height of the new window. Change these values as needed to suit the page you are opening. Specify dimensions smaller than the average Internet surfer's desktop size of 800 x 600.

If your Flash movie references more than one new window, copy lines 2 through 4 of the above code and change the first line to **newwin2**, entering the URL for the second URL on the second line.

Designer Notes

In this chapter, you learned how to take control of your movie's timeline with ActionScript. You learned how to apply ActionScript to keyframes and buttons as well as how to use basic actions to direct the flow of your designs. In the next chapter, you'll take your knowledge one step further and learn how to create movie clips. Mouse events and clip events are also covered.

✦   ✦   ✦

Creating Basic Interactivity

♦   ♦   ♦   ♦

In This Chapter

Creating movie clips

Assigning actions to an object

Embedding video files

Understanding clip events

Understanding mouse events

Using buttons for navigation

Using buttons for interactivity

♦   ♦   ♦   ♦

In the last chapter, you learned how to assign actions to buttons and keyframes. Buttons can be used for many things. One of the most obvious is navigating to another part of your design: When the button is clicked, the movie advances to a predetermined frame. Buttons can also be used to trigger a change, for example, moving an object on Stage. You can also use buttons to load additional content or open up another Web page.

Actions can also be assigned to objects in your Flash movies. However, you can't just assign an action to a graphic symbol. If you want to modify a graphic object, it must reside in a movie clip. And in order for Flash to locate that movie clip, it must have a name.

In this chapter, you learn how to create movie clips and label them. You also learn how to assign multiple actions to a button that does different things depending on how the user's mouse interacts with the button. When the mouse interacts with the button, it is an *event*. The code you assign to an event determines what happens when the event occurs. Movie clips also have events. As you progress through this chapter, you learn how to use these ActionScript event handlers.

Note   The Actions panel's got lots of books. And some of these books have books within a book. To add some actions to your scripts, you have to click this book icon, then click that book icon, then click another book icon, and so on. Rather than bore you with a lot of words, I'm going to show the path to each action as shown in the following example: Click Actions⇨Movie Control and then double-click `goto`.

Creating Movie Clips

You can use a movie clip symbol in numerous places in a design — wherever you need animation on demand. A movie clip can consist of a single frame containing a single bitmap or graphic symbol you need to modify, or it can contain several frames of animation or even a video clip. When you create a named instance of a movie clip symbol, you can address it with ActionScript.

To create a movie clip:

1. Choose Insert New Symbol to open the Create New Symbol dialog box shown in Figure 5-1.

2. Enter a name for the symbol, choose the Movie Clip behavior, and click OK to enter symbol-editing mode.

3. Create the keyframes and desired animation using either frame by frame methods or tweening.

4. If the movie clip is to be a container for ActionScript, select the first frame, open the Actions panel, and create the desired script.

5. Click the Back button to exit symbol-editing mode.

Figure 5-1: You define a symbol's behavior with this dialog box.

Using movie clips for interactive content

Many Flash authors create single frame movies and rely on movie clips to supply all the action. You can do the same and rely on buttons or a navigation menu to play a movie clip on demand. When you create a movie in this fashion, all of your movie clips are on Stage. When your movie loads, you don't want the movie clips to play until summoned by the click of a button. Therefore, when you create the movie clip, leave the first frame blank. The only ActionScript on the first frame is a stop action, which prevents the movie clip from playing when it loads. Select the second frame and create a blank keyframe by pressing F7. Then you can begin adding your content. On the root timeline, create a separate layer for each movie clip. If you have several movie clips in your movie, consider creating a layer folder. Figure 5-2 shows a document with several movie clips housed in a layer folder.

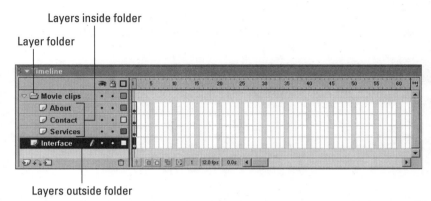

Figure 5-2: You can create individual movie clips for your design's content.

When you create a movie clip that will play on demand, you need the clip to cycle back to the first frame when it's finished playing. You do this by adding the goto action to the last frame of the clip. Figure 5-3 shows the timeline of one of the movie clips from Figure 5-2 with ActionScript on the last frame that returns the clip to the first frame.

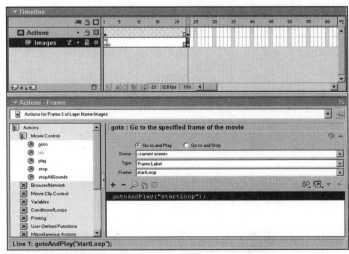

Figure 5-3: After a movie clip plays, this ActionScript returns it to the first frame.

Importing a video file into a movie clip

In prior versions of Flash, you could import QuickTime .MOV videos and incorporate them in your designs. However, you could only export the file from Flash in the QuickTime .MOV format.

In you have QuickTime 4.0 or better installed on your machine (Windows or Macintosh), you can import the following video file formats:

File Type	Extension
Audio Visual Interleaved	*.avi
Digital Video	*.dv
Motion Picture Experts Group	*.mpg, *.mpeg
QuickTime Movie	*.mov

If you have DirectX 7.0 or greater installed on your machine (Windows only), you can import the following video file formats:

File Type	Extension
Audio Video Interleaved	*.avi
Motion Picture Experts Group	*.mpg,*.mpeg
Windows Media Video	*.wmv,*.asf

If you work on the Windows platform and have both QuickTime and DirectX 7.0 or better installed, you can import all of the formats listed above.

Tip   If you are importing a video to play in a movie clip, follow the preceding steps to create a movie clip symbol with a `stop` action on the first frame. If the finished movie clip will be on Stage at all times, create a blank keyframe on frame 2 and select it prior to importing the video.

To import a video file into Flash:

1. Choose File⇨Import.

2. Navigate to the file you want to import and click Open. The Import Video dialog box appears. Choose one of the following options:

    • Embed video in document embeds the video file. Choose this option and you can publish the file as a *.SWF movie.

  • Link to external file creates a link from the document to the external
    video file. If you choose this option, you can only export the document
    as a QuickTime *.MOV movie. This option is available only if you are
    importing a QuickTime *.MOV movie.

 3. If you choose to embed the video, the Import Video Settings dialog box
    appears (see Figure 5-4).

 4. Drag the Quality slider to set the level of compression for the imported video.
    Alternately, you can enter a value between 0 and 100. Choose a high setting,
    and little compression is applied to the video, resulting in a higher quality clip
    at the expense of a larger file size. Lower settings result in higher compres-
    sion, which yields a smaller file size with a tradeoff in image quality.

 5. Drag the Keyframe slider to determine how often a keyframe is created. A
    keyframe is a frame with complete data. The frames before and after the
    keyframe only contain data that is changed from the keyframe. Enter a lower
    value and the embedded video will have more keyframes, resulting in a faster
    seek time at the expense of a larger file size.

 6. Drag the Scale slider to reduce the image size of the embedded video.
    Alternately, enter a value between 1 and 100. A setting of 50 percent effec-
    tively halves the image size. If your published movie will be viewed by users
    with slower processors, reducing the image size improves playback perfor-
    mance.

 7. Enable the Synchronize to Flash document frame rate option and the playback
    of the embedded video will be synchronized to the document frame rate.

 8. Click the button to the right of the Number of Frames to Encode per Number
    of Flash Frames field and choose an option from the drop-down menu. The
    default rate of 1 to 1 plays one video frame for each Flash frame. Choose a dif-
    ferent setting to create a smaller file size at the expense of choppy motion. For
    example, if you choose a rate of 2 to 1, the embedded video plays 1 frame for
    every 2 Flash frames; in other words, 1 frame out of 2 is dropped resulting in
    uneven motion.

 9. If audio is present in the video you are importing, the Import Audio option is
    enabled by default. Deselect this option to import the video without sound.

10. Click OK to import the video. If the file is large, Flash displays the Importing
    dialog box, which gives you a visual representation of the operation's
    progress.

11. After the file finishes importing, Flash displays a dialog box telling you how
    many frames must be created to play the video from beginning to end. Click
    Yes, and Flash creates the necessary frames.

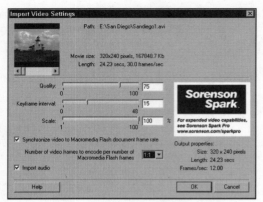

Figure 5-4: You control the quality and size of the embedded video by modifying import settings.

After importing the video, you can add the necessary ActionScript to finalize your movie clip. For example, you may want to create a new layer and a blank keyframe at the last frame of the video and use the `goto` action to return to the first frame of the movie clip, which if you've created it as outlined in the previous section, will be a blank frame with a `stop` action. If you don't add some type of control to the embedded video, it will loop continuously.

Tip

If you have a large number of videos in your design, embedding them all in a single movie results in a large file size and a lengthy download. Create separate documents for each video file and publish them as .SWF movies. Use the `loadMovie` action to load each file on demand. (You learn to use the `loadMovie` action in Chapter 7.)

Creating instances of movie clips

After you create a movie clip symbol, it's added to the document Library. To use the symbol in your design, select a keyframe and drag an instance of the symbol from the document Library to the desired spot on Stage.

Labeling the movie clip with the Property inspector

In order to have interactive control of the movie clip with ActionScript, you must create a name for the symbol instance. You use the Property inspector to label a symbol.

To name a symbol:

1. Select the symbol.

2. Open the Property inspector (see Figure 5-5).

3. In the <Instance Name> field, enter a name for the symbol. When you name an instance, you create a target for your ActionScript. Remember to choose a name that describes what the symbol does. This is especially import if you have a document with several named instances in it. Every named instance appears as a button in the Target Path dialog box. Without having a descriptive name to go by, you can easily select the wrong target.

Figure 5-5: You name an instance to provide a target for your ActionScript.

Assigning Actions to an Object

After you create an instance of a movie clip, you can use ActionScript to modify it. For example, you can use the `duplicateMovieClip` action to create several clones of a movie clip and apply future actions to the clones of the parent movie clip. You learn how to use the `duplicateMovieClip` action in Chapter 16 to create a background of sparkling stars. But before you can use ActionScript to create special effects in your designs, you must first know how to write a script for an object.

To assign ActionScript to an object:

1. Select the movie clip object you want to modify with ActionScript.

2. Open the Actions panel. Notice that panel's title reads Actions – Movie Clip.

3. Navigate to the action you want to assign to the object and use your favorite method to add it to the script.

Figure 5-5 shows an ActionScript that changes the x and y scale properties of a movie clip named placeHolder. Before the name of the movie clip is _root., which is the target path to the movie clip. In this case, the movie clip resides on the main or root timeline.

In Figure 5-6, the first line of code that reads `onClipEvent (load)`. The code that follows executes when the movie clip loads, which is known as a *clip event*.

About clip events

When you write ActionScript for an object, you control when the actions occur. By default, code you assign to a movie clip executes when the movie clip loads. However, you have several different events to choose from. When you create ActionScript in normal mode, Flash automatically adds the default on load clip event before the selected action. You can modify the clip event by clicking the line of code that lists the clip event. Doing so opens the text parameter boxes shown in Figure 5-7.

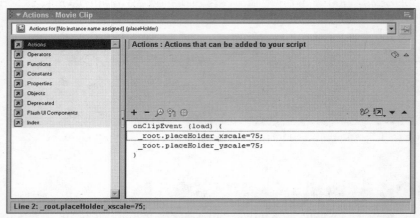

Figure 5-6: You can use ActionScript to modify the properties of an object.

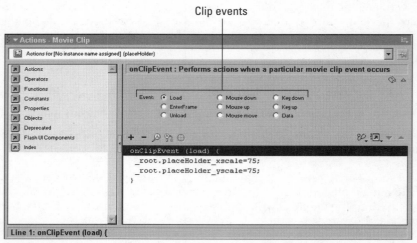

Figure 5-7: The clip event you choose determines when the ActionScript executes.

When you create ActionScript for an object, you can choose any of the following clip events:

    ✦ **Load:** The actions that follow this clip event execute when the movie clip loads.

✦ **EnterFrame:** The actions that follow this clip event execute when entering a frame of the movie clip. If the movie clip is a single frame, the actions that follow are constantly evaluated and executed.

✦ **Unload:** The actions that follow this clip event are handled after the first frame of the movie clip plays.

✦ **Mouse down:** The code that follows the Mouse down event occur after the down stroke of the user's mouse button.

✦ **Mouse up:** The actions that follow this clip event are handled after the user releases the mouse; the upstroke of the mouse button.

✦ **Mouse move:** The code that follows this clip event occurs whenever the user's mouse is moved.

✦ **Key down:** The actions following this clip event occur when a key is pressed. You use the getCode method of the Key object to tell Flash which key must be pressed.

✦ **Key up:** The action associated with this clip event occurs when a key is released. You use the getCode method of the Key object to tell Flash which key must be pressed.

✦ **Data:** The script associated with this clip event occurs when data is loaded as a result of the `loadMovie` action or `loadVariable` action.

If you prefer, you can specify the clip event before creating your code. To do this, you add the `onClipEvent` action to your script before adding other actions. To assign the event handler to a movie clip object:

1. Select the movie clip instance to which you want to apply the code.

2. Open the Actions panel.

3. Click Actions⇨Movie Clip Control and then double-click the `onClipEvent` action.

   After you select the action, Flash opens the parameter text boxes previously seen in Figure 5-7.

4. Accept the default Load event or select another event.

5. Select the action you want to occur after the clip event.

Using the with action

When you use ActionScript to address a movie clip object from a button or another movie clip, you must supply a target path for the Flash Player to follow. You may have seen Flash documents with many lines of code that begin `_root.` followed by the name of a movie clip, a dot, and then an action or property. When several actions or property changes are assigned to the same movie clip, you end up entering the target path every time you use a different action. You can alleviate some of this repetitive action using the `with` action. When you use the `with` action, you specify the target path to the movie clip once. The actions that follow occur with the specified target. The `with` action is quite handy when you have a number of actions that occur when a button is clicked.

To add the with action to a script:

1. Select the object you want to which you want to assign the action.

2. Open the Actions panel.

3. Click Actions⇨Variables and then double-click the `with` action.

   After you select the action, Flash displays it in the Script pane followed by <not set yet>, which is highlighted in red (see Figure 5-8).

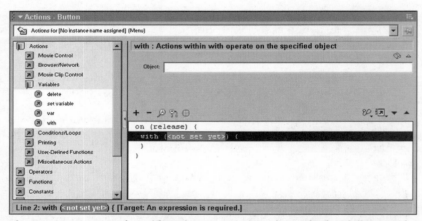

Figure 5-8: You use the with action to associate the code that follows with a specific object.

4. Place your cursor inside the object field and then click the Insert a Target Path icon that looks like a cross-hair to open the Insert Target Path dialog box shown in Figure 5-9.

5. Click the button that matches the symbol you want to target. Flash adds the target path to the script.

6. Add the actions that you want to occur with the targeted clip. Listing 5-1 shows code that changes the opacity, x scale, and y scale properties of a movie clip named myGirl when the user release the mouse button.

Indicates main (root) timeline

Labeled movie clips

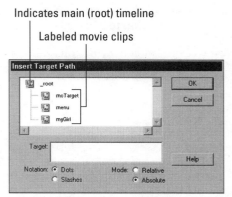

Figure 5-9: Every named instance of a symbol appears in this dialog box.

Listing 5-1: **Using the With Action**

```
on (release) {
  with (_root.myGirl) {
    _alpha=75;
    _yscale=50;
    _xscale=50;
  }
}
```

Assigning Actions to a Button

When you assign actions to a button, you can assign multiple actions. You can also use more than one mouse event on a button. For example, you can program a button to display a tooltip when users move their mouse over the button's target area, play a sound when the button is clicked, and load additional content or go to a specific frame when the button is released. Here's how to assign an action to a button:

1. Select the button that you want to program.

2. Open the Actions panel. The title of the Actions panel should read Actions – Button. If it doesn't, reselect the button.

3. Navigate to the action you want to assign to the button and double-click it to add it to the script. When you assign an action to a button, Flash uses the default on(Release) event handler.

4. To change the mouse event, click the line of code that contains the event handler and choose one of the events in the parameter text box area. Note that
you can use more than one event to trigger an action. Make sure that the only
events selected are the ones you want to trigger the actions that follow. Each
mouse event is covered in detail in the next section.

About mouse events

A mouse event describes how the viewer's mouse interacts with a button in your
design. For example, when a viewer's mouse passes over the button's target area, it
rolls over the button — the mouse event is a *rollover*. You can make the button
interactive by creating ActionScript for the rollover event. You can program a button to be multi-functional by taking advantage of several mouse events. When you
program a button, you can use any of the following mouse events:

✦ **Press:** Triggers the action when the button is pressed (the down stroke of a
mouse click).

✦ **Release:** Executes the action when the button is released (the up stroke of a
mouse click).

✦ **Release Outside:** Triggers the action when the user clicks the mouse while in
the button's target area, but releases the mouse button outside of the target
area.

✦ **Key Press:** Executes the action when the user presses a key.

✦ **Roll Over:** Triggers the action when the user's mouse rolls over the button's
target area.

✦ **Roll Out:** Executes the action when the user's mouse moves outside of the
button's target area.

✦ **Drag Over:** Triggers the action when the user's mouse is clicked and then
dragged over the button's target area.

✦ **Drag Out:** Executes the action when the user's mouse button is clicked,
dragged over the button's target area, and then moved beyond the button's
target area.

When you create an interactive button, it is often necessary to use mouse events in
conjunction with each other. For example, you can create a design where you program each button to display a an animated text movie clip that displays the title of
the section when a user's mouse rolls over the button . However, if users quickly
roll over the buttons in succession, you'll have several movie clips playing at once.
To prevent this, program each button to stop playing when a viewer's mouse rolls
out of each button's target area. Listing 5-2 shows a button programmed in this
manner.

Listing 5-2: **Assigning Multiple Events to a Button**

```
on (rollOver) {
  with (_root.sexysadie) {
    gotoAndPlay(2);
  }
}
on (rollOut) {
  with (_root.sexysadie) {
    gotoAndStop(1);
  }
}
```

The movie clip associated with the ActionScript in Listing 5-2 has a `stop` action on frame 1. When a user rolls over the button, frame 2 plays and the movie clip begins playing. As soon as the user rolls past the button's target area, the action associated with the `rollOut` event begins and the movie clip goes to frame 1 and stops.

Tip
Notice that the code for the `rollOver` and `rollOut` events are similar. When you create lines of code that you know will be similar, you can save yourself a lot of time using the Actions panel's context menu's Copy and Paste commands. Select the lines of code that are similar and then right-click (Windows) or Ctrl+click (Macintosh) and choose Copy. Click the last line of code in the Script pane, open the context menu, and choose Paste. You can now select an individual line of the code you just pasted and change parameters such as the mouse event that will be used or frame that will play when the code is executed.

Using the Key Press mouse event

You can program a button so that an action is executed when users press a key on their computer's keyboard. Triggering ActionScript with a key press is quite a useful feature. For example, you can create an object the moves in a certain direction when a button is clicked and also have the action execute when a user presses one of the arrow keys.

To use the Key Press event:

1. Assign an action to a button as discussed previously.
2. In the Actions panel, select the line of code that specifies the mouse event.
3. Select the Key Press event. After you select this event, a text field opens.
4. Using your computer keyboard, press the key you want to trigger the event. After you press a key, it appears in the Key Press field. Certain keys such as Ctrl, Shift, and Caps Lock are reserved for your computer's operating system. If you press one of these keys, the text field remains blank. Figure 5-10 shows a script that executes when the Up arrow is pressed.

Key Press mouse event handler

Key Press field

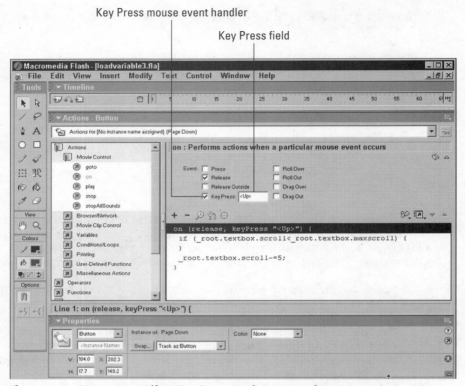

Figure 5-10: You can specify a Key Press to trigger an action.

Using the on action

When you assign an action to a button while creating ActionScript in normal mode, Flash automatically adds the on(Release) event to your script. If you know the event you want to use to trigger the action, or if you work in expert mode, you can use the on action to specify the mouse event you want to trigger the action.

To use the on action:

1. Select a button.

2. Open the Actions panel.

3. Click Actions⇨Movie Control and then double-click the on action.

   Flash displays the action in the Script pane, and the Release event is selected.

4. Select the event(s) you want to trigger the action.

5. From the left pane of the Actions panel, select the actions that you want to execute with the event(s).

Using buttons for navigation

When you use Flash to create a full-fledged Web site, you can use buttons as navigation devices. You can program individual buttons to navigate to different frames on your movie, play different movie clips, or load additional content on demand.

Interactive interface elements are discussed in greater detail in Chapter 12. In Chapter 4 you learned to use some basic actions to navigate to different parts of a movie.

You can quickly create navigation for a design by using the actions in the Movie Control book in conjunction with a button symbol. Figure 5-11 shows a navigation menu created for a photographer's Web site.

Buttons for graphic navigation menu

Figure 5-11: You can use buttons to create navigation for your designs.

If you study Figure 5-11, you notice the buttons are all the same size yet have a different look. Instead of creating a new symbol for each button, create one button, open the Document Library, and duplicate the button. You can then edit the duplicated button symbol to change the graphics and text displayed. Repeat this for the other buttons, and you can quickly create a navigation menu.

Using buttons for interactivity

In addition to using buttons for navigation, you can also use them to affect changes in your design. You can program buttons to open navigation menus, a feat you learn in Chapter 12. You can also use buttons to accept data from viewers and store the data in variables for future use. You can use buttons to change an object's properties. In Chapter 15 you learn to program a button to change the color of an object displayed in an e-commerce design. As you gain more familiarity with ActionScript, you'll think of new and exciting ways to add interactivity to your designs with buttons.

Navigate to this chapter's folder and copy the file button.fla to your hard drive. Use your operating system to disable the file's read-only attributes. Open the file in Flash and choose Control⇨Test Movie. Click the various buttons to get an idea of what you can create for your own designs. After you finish exploring the interactive buttons, return to movie-editing mode to select a button and open the Actions panel to find out what makes the button tick.

Designer Notes

In this chapter you learned how to create the basic elements for interactive Flash designs. You learned how to create movie clips and how to choose a clip event to trigger an action. You also learned to program buttons for use as navigation devices and as triggers for interactivity in your designs. Finally, I showed you how to trigger an action upon a key press. In the next chapter, you'll learn to work with symbols, create loops, and more.

✦   ✦   ✦

Creating Elements for Your Movie

✦ ✦ ✦ ✦

In This Chapter

Working with symbols

Creating loops

Generating random numbers

Creating functions

Creating modular ActionScript

Chapter project: Navigating to a random frame

✦ ✦ ✦ ✦

When you take you designs to the next level with ActionScript, you modify garden variety graphic symbols by incorporating them in movie clips. This technique is known as *nesting* a symbol within a symbol. You address the movie clip with ActionScript to make the symbols nested within jump through the virtual hoop, so to speak.

You can also nest a movie clip within a movie clip. You use nested movie clips to pull off all manner of effects, one being the motion blur effect you learn to create in Chapter 16. One movie clip has the animation, and the other movie clip houses the ActionScript that causes the blur effect.

Prior to using ActionScript, you probably used the time-honored motion-tween to create your animations, or perhaps you used frame-by-frame animations to get the job done. When you animate movie clips with ActionScript, you can add a certain randomness to the equation by creating a script that directs the movie towards a random frame. You do this by creating ActionScript that generates a random number equal to or less than the last frame in a movie clip. When the code executes, the Flash Player jumps to a random frame in the movie clip.

In this chapter, you learn how to work with symbols and create frame-based loops and ActionScript loops. You also learn how to create ActionScript to generate random numbers and create your own functions. The latter part of the chapter shows you how to create modular ActionScript that you can use in any movie.

Note   The Actions panel's got lots of books. And some of these books have books within a book. To add some actions to your scripts, you have to click this book icon, then click that book icon, then click another book icon, and so on. Rather than bore you with a lot of words, I'm going to show the path to each action as shown in the following example: Click Actions⇨Movie Control and then double-click goto.

Working with Symbols

As you know, symbols are key ingredients in any Flash design. When you create a symbol, it's reusable. When you create a movie clip symbol, you can create code to modify the movie clip or communicate with it. When you begin to add movie clips to your design, you plant the seeds for interactivity with ActionScript. When you begin to nest other symbols within a movie clip, you take your production to a higher level.

Converting a graphic to a symbol

There will be times during the heat of creation that you begin creating an object on Stage for your design. After you finish creating the symbol, you may realize you're going to need it repeatedly throughout your production or that you'll need the ability to modify the symbol with ActionScript. You can quickly convert the object to a symbol by doing the following:

1. Select the object.

2. Choose Insert⇨Convert to Symbol or press F8. Flash opens the Convert to Symbol dialog box shown in Figure 6-1.

3. Enter a name and choose the appropriate symbol behavior. Remember the symbol behavior is not cast in stone; you can change it at any time by using the Property inspector or by selecting the object in the document Library, clicking the Properties icon, and then assigning a new behavior to the symbol.

4. Click OK. The object is converted to a symbol and is added to the document Library.

Converting a timeline animation to a movie clip

You can also convert animations on the main timeline to movie clip symbols. You can create the movie clip symbol with as many frames and layers from the main timeline as needed. After you convert the animation to a movie clip symbol, you can use ActionScript as needed on the movie clip. To convert a main timeline animation to a movie clip symbol:

1. Select all of the frames and layers used to create the animation.

2. Choose Edit⇨Copy Frames.

3. Choose Insert⇨New Symbol.

The Create New Symbol dialog box opens.

4. Enter a name for the symbol, choose the Movie Clip behavior, and click OK.

Flash enters symbol-editing mode.

5. Select the first frame and then choose Edit⇨Paste Frames.

Flash pastes the frames and layers you copied from the main timeline.

If the movie clip is displayed on Stage at all times, you don't want it to play until called by the click of a button. To prevent the movie clip from playing when it loads, follow Steps 6 through 8; otherwise, go to Step 9.

6. Select every frame in every layer by clicking the first frame on the first layer and then dragging across and up.

7. With all the frames selected, click the first frame and drag it one frame to the right to create a blank keyframe in the first frame.

8. Add the `stop` action to the first frame of the top layer. If the movie clip will have actions on several keyframes, it's advisable to insert a layer for your actions.

9. Click the Back button or click the current scene button to exit symbol-editing mode. The new movie clip is added to the document Library for future use.

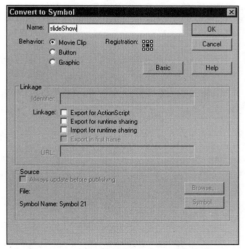

Figure 6-1: You can convert an object to a symbol when needed.

Nesting symbols

When you need to include other graphics or movie clips within a shell movie clip that contains your ActionScript, you create a new symbol and drag an instance of the symbol from the document Library into the newly created symbol. For example, when you create drag-and-drop elements for your Flash designs, you nest an invisible button in the movie clip and then assign the `startDrag` action to the invisible button.

Remember you can also import objects such as bitmap images when you're modifying a symbol. Nesting a bitmap within another symbol keeps everything compact and tidy. And if for any reason you need to change the bitmap currently nested in the movie clip, you can use the Swap Bitmap command, which will be discussed before the end of this chapter.

To nest one or more symbols within another movie clip:

1. Create a new movie clip as discussed previously.

2. Choose Window⇨Library.

3. Select the Library item you want to nest in the symbol and position it on Stage.

4. If the nested symbol is a movie clip and you're going to use ActionScript to modify it, open the Property inspector and enter a name in the <Instance Name> field.

5. At this point you can drag other symbols from the document Library and nest them within the newly created movie clip. After you add the other graphics needed for the symbol, click the Back button to exit symbol-editing mode. Alternately, you can double-click anywhere on Stage. Figure 6-2 shows an example of symbol nesting.

Nested graphic symbol

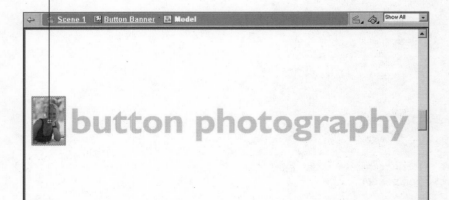

Figure 6-2: When you nest symbols, you can create a movie with a smaller file size.

Swapping symbols

A Flash document is often a work in progress, especially when you're creating a design for a client. Clients have been known to change their minds more frequently than politicians change their opinions. If your design is peppered with symbols that are nested in other symbols, you can quickly change the look of a symbol by swapping one symbol with another. If you design for clients who frequently change artwork while the design is still in production, this feature is invaluable.

To swap one symbol with another:

1. Select the symbol you want to swap. If the symbol is nested within another symbol, double-click the parent symbol to enter symbol-editing mode and select the nested symbol.

2. Open the Property inspector and then click the Swap button. Alternately, you can choose Modify⇨Swap Symbol.

   The Swap Symbol dialog box opens, as shown in Figure 6-3. Every symbol in the document Library is listed in this dialog box.

3. Click a symbol to view it in the preview window.

4. Click OK to swap the symbol. Alternately you can double-click the symbol's name.

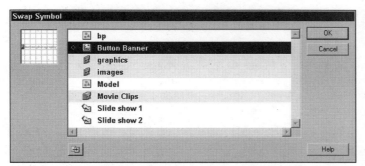

Figure 6-3: You can quickly swap one symbol for another to change your document.

Swapping bitmaps

Designers are fond of using bitmaps in their work. Bitmaps liven up your design, but you must use them judiciously to avoid bloating the file size of the published movie. If you create a document with bitmaps and decide a bitmap in your production isn't quite right, you can easily swap it for another bitmap in the document Library. The ability to swap bitmaps is new to Flash MX.

To swap one bitmap for another:

1. Select the bitmap you want to swap. If the bitmap is nested in another symbol, double-click the parent symbol to enter symbol-editing mode and then select the bitmap.

2. Open the Property inspector and click the Swap button. Alternately, you can choose Modify➪Swap Bitmap.

   The Swap Bitmap dialog box (shown in Figure 6-4) opens displaying a thumbnail of the currently selected bitmap and a list of other bitmaps in the document Library.

3. Click a bitmap to view it in the preview window.

4. Click OK to swap the bitmap.

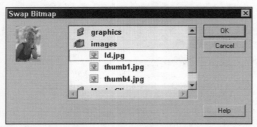

Figure 6-4: You can quickly update content by swapping bitmaps.

Tip If you work for a client who frequently changes bitmap content in a Flash design, when it comes time to update the movie, open the *.FLA file you created the document with. Import the new bitmaps and then swap them.

Creating Loops

You can create two kinds of loops in Flash: frame-based loops and ActionScript loops. You create a frame-based loop when you want a certain number of frames to continue playing. A frame-based loop is the basic ingredient in a preloader; the same frames loop until the movie content is loaded. You use actions to create the frame loop and then use ActionScript to launch the main movie when enough content has loaded for the production to play without interruption.

When you have ActionScript code that is repeated several times, you can simplify things by creating a loop. When you create a loop, you save the hassle of having to write the same bit of code several times. For example, if you use the `duplicateMovieClip` action to populate the movie with shimmering stars, you have to create a new name for each new clip the action creates. Instead of manually entering the code and naming the clips MC1, MC2, MC3, and so on, you create a loop for the number of clips you want to create.

Looping frames

To create a frame loop, you use the `goto` action on the last frame of a movie clip. If the movie clip is always on Stage, use the `stop` action on the clip's first frame, which is blank, and have the movie loop back to the second frame. A frame-based loop is what keeps repeating the animation in a preloader.

Creating ActionScript loops

You use ActionScript loops to speed up your work. With an ActionScript loop, you can repeat the same set of actions for a set number of times or create a loop that occurs while a set of conditions are true. An ActionScript loop occupies a single frame of the movie. Therefore, the loop must be capable of executing within a single frame. If you use the default frame rate of 12 FPS, the loop must execute within one-twelfth of a second. It is possible to create a loop so complex that it cannot execute within a single frame. If you create such a loop, when you test the movie, Flash displays the warning dialog box shown in Figure 6-5. When you see this warning dialog box, click No; otherwise, Flash may crash and you'll lose your current work.

Figure 6-5: If you create a loop that can't execute in a single frame, Flash displays this warning.

You have three types of ActionScript loops:

✦ **Do While:** This ActionScript loop repeats while a given set of conditions is true. When the condition is false, the loop terminates.

✦ **For:** This type of loop executes a specified number of times before termination. When the loop finishes, the next action in the script occurs.

✦ **While:** This loop is similar to the do while loop, but the condition takes precedence over the action being performed while the condition is true. When you create a while loop, the loop terminates as soon as the condition is false. With a do while loop, the action following the condition executes once more after the condition is false.

Creating a for loop

When you want to repeat an action for a given number of iterations, you create a for loop. When you create a for loop, you specify three parameters: the initial value of the variable, the condition that must be true for the loop to continue, and the increment the loop increases by. You can use the for action to create several lines of text on Stage that are stored as data in an array. Instead of writing several lines of code to transfer the text from the array to the movie, you create a for loop. Listing 6-1 shows a loop created with the for action.

Listing 6-1: **Example of a For Loop**

```
mc = new Array();
for (i=0; i<=5; ++i) {
  mc[i] = eval("mc"+i);
  mc[i]._alpha = 75;
  mc[i]._yscale = 80;
  mc[i]._xscale = 80;
}
```

In the example above, the properties of six instances of a movie clip called mc0 through mc5 are being changed. Lines 4 through 6 change the properties of each clip. Without the loop, you'd have to codes each property change for each clip, resulting in a whopping 18 lines of code. When you use a for loop, you eliminate many lines of code and free your time for more products tasks. The second line of code initializes the loop. The parameters for the action appear between the parentheses. The first parameter sets the initial value of i equal to 0, which is identical to the first element in an array. If you're not familiar with using an array to store data, you'll be up to speed after reading Chapter 9. The second parameter of the for action is the condition that must be true for the loop to continue. The loop in the above example continues as long as i is less than or equal to 5. The third parameter in the code determines the increment for each loop. In this case, the increment is 1. The third parameter could have been written as i+1, but ++i is a code shortcut that does the same thing. The lines of code between the curly braces execute as long as the condition is true. In the above example, each movie clip's opacity is reduced by 25 percent and scaled to 80 percent of its original size.

Note   There is also a post increment operator that would be written as i++. The post increment operator is used when two variables are present. The post increment operator increases the value of the first variable, but not the variable the operator is attached to. If you use a post increment operator in a loop with a single variable, the loop will fail because the value of the variable will never increase.

You can use the for action on a keyframe, a movie clip, or a button. To add a for loop to your script:

1. Select the object or keyframe where you want the loop to occur.

2. Open the Actions panel and then click Actions⇨Conditions/Loops. Then double-click for.

   The action is added to your script, and three parameter text boxes appear above the Script pane.

3. In the Init field, enter the beginning value for the loop.

   You assign the beginning value to a variable. You can create any variable name, but it's easier to use a single letter. Standard programming practice favors the letters *i, j,* or *k* for loop variables. Note that you do not have to begin a loop with 0 or 1. In the example in Listing 6-1, you enter an initial value of 3 to change the properties of the last three clips. Note that you can also create a loop that counts down (decrements) by starting with a high value and decreasing the value during each iteration of the loop. To begin the loop with a variable named i with a value of 1, enter i=1.

4. In the Condition field, enter the condition that must remain true for the loop to continue.

   The condition is the number of iterations before the loop ends. If you set the variable's value less than or equal to a given value, the loop ends when that value has been reached. For example, i<=10 stops the loop when the value of i is equal to 10.

5. In the Next field, enter the value the loop will increment by.

   You can use any applicable value in this field. For example, if you create a loop to change the property of every other movie clip, you'd enter a value of i+2, assuming your initial variable is i. To increase the initial loop value by a value of 1, you can use the code shortcut ++i, to decrease the value of the loop by 1 enter -i.

6. Enter the code that you want to occur during the loop. Figure 6-6 shows the Actions panel with the for action selected.

   The code in this figure uses the trace action to record the loop as it counts down from 10 to 1. The trace action is used when you need to trace the value of a variable when debugging a document. In Figure 6-6, it is used for demonstration purposes. To gain a bit of experience with the for action, launch Flash, duplicate the code in Figure 6-6, and choose Control⇨Test Movie. Flash publishes the movie in another window and the Output Window displays the variable as the for loop counts down to 1. After you successfully run the script, close the window. Open the Actions panel and modify the script, entering different values and conditions to count up or count down by different increments.

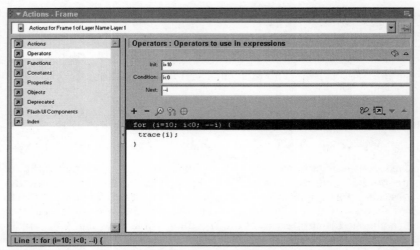

Figure 6-6: This for loop counts down from 10 to 1.

Understanding the while loop

You use a while loop to repeat a set of actions while a condition is true. When you create a while loop, the condition takes precedence over the action being performed. In other words, the condition is evaluated before the action executes. When the condition is false, the loop terminates. Listing 6-2 shows the syntax format of the while loop.

Listing 6-2: **Using a While Loop**

```
while (this condition is true) {
     these actions are executed
}
```

You find the while loop in the Loops/Conditions book. When you add it to a script, you have only one parameter: Condition. Enter the condition that must occur for the loop to continue and then enter the actions you want to execute while the condition is true.

Understanding the do while loop

You use a do while loop when the actions take precedence over the condition being evaluated. In other words, the actions are executed prior to the condition being evaluated. The syntax for a do while loop is shown in Listing 6-3.

Listing 6-3: Syntax of the Do While Loop

```
do {
     execute these actions
} while (this condition is true);
```

You also find the do while action in the Loop/Conditions book. When you add the action to your script, you have only one parameter to specify, the condition. After you specify the condition, select the first line of code and then add the action(s) you want to execute before the condition is evaluated.

Generating Random Numbers

Another useful element you can use for your designs is the ability to generate random numbers. You can use random numbers to create quiz games where a question is drawn from an array of questions in a random manner. You can also use random numbers to create random patterns, and patterns are something near and dear to a designer's heart. For example, you can generate a random number to position a movie clip on Stage. Furthermore, you can create additional ActionScript to duplicate the movie clip a random number of times. You learn how to use random numbers and the `duplicateMovieClip` action to create a starburst background in Chapter 16.

Using the random method of the Math object

When you need to generate a random number in one of your scripts, you use the random method of the Math object. The random method generates a random number between 0 and 1. To generate a random number within a specific range, you multiply the number generated by the random method by the largest number in the range of random numbers you want to generate. Listing 6-4 shows a script that generates a random number of movie clips.

Listing 6-4: Using the Random Method to Duplicate Movie Clips

```
k = 0;
i = Math.random()*50;
while (k<i) {
  duplicateMovieClip("myClip", "myClip"+k, k);
  k = ++k;
}
```

In the above listing, the value of the variable i is set to a random number between 1 and 50. The next line of code is a while loop that creates duplicates of the movie clip as long as the value of k is less than the value of i, which is a random number. The fifth line of code increase the value of the variable by k by 1 with each loop.

Cross-Reference

The `duplicateMovieClip` action is discussed in detail in Chapter 9.

You can also generate random motion, change an object's size to a random value, and more. To achieve this, all you have to do is set a property of an object equal to a random value. Listing 6-5 shows ActionScript that changes a movie clip's position, size, and alpha settings.

Listing 6-5: **Using the Random Method to Change an Object's Properties**

```
_root.myclip._x=Math.random()*540;
_root.myclip._y=Math.random()*280;
_root.myclip._xscale=Math.random()*100;
_root.myclip._yscale= Math.random()*100;
_root.myclip._alpha=Math.random()*100;
```

Each line of code in the above example is an expression that sets the object property equal to a random number. The steps that follow show you how to create a variable with a value equal to a random number. If you've used variables before, you know they are placeholders for data. If you're not familiar with variables, consider this your baptism by fire.

Cross-Reference

Variables are covered in detail in Chapter 8.

To create a variable with a value equal to a random number using the Math object, do the following:

1. Select the keyframe or object you where you want to declare the variable.

2. Open the Actions panel and then click Actions⇨Variables.

3. Double-click the `set variable` action to add it to your script.

   Two text parameters boxes appear above the script pane.

4. In the Variable field, enter a name. You can choose any name for a variable except a reserved keyword. (Naming variables are covered in detail in Chapter 8.) For the purpose of this demonstration, enter **myRandomNum**.

5. Place your cursor inside the Value field.

6. In the left pane of the Actions panel, click Objects⇨Core⇨Math⇨Methods.

7. Double-click the `random` method to add it to your script. In the Value field, the following code appears: `Math.random()`. This code is sufficient to generate a random number between 0 and 1. To generate a random number within a specific range, go to Step 8.

8. In the Value field, click to the right of the last parentheses and type `*` followed by the highest number you want to generate.

9. Click the Expression checkbox to the right of the Value field. When you generate create a variable equal to a number, it is a mathematical expression. If you fail to check the Expression checkbox, Flash reads this as text data. The code in Listing 6-6 creates a variable with a random value between 0 and 50.

Listing 6-6: Generating a Random Value

```
myRandomNum = Math.random()*50;
```

Rounding numbers

When you use the random method, Flash generates a random value between 0 and 1. When you multiply this value by a whole number, Flash does not round the number up or down. If you're creating a random value to reference a frame or need a randomly generated whole number for your script, you need to add additional code to round the number up or down. To do this, you use the round method of the Math object. The example below shows you how to create a variable that has a value equal to a variable number that has been rounded off.

To round a random value:

1. Follow Steps 1-4 of the previous section to create a variable called myRandomNum.

2. Place your cursor inside the Value field.

3. In the left pane of the Actions panel, click Objects⇨Core⇨Math⇨Methods.

4. Double-click the `round` method to add it to your script. In the Value field the following code is added: `Math.round()`. You enter the value you want Flash to round between the parentheses.

5. Place your cursor between the parentheses and in the left pane of the Actions panel, double-click `random`. The code in the Value field should now read: `Math.round(Math.random())`.

6. Place your cursor before the last parenthesis, type an asterisk (*****) followed by the highest number you want to randomly generate.

7. Click the Expression checkbox to the right of the Value field. Listing 6-7 shows the code needed to generate a random value between 0 and 150 that is rounded in accordance with mathematical principles.

Listing 6-7 Using the Round Method of the Math Object

```
myRandomNum = Math.round(Math.random()*150);
```

Saving Time with Functions

Flash has several built-in ActionScript functions that you use to perform certain tasks. For example, there are functions to convert text data to numbers, functions to get an object's property, functions that return the amount of time a movie has been running, and more. These functions are addressed as they apply to particular tasks or operations. In addition to the built-in Flash functions, you can create your own functions.

Creating a function

When you use several lines of code repeatedly in a design, assigning the same code to different movie clips can become tedious. You can save a considerable amount of time if you create a function for the repetitive code and then call the function when you need it. You can specify the parameters of a function, the type of object the function can be used with, or create a function with no parameters that you can use with movie clips, and other programmable objects. If you use a function repeatedly in a movie, it's a good idea to create it on the movie's first frame.

To create a function, do the following:

1. Select the object or keyframe where you want to create the function.

2. Open the Actions panel. Then in the left pane of the Actions panel, click Actions⇨User Defined Functions and then double-click `function`.

   Flash adds the action to your script and opens two parameter text boxes, as shown in Figure 6-7.

3. In the Name field, enter a name for the function.

When you choose a name, choose one that reflects what the function does. This makes it easier for you to remember what the function does as well as other designers working on the project. Don't include any spaces in the function name. If you must designate the difference between two words in a function name, use an underscore or capitalize the first letter of the second word, similar to the way the Flash programmers designate between words in an action. Remember you can use a reserved keyword as part of a function name, but you cannot use just a keyword.

4. In the Parameters field, enter the parameters for the function.

For example, if you are using the function exclusively with movie clips, mc is the proper parameter. If you're not sure which objects you're going to use the function with, leave this field blank.

5. After you enter the parameters, enter the actions you want the function to perform. Listing 6-8 shows a function that sends the movie to a random frame in a movie clip on the root timeline.

Listing 6-8: **Creating a Function**

```
function rndFrame(mc) {
  frmLabel=Math.round(Math.random()*(_root[mc]._totalframes))
  _root[mc].gotoAndPlay(frmLabel);
  ;
}
```

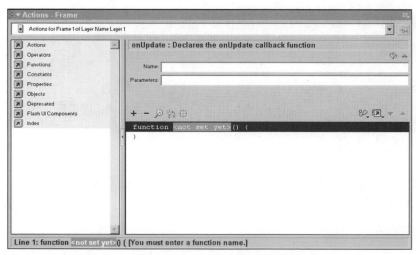

Figure 6-7: You create a function to streamline your work.

Calling a function

When you need to use a function, you call it. You can call a function from a keyframe in the movie or call it from a movie clip or button. When you call the function, you associate it with a named instance of a movie clip in your production.

To call a function, do the following:

1. Select the keyframe or button you want to call the function from.

2. Open the Actions panel. Click Actions⇨User Defined Functions and double-click `call function`.

   The action is added to your script and three parameter text boxes appear as shown in Figure 6-8.

3. In the Object field, enter the path to the function.

   If the function is declared in a keyframe before the function is called, you can leave this parameter blank. If the function is in a keyframe on another timeline, click the black Insert a Target Path button. In the Insert Target Path dialog box that appears, click the button that represents the movie clip the function is stored in.

4. In the Method field, enter the name of the function.

5. In the Parameters field, enter any parameters associated with the function.

   For example, if the function parameters address a movie clip, enter the name of the movie clip with quotation marks. Listing 6-9 shows the code used to call the function `rndFrame` that is embedded in a movie clip called My Function. The function is being used to send the movie to a random frame in a movie clip called *diva*.

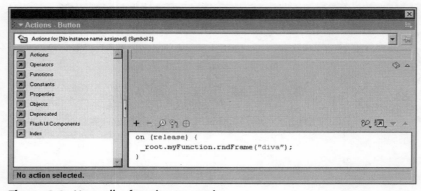

Figure 6-8: You call a function to use it.

Listing 6-9 **Calling a Function**

```
on (release) {
  _root.myFunction.rndFrame("diva");
}
```

Creating Modular ActionScript

Creating ActionScript is tedious work. If you're like most designers, you'd rather spend your time creating artwork for your Flash designs than writing code. If you end up creating a dazzling effect that involves several lines of code, you'll be further ahead if you create the effect in a movie clip instead of on the root timeline. Creating the effect in a movie clip does two things for you: First, you can use the effect in another part of your movie by just creating an instance of the movie clip on the timeline. Second, you can use the effect in another production by choosing File⇨Open as Library and then dragging the movie clip with the effect you need into the current document Library. If there are images or other graphic symbols in the effect that aren't suited to the document you're creating, you can import or create the objects you need and then swap them as outlined previously in this chapter. Several of the projects in this book may be useful in your own design work; for example, the moving navigation bar you'll create in Chapter 12. By creating this in a movie clip, you can use it in any other document; all you need to do is change the color of the buttons and the text description.

You can even create your own custom library of effects. After you've created several ActionScript effects that you've embedded in movie clips, do the following:

1. Create a new document.

2. Choose File⇨Open as Library, locate the file one of your favorite effect movie clips is stored in, and drag the effect into the document library.

3. Repeat Step 2 for the other effects you want to store as a custom library.

4. Choose File⇨Save As.

   Name the folder as you want it to appear in the Common Libraries menu, navigate to the Libraries folder in the Flash MX directory, and then save the file.

The next time you launch Flash, choose Window⇨Common Libraries, and your special effects library appears on the Common Libraries menu. Click your library to open it and drag the movie clip on Stage or into the current document Library.

Chapter Project: Navigating to a Random Frame

Now that you've been exposed to some of the ActionScript elements you can add to your designs, it's time to put your knowledge to use in a real world application. In this project, you'll be creating a function that generates a random number that is used to navigate to a different frame in a movie clip. To demonstrate the power of a function, you'll be using it on two different movie clips of different lengths.

On the CD-ROM Open this chapter's folder on the CD-ROM and copy the buttonPhotography.fla file to your hard drive. Use your operating system to disable the file's read-only attributes.

Creating a function to generate a random frame number

To create a function that generates a random frame number, do the following:

1. Launch Flash and open the buttonPhotography.fla file.

   Flash opens the document you see in Figure 6-9. The majority of the project has been created for you. All you have to do is create the function and program the buttons.

2. Click the first frame on the Actions layer and then open the Actions panel.

3. Click Actions⇨User Defined Actions and then double-click `function`.

   The action is added to your script and two parameter text boxes appear above the Script pane.

4. In the Name field, type **rndFrame**.

   You can enter any name for a function as long as it's not a reserved keyword. Refrain from using a function name with spaces.

5. In the Parameters field, type **mc**.

6. In the left pane of the Actions panel, click Actions⇨Variables; then double-click `set variable`.

   The action is added to your script and two parameter text boxes open above the Script pane.

7. In the Name field, type **rndLabel**.

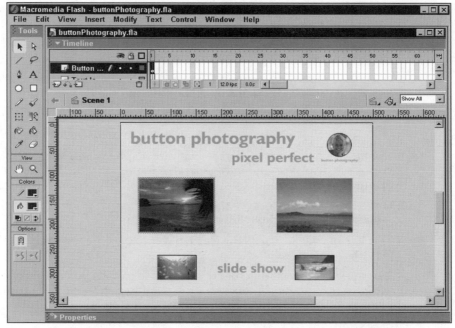

Figure 6-9: You can use a function to go to a random frame when a button is clicked.

8. Place your cursor inside the Value field, and in the left pane of the Actions panel, click Objects⇨Core⇨Math⇨Methods book and then double-click round.

The action is added to your script and your cursor is flashing between parentheses.

A frame label is a whole number. Without the round method of the Math object, Flash would never be able to equate the value generated by the random method of the Math object with a frame and the script would fail.

9. From the Methods book, double-click random.

The random method of the math object is added to your script. This is where you add the number that represents the upper limit of numbers you want randomly generated with the function. In this case, you're dealing with two movie clips with a different number of frames. In order to generate a number that represents the last frame of each movie, you use a movie clip property called *total frames* that returns the total number of frames in an instance of a movie clip.

10. Place your cursor between the parentheses after the word random and type **_root[mc].**.

    You enter mc between the square brackets to reference the parameter you declared in the function, mc for movie clip.

11. Open the Properties book and then double-click `_totalframes`. Click the Expression checkbox. Your second line of code should now read:

    ```
    rndLabel=Math.round(Math.random()*(_root[mc]._totalframes))
    ```

12. Click Actions⇨Miscellaneous Actions and then double-click `evaluate`.

    You have one parameter box to work with: Expression. The expression you create will display a randomly generated frame when the function is applied to a movie clip.

13. In the Expression field, type the following code: **_root[mc].gotoAndPlay(rndLabel)**.

    This line of code instructs the Flash player to play the frame number generated in the last line of code.

    This looks quite a bit different than the lines of code you normally associate with the `goto` action. In this case, you're addressing a movie clip on the root timeline, which is why you end up manually entering the expression rather than selecting the `goto` action from the Actions panel.

Putting the function to work

Now that you've created the function, it's time to put it to work in your movie. You'll be using the function with each button. Each button references a different movie clip.

To use the function with a button:

1. Select the button on the left side of the Stage and open the Actions panel.

2. Click Actions⇨User-Defined Functions and then double-click `call function`.

    The action is added to your script and three parameter text boxes appear.

3. In the Function field, type **rndFrame**. If for any reason you used a different name for the function, type that name.

4. In the Parameters field, enter **"ss1"**.

    This is one of the few times you don't refer to a movie clip by its path. Your finished code for the button should read:

    ```
    on (release) {
            rndFrame("ss1");
    }
    ```

The object field is left blank because the function resides on the root timeline. If you make the function modular by creating it in a movie clip, you would enter the movie clip's path in the object field.

5. Select the button on the right side of the Stage and repeat Steps 2 through 4, with the exception of typing **"ss2"** in the Parameters field this time around.

Test the movie and when you click the left button, the function directs your attention to a random frame in the first movie clip. Continue clicking the button and the function displays another frame. Click the right button and you see different frames generated in the second movie clip.

When you tested the movie in the preceding project, you may notice that clicking the button did not change the image. There are two reasons for this: The random number generated may have been 0 and there is not a frame 0 on the timeline, or the same number was generated twice in succession. You can add conditional statements to your script that cause a different number to be generated if the number is a duplicate or 0.

Cross-Reference You learn how to create conditional statements in Chapter 8.

Designer Notes

In this chapter, you started delving into your ActionScript tool kit. You learned to use symbols as ActionScript elements in your design and how to generate random numbers. You were introduced to a powerful ActionScript tool, the loop, which takes the drudgery out of writing repetitive code. Creating a user-defined function was also covered in detail. In the next chapter, you learn how to manage the content of your movies and keep the file size of your movies impressively small.

✦   ✦   ✦

Taking Control of Your Movie

✦   ✦   ✦   ✦

In This Chapter

Breaking a movie
into segments

Using the loadMovie
and unloadMovie
actions

Loading a movie into
a target

Communicating
between timelines

Demystifying targets
and paths

Chapter project:
Creating an
organizational chart

✦   ✦   ✦   ✦

Designers have a grand vision of their creations, often before they begin creating them. Even though Flash's strong suit is giving designers the capability to create fast loading, impressively small Web files (hence the acronym SWF), it is possible to break the bandwidth barrier by using every bit of eye candy known to Flash designers. If you've ever visited a Flash Web site that takes a long time to download, you have experienced the everything-but-the-kitchen-sink Flash designer at work. That doesn't mean that you can't include everything but the kitchen sink in your Flash movie; you just need to take control of the process so you don't break the bandwidth barrier and lose visitors because of lengthy downloads.

In this chapter, you learn a couple techniques to effectively manage the size of your grand design. First and foremost, you learn to break a Flash movie into logical segments. After all, you may be the greatest designer in the world, but people who view your Flash creation may not want to see all of it in one sitting or be patient enough to wait for it all to download. Then you'll learn to load a movie into a target window.

Note The Actions panel's got lots of books. And some of these books have books within a book. To add some actions to your scripts, you have to click this book icon, then click that book icon, then click another book icon, and so on. Rather than bore you with a lot of words, I'm going to show the path to each action as shown in the following example: Click Actions⇨Movie Control and then double-click `goto`.

Breaking Movies into Segments

When creating a large Flash Web site, the first step in the design process is to think of your movie as if it were a conventional HTML Web site. HTML Web pages are broken down into sections. You can do the same with your Flash movie. For example, if you are creating a site for a photographer, you can break the movie into four sections: the photographer's biography, the photographer's portfolio, services offered by the photographer, and the photographer's contact information. Each of these sections becomes an individual movie that is loaded when the visitor clicks a button on the navigation menu.

Dividing a Flash site into individual movies

After you make the decision to break the Web site into individual movies, create the base movie. Generally, the base movie includes the navigation menu for the site as well as the Web site's banner and other pertinent information. Figure 7-1 illustrates a base movie for a large Flash Web site. Notice that the center area of the Stage is blank. This is where the content of each section movie will appear.

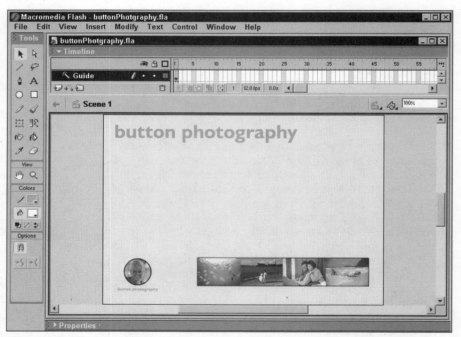

Figure 7-1: The base movie for the Web site contains the navigation menu and banner.

When you plan the site, keep the overall size of each movie in mind. If you've created a compelling introduction, visitors will wait several seconds for a section to load, but not much longer than that. If you're forced either by a client or by design considerations to create section content that will take considerable time to load, consider creating an animated preloader as discussed in Chapter 14.

Understanding levels

When you load a movie you assign it a level, which determines how the content of the new movie is displayed. The base movie is always level0 — in other words, the bottom floor. If you load another movie into level0, the base movie is erased with the new content. If, however, you load a movie into a higher level, the content is displayed on top of the base movie. If you're familiar with photo editing programs such as PhotoShop, levels in Flash work the same way layers in Photoshop do. For that matter, they work like the layers in Flash MX as content on a higher level eclipses anything on the level below it.

Creating movies for site sections

The first step in the process is creating the base movie for the site. If you've planned the site as described in Chapter 4, you'll know exactly what size to create the movie and which additional assets are needed to create the navigation menu, site banner, and so on. Planning is especially important when creating a site that you intend to break into sections. You can create a base movie as follows:

1. Create the base movie using the assets and navigation items that will remain visible throughout the movie. Remember your movie will be smaller in file size if you create symbols for any item that will be used more than once in the production.

2. Leave a blank area on Stage where you want additional content to be displayed. You'll have better control over the exact placement of your movie's assets if you enable rulers by choosing View⇨Rulers.

3. Create the ActionScript for each button as described in the upcoming "Using the loadMovie and unloadMovie Actions" section.

4. Choose File⇨Publish Settings. Remember to publish the movie using the version of Flash that your anticipated viewing audience is likely to have available. If you publish the movie using version 6 and the majority of your viewing audience only has the Flash 5 Player plug in, the version 5 player may not display the movie correctly.

5. Choose File⇨Save. Remember to choose a name that aptly describes your movie.

6. Choose File⇨Publish and Flash creates the base movie for your site.

After you create the base movie, your next task is to create the content that loads when a visitor clicks a navigation button. When you load a movie into a base movie, Flash resizes the loaded movie to the dimensions of the base movie. When you produce the movies for each section, create each one with the same dimensions as the base movie; otherwise, the graphics in the loaded movies distort when resized to the dimensions of the base movie. Use an area equivalent to the blank section of the base movie's Stage to create the content for the other movies. You can create a template to simplify the process of determining which part of the Stage is blank.

To create a template for section movies, follow these steps:

1. Open the base movie and choose File➪Save As.

2. Name the file *template*.

3. Create a new layer and name the layer *template*. Remember that you can create a layer by choosing Insert➪Layer or by clicking the Insert Layer icon in the Timeline window.

4. Right-click (Windows) or Ctrl+click (Macintosh) and choose Guide from the drop-down menu. Any object you create on a guide layer will not be visible when the movie is published. You can also display objects on the guide layer (or any layer, for that matter) as outlines by clicking the rectangular icon to the left of the layer's timeline.

5. Select the template layer and, using the Rectangle tool, create a rectangle that encompasses the blank area of the Stage. This rectangle serves as a visible guide to the area you use to create content for each movie you load into the base movie. Leave yourself a margin for error. Remember you can use rulers and the Property inspector to precisely size and place the template rectangle.

6. Delete all of the elements from the base movie.

7. Choose File➪Save and you'll have a template that resembles Figure 7-2.

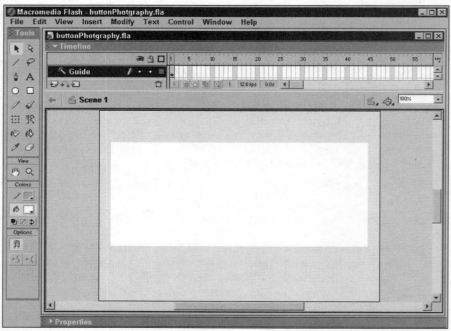

Figure 7-2: Create a template to accurately place objects on Stage in section movies.

Notice the difference between this figure and Figure 7-1. The objects you create in the white rectangle will fill the blank area in Figure 7-1 when movies you create from the template are loaded into a higher level.

After you've created the template, you can use it to create content for each section's movie. After you create a section movie using the template, choose File➪Save As and christen the movie to reflect the section content; for example, *about.swf*. This is the name you'll use in conjunction with the `loadMovie` action discussed in the next section.

Using the loadMovie and unloadMovie Actions

After you create the content for your movie, use the `loadMovie` action to load individual sections on demand. When a user clicks a button, the `loadMovie` action takes over and loads the specified content into the level you specify. If you load additional movie content into the same level, the previous movie is erased. If, however, you load additional content into a higher or lower level, you can use the `unloadMovie` command to remove unwanted content.

Loading a movie

You can use the `loadMovie` action in one of two ways. You can assign the action to a button, which when clicked loads the desired movie, or you can assign the action to a keyframe, whereupon the movie is loaded when the keyframe is reached.

To use the `loadMovie` action, follow these steps:

1. Select the button or keyframe that will trigger the `loadMovie` action.

2. Open the Actions panel and click Actions➪Browser/Network Control and then double-click `loadMovie` to add it to the script. If you assign the action to a button, choose the mouse event that will trigger the action. (For more information on mouse events refer to Chapter 5.)

3. In the URL field, enter the path to the movie you're loading. If the movie is in the same Web site, you can enter the relative path to the movie, for example, *about.swf*. If the movie is part of another Web site, enter the absolute path to the movie, for example, *http://www.dasdesigns.net/about.swf*.

4. In the field to the right of Level, enter the level you want to load the movie into. A Flash movie can have up to 99 levels.

5. If the movie you are loading contains variables and you want to load the variables into the base movie, click the triangle to the right of the Variable field and from the drop-down menu choose either Send Using Post or Send Using Get.

6. Close the Actions panel.

After you publish the movie, the specified movie will load when the keyframe is reached or the mouse event assigned with the button occurs. Figure 7-3 shows a typical ActionScript for the loadMovie action.

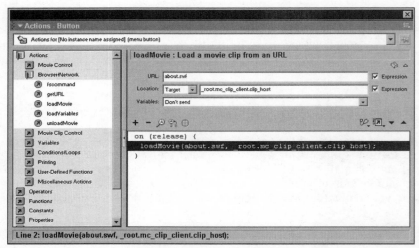

Figure 7-3: Use the loadMovie action to load additional content into your base movie.

Unloading a movie

As discussed previously, when you load a movie into a level, the loaded movie replaces the previous content of the level. If, however, you have movies loaded on different levels and load a movie into a level not previously used, the movies on the other levels continue to play and be visible. If this is not the effect you are after, you need to unload the movie(s) you no longer want to play. The unloadMovie action has one parameter: Location. To unload a movie, follow these steps:

1. Click the button or keyframe that will cause the movie to unload.

2. Open the Actions panel and click Actions⊃Browser/Network Control and then double-click unloadMovie. If you assign the action to a button, specify the mouse event that must occur to initiate the action.

3. Click the triangle to the right of the Location field and from the pop-up menu, choose either Target or Level.

4. If you choose Target, click the Insert a Target Path button and click the target you want to unload the movie from. If you choose Level, enter the level the movie you want to unload was loaded into.

5. Close the Actions panel.

If you have more than one movie to unload, repeat Steps 2 and 3. By using the `loadMovie` and `unloadMovie` actions, you can take control of your movies and create an interactive experience for viewers of your Flash movies. You can also load movies of different dimensions by loading a published Flash movie into a target movie clip.

Loading a Different-Sized Movie into a Target

When you use the `loadMovie` action to load content into a Flash movie, by default Flash sizes the new content to the same dimensions as the base movie. This works well in most cases, except when you need to load content of a specific size onto a specific area of the Stage. For example, you may want to change the movie's header when the user clicks a button. When this need arises, you can load a movie of a specific size into a target movie clip that is the same size as the movie you are loading. When you load a movie into a target, you load the movie into a named instance of a movie clip symbol. The first step in the process is creating the target movie clip.

Creating a target movie clip

When you create a target movie clip, in essence you are creating a placeholder for the content you want loaded when either a keyframe is reached or a button is clicked. When a designer creates a movie clip containing a graphic element, the norm is to center the content to Stage. The designer then positions the movie clip where desired when inserting an instance of it into the movie. However, when Flash loads a movie, it loads it from the upper-left corner, Stage coordinates (X=0,Y=0). If the target movie clip is centered to Stage, when you load a movie into the target, it will be positioned incorrectly. To accommodate for this, you must position the movie clip so that the uppermost left corner of the target is aligned to the center of the Stage.

Another factor you must consider is the movie's background. If you are loading the content into a blank area of the Stage, you create a rectangle the same size as the movie you are loading with no fill and a stroke color that matches the movie's background. However, if your design uses a bitmap background, the rectangle may be visible on certain parts of the Stage. To create a target movie clip that is not visible, follow these steps:

1. Choose Insert⇨New Symbol and choose the Movie Clip behavior.
2. Name the movie clip and click OK to enter symbol-editing mode.
3. Select the Rectangle tool.
4. Drag the tool on Stage to create a rectangle the approximate dimensions of the target movie.
5. Select the Arrow tool and double-click any part of the rectangle to select it.

6. Open the Property inspector.

7. In the W and H fields, enter the width and height of the movies you'll be loading into the target clip.

8. In the X and Y fields, enter a value of exactly half the x dimension and half the y dimension. This aligns the upper-left corner of the target movie clip for proper loading. Your movie clip should resemble Figure 7-4.

9. If the target movie clip will reside on a Stage with the same background color, open the Stroke panel, click the color swatch, and then click anywhere on Stage to match the rectangle's stroke to the background color. After changing the rectangle's stroke color, proceed to Step 13. If your background is a bitmap image, proceed to Step 10.

10. On the timeline, click the first frame to select it and drag it to frame 2.

11. Select the first frame and choose Window⇨Actions to open the Actions panel. Then click Actions⇨Movie Control and then double-click the stop action to add it to your script. Assigning the stop action to the first keyframe prevents the rectangle on frame 2 of the target movie clip from being visible when the movie loads.

12. Select the second keyframe and assign the stop action to it.

13. Click the current scene button to exit symbol-editing mode.

14. Select the target movie clip from the document Library and drag an instance of it on Stage.

15. Position the target movie clip where you want the content to appear when a user summons it by clicking a button or when a keyframe on the timeline is reached. If you create a movie clip with a blank first frame, the only clue you'll have to position the target is the movie clip's registration point, a small filled circle sign. Remember that this is the upper-left corner of the target movie clip. If you created a storyboard and know the precise coordinates of the target clip, you can use the Info panel to position it.

16. Open the Property inspector and in the <Instance Name> field, enter a name, and then press Enter or Return.

Tip   When you create a complex movie with many elements, it's good practice to first create a storyboard, as described in Chapter 3. The storyboard serves as your blueprint to precisely placing items such as target movie clips. Many designers have the ability to think visually. However, what looked great in your mind's eye may not work when you try to do it in Flash. A few minutes with pencil, paper, ruler, and calculator can save you hours of frustration when you're under deadline to get a project ready for a client.

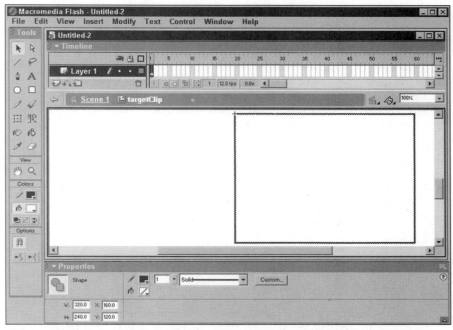

Figure 7-4: This target movie clip is properly aligned for loading a Flash movie.

Loading a movie into a target

After you create the target movie clip and position it on Stage, all that's left to do is create the ActionScript to load the desired movie into the target on command. If your target movie clip is a single frame, you can use the loadMovie action to load the content when a button is clicked or a keyframe is reached. If your movie clip has a blank first frame, you must communicate directly with the movie clip as outlined in the upcoming "Communicating between Timelines" section. If, however, your target movie clip is a single frame placeholder, you load the movie into the target clip by following these steps:

1. Select the button or keyframe that will trigger the loading of the movie.

2. Open the Actions panel.

3. Click Actions⇨Movie/Browser Control and double-click the loadMovie action. Alternately, you can drag and drop the action directly into the Script pane. If you assign the action to a button, choose the proper mouse event.

4. In the URL field, enter the name of the movie to be loaded. Remember to include the .swf extension.

5. Click the triangle to the right of the Location field and choose Target from the drop-down menu.

6. In the field to the right of Location, select the default entry of 0 and then click the Insert a Target Path button to open the Insert Target Path dialog box and choose the Absolute Mode. Within the dialog box you'll find an icon for every named movie clip instance in your movie, as shown in Figure 7-5.

7. Click the icon that corresponds to your target movie clip.

8. Click OK to close the Insert Target Path dialog box and within the Location field Flash replaces the default value of 0 with the correct target path, as shown in Figure 7-6. This figure shows the action applied to a button. Your ActionScript will differ if you apply the action to a keyframe.

9. Close the Actions panel.

After you publish the movie, when the event that triggers the loadMovie action occurs, Flash loads the movie into the specified target movie clip.

Tip   Whenever you complete a milestone such as programming a button, it's a good idea to test your handiwork. You can test the movie at its current stage of completion by choosing Control⇨Test Movie, or you can test a scene's current stage of development by choosing Control⇨Test Scene. If everything works as planned, save the file. It's always a good idea to periodically save a file in case a computer glitch causes Flash to become unresponsive.

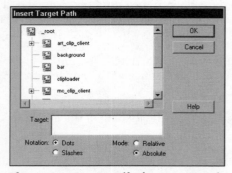

Figure 7-5: You specify the target movie clip by selecting it in the Insert Target Path dialog box.

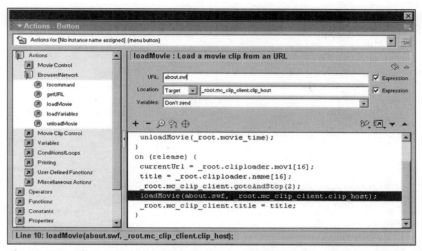

Figure 7-6: After you choose the target movie clip, Flash adds the path to your ActionScript.

Communicating between Timelines

When you create a target movie clip or need to access any movie clip, you must communicate between timelines. The base movie has its own timeline, and each movie clip you create has a timeline. A movie clip's timeline can be a single frame, or in the case of an animated clip, several frames. Computer geeks and programmers prefer the cold hard logic of code to get things done. Designers prefer a simpler method of performing this task so they can get back to the job at hand — being creative and designing unique content for their Flash movies. Designers prefer to do things with objects. They edit images with photo-editing software. They design Web pages with WYSIWYG (What You See Is What You Get) HTML editors. They create interactive animations with Flash. When designers have to work with anything resembling true code, they break out in a cold sweat and caress their digital tablets for comfort. Fortunately, the Flash programmers created a way for designers to communicate between timelines without having to write a single line of code. Designers can communicate between a movie's main timeline and the timeline of any movie clip by using the with action. The with action targets a movie clip that an action you specify occurs with (hence the name *with*).

When you communicate between the main timeline and one or more movie clips, you unleash some of Flash's interactive power. For example, you can create movie clips with animated text that plays when a user's mouse rolls over a button. You can also create movie clips with sound bytes that play when the movie advances to a specific keyframe.

Use the `with` action with target movie clips when the first frame of the clip is blank. Add the `with` action to the script and instruct Flash to go to and stop at frame 2. You then use the `loadMovie` action to load a specific movie into the target.

Cross-Reference   For more information on the `with` action, refer to Chapter 5.

Demystifying Targets and Paths

As you may have noticed in Figure 7-6, Flash has two different modes for target paths: Absolute and Relative. You can communicate from the base movie timeline (also known as *root*) to any other movie clip's timeline. You can also communicate from a movie clip to the root timeline, from a movie clip to another movie clip, or from a movie clip to itself.

You increase the amount of interactivity in your designs (and increase the indefinable but instantly recognizable WOW factor) when you use movie clips. When you create an action on a timeline and want it to affect another timeline, you must supply the proper path so Flash can find the target. To insert a target path, open the Actions panel and click the Insert a Target Path button (the black circle with a cross hair) just above the Script pane as shown in Figure 7-7.

Insert a Target Path button

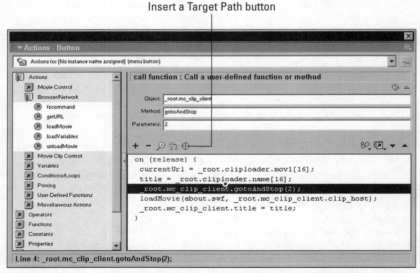

Figure 7-7: Click this button to open the Insert Target Path dialog box.

After you click the button, the Insert Target Path dialog box appears. Within this dialog box, you'll find an icon for every named movie clip instance in your production. Click the desired icon, and the name of the target path appears in the Target Path dialog box. You can now add an object to the target path, for example, the name of a variable you need to address within the target timeline. After you close the Insert Target Path dialog box, Flash adds the name of the target path to the ActionScript. If you look at the Insert Target Path dialog box shown in Figure 7-8, you see that it's not quite as simple as point and click. You have a decision to make in order to give Flash the information it needs to properly access the desired timeline. In the lower-right corner of the dialog box are two modes to choose from: *Absolute,* which uses the root timeline as the path starting point, and *Relative,* which uses the current timeline as the path starting point.

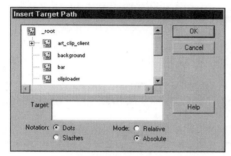

Figure 7-8: The mode determines the beginning point of the path.

Using absolute mode

When you use absolute mode, the path has its starting point on the movie's root timeline. You can easily spot a path in absolute mode as it begins with _root followed by a dot, which is then followed by the named instance of the movie clip. If a movie clip is nested within another movie clip, it is a *child* of the *parent* movie clip. For example, a path with the name _root.myclip.clip refers to a movie clip called "clip", nested within a movie clip called "myclip". You don't have to bother yourself with writing out extensive path names like this, Flash does it automatically when you click the child movie clip's icon within the Insert Target Path dialog box.

Using relative mode

When you use relative mode, you address the timeline of the movie clip that calls the action. For example, if you want to get the x property of a movie clip named *box* that is nested within a movie clip called *bigbox,* the path is _x.box. Whenever you see a path that is not preceded by root, it's a dead giveaway you're dealing with a path in Relative mode. Again, it is not necessary to enter the path when creating ActionScript. Simply switch to relative mode, click the icon that corresponds to the movie clip, and Flash creates the proper nomenclature.

Tip

If you prefer to venture boldly into the world of the programmer, you can save yourself some time by referencing a target path alias rather than using the Insert Target Path dialog box. You have three aliases to work with: _root, _this, and _parent. Use the _root alias to address the root timeline. Use the _this alias when you want to address the timeline of the movie clip calling the action. Use the _parent alias to address the parent movie clip from which the movie clip calling the action is nested.

Introducing the User-Defined Component

Another excellent way to take control of your movies is by using the user-defined component. The user-defined component is a movie clip with parameters that you can update on the fly. For example, if you have a movie with variables such as prices of objects in an e-commerce Flash movie, you can quickly change the prices by modifying the variables within the user-defined component. The movie clip that is the basis for the user-defined component need not have graphics. User-defined components can house nothing more than variables or an array, the contents of which are displayed in blocks of dynamic text. User-defined components are used in an upcoming chapter project. To learn the mechanics of creating a user-defined component, follow these steps:

1. Create a movie clip with variables or properties that you want to be able to easily update.

2. Choose Window⇨Library to open the document Library.

3. Select the movie clip you want to convert to a user-defined component and then right-click (Windows) or Ctrl+click(Macintosh) and choose Component Definition to open the dialog box shown in Figure 7-9.

4. Click the plus sign (+) to add an object to your component.

5. In the Name column, double-click varName and replace it with the name of the object as you want it defined in the Property inspector.

6. Double-click inside the Variable column and enter the name of the variable as it appears in your movie clip.

7. In the Type column, double-click Default, and a triangle appears to the right of the field. Double-click the triangle and choose one of the following:

   • **Default:** Use this option to specify a string literal or numeric literal value. Choose this option for values such as an object's name or price.

   • **Array:** Use this option to create a blank array that you can populate with several string or numeric values.

   • **Object:** Use this option to create a group of objects. This is similar to creating an array, but the number of objects can grow or shrink according to your needs.

- **List:** Use this option to create a list. This option is similar to an array, but the list cannot be changed after an instance if the user-defined component is in your movie. The user can choose only one item from the list.

- **String:** Use this option to create a string literal object. Add this object to your component when you need the ability to frequently update text within a dynamic text box.

- **Number:** Choose this option when you need to create numeric data. You can use ActionScript to perform mathematical calculations on this type of data whereas if you enter numbers into a string object, Flash reads them as text objects.

- **Boolean:** Use this object type to define whether a particular object the user-defined component refers to is enabled (true) or disabled (false).

- **Font type:** Use this object type to refer to the font in a text object.

- **Color:** Choose this data type to define a text object's color. You can also use this object type if your component contains ActionScript that modifies and object's color with the setRGB method of the Color object.

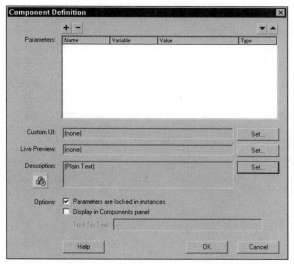

Figure 7-9: Use this dialog box to define a user-defined component's parameters.

8. In the Value field, double-click the default value to define it. If you define a variable (the default option), enter the value. If you choose Array, List, or Object, the dialog box shown in Figure 7-10 appears. Click the plus sign (+) to add a value; click the minus sign (−) to delete a value. To rearrange the order of a value, click the value and then click the Up arrow to move the value higher in the list; click the Down arrow to move the value lower in the list.

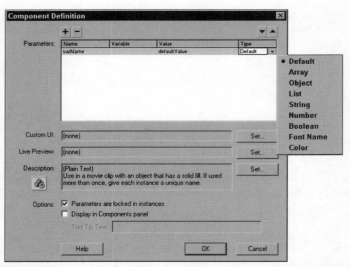

Figure 7-10: You can define the values of an array, list, or object with this dialog box.

9. Repeat Steps 3 through 7 for any other values you need to define in the user-defined component. You can mix different items within the rows of a user-defined component. For example, you can include variables and an array within the same user-defined component.

10. In the Description field, enter any notes that define what the user-defined component does. Think of the Description field as a memory jogger for when you modify the user-defined component as you update your client's site. The information you put in this field is also beneficial for other designers working on the same project.

11. Choose the Lock In Instance option to prevent modification of the Type parameters after an instance of the user-defined component is added to a movie.

12. Click OK to assign the objects to the component and close the dialog box. Figure 7-11 shows a user-defined component for a catalog item at an e-commerce Web site. Whenever a product description or catalog number changes, the designer updates the parameters of the user-defined component without having to revise any ActionScript.

After you create a user-defined component, you create instances of the symbol on Stage. You can then modify the value of each parameter to suit the movie you are working on. After you create a user-defined component, you can use it in any other movie. Use the Open As Library command to open the document Library the user-defined component is stored in, drag it into the current document Library, and modify the parameters to suit your current production. Create user-defined components for items you commonly use in your movies such as arrays and lists. When you create a user-defined component, you eliminate the drudgery of creating ActionScript and free your time up for adding more design elements to your production.

Tip   Macromedia has an extensive library of user-defined components available as extensions. You can download the free Macromedia Extension Manager, as well as user-defined components and extensions, from this Web site: www.macromedia. com/exchange/flash.

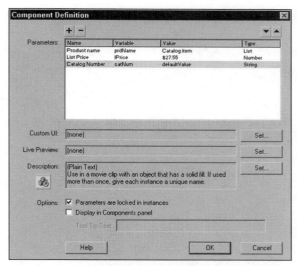

Figure 7-11: Update the parameters of a user-defined component instead of writing new ActionScript.

Chapter Project: Creating an Organizational Chart

Breaking a large site down into sections makes it easier for you to take control of your production. As an added benefit, each section of the site loads quickly, which ensures more people will view your Flash design instead of becoming impatient during a lengthy download and clicking their browser's Back button. This chapter's project shows you how to create an organizational chart. The base movie for the site is a simple interface that lists each office in the organization. The label for each office is a button. The pertinent information about each officer is stored in a variable and is displayed in a dynamic text box when a button is clicked. In addition, an officer's picture loads into a target when a button is clicked.

On the CD-ROM To follow along with this exercise, copy the Orgchart folder from this chapter's folder on the CD-ROM that accompanies this book to your hard drive. Use your operating system to disable the read-only attributes of each asset in the folder.

Beginning the design

The majority of the organization chart project has already been created for you. You'll finish the project by publishing a movie for the mythical organization's CEO and then create ActionScript to load a JPEG image into a target movie clip. To begin the project, launch Flash and then choose File⇨Open and open the orgChart.fla file shown in Figure 7-12.

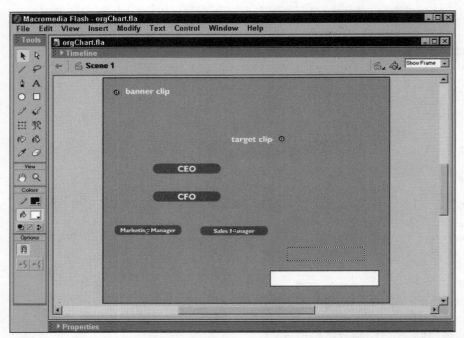

Figure 7-12: The base movie consists of an organization chart and a target movie clip.

Take a few minutes to examine the design of the movie before beginning the next section. Notice there is a blank placeholder at the top of the movie. An animated Flash banner named *banner.swf* loads into the placeholder when the movie begins. The ActionScript that loads the movie resides in the first frame of the movie on the Actions layer. This ActionScript also loads the image logo.jpg into the target movie clip on the right side of the Stage.

Notice the guide layer in Figure 7-12. This is set up so you know where the target movie clip resides. When you load a movie or image into a target movie clip that is the same color as the background, all you see is the movie clip's registration point. On the guide layer, a circle has been created to highlight the movie clip's registration point, and the movie clip's instance name is displayed beside it. For the purpose of this project, the movie clip instance is called *target.* The guide layer will not be visible when the movie is published, yet it serves as a handy reference to each movie clip instance's location and name. Create a guide layer whenever you have more than one target movie clip to identify in a movie.

To view the movie at this stage of creation, choose Control⇨Test Movie. After Flash publishes the movie, you see the animated banner and corporate logo, as shown in Figure 7-13. Click any button other than CEO (the button you'll be programming in a few minutes) and watch as the logo is replaced by the officer's picture and name. After you finish examining the movie, close the file.

Creating the ActionScript

After you create each movie for the site, you create the ActionScript that loads each movie into the target movie clip. The ActionScript you create will load the ceo.jpg into the *target* movie clip. The script executes when the user releases the mouse button after clicking the CEO button.

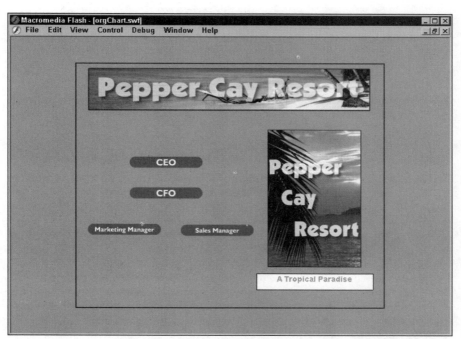

Figure 7-13: Each button is programmed to load a published movie into the target movie clip.

To program the CEO button:

1. Choose File⇨Open, navigate to the orgChart.fla file, and click Open.

2. Using the Arrow tool, select the CEO button.

3. Open the Actions panel.

4. Click Actions⇨Browser/Network and then double-click loadMovie to add the action to your script. Accept the default (on)Release mouse event.

5. In the URL field, type **ceo.jpg**.

Note The ability to load a JPEG image into a movie is a new and exciting feature of Flash MX. Previously, you needed to create a separate movie and import a JPEG when you wanted the ability to load a JPEG image from an external source.

6. Click the triangle to the right of the Location field and choose Target from the drop-down menu.

7. Select the 0 in the window to the right of the Location field and then click the Insert a Target Path button to open the Insert Target Path dialog box.

8. Click the button named *target* and then click OK to close the dialog box.

9. Click Actions⇨Variables and then double-click set variable. Two parameter text boxes appear above the Script pane.

10. In the Variable field, type **Name** and in the Value field, type **John Walker**.

Name is the variable assigned to the dynamic text box used to display the officer's name. When the button is clicked, text changes to reflect the new value of the variable. If for any reason you don't like the name John Walker, feel free to change it. However, Name needs to remain the same.

11. Repeat Step 10 to create a new variable named *Title* with a value of *Chief Executive Officer*. Your finished ActionScript should be identical to Figure 7-14.

12. Close the Actions panel and then choose Control⇨Test Movie. When you click the CEO button, the ceo.jpg file loads into the target movie clip.

13. Choose File⇨Publish, and Flash republishes the file to reflect the added ActionScript. Congratulations. Your movie is complete.

Tip If you create a design or technique you're especially proud of and don't want the rest of the world to know how you did it, create a base movie with no graphic elements and one keyframe. Assign the loadMovie action to the keyframe and use it to load the interface or intro movie. You can then use the loadMovie action to load additional content when a button is clicked. Although you can choose Protect From Import when you publish the movie to prevent other designers from opening the movie in Flash, savvy designers will still be able to find a published movie from their browser cache. When you create a movie in this fashion, other Flash designers won't be able to pull your design from their browser's cache because the base movie is blank.

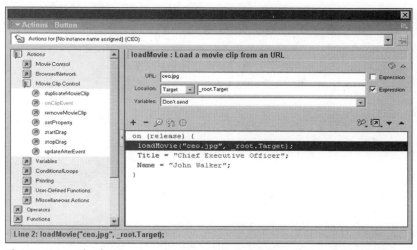

Figure 7-14: The button is programmed to load the movie when clicked.

The techniques you used to finish the organizational chart movie can be used with any movie. For example, you can create an effective movie for a client's product catalog by creating a main movie with an interface and banner and then creating a movie for each product category the company represents. You then use the `loadMovie` action to load each product category movie into the main movie on demand. Within each section, create a text button for each product and a target clip. Create an individual movie for each product that loads into the target movie clip. When the client's catalog needs to be updated, you simply modify the appropriate movies rather than redesigning the whole site. You can streamline the process even further by creating a user-defined component with an array of product names. When the client decides to refresh the product offerings, you update the array in the user-defined component.

Designer Notes

In this chapter, you added more ammunition to your ActionScript arsenal. You learned to manage a movie by breaking it into logical sections and then learned to program buttons to load content upon demand. Additionally, you learned to load movies and JPEG images of different sizes into a target movie clip. You experienced the power and flexibility you can add to your designs by creating user defined components. In the next chapter, you learn to use variables to store and dispense information.

✦   ✦   ✦

Creating Variables to Store and Dispense Information

CHAPTER

8

✦ ✦ ✦ ✦

In This Chapter

Understanding the different variable types

Creating variables

Understanding data types

Creating arrays

Evaluating conditions with statements

Using logical operators

Chapter project: Generating random quotes

✦ ✦ ✦ ✦

Up to this point, you've learned to use some basic ActionScript that you can use for navigation and to control the flow of a movie. When you add variables to your document, you add the capability to store information in the published movie and retrieve information.

With variables you have a wealth of possibilities. You can collect information from viewers of the published movie and forward the information to a CGI (Common Gateway Interface) mail forwarding script at a host site. When you create a variable, the contents are not cast in stone. If you break the word variable down, you have *able* and *vary*. Therein lies the power of the variable — it's an ActionScript object whose content can vary. At the start of an ActionScript movie, a variable's content can be one thing and with input from a user, or a few carefully crafted lines of code, the variable can contain something else entirely.

This chameleon ability of a variable makes it possible for you to create some interesting things in your design. In past chapters, you received a brief taste of the power of variables when used with functions. In this chapter, you learn about the different data types you can store in a variable as well as how to use them in your scripts. You also learn how to create an *array*. Think of an array as a supercharged variable. It's like a file cabinet filled with neatly organized folders of data you can retrieve in an instant. You also learn how to create conditional statements. A *conditional statement* evaluates an outcome. In plain English, a conditional statement does something if a given set of conditionals evaluate as true.

Note   The Actions panel's got lots of books. And some of these books have books within a book. To add some actions to your scripts, you have to click this book icon, then click that book icon, then click another book icon, and so on. Rather than bore you with a lot of words, I'm going to show the path to each action as shown in the following example: Click Actions⇨Movie Control and then double-click `goto`.

Understanding Variable Types

When you create a variable, it can hold one of three types of information: text data (known as *strings* to programmers), numeric data that you can use to perform calculations, or Boolean data. The following is a brief explanation of each data type.

✦ **Text or string data** is data that is comprised of text characters. You can use string data to display text and numbers. However, when you have a string variable, you cannot add numbers and use them in calculations. String literal data can be a single character, several words, or several sentences. You can use string literal data to store large amounts of text that are displayed in dynamic text boxes. In Chapter 11, you learn to create scrolling text that is stored in a variable. Examples of string data are: "Fred," "Mary," "That is the correct answer," and so forth. Note that each example is surrounded by quotes. That is exactly how string data appears in your scripts.

✦ **Numeric literal data** are numeric characters that are used to describe object but cannot be used in calculations. You can combine numeric literal and string literal data, for example, to describe a street address: 123 Mockingbird Lane.

✦ **Numeric data** are values that you can use in calculations. You can also use information stored in variables of this type to change an object's characteristics. In addition, you can use numeric data to retrieve information from an object on Stage, such as its current position, and then pass that information to another variable. When you create a variable that will be evaluated, you specify it as an expression. Examples of numeric data are: 56, 2.56, and 956.

✦ **Boolean data** can have only two possible values: true or false. Booleans are used in conditional statements, a topic that is covered later in this chapter.

In other types of programming, variables can only contain one type of data. In other programming languages, the type of data must be specified when the variable is declared. In Flash MX ActionScript, variables are much more forgiving. You can house numeric data in a variable at the start of a movie and replace it with string literal data as the movie progresses. When you change the type of data stored in a variable, the Flash Player adjusts for it and the script executes as you planned.

About string data

When you create a variable that stores string values, you have two types of information: *string literal*, which is comprised solely of words or characters from the alphabet; and *numeric literal*, data that contains numeric characters.

You can use string literal data to dispense and retrieve text information. If you design a movie for a client who wants to password protect a site, you retrieve the password the user enters into an input text box and store the data in a variable. You can also use a string literal variable to store a person's name and display it when needed in a dynamic text box, a technique you were introduced to in the project in Chapter 7. When you see string literal data in ActionScript, it is surrounded by quotation marks; for example, customerName= "Harry Smith", where customerName is the variable name and Harry Smith is the value of the variable. You can also create a new variable to combine (or *concatenate* as programmers refer to this) the contents of two or more variables. Listing 8-1 shows an example of this process in action.

Listing 8-1: **Combining the Contents of Two Variables**

```
firstName = "Jane";
lastName = "Doe";
fullName = firstName + " " + lastName;
```

When the variable full name is displayed, the result is as you would expect, Jane Doe. Notice the space between the quotation marks between firstName, and lastName. You know this is a string literal value because it is surrounded by quotation marks. Without this space, the variables would run together and you'd end up with JaneDoe. One more thing you need to notice about the third line in the above example is that the value of the variable fullName, which combines two string literal values, is not surrounded by quotation marks. That's because the variable must be evaluated by Flash as an *expression*. An expression is when you combine:

✦ The values of two variables

✦ Different kinds of variables

✦ Hard numeric values and variables to perform a mathematical computation.

In the above example, the expression is combining two string literal values to produce a third. If the variable fullName is not designated as an expression, the third line of code in the example above reads as follows: fullName = "firstName +\" \" + lastName"; and when the movie is published or tested variable fullName is displayed as: firstName +" " + lastName. Whenever you create a variable to combine the values of two or more variables with string literal data, you must specify it as an expression.

While on the subject of combining variables, it's important to understand how Flash combines numeric literal values. Consider Listing 8-2. In this example, you see two variables that are numeric literal data. The third line of code uses an expression to combine them. Everyone knows that 4 + 6 = 10, but the variables in the first two lines of code are not specified as expressions. The quotes around each value identify the value to the Flash Player as a numeric literal value, and Flash combines the literal data to produce a result of 46 when the script is executed. In order to add the two values as a numbers, you specify each value as an expression. When you specify a value as an expression, the Flash Player no longer recognizes the value as numeric literal data. Listing 8-3 shows the subtle difference (the lack of quotation marks around the variable's values) in the code when a variable's value is designated as an expression. The value of the variable designated in the third line of code will now be 10.

Listing 8-2: **Combining Two Numeric Literal Values**

```
numLiteral1 = "4";
numLiteral2 = "6";
combined = numLiteral1 + numLiteral2;
```

Listing 8-3: **Combining Two Numeric Values**

```
numLiteral1 = 4;
numLiteral2 = 6;
combined = numLiteral1 + numLiteral2;
```

About expressions

When you create a variable and designate its contents as an expression, you create a variable that can be evaluated using mathematical functions. In Listing 8-3, each variable is designated as an expression. The third variable uses a mathematical expression to produce a result that you'd expect when adding two numbers. You can also create an expression that performs multiple operations. An example of this is the expression you created to generate a random frame in Chapter 6's project.

In addition to using numeric data to perform mathematical operations, you can also use a variable whose value is designated as an expression to evaluate the properties of an object. For example, if you need to use the x position of movie clip named myClip, you create a variable and set it equal to the x position of the movie clip. After you declare the value of the variable as an expression, you end up with a variable that looks something like this: xPos=_root.myClip._x where xPos is the name of the variable and _root.myClip._X is the value. Because the value of xPos is declared as an expression, you can now use it as part of a mathematical expression.

Creating mathematical expressions

You can use mathematical expressions for many things in your designs. If your client wants you to create an e-commerce design with online shopping, you can tally up a customer's purchase by creating variables and using expressions to add up the customer's purchase plus applicable taxes. You can also use expressions to keep score of quiz games.

When you create expressions in your scripts, you use the standard math operands. You can add math operands to your scripts by manually entering them in a text parameter box, or you select an operator from the Arithmetic Operators book in the Actions panel. Table 8-1 shows the standard operators you can use in your expressions.

Table 8-1
Arithmetic Operators

Operand	Operation performed	Proper syntax
+	Adds two numbers	a+b
++	Increments a value by 1	++a or a++
–	Subtracts the second value from the first	a–b
––	Decrements a value by 1	––a or a––
*	Multiplies two values	a*b
/	Divides the first value by the second	x/y
%	Returns the remainder of a division. For example (16%3) returns a value of 1	(a%b)

The ++ operand and — operand are shortcuts. Whenever you need to increase or decrease a value by 1, you can use these shortcut keys. However, notice there are two ways to format these operands; you can put them before or after the variable you are incrementing or decrementing. Where you place the operand is all important when creating a script, especially when using these operands in a loop. Listing 8-4 and Listing 8-5 show the different values returned by placing the operand before or after a value being increased or decreased by 1.

Listing 8-4 **Pre-Increment Syntax of the Operand**

```
a = 124;
b = ++a;
```

The code in Listing 8-4 returns a value of 125. You would use this syntax if your script called to increase the value of variable a by a value of 1 while leaving the value of variable b unaffected.

The code in Listing 8-5 returns a value of 124 for b, but returns a value of 125 for a.

Listing 8-5: **Post-Increment Form of the Operand**

```
a = 124;
b = a++;
```

 Caution If you create a for loop and use the post-increment syntax to increase the value of the variable, the script will fail because the value of the variable would never increase. This in effect creates an endless loop, which causes the Flash Player to crash.

When you create expressions for your ActionScript, you can create an expression that uses multiple operations. For example, you can multiply a variable by a randomly generated number and then divide that computation by another value. Just remember to separate each operation with parentheses and remember which operators take precedence over the others so the expression generates the expected result.

About operator precedence

When you create a complex expression involving multiple operations, you must take operator precedence into account. The rules of mathematics dictate that certain operations are performed before others. These rules of precedence also apply to the expressions you create with ActionScript. As an example, consider the following equations:

$$x = 7 + 3 \times 10$$

$$x = (7 + 3) \times 10$$

The result of the first operation is 37, the second operation yields a result of 100. In the first equation, multiplication takes precedence over addition; in the second equation, the operation in brackets takes precedence over multiplication. It may help to remember the acronym *BODMAS* to keep the order of precedence straight: Brackets, Open (no brackets), Division, Multiplication, Addition, and Subtraction. Operations in brackets have priority over operations not in brackets; operations not in brackets have precedence over division, which has precedence over multiplication, which has precedence over addition, and last but not least is subtraction.

Creating a Variable

You create a variable whenever you need to store data in your movie or retrieve data input from a movie viewer. You've already created a few variables in projects presented earlier in this book. When you branch out and begin creating variables for your own designs, there are a few things you need to remember. Like everything else in ActionScript, variables have a set of rules you must adhere to — otherwise, your script will fail or you'll get unexpected results.

Naming a variable

When you name a variable, it's in your best interests to choose a name that describes what the variable does, yet at the same time remember the acronym *KISS:* Keep It Short, Simple. This is especially important when you use the same variable repeatedly in a design. One typo and Flash won't pass the value of the variable and your script will fail. Mistyped variables are one of the main reasons an ActionScript fails. Fortunately, you have tools to track the value of variables when debugging your ActionScript.

Cross-Reference   Debugging is covered in Chapter 14.

There are other things to consider when naming a variable. You cannot include any of the following when naming a variable:

✦ **Reserved words and commands:** If you use a reserved keyword or command to name a variable, Flash may mistake it as an action. Therefore, you cannot use `break`, `case`, `continue`, `date`, `default`, `delete`, `else`, `function`, `if`, `in`, `instanceof`, `new`, `on`, `return`, `sound`, `switch`, `this`, `typeof`, `var`, `void`, `while`, or `with` as a variable name. You can use reserved words as part of a variable name; for example, the name `dateToday` doesn't cause the script to run improperly.

✦ **Punctuation:** You cannot use any of the following punctuation as part of a variable name: {}, ; , or (). Also, if you begin a variable name with two forward slashes (//), Flash mistakes the variable as a comment.

✦ **Flash objects:** You cannot use any of the Flash objects as variable names as they will render the object inoperable. Date, Sound, Key, Math, and so on are all names of Flash objects.

Note   When you choose a Flash object as a variable name and test the movie, Flash displays a warning in the Output window telling you the variable conflicts with a Flash object and will obscure it. When you see this warning, it's best to choose another variable name.

✦ **Mathematical operators:** If you use +,-, *, or / as part of a variable name, Flash mistakes the variable for an expression.

✦ **Spaces:** You cannot include a spaces between words when naming a variable. For example, site password causes the script to fail. If you need to separate two names in a variable, use an underscore, as in site_password, or capitalize the second word, as in sitePassword.

✦ **Numbers:** You cannot precede a variable name with a number. A variable name of 4tier won't work; tier4 will.

When you create a name for a variable, it should be displayed in black in the Script pane. If you violate a syntax rule when creating a variable, the offending variable is highlighted in red with the message The variable name you have entered contains a syntax error.

Another thing to remember about variable names is case sensitivity. When you write ActionScript mode in expert mode, you must use the proper case. If you create a line of script gotoandplay (2) instead of gotoAndPlay (2), your script will fail. However, if you create a variable and initially name it myVariable and refer to it later as Myvariable, the Flash Player reads them as the same variable.

When you need to retrieve the value of a variable on a different timeline, you must include the path to the variable in the variable name. If you create a variable called currentTime in a movie clip called digitalClock and add the movie clip to the main timeline of the movie, the path to the variable is _root.digitalClock.currentTime.

Another thing to remember about variable names is that you can assign the same variable to a different timeline and Flash thinks it a different variable. For example, if you create another movie clip with the variable currentTime, Flash recognizes them as two separate variables, even though you may not.

Declaring a variable

When you decide to add a variable to your design, you must first create it, or as programmers are fond of saying, *declare* the variable. If you use a variable several times throughout the course of a movie, declare the variable on the movie's first keyframe. If you use variables in a movie clip, declare them on the movie clip's first keyframe.

To create a variable, do the following:

1. Select the keyframe or object where you want to declare the variable.

2. Click Actions⇨Variables and then double-click setVariable.

   The action is added to the script and two parameter text boxes appear above the Script pane.

3. In the Variable field, enter a name for the variable.

   Remember to adhere to the variable naming conventions presented earlier in this chapter.

4. In the Value field, enter the value you're assigning to the variable. Click the Expression checkbox if the value will be evaluated. Figure 8-1 shows a typical script to create a new variable.

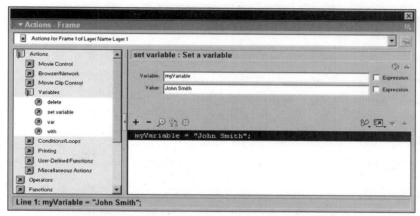

Figure 8-1: To use a variable in your design, you must first declare it.

Creating a local variable

If you use variables in a movie clip that won't be called from the root timeline, you can save yourself the hassle of having to refer to a timeline by declaring a local variable. When you declare a local variable, you can still change its value when a button in the movie clip is clicked for example. Creating local variable can be a tremendous time saver if you're creating modular ActionScript in a movie clip.

To declare a local variable:

1. Select the object or keyframe where you want to declare the local variable.

2. Click Actions⇨Variables book, and then double-click `var`.

   A single parameter text box named Variables appears above the Script pane. You can declare more than one local variable in this field.

3. Enter the name of the variable followed by an equal sign (=) and the variable's value. If you declare more than one local variable, separate each variable with a comma. If the value of the local variable is string data, remember to put the value between quotation marks. Figure 8-2 shows an ActionScript declaring a few local values.

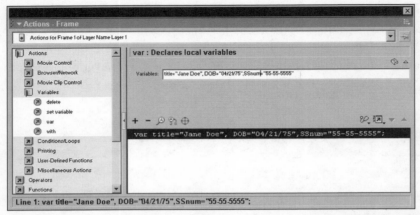

Figure 8-2: You can declare several local variables for a movie clip with a single line of code.

Passing a variable's value to other objects

When you have several variables in your movie, you can pass a variable's value to another value or create the value for another variable by combining the values of two or more variables. You can combine the numeric and string data to create new string data. You can combine the values of two or more variables with expression data to create numeric data for a new variable.

To pass the value of one variable to another, create a new variable and set its value equal to another variable. When you create the new variable, be sure to check the Expression checkbox or Flash will set the value of the new variable equal to the variable's name instead of the variable's value. Figure 8-3 shows a new variable whose value is equal to the value of another variable.

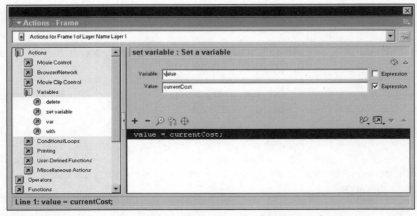

Figure 8-3: You can pass values from one variable to another.

You can also set the value of a new variable equal to two variables that contain string literal data. You can use this to personalize a user's experience. Users enter their names in an input text box, and you create a new variable to display a user's name combined with a greeting message, as shown in Figure 8-4. Again notice that the Expression checkbox is checked. If you're combining string literal data with a variable as in this example, add a space after the string literal data (the word *Welcome* in this example) and the variable's contents are correctly spaced when displayed in a dynamic text box. If you combine two variables with string literal data and need to place punctuation or a space between the two values, add the punctuation or space between the two variable names. Be sure to enclose the punctuation between quotation marks so it displays properly in a dynamic text box.

Cross-Reference   The subject of dynamic and input text is covered in Chapter 11.

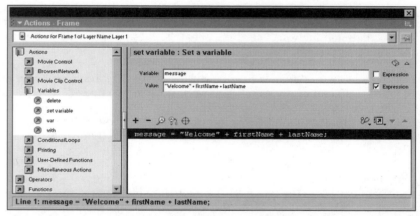

Figure 8-4: You can combine the contents of variables with string literal data.

Storing Data with an Array

When you need to store a lot of similar data for a design you are creating, you can use an array. An array is like a variable due to the fact that both store data. When you create an array, you can store many pieces of data. An array is like a neatly organized file folder in your file cabinet. For example, if you use a file drawer for client proposals, you create a folder for each client and arrange them in alphabetical order. To follow this analogy a step further, the file drawer is the array, and each client folder is an *element* in the array. Within each folder is all of the information related to that client. When you need the information, you simply pluck the folder from the file drawer. Arrays are like that. If you were to store your clients' names in a Flash movie, you could create a variable for each client, as shown in Listing 8-6.

Listing 8-6: **Comparing Multiple Variables to an Array**

```
// creating individual variables for each client
client1 = "Acme Enterprises";
client2 = "ABC Engineering";
client3 = "Collage Computers";
client4 = "Laxon Enterprises";
client5 = "Smith Auto-bionics";
client6 = "Zanadu Xylophones";

// Storing client names in an array
clients = new Array("Acme Enterprises","ABC Engineering","Collage
Computers","Laxon Enterprises","Smith Enterprises","Zanadu Xylophones");
```

In the above example, six client names have been neatly grouped in one array. In this example, you still have to enter each client's name into the array but you save the bother of creating numerous variables. What would you rather do — create 50 variables or create one array with 50 elements?

The clients array in the previous listing has six elements. The first element in an array's position (also known as *offset*), is always 0. When you need to refer to an element in the array, you refer to it by its offset. Therefore, if you wanted to create a variable named customer that retrieves information about your third client, the variable would look like this: `customer=clients[2]`. Notice that the array element is surrounded with square brackets.

You can use the elements from two arrays and combine them in a single variable. For example, you can store the names of each client contact person in a different array called contacts. When you create the array, you use the same array offset for the client contact person as you did in the clients array. The array offset for the client and contact person are the same. If you need to create a variable that displays the name of the client and the contact person, it would look something like this: `custContact = "The CEO for "+clients[2]+ " is " + contacts[2] +".".` When you cross reference different arrays, this is known as *cross indexing*. In the example above, each element for the clients array corresponds with the same element in the contacts array. In the custContact variable example, notice the addition of the string literal data. You can combine string literal data and array data to display just about anything in your designs. At the end of the chapter, you'll be using array data to generate random quotes.

Creating an array

When you create an array, you create an instance of the Array object. You set the instance of the Array object equal to a variable. The Array object has various methods you can use to manipulate the contents of an array and join the contents of one array to another. The Array object also one property that you can use to measure the number of elements in an array. You'll be using this property in the project at the end of this chapter.

When you decide to add an array to your design, you create a variable and set its value equal to the Array object. After you create the array, you add elements to it. When you go to the trouble of creating an array, chances are you use it often in the design. Therefore, it's good practice to define the array on the first keyframe of the movie or the first keyframe of the movie clip the array is housed in.

To create an array:

1. Select the keyframe where you want to create the array.
2. Click Actions⇨Variables and then double-click `setVariable`.
3. In the Variable field, enter the name of the variable you want associated with the array.
4. Place your cursor inside the Value field.
5. In the left pane of the Actions panel, click Objects⇨Core⇨Array and then double-click `newArray`.

   The code `newArray()` is added to your script.
6. Click the Expression checkbox.

That's all you need to do to create an array. The next step is to add the individual elements to the array.

Creating elements for an array

The elements in an array can be string literal data, numeric literal data, or numeric data. Flash ActionScript doesn't require that the elements of an array contain the same type of data, but it will be much easier to keep a handle on things if you keep string data and numeric data separate. Each array element is separated by a comma. If an array element is string literal data, it must be surrounded by quotation marks.

To create the elements for an array:

1. Repeat Steps 1 through 6 from the previous section.
2. Position your cursor between the parentheses in the Value field.
3. Enter each element of the array followed by a comma. If the data is string literal data, remember to sandwich the element between beginning and ending quotation marks. Figure 8-5 shows an array populated with similar data.

Tip   If you create arrays with multiple elements, create the data in your favorite word processing program. Enter the name for each element, remembering to separate the elements with a comma and include quotation marks for string literal data. If your word processor has smart quotes, turn them off as they will cause your script to fail if you copy them into the Actions panel. Select the array data and then copy it to the clipboard. In Flash, place your cursor between the parentheses and then choose Paste from the context menu. Working in a word processor is easier than creating copious amounts of data in the Script pane. As an added bonus, your word processor probably has a spell checker.

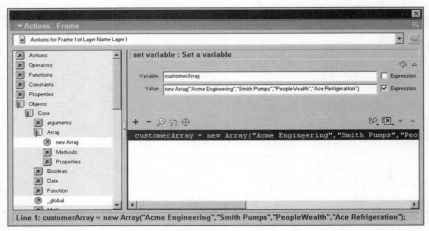

Figure 8-5: You populate an array with similar data.

Creating an associative array

You create an *associative array* when you need placeholders to accept data that will be displayed later. Each element in an associative array is linked to a variable in the movie. For example, if your client wants you to create a customer survey form, you can create an associative array to accept the data the customer enters. After the customer answers a question, the result is transferred to an element in the associative array. After the customer answers all the questions, they can be reviewed by transferring the element from the array to a variable, which is displayed in a dynamic text box. When you create an associative array, you create blank placeholders for data to be transferred to.

To create an associative array:

1. Create a variable and assign its value to the newArray method of the Array object as outlined previously.

    After you create the new array, your cursor blinks between the parentheses in the Value field.

2. Enter the number of elements in the array. Remember that the first element of an array is 0. If you're creating an array with 20 elements, enter 19. Listing 8-7 shows the code for an associative array with 20 elements.

Listing 8-7: **Creating an Associative Array**

```
surveyResults=newArray(19);
```

You finish your code for an associative array by creating a variable with the name of the array element you want to store the data in and set the variable's value equal to the data of the variable associated with the element. You do this by using the `eval` action, which evaluates the contents of the variable. Listing 8-8 shows the code needed to transfer data from the variable to its associated element in the array when the user clicks a button.

Listing 8-8: **Transferring Data to the Array**

```
on (release) {
  surveyResults[0] = eval("result1");
  }
```

Working with Conditional Statements

You add a conditional statement to a script when you want a certain set of actions to occur if the set of conditions are met and a different set of actions to occur if the conditions are not met. When you add a conditional statement to a script, the Flash Player evaluates the condition. If the condition is true, the actions associated with the statement are executed. If the condition evaluates as false, the next line of code is executed. You can create a conditional statement to evaluate the answer to a question in a quiz, or you can create a conditional statement that evaluates certain properties of an object in your movie. For example, in Chapter 16, you create a slide show that scrolls across the screen. To prevent the images from scrolling beyond the boundaries of the movie, you create a conditional statement. As long as the movie is less than or equal to the boundary, the condition evaluates as false and the clip continues moving. As soon as it reaches the boundary the condition evaluates as true and the next set of actions occur, which sets the position of the clip equal to the boundary, effectively stopping all movement. Listing 8-9 shows the conditional statement and associated action that halts the clip at the right boundary.

Listing 8-9: A Conditional Statement

```
if (reelPos>rightStop) {
  reelPos = rightStop;

  }
```

Notice that the code in Listing 8-9 begins with the if action. As long as the value of reelPos is less than the value of rightStop, the statement is false. As soon as the value of reelPos (the position of the moving slide show) is greater than the value of rightStop, the condition evaluates as true and the next line of code executes and sets the value of reelPos equal to rightStop (the boundary of the movie clip), which stops the clip from advancing further.

Creating conditional statements

When you need a different set of actions to occur based on an outcome, you create a conditional statement. You use operators to evaluate the statement; the operators you use differ depending on the type of data the statement is evaluating. The conditional statement in Listing 8-9 is an expression; therefore, mathematical operators evaluate the expression, in this case the greater than (>) operand. When you compare string data, you use logical operators.

To create a conditional statement:

1. Select the object or keyframe where you need to create a conditional statement.
2. Open the Actions panel.
3. Click Actions⇨Conditions/Loops and then double-click if.

    The action is added to the script and the Condition parameter text box appears.
4. Enter the condition that must be true for the next set of actions to occur.
5. Enter the actions that will occur when the condition evaluates as true.

Working with conditional statements that have multiple outcomes

You often end up creating scripts where you need more than one outcome depending on the properties of an object. As an example, when you display the results of a quiz, you display a different message depending on the player's score. When you need to evaluate more than one outcome, you use the elseif action and the else action.

To create a conditional statement with multiple outcomes:

1. Select the keyframe or object where you want to create the conditional statement.

2. Add the if action to your script as outlined previously and add the actions that occur when the condition evaluates as true.

3. Click Actions⇨Conditions/Loops and then double-click elseif.

    Like the if action, the elseif action has only one parameter: Condition.

4. Enter the condition that must be true for the associated action to occur.

5. Create the code that executes if the condition is true.

6. Repeat Steps 3 through 6 for other possible outcomes to the first condition.

7. When you arrive at the final possible outcome for the first condition, double-click the else action from the Conditions/Loops book.

8. Enter the condition that must be true in order to execute the associated action.

9. Enter the actions that you want to execute when the condition in the else statement evaluates as true. Listing 8-10 shows an example of the elseif and else actions used to display different messages depending on how well or poorly a player scored on a current events quiz.

Listing 8-10: A Conditional Statement with Multiple Outcomes

```
if (score <70) {
     message ="Take out a subscript to your local paper." ;
} else if (score<=79) {
     message = "Not bad, but you can do better.";
} else if (score<=89) {
     message = "Well done. You keep up with the news.";
} else if (score<=99) {
     message = "Excellent.You know your current events.";
} else {
     message ="Congratulations. You achieved a perfect score." ;
}
```

In the above example, the first statement checks to see if the player scored below 70. If the condition evaluates as false, the condition in the first elseif statement is evaluated. The Flash Player continues evaluating the possible outcomes until a conditional statement evaluates as true. If none of the elseif statements are true, the else statement takes control. The else statement is the last possible outcome; therefore, no parameters are required. If all conditions evaluate as false, the next line of code executes.

Using Logical Operators

You can also create conditional statements where two conditions are evaluated. When you compare two conditions in a single statement, you can specify that both conditions must be true to execute the actions associated with the statement or either condition must be true for the actions to occur. To create statements like these, you use the logical AND operator or the logical OR operator. There is a third logical operator that checks for the opposite of a condition: the logical NOT operator. Table 8-2 shows the logical operators you find in the Logical Operators book.

Table 8-2
The Logical Operators

Operator	Description
&&	Logical AND Operator
||	Logical OR Operator
!	Logical NOT Operator

When you use a logical operator, you insert it between the statements you're comparing. In the case of the NOT logical operator, you insert if before the condition you want to evaluate. Listing 8-11 shows the correct syntax for the logical operators.

Listing 8-11: **Proper Syntax for the Logical Operators**

```
// The Logical AND Operator evaluates the next statement.
if (password=="Enter"&&username=="Bill") {
  message = "Welcome Bill.";
}
// The Logical OR Operator evaluates the next statement.
if (password=="Enter"||username=="Bill") {
  message = "Welcome to our Web site.";
}
// The Logical NOT Operator evaluates the next statement.
if (!password) {
  message = "You are not authorized to view this site.";
}
```

In the above example, the first statement evaluates as true if the password AND the username are correct. The second statement evaluates as true if the password OR the username are correct. In the third example, the statement evaluates as true if an incorrect password is entered and a Boolean statement preceding the code defines what the contents of the password variable must be for the password to evaluate as true. You can create a statement that evaluates more than two conditions by placing the appropriate logical operator for your script between the conditions you want Flash to evaluate.

Working with Boolean Expressions

When you decide to do something, you evaluate a number of parameters. For example, if a potential client contacts you to create a Web site, you must weigh several factors. Do you have the time to create the site? Do you have the knowledge to meet the client's expectations? Based on your initial meeting, will the client be easy to work with or is the client from you-know-where? You have many possible outcomes, but when a computer evaluates a situation, there are only two possible outcomes: true or false. If you're familiar with the binary system, everything done by your computer is comprised of a long string composed of the numbers 0 and 1. Granted, a powerful computer can evaluate hundred of situations in the blink of an eye, but each situation is evaluated one at a time and each situation evaluates as either true or false.

So how do you use Boolean expressions in your designs? You can have one set of actions execute if an expression is true and another execute when the expression evaluates as false by creating a conditional statement as outlined previously. Listing 8-12 shows a Boolean expression in action.

Listing 8-12: **Boolean Expression**

```
on (release) {
  if (password==="Bill") {
    passed=true;
    if (passed) {
      gotoAndPlay("Enter");
    }
  } else {
    message = "You are not authorized to enter this Web site.";
  }
}
```

In the previous listing, if the password is Bill, the variable passed is assigned the Boolean value of true. The next line of code evaluates checks to see if passed has a value of true. If so, the movie advances to a frame labeled Enter, and Bill is granted permission to visit the Web site. If the password is not equal to Bill, the statement evaluates as false and passed evaluates as false; the visitor sees a message instead of gaining entry to the site.

Chapter Project: Generating Random Quotes

You've been exposed to a lot information about variables and arrays. Granted, it's not the most stimulating subject in the world, but as you'll find out in future chapters, arrays and variables are useful objects. Now that you've absorbed all of this information, it's time to put your hard-won knowledge to work. In this project, you create a movie clip with an array that stores 70 quotes. The quotes appear in random order. You'll be using a user-defined component that contains a timer, which displays the quote for a few seconds before another one is generated.

 On the CD-ROM   Open up this chapter's folder on the CD-ROM that accompanies this book and copy the rndQuote.fla and quotes.txt files to your hard drive. Use your operating system to disable the file's read-only attribute.

To begin the project:

1. Launch Flash and open the rndQuote.fla file.

2. Open the document Library and double-click the Random Quote movie clip.

   The clip opens in symbol-editing mode. Notice you have two layers to work with: Text and Actions. The Actions layer has three keyframes.

3. Click the first frame on the Actions layer and then open the Actions panel.

4. Click Actions⇨Variables book and double-click set variable to add the action to your script.

5. In the Variable field, type **rndQuote**.

6. Place your cursor inside the Value field and in the left pane of the Actions panel, click Objects⇨Core⇨Array.

7. Double-click newArray to add it to the script.

   The code newArray() appears in the value field. Your cursor blinks between the parentheses.

8. Minimize Flash, open your word processing software, and open the quotes.txt file you copied to your hard drive.

9. Select all of the text and copy it to the clipboard.

10. In Flash, place your cursor between the parentheses after newArray and right-click (Windows) or Ctrl+click (Macintosh) and choose Paste from the context menu.

11. Click the Expression checkbox. The array is now populated with 70 quotes.

In the next section, you'll be creating the code to generate the random number. Leave the Actions panel open — you'll need it again in a minute or so.

Generating the random number

Now that you've got the array populated, it's time to generate the random number that plucks a quote from the array. When you use the random method of the Math object, it generates a random value between 0 and 1. You could just multiply the random method of the math object by 70 to generate a quote, but that wouldn't leave you any room for future expansion. If you add or delete elements from an array, you have to remember how many elements are currently in the array and change the script accordingly. Instead of relying on a set numeric value to generate the random number, you use the length property of the Array object. When you add this to your script, Flash checks the array length and knows the exact number of elements in the array. In the future, when you add or subtract elements from the array, Flash evaluates the array length and knows the number of elements currently in the array.

To generate the random number:

1. Click Actions⇨Variables and double-click `setVariables`.

2. In the Variable field, type **rndNum** and then place your cursor in the Value field.

3. Click Objects⇨Core⇨Math⇨Methods and double-click `round`.

    The text `Math.round()` appears in the Value field.

4. Place your cursor between the parentheses, and in the left pane of the Actions panel, Click Objects⇨Core⇨Math⇨Methods and then double-click `random`.

    The method is added to your script, and the text `Math.random()` appears in the Value field.

5. Place your cursor between the parentheses and type **rndQuote**.

6. In the left pane of the Actions panel, click Objects⇨Core⇨Array⇨Properties and then double-click `length`. Click the Expression checkbox. Your finished ActionScript for the first frame should look like Figure 8-6.

Adding a timer and accessing the array

The first frame of the movie generates the first random number. In the second frame of the movie, you use the first random number to pluck the first quote from the array. However, if you don't have some way to pause the movie, the quote will be visible only for a fraction of a second — one-twelfth of a second to be exact, which is the amount of time it takes to reach the next frame. You could add 36 frames before the next keyframe, which pauses the movie for three seconds before the keyframe's ActionScript generates the next random number, but there's a much easier way to do it using a programmable timer.

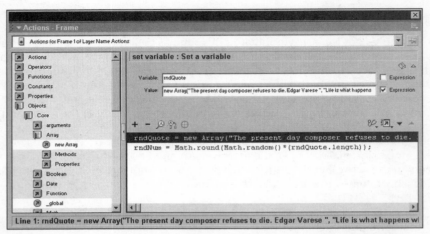

Figure 8-6: In the first frame, you create the array and generate the random number.

To add the timer and access the array:

1. Click the second keyframe on the Actions layer.

2. Open the document Library and drag the timer component on Stage. Place it anywhere—it won't be seen when you publish the movie.

3. With the timer component still selected, open the Property inspector and click the Parameter tab. Notice you have one parameter displayed in the window, seconds. To the right of the word *seconds,* you see the number 10.

4. Double click the 10, enter 3, as shown in Figure 8-7. and press Enter or Return.

   The timer is now programmed to pause on the frame for three seconds. If that's too much or too little time for your taste, you can change the value at any time.

5. Close the Property inspector, click the second frame on the Actions layer, and open the Actions panel.

6. Click Actions⇨Variables and then double-click `set variable`.

7. In the Value field, type **quote**.

   This is the same name as the variable in the dynamic text box that is already created for you. When the movie is published, the value of the variable you're now creating is displayed in the dynamic text box.

8. In the Value field, type **rndQuote[rndNum]**.

   The first part of the variable value, rndQuote, is the name of the array you created in the first keyframe. The brackets are used to designate the number of the array element (offset). The element offset is the value of the rndNum variable, a random number between 0 and the length of the array.

9. Click the Expression checkbox.

10. Click the third frame on the Actions layer. The code in Listing 8-13 has already been created for you.

11. Click the Back button to exit symbol-editing mode.

Figure 8-7: The timer component has one parameter: Seconds.

Listing 8-13: **Code for the Third Frame**

```
currentNum = rndNum;
rndNum = (Math.round((Math.random()*(this.rndQuote.length))));
if (rndNum == currentNum) {
  rndNum = Math.round(Math.random()*currentNum);
}
gotoAndPlay(2);
```

The code in Listing 8-13 checks to make sure the last random number is not duplicated. A new variable currentNum is set equal to the value of rndNum, the last random number generated. The second line of code generates a new random number using the same code as you created on the first keyframe. The conditional statement in the third line of code checks to see if the new random number is the same as the old one. If the condition evaluates as true, a new random number is created by multiplying the previous random number by the random method of the Math object. Granted, the new number could be the same as the old, but with an array of 70 elements, the odds are against it. The last line of code loops the movie clip to the second keyframe and displays another quote.

Finishing the project

To finish the project, open the document Library, drag the Random quote movie clip on Stage, and center it using the Align panel. To test the movie, choose Control⇨Test Movie. You should see a quote appear followed three seconds later by another quote. If the timing is too fast or slow, select the timer component and change the seconds parameter to a different value.

The finished product may seem a little bland. After all, there's nothing but text on Stage. But this little gem is stored in a movie clip, which means the ActionScript is modular, you can use it in any other movie by using the Open as Library command to open this library and then transfer the movie clip to another document. When you use the Random quote movie clip in another document, you bring the timer right along with it. As a matter of fact, the timer is modular as well.

When you use the Random quote movie clip in another document, you can modify the contents of the array to suit the movie. For example, if you have a client who wants to display customer quotes in the header of the Flash movie you are designing, here's the perfect way to do it. After the customer supplies you with the quotes, replace the quotes currently in the array with your client's quotes. You can modify the amount of time each quote is displayed by changing the seconds parameter of the timer component. If need be, you can modify the font style and color by changing the parameters of the dynamic text box that displays the quote.

Dynamic text is covered in Chapter 11.

Designer Notes

In this chapter, you learned to work with variables and arrays. The project at the end of the chapter demonstrates the amount of power you can add to your designs with variables and arrays. When you add arrays to your designs, you can pack an impressive amount of data into a small package. When you take it one step further and put all your code in a movie clip, you can use the movie clip in another document and modify it to suit the design. In the next chapter, you take your knowledge of ActionScript to the next level by using variables and expressions to modify the properties of objects.

✦   ✦   ✦

Creating ActionScript Elements for Your Movie

P A R T

III

◆   ◆   ◆   ◆

In This Part

Chapter 9
Generating
ActionScript to
Modify Objects

Chapter 10
Designing Interactive
Navigation

Chapter 11
Composing
Dynamic Text

Chapter 12
Building Interactive
Interfaces

Chapter 13
Creating ActionScript
Sound Objects

Chapter 14
Debugging an
ActionScript

◆   ◆   ◆   ◆

Generating ActionScript to Modify Objects

✦ ✦ ✦ ✦

In This Chapter

Modifying object properties

Changing object opacity

Using the Color object

Using the Key object

Duplicating an object

Chapter project: Creating an interactive animation

✦ ✦ ✦ ✦

Your previous Flash work probably featured some interesting animations using motion and shape tweening. The problem with motion and shape tweening is that after a while, the results are fairly predictable. Veteran Web surfers have seen a zillion Flash movies and tend to become a bit jaded. If a Web page doesn't jump up and grab them by the throat, they click the Back button and meander elsewhere.

You can take your designs to a higher plateau when you use ActionScript to modify the properties of objects in your designs. Instead of creating plain-Jane, me-too Flash designs, you can use ActionScript to create compelling designs that capture the attention of your audience and leave them wanting more.

When you place a graphic symbol in a movie clip, you can modify the properties of the object. You can make the object move on demand, create random motion, change the color of an object, scale an object, and vary its opacity. In this chapter, you learn how to modify many object properties. You also learn how to create a Color object. When you create a Color object, you can use it to modify the color of objects. Finally, I show you how to create code that modifies an object's properties with keystrokes from the user's keyboard.

Note The Actions panel's got lots of books. And some of these books have books within a book. To add some actions to your scripts, you have to click this book icon, then click that book icon, then click another book icon, and so on. Rather than bore you with a lot of words, I'm going to show the path to each action as shown in the following example: Click Actions⇨Movie Control and then double-click `goto`.

Modifying an Object's Properties

Every object you create has properties. Objects have a width and height (x and y) coordinates that represent the object's position on Stage, properties that reflect the object's opacity, and more. When you create an object and embed it in a movie clip, you can modify these properties with ActionScript.

Setting an object's properties

You can modify an object's properties by creating a variable that includes the path to the object, the property you want to modify, and set the variable's value to the amount you want to modify the property by. If you modify several properties of an object, you can use the `with` action to save some hard coding. You can also use the `setProperty` action to modify a specific property. Listing 9-1 shows the three methods.

Listing 9-1: Changing an Object's Properties

```
// Using the with action to modify properties
with (_root.sphereClip) {
  _x=125;
  _y=125;
}
// Changing properties by addressing the object's path
_root.sphereClip._x=125;
_root.sphereClip._y=125;
// Changing properties using the setProperty action
setProperty("_root.sphereClip", _x, 125);
setProperty("_root.sphereClip", _y, 125);
```

When you change an object's properties using the `with` action or by directly addressing the object's target path, you use the Properties book to locate the properties you add to your script. If you use either of these methods, you can access the target path using the Insert Target Path dialog box. Remember, you can assign ActionScript only to a named instance of a movie clip, and all named instances in your movie are listed in this dialog box. The third method is probably the simplest — you get the object's target path and the property and assign the value with a single action. However, this method is also the most time consuming if you have several properties to change.

The method you use to modify an object's properties depends on how comfortable you are, or how comfortable you plan to be, with ActionScript. Table 9-1 lists the properties you can modify with a brief description of each and the parameters you can modify, along with the properties you use to return a the current property of an object, such as the frame number the playhead is over in a movie clip.

Table 9-1
ActionScript Properties

Property	What It Modifies	Property Parameters
_alpha	An object's opacity	Any value between 0 (transparent) and 100 (opaque)
_currentframe	Returns the frame number currently being played	None, read only
_droptarget	Returns the absolute path of an object in slash (\) where a dragged movie clip is dropped	None, read only
_focuserect	A Boolean value that specified whether a movie clip has a yellow rectangle around it when it has keyboard focus	True or false
_framesloaded	Returns the number of frames loaded from a streaming movie	None, read only
_name	An instance's name	None, read only
_height	An object's height in pixels	Any numeric value
_quality	Render quality	Low, medium, high, best
_rotation	Degree of rotation	Any value between 0 and 360
_soundbuftime	Time before a movie begins to stream	An integer
_target	Returns the target path of the specified movie clip	None, read only
_totalFrames	Returns the total number of frames in a movie clip	None, read only
_url	Returns the URL of the .swf file from which the movie clip is downloaded	None, read only
_visible	Toggles visibility on or off	True or 1 (visible); false or 0 (invisible)
_width	An object's width in pixels	Any numeric value
_x	An object's x position	Any numeric value
_xmouse	Returns the current x coordinate of the mouse	None, read only
_xscale	An object's x scale	Any numeric value
_y	An object's y position	Any numeric value
_ymouse	Returns the current y coordinate of the mouse	None, read only
_yscale	An object's y scale	Any numeric value

It is possible to enter a value for many of the properties in the preceding table that is acceptable to the Flash Player but not realistic. For example, you can enter a value for an object's _x property that moves it beyond the boundaries of the Stage.

Using the setProperty action

When you use the setProperty action, you can address the movie clip root path, select the property to modify, and set the value using one action. The drawback to this action is that when you need to modify several properties of an object, you have to add the action for each property you need to modify. That is, you have to unless you use the ActionScript context menu to copy the line of code that contains the setProperty action and paste it as needed. You can then go back and select a different property and value.

To add the setProperty action to a script:

1. Select the object or keyframe that will trigger the property change.

2. Open the Actions panel and then click Actions⇨Movie Clip Control.

3. Double-click the setProperty action.

   The action is added to the script and three parameter text boxes appear. Your cursor flashes in the Target field.

4. Click the Insert a Target Path button and from the Insert Target Path dialog box, click the button for the movie clip's target path.

5. Click the triangle to the right of the Property field and choose a property from the drop-down menu.

6. In the Value field, enter an appropriate value for the property you are modifying, as shown in Figure 9-1. If you enter an inappropriate value, Flash does not display a warning dialog box. Refer to Table 9-1 for examples of applicable values.

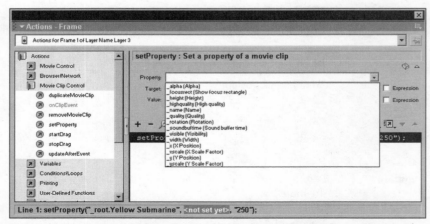

Figure 9-1: *Use the setProperty action to change an object's characteristics.*

Modifying an object by addressing its target path

You can modify an object's properties by creating a variable that addresses the target path of the object and the property you are modifying. You set the variable's value equal to an applicable value for the property you are changing. Refer to Table 9-1 for the range of values for each property. You can also use a variable for a value.

To modify an object's property by addressing its target path:

1. Select the keyframe or object that will trigger the object's property change.

2. Click Actions⇨Variables and then double-click `set variable` to add the action to your script.

3. In the Variable field, enter the target path to the object whose properties you want to change.

   You can enter the path directly in the field, or click the Insert a Target Path button to insert the target path from the Insert Target Path dialog box. Remember that you can only change the property of a named instance of a movie clip.

4. In the Variable field, type a dot (.) after the target path.

5. In the left pane of the Actions panel, click Properties and double-click the property you want to change.

6. In the Value field, enter a value or the name of a variable that contains the value of the property you are changing.

7. Click the Expression checkbox. Listing 9-2 shows several properties of a movie clip being changed. The lines of code preceded by two forward slashes are comments. Comments are notes you can add to ActionScript to describe the code that follows. (Comments are covered in Chapter 14.)

Listing 9-2: **Changing an Object's Properties by Addressing Its Target Path**

```
// Increases the xscale of a movie clip named bigSphere by 50%
_root.bigSphere._xscale = 150;
// Increases the yscale of a movie clip named bigSphere by 20%
_root.bigSphere._yscale = 120;
// Change the alpha value of bigSphere to 75%
_root.bigSphere._alpha = 75;
// Moves bigSphere to the X coordinate 525
_root.bigSphere._x = 525;
// Moves bigSphere to the y coordinate 25
_root.bigSphere._y = 25;
// Changes the width of bigSphere to 25 pixels
_root.bigSphere._width = 25;
// Changes the height of bigSphere to 75 pixels
_root.bigSphere._height = 75;
```

You can also create code that changes an object's property by a certain increment or decrement every time a button is clicked or a key is pressed. You can use this technique to create an interactive animation where the user can move objects with button clicks or key presses.

To create an expression that changes an object property by a given value:

1. Select the object or keyframe that triggers the property change.

2. Click Actions⇨Miscellaneous Actions and then double-click `evaluate`.

   One parameter text box named Expression appears.

3. Enter the target path of the object you want to apply the property change to.

4. Type a dot (.) after the target's name.

5. Enter a plus sign (+) to increase (increment) the value of the property or a minus sign (–) to decrease (decrement) the value of the property.

6. Type an equals sign (=) followed by the amount you want to increment or decrement the property by.

   Figure 9-2 shows the Expression field and several lines of code where an object's property is incremented or decremented by a set amount. You can also use a variable for the value. When you use a variable for a value, you can modify the variable to change the amount the property is incremented of decremented by. For example, you can speed up an object by increasing the value of a variable when a key is clicked.

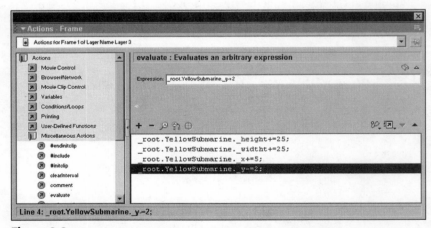

Figure 9-2: *You create an expression to increment or decrement a property value by a given amount.*

Getting an object's properties

You can use the properties of an object to modify other objects in your movie. For example, if you have a movie clip with an object that can be dragged exactly 100 pixels along the x axis, you can use the _x property of the object to control the volume of a sound in your movie. When the object's _x property is 0, the sound cannot be heard; when the value of _x property changes to 100, the sound plays at full volume. The _x property changes as the object is being dragged; therefore, you can use a variable to record the property of the object and modify the sound.

 Cross-Reference You find out how to make a sound controller in Chapter 13.

You can get an object's property using two methods. You can address the object directly by referring to its target path, or you can use the getProperty function. The resulting code for both methods is shown in Listing 9-3.

Listing 9-3: **Getting an Object's Properties**

```
// The following line of code addresses the clip target path to get a property
yPos = _root.sphereClip._y;
// The following line of code uses the getProperty function to return the
property
yPos = getProperty(_root.sphereClip,_y);
```

Both examples in the previous listing retrieve the same result. When you get an object's property, you set it equal to a variable so that as the property changes, the value of the variable also changes. To address the clip directly by its path, do the following:

1. Select the object or keyframe where you want the action to occur.

2. Click Actions⇨Variables and then double-click set variable.

3. In the Variable field, enter a name.

   Choose a name that reflects the property you are retrieving. In the previous example, the variable's value is equal to _y property of the movie clip, hence the name yPos.

4. Click inside the Value field, click the Insert a Target Path button, and from the Target Path dialog box, click the button that corresponds to the movie clip you whose property you want to use in your script. Then close the Insert Target Path dialog box.

5. In the Value field, type a dot (.) to the right of the target path.

6. Enter the property you want the variable to return. In the above example, the sphereClip's _y property is returned by the yPos variable. If you're not sure of the proper syntax for a property, position your cursor to the right of the dot, open the Properties book, and then double-click the property you want the variable to return.

You can also use the `getProperty` function to return the value of an object's property. This function is not as easy to use as the `setProperty` action because the `getProperty` function does not have object properties listed on a menu. You'll probably find it easier to address the movie clip target directly and then choose the desired property from the Properties book (as outlined in the previous steps). If you prefer to use the `getProperty` function, follow these steps:

1. Select the object or keyframe where you want the action to occur.

2. Click Actions➪Variables and then double-click `set variable`.

3. In the Variable field, enter a name that reflects the type of property the variable is returning.

4. Click inside the Value field and in the left pane of the Actions panel, click Functions and then double-click `getProperty`. The function is added to your script and the Value field `getProperty()` appears.

5. Place your cursor between the parentheses and click the Insert a Target Path button to add the movie clip's target path to the script.

6. To the right of the movie clip's path, type a comma and then enter the property you want the variable to return. If you're not sure of the syntax, in the left pane of the Actions panel, click Properties and then double-click the applicable property. Figure 9-3 shows a variable whose value is set using the `getProperty` function to return an object's property.

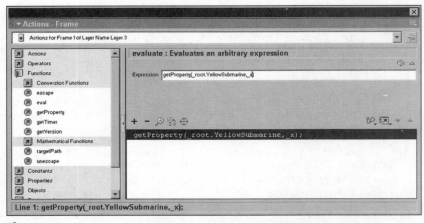

Figure 9-3: *Getting an object's property with the getProperty function.*

Using the Color Object

You can also use ActionScript to modify the colors of objects in your designs. When you modify an object's color, you work with the Color object. The Color object has methods that allow you to modify an object. The Color object has the following methods:

- **getRGB:** Returns the value of the last color transform applied to an object in hexadecimal format.
- **getTransform:** Returns the parameters used the last time an objects color was transformed using the setTransform method.
- **setRGB:** Sets the color of an object as specified in hexadecimal format.
- **setTranform:** Sets the transformation parameters for a color transform object.

Creating a Color object

When you modify the color characteristics of an object in your design using the Color object, you must first create an instance of the Color object. When you create an instance of the Color object, you specify the target path of the movie clip instance to be transformed.

To create a Color object:

1. Select the object or keyframe that will be used to trigger the change.
2. Click Actions⇨Variables and then double-click set variable.
3. In the Variable field, enter a name for the Color object.
4. Click Actions⇨Objects⇨Movie⇨Color and then double-click newColor.

    The action is added to your script and your cursor is flashing between parentheses.

5. Enter the target path to the movie clip that will be linked to the Color object.
6. Click the Expression checkbox.

That's the first step in modifying an object's color characteristics. After you set up an instance of the Color object, you use one of the methods to modify the color of the movie clip linked to the Color object.

Modifying an object's color

After you create a Color object, you can use the setRGB method to change an object's color by specifying a new color value in hexadecimal format, or you can use the setTransform method to modify the color characteristics of the original object and then transform them. You use the setRGB method to modify a solid color and the setTransform method to tint a multi-colored object such as a bitmap image or a vector object with a gradient fill.

Using the setRGB method to modify a solid color

You use the setRGB method of the Color object to transform a solid color to a new hexadecimal value. If you use the setRGB method with a multicolored object, the entire object is transformed to the color specified.

To modify an object's color using the setRGB method:

1. Create an instance of the Color object as outlined previously.

2. Click Objects⇨Movies⇨Colors⇨Methods book and then double-click `setRGB`.

    The method is added to the script and two parameter text boxes open.

3. In the Object field, enter the name of the Color object the method will be used with. This is the Color object you created an instance of as outlined in the previous section.

4. In the Parameters field, enter the hexadecimal value of the color you want to set using the following format: 0xRRGGBB.

    The 0x informs the Flash Player that the numbers are in hexadecimal format. RR is the hexadecimal value of red, GG the hexadecimal value of green, and BB the hexadecimal value of blue. You can enter any combination of letters from a through f; numbers from 0 through 9. For example, the proper syntax to convert an object to bright red is 0xFF0000.

Tip

If you're not sure of the hexadecimal value of the color you want to apply, choose Window⇨Color Mixer to open the Color Mixer panel. Click the swatch in the Fill Color well and choose a color from the palette. If you work with the Color Mixer expanded to show all windows, the hexadecimal value of the selected color is displayed below the Color Sample window.

5. Click the Expression checkbox. When the movie is published and the event to trigger the setRGB method occurs, the object will be changed to the colors specified.

**Cross-
Reference**

You work with the setRGB method in Chapter 12.

Using the setTransform method to tint an object

When you want to transform the color characteristics of a multi-hued object, use the setTranform method. If you've used the Advanced Color effect in the Property inspector to transform an object, the process is similar. You can modify eight sets of parameters. You use four of the parameters to vary the percentage of red, green, blue, and alpha in the original color, and four sets of parameters to specify the offset values of the original color. The offset values for the red, green and blue components correspond to the 8-bit, 256-color model. Each of the parameters is described in the following list:

- ✦ **ra:** Specifies the percentage to change the red component. Acceptable values are from –100 to 100.

- ✦ **rb:** Specifies the amount to offset of the red component. Acceptable values are from 255 to 255.

- ✦ **ga:** Specifies the percentage to change the green component. Specify a value from –100 to 100.

- ✦ **gb:** Specifies the amount to offset the green component. Specify a value from –255 to 255.

  ba: Specifies the percentage to change the blue component. Use a value between –100 and 100.

- ✦ **bb:** Specifies the amount to offset the green component. Use a value between –255 and 255.

- ✦ **aa:** Specifies the percentage to change the alpha component. Acceptable values are from –100 to 100.

- ✦ **ab:** Specifies the amount to offset the alpha component. Acceptable values are from –255 to 255.

It may help to think of these changes as before and after. The percentage values modify the values in the original color. They either add or remove a percentage of the component. This is similar to adjusting an object's color characteristics in an image editing program such as Photoshop. The offset values are the equivalent of tinting an object. For example, if you specify a value of 255 for the rb setting, it's the equivalent of applying a red tint over an object.

Tip   Before you decide on what settings to use with the setTransform method, select the movie clip and open the Property inspector. Click the triangle to the right of the Color field and choose Advanced from the drop-down menu. Click Settings to open the Advanced Effect dialog box. Drag the sliders in the two columns until you have the desired transformation. Jot the percentage figure for each component in the left window. They correspond to the ra, ga, ba, and aa parameters. Write down the offset values from the right column. These correspond to the rb, gb, bb, and ab settings. After getting the values, be sure to choose None from the Color field as you want to use ActionScript to transform the color. The Advanced Color effect will yield a larger file size than if you apply the change with ActionScript.

When you use the setTransform method to tint a bitmap, you need to create a new object. The object passes the transformation data to the Color object.

To tint an object with the setTransform method, do the following:

1. Create a Color object as previously outlined.

2. Click Actions⇨Variables book and double-click `set variable`.

3. In the Variable field, enter a name for the color transformation object. A logical choice is `myColorTransformation`.

4. Click inside the Value field and then in the left pane of the Actions panel, click Objects⇨Core⇨Objects.

5. Double-click `newObject`.

   After you create the color transformation object, you need to specify the parameters for the transformation. There are two different ways to do this. You can specify each parameter individually by creating an expression. This is handy when you're just modifying one or two parameters. For example, to apply a light blue tint to a bitmap, you need to use only the bb parameter. If you're modifying all the parameters, you create a single expression. The following list shows both ways of specifying the parameters for a transformation. The last item on the last specifies a value for each parameter, while the other items address a single parameter.

   • myColorTransform.ra=75

   • myColorTransform.rb=175

   • myColorTransform.ga=25

   • myColorTransform.gb=215

   • myColorTransform.bb=65

   • myColorTransform.bb=240

   • myColorTransform.aa=-52

   • myColorTransform.ab=15

   • myColorTransform={ ra: '80', rb: '204', ga: '30', gb: '212', ba: '12', bb:'90', aa: '40', ab: '70'}

6. Click Actions⇨Miscellaneous Actions book and then double-click `evaluate`.

   The Expression parameter box appears (see Figure 9-4).

7. In the Expression field, type **myColorTransform** and then use one of the methods outlined in Step 5 to set the parameters.

   • You address individual parameters by typing a dot (.) after the parameter followed by an equals sign (=) and then the value.

   • If you use the last method outlined in Step 5, enter the equals sign (=) and then curly braces. Between the curly braces, list each parameter is followed by a colon and the parameter value, which is enclosed in single quotes.

8. Click Objects⇨Movie book⇨Color book⇨Methods book and then double-click `setTransform`.

   The action is added to the script and two parameter text boxes appear above the Script pane.

9. In the Object field, enter the name of the Color object linked to the movie clip you're transforming.

10. In the Parameters field, enter the name of the color transformation object you created in Step 7.

    When the movie is published and the event that triggers the code occurs, the object is transformed to the parameters of the color transformation object. Figure 9-5 shows a typical script using the `setTransform` method. Figure 9-6 shows four bitmaps. The original is in the upper-left corner; the other three have been transformed using the `setTransform` method.

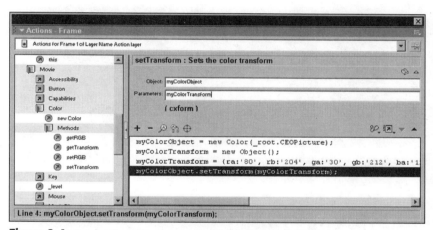

Figure 9-4: *You use the setTransform method to modify a bitmap's colors.*

On the CD-ROM

In this chapter's folder on the CD-ROM, you'll find a file called colorComponents.fla. Open the document Library and you'll find two components. You can add the setRGB component to a movie clip that includes a graphic with a solid fill. After adding the component to the movie clip, open the Property inspector and click the color swatch to specify the color you want the object to change to. You can use the setTransform component in a movie clip that has a bitmap object whose color characteristics you want to modify. If you use the component more than once in a document, give each instance a unique name.

Figure 9-5: You can achieve some interesting effects by modifying an object's color properties.

Using the Key Object

When you program a button, you can get it to accept keyboard input using the Key object. You can also program a movie clip to execute when a key is pressed using the Key Down or Key Up events. When your design calls for different things to happen based on a user's keyboard input, you use methods of the Key object. For example, you can program an object to do different things by using the Arrow keys as triggers. If the up arrow key is pressed, one thing happens; when the Down arrow key is pressed something different happens, and so on.

When you use the Key object, you create a conditional statement. If a certain key is pressed, the actions that follow occur. The actions that occur can be anything from an object moving to images appearing from off Stage. You can even use the Key object to load additional content. You can have a key press as a button event, and a key press can also be used to trigger actions in a movie clip. With a button mouse event or a clip event, you can only use one key as a trigger. When you use the Key object, you can use multiple keys for your ActionScript. You can address each key by its key code or take the easy way out and use one of the constants that addresses most of the popular keys you'd use in ActionScript, for example the arrow keys, Page Up, Page Down, spacebar, and so on.

You can use the Key object with other actions on a keyframe; however, you need to loop back and forth between two keyframes. If you don't loop back and forth, Flash will execute the action once when the keyframe is reached and not read additional key presses. A better way to use the Key object is with a single-frame movie clip using the onFrameEnter event. Flash executes the script every time the frame is entered.

To use the Key object in a script, do the following:

1. Select the object or keyframe that you want to use to trigger the script. Your best bet is to use a movie clip and use the onEnterFrame clip event.

2. Click Actions⇨Conditions/Loops and double-click if.

   The action is added to your script and the Condition parameter text box opens.

3. Click Objects⇨Movie⇨Key⇨Methods and double-click isDown.

   The text Key.isdown() appears in the Condition parameter box and your cursor flashes between the parentheses.

4. In the left pane of the Actions panel, click Objects⇨Movie⇨Key⇨Constants and then double-click the key you want to trigger the actions that follow.

5. Create the code you want to execute when the key is pressed. The code in Listing 9-4 makes it possible for the user to navigate the movie clip the code is assigned to by clicking one of the arrow keys. Notice that an expression has been used to increment or decrement the object's _x or _y property. By pressing the two of the arrow keys that trigger the objects movement in different axes, diagonal movement occurs.

Listing 9-4: **Creating Movement with the Arrow Keys**

```
//the right arrow key moves the object right in 5 pixel increments
if (Key.isDown(Key.RIGHT)) {
  this._x+=5;
}
//the left arrow key moves the object left in 5 pixel increments
if (Key.isDown(Key.LEFT)) {
  this._x-=5;
}
//the up arrow key moves the object up in 5 pixel increments
if (Key.isDown(Key.UP)) {
```

Continued

Listing 9-4 *(continued)*

```
  this._y-=5;

}
//the down key moves the object down in 5 pixel increments
if (Key.isDown(Key.DOWN)) {
  this._y+=5;
}
```

You can create additional statements that rotate the object if, for example, the right and up arrow keys are pressed at the same time.

Duplicating an Object Using the duplicateMovieClip Action

Before you used ActionScript to add a little magic to your designs, you probably dragged instances of graphic symbols from the document Library and put them through their paces using motion tweening. With ActionScript, you can create a screen full of moving objects with a few lines of code.

When you need to create one or several clones of a movie clip, use the duplicateMovieClip action. The duplicateMovieClip action takes a movie clip and creates the number of duplicates you specify. Combined with a while loop, this action is a powerful addition to any designer's arsenal. Figure 9-6 shows the action in use to create multiple copies of a bitmap image.

When you use the action, the duplicated movie clip begins playing on its first frame, no matter what frame of the parent clip is playing when the duplicate is created. The action has parameters that you use to specify the name of the duplicated clips as well as the depth, or number of copies you want to create. (In Chapter 16, you use the action to create a background of twinkling stars.)

Listing 9-5 shows the action used to create 20 duplicates with a while loop.

Listing 9-5: **Using the duplicateMovieClip Action**

```
k = 0;
while (k<20) {
  duplicateMovieClip("Sphereclip", "Sphereclip"+k, k);
  k = ++k;
}
```

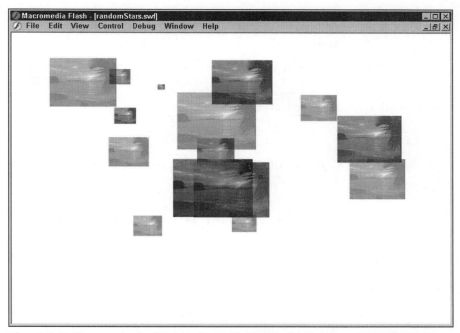

Figure 9-6: You create duplicates of an object with the duplicateMovieClip action.

Chapter Project: Creating an Interactive Animation

In Chapter 9, you learned to create conditional statements. In this chapter, you learned how to use keyboard input to trigger actions. In this project, you'll combine both of these skills to create an interactive animation.

On the CD-ROM Locate the submarine.fla file in this chapter's folder on the CD-ROM that accompanies this book. Copy the file to your hard drive and use your operating system to disable the file's read-only attributes.

In this project, you'll be animating a submarine (see Figure 9-7) by creating code that checks for a key press. The arrow keys will be used to navigate the submarine. You won't be creating each and every line of code. Much of the script has been written for you. You will create a conditional statement that checks for a key press and moves the sub in a specific direction.

To create an interactive animation:

1. Launch Flash and open the file submarine.fla. The file consists of a solitary submarine on a sea bottom.

2. Select the submarine and open the Actions panel.

You see several lines of code have been created for you. Notice that the first lines of code use the load clip event. This initializes the variable speed. The next several lines of code check to see if one arrow key is pressed and the opposite arrow key is not pressed. This code determines the direction and rotation of the submarine. You'll be creating a few lines of code to move the submarine towards the top of the Stage.

3. Place your cursor over the line of code that reads `// Check for keys that are pressed, set direction and rotation`.

4. Click Actions⇨Conditions/Loops book and double-click `if`.

5. Place your cursor in the Condition field, and in the left pane of the Actions panel, click Object⇨Movie⇨Key⇨Methods and then double-click `isdown`.

The action is added to your script and in the Conditions field, your cursor is flashing between parentheses.

6. In the left pane of the Actions panel, open the Constants book and double-click `UP`.

The words `Key.Up` appear between the parentheses.

7. In the Conditions field, click to the right of the parenthesis, type a space and then type **&& !**

You may recognize the double ampersand (&&) as the logical AND operator from Chapter 8. The single exclamation point is the Logical NOT Operator. It checks for the reverse of the next condition in the statement.

8. In the left pane of the Actions panel, Object⇨Movie⇨Key⇨Methods double-click `isdown`.

9. In the left pane of the Actions panel, click Object⇨Movie⇨Key⇨Constants and then double-click `Down`. (At this point, you may find it convenient to close one or two of the books to make navigating the Actions panel a bit easier.)

10. Click Actions⇨Miscellaneous Actions and double-click `evaluate`.

The Expression pane appears above the Script pane.

11. In the Expression field, type the following code: **_y- = speed**

This line of code decrements the _y property of the movie clip by the value of the variable speed.

12. In the Script pane, click the line of code you just created.

13. In the left pane of the Actions panel, double-click `evaluate`.

14. In the Expression field, type the following code: **_rotation = 0**

This line of code sets the rotation of the sub to 0 degrees when the up arrow key is pressed. Your finished code should look like this:

```
if (Key.isDown(Key.UP) && !Key.isDown(Key.DOWN)) {
    _y -= speed;
    _rotation = 0;
}
```

15. Close the Actions panel and then choose Control➪Test Movie.

After Flash publishes the movie and opens it in another window, press any of the arrow keys to set the sub in motion. After the sub is moving, press the right arrow key and the up arrow key. Notice that the sub veers to the right. When the sub moves beyond the range of the movie, it pops out on the other side. The sub's moving at a snail's pace, though. Press the Shift key to kick it into overdrive; press the spacebar to slow it back down again. After you're finished navigating your yellow submarine, save your work and study the complete code for the movie clip, as shown in Listing 9-6.

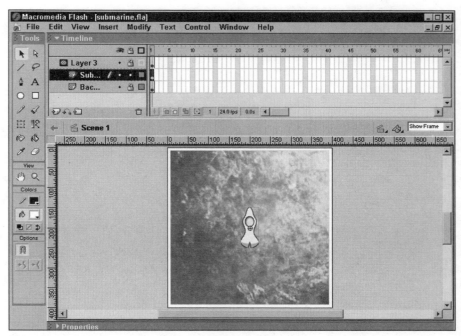

Figure 9-7: *To animate the submarine, you use the Key object.*

Listing 9-6: **Setting the Sub in Motion**

```
onClipEvent (load) {
  // sets initial speed
  speed = 2;
}
onClipEvent (enterFrame) {
  // Check for keys that are pressed, set direction and rotation
  if (Key.isDown(Key.UP) && !Key.isDown(Key.DOWN)) {
    _y -= speed;
    _rotation = 0;
  }
  if (Key.isDown(Key.RIGHT) && !Key.isDown(Key.LEFT)) {
    _x += speed;
    _rotation = 90;
  }
  if (Key.isDown(Key.DOWN) && !Key.isDown(Key.UP)) {
    _y += speed;
    _rotation = 180;
  }
  if (Key.isDown(Key.LEFT) && !Key.isDown(Key.RIGHT)) {
    _x -= speed;
    _rotation = 270;
  }
  // Sets diagonal motion if 2 keys are pressed
  if (Key.isDown(Key.LEFT) && Key.isDown(Key.UP) && !Key.isDown(Key.RIGHT) &&
!Key.isDown(Key.DOWN)) {
    _rotation = 315;
  }
  if (Key.isDown(Key.RIGHT) && Key.isDown(Key.UP) && !Key.isDown(Key.LEFT) &&
!Key.isDown(Key.DOWN)) {
    _rotation = 45;
  }
  if (Key.isDown(Key.LEFT) && Key.isDown(Key.DOWN) && !Key.isDown(Key.RIGHT) &&
!Key.isDown(Key.UP)) {
    _rotation = 225;
  }
  if (Key.isDown(Key.RIGHT) && Key.isDown(Key.DOWN) && !Key.isDown(Key.LEFT) &&
!Key.isDown(Key.UP)) {
    _rotation = 135;
  }
  // Checks to see if sub is out of range and changes x or y property so sub
appears on the other side of the stage
  if (_x<5) {
    _x = 435;
  }
  if (_x>435) {
    _x = 5;
  }
  if (_y<5) {
    _y = 435;
```

```
  }
  if (_y>435) {
    _y = 5;
  }
  // Increases and decreases sub speed
  if (Key.isDown(Key.SHIFT)) {
    speed = 7;
  }
  if (Key.isDown(Key.SPACE)) {
    speed = 2;
  }
}
```

As you study the above listing, you'll see several comments (the text preceded by two forward slashes) that explain what the following lines of code accomplish. All of the code that sets the sub in motion follows the enterFrame clip event. When you use the enterFrame clip event with a single frame movie clip, Flash continually reevaluates the code that follows.

Designer Notes

In this chapter, you learned to modify objects by changing their properties. Modifying an object's color characteristics was another key topic in this chapter. You were introduced to the duplicateMovieClip action, which you'll use in upcoming chapters to create eye candy for your Flash designs. You also learned to generate action after a key is pressed. The chapter project combined your knowledge of conditional statements with the Key object to create an interactive animation. In the next chapter, you learn to work with dynamic and input text objects.

✦   ✦   ✦

Designing Interactive Navigation

◆ ◆ ◆ ◆

In This Chapter

Breaking a movie
into scenes

Working with named
anchors

Creating a
navigation bar

Designing an On
When Pressed button

Creating an
animated button

Chapter project:
Creating a flyout
menu

◆ ◆ ◆ ◆

One of the most important parts of any design is the navigation. Navigation should be intuitive for the novice Web user, yet at the same time have enough bells and whistles to entertain experienced Web surfers. In this chapter, you learn how to create navigation that appeals to both types of users. You also learn the importance of breaking a movie down into scenes. If you've ever toiled over creating several symbols to create navigation for a site, you'll appreciate the quick and simple way to create a navigation (also called *nav*) bar. To add interesting variation to your designs, consider adding an animated button, a technique you'll learn before the end of the chapter. And if your designs are viewed by Web surfers from the old school who prefer to navigate with their browser's Back and Forward buttons, you'll learn to harness a new Flash MX feature known as the *named anchor*. When you add named anchors to your design, users can navigate between named anchors by clicking the Back or Forward buttons in their Web browser.

Note The Actions panel's got lots of books. And some of these books have books within a book. To add some actions to your scripts, you have to click this book icon, then click that book icon, then click another book icon, and so on. Rather than bore you with a lot of words, I'm going to show the path to each action as shown in the following example: Click Actions⇨Movie Control and then double-click `goto`.

Navigating to Scenes

When you create a movie that uses an introduction before the main movie, you can save yourself a lot of time by breaking the movie into scenes. Breaking a movie into scenes makes it easier to find objects, especially if you end up adding a lot of frames to the design. If the movie is large enough to warrant a preloader, that's yet another reason to break the movie into scenes. If the movie has a logical beginning, middle, and end (meaning, for example, an introduction, the main movie, and an exiting trailer), break the movie into three scenes. If you've created a particularly compelling introduction, you can create a button to replay the introduction.

You can break a movie into scenes like you'd break a Web design into separate pages. Create a separate scene for each section of the movie and create a navigation menu viewers can use to navigate from scene to scene.

Adding a scene

You can add a scene to a movie at any time. When you add a scene to a movie, you've got a blank Stage and a single timeline with one keyframe. Consider adding a scene whenever you reach a logical breaking-off point or if the sheer magnitude of frames is more than you're willing to deal with on one timeline.

To add a scene to your movie: do one of the following:

1. Choose Insert➪Scene. A new scene is added to your movie.

2. Choose Window➪Scene to open the Scene panel shown in Figure 10-1 and then click the Add Scene button that looks like a plus sign (+).

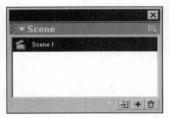

Figure 10-1: You can create separate scenes for your designs.

Naming a scene

When you add a scene to a movie, it is given the default name of *Scene* followed by the next available number. While this is perfectly logical, the name is not very intuitive, especially if you're working with other designers. Whichever way you go about adding a scene to a movie, you use the Scene panel to name it.

To name a scene:

1. Choose Window➪Scene.

2. Double-click the scene name. A text box appears and the current scene name is highlighted.

3. Type a new name for the scene and press Enter or Return.

Navigating to a scene

After you have a movie divided into scenes, you can quickly navigate from one scene to another as needed. There are three methods you can use to navigate to a scene.

To navigate to a scene, do one of the following:

✦ Choose View➪Go To and choose a scene name from the submenu.

✦ Choose Window➪Scene to open the Scene panel and then click the scene name.

✦ Click the Scene button (looks like a movie clapper) and select a scene from the menu, as shown in Figure 10-2.

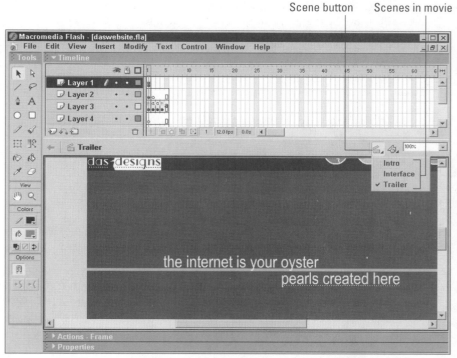

Scene button   Scenes in movie

Figure 10-2: You can navigate to a scene by choosing it from this menu.

Deleting a scene

After you break a movie into scenes, you may find a scene is no longer needed. You can delete a scene at any time. You can delete a scene in one of two ways.

To delete a scene:

✦ Navigate to a scene and then choose Insert⇨Remove Scene.

✦ Choose Window⇨Scene to open the Scene panel. Select the scene name and then click the Delete button, which looks like a trash can.

After you choose to delete a scene, you are prompted to confirm the deletion. Click OK to delete the scene from your design.

Duplicating a scene

You can duplicate a scene when it becomes necessary to create a new scene with elements from the preceding scene. This option is useful when, during the planning stage of your design, you decide to break a movie into scenes. Create the main scene with all the elements that will be used in every scene; for example, the movie's banner and navigation buttons. Duplicate the scene as needed and change the scene name to reflect what the scene does. Remember, you can use the scene name when creating ActionScript for navigation. Remembering a unique scene name is easier than remembering which scene number the navigation button needs to link to.

To duplicate a scene, do the following:

1. Choose Window⇨Scene to open the Scene panel.
2. Select the scene you want to duplicate.
3. Click the Duplicate Scene button.
4. Name the scene.
5. Close the Scene panel.

Rearranging scene order

When you add several scenes to a movie, the Flash Player rolls the scenes in the order they were created. If you decide that the order in which the scenes play needs to be changed, you can quickly rearrange the order of scenes from within the Scene panel.

To rearrange the order of scenes:

1. Choose Window⇨Scene to open the Scene panel.
2. Select the name of the scene whose order you need to rearrange.
3. Drag the name to a different position in the list. Drag up the list to play the scene earlier, down to play it later.

Using Named Anchors

If the audience viewing your design is from the old school, you may find it beneficial to take advantage of a new feature in Flash MX: *named anchors*. You can add a named anchor to any keyframe, and it will serve as a navigation device that can be accessed through the user's Web browser.

Creating a named anchor

When you need to create a named anchor, it's done in the same manner as labeling a frame. If you've created the document using scenes, you can create a named anchor at the beginning of each scene. If you've created a particularly compelling introduction (or *intro* as Flash designers are fond of calling them), you can create a named anchor at the beginning of the intro.

To create a named anchor:

1. Select the keyframe you want the viewer to navigate to when clicking the browser Back or Forward button. Remember, you can use a named anchor only on a keyframe. If you attempt to add it to a regular frame, it is applied to the previous keyframe.

2. Click the arrow to the left of the word Properties to open the Property inspector.

3. In the <Frame Label> field, enter a name for the anchor.

4. Click the Named Anchor checkbox.

5. Continue labeling frames you want to be named anchors.

After you create the named anchors, you must choose the proper template before publishing the document or testing the named anchors (by choosing File⇨Publish Preview⇨HTML).

Publishing a document with named anchors

When you create a document with named anchors, you must choose the proper template; otherwise, the named anchors will not work. Before you test or publish your document, you can modify the publish settings in order for the named anchors to be functional.

To modify the settings of a document with named anchors:

1. Choose File⇨Publish Settings to open the Publish Settings dialog box.

   By default, all Flash documents are published as Flash *.SWF files embedded in an HTML document. When the dialog box opens, you have three tabs: Formats, Flash, and HTML.

2. Click the HTML tab to open the HTML section of the dialog box.

3. Click the triangle to the right of the Template field, and from the drop-down menu, choose Flash with Named Anchors (see Figure 10-3).

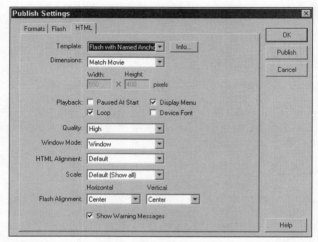

Figure 10-3: You must choose the proper template to activate named anchors.

Creating an On When Pressed Button

If you create designs with buttons that require viewers to frequently click them, viewers quickly become bored and wander off to view someone else's handiwork. For example, if you create a scrolling text block using a standard button, viewers must click the button each time they want to advance to another line in the document. A much more elegant solution is to create a button that is continually active when pressed. The ActionScript to create an On When Pressed button is surprisingly simple. All you have to do is nest the button in a movie clip and create a Boolean expression.

To create an On When Pressed button:

1. Choose Insert⇨New Symbol to open the Create New Symbol dialog box. Choose the button behavior and click OK to enter symbol-editing mode.

2. Create a button.

   You can use as many states as needed to create the button. After you create the button, click the Back button to exit symbol-editing mode and add the button to the document Library.

3. Choose Insert⇨New Symbol to open the Create New Symbol dialog box.

4. Enter a name for the symbol, choose the Movie Clip behavior, and then click OK to enter symbol-editing mode.

5. Open the document Library and drag an instance of the button symbol you created in Steps 1 and 2 into the movie clip.

6. Center the button to Stage using the Align panel.

7. With the button still selected, click the arrow to the left of the word Actions.

8. In the left pane of the Actions panel, click Actions⇨Variables and then double-click set variable.

9. In the Variable field, type **clicked**.

10. In the Value field, type **true** and click the Expression checkbox.

11. Click the first line of code to select it and change the event handler to Press.

12. Repeat Steps 8 through 10 using the set variable action to set the value of clicked to false. Accept the default release event handler. Your code should look like Listing 10-1.

13. Click the Back button to return to movie-editing mode.

Listing 10-1: **Creating Code for an On When Pressed Button**

```
on (press) {
  clicked = true;
}
on (release) {
  clicked = false;
}
```

The code in Listing 10-1 sets the value of clicked to true as long as the button is pressed. When the button is released, the value of clicked is false. To finish creating an On When Pressed button, you program the movie clip the button is nested in.

To program the movie clip, you use a conditional statement. A *conditional statement* evaluates a statement, and if the condition is true, executes the code that follows. If the statement evaluates as false, the next bit of code executes.

To program the movie clip, do the following:

1. Click the arrow to the left of the word Actions.

2. In the left pane of the Actions panel, click Actions⇨Conditions/Loops and double-click if.

   The action is added to your script and the Condition field appears above the Script pane.

3. In the Condition field, type **clicked**.

That's all that's needed. You *don't* have to create a statement like clicked=true. Flash knows that the clicked variable is a Boolean expression. To create a statement to evaluate if the button isn't clicked, you use the Logical NOT operator discussed in Chapter 9 and create a statement that reads `!clicked`.

4. Create the code that executes when the button is clicked.

5. Click the first line of code and choose the EnterFrame clip event.

When you choose the EnterFrame clip event, Flash executes the code in the movie clip every time the frame is entered, which is just what you want. When the user presses the mouse button and holds it down, the script is executed until the button is released, upon which time the Boolean value of clicked is false. Listing 10-2 shows a script that continually scrolls a block of text while a button is clicked. You'll be creating a scrolling text box in Chapter 11.

Listing 10-2: **Programming the Movie Clip**

```
onClipEvent (enterFrame) {
  if (clicked) {
    _root.ScrollBox.scroll+=1;    }
  }
}
```

Creating a Navigation Bar

In your role as a designer, you've probably created quite a few navigation bars for your HTML designs. Navigation bars in Flash are similar; however, you can take advantage of symbols to streamline your work. As you may know, symbols are reusable graphic objects. When you create a button symbol for a navigation bar, it uses the same shape with different text. Therefore, you can streamline your work by creating a template for the button and a template for the button label. After you create the template, it's a simple matter of duplicating each template, giving it a different name and editing the contents.

When you plan a movie that will have a navigation bar, create the document to suit the navigation bar. For example, if your client needs you to design a movie with six buttons and you decide a navigation bar is the way to go, you'll need to create a document 600 pixels wide and six buttons 100 pixels wide. The font size you use for the text label is dictated by the longest word. In this case, choose a font size that keeps the width of the label less than 95 pixels to allow for space between the label and the border of the button

Creating a label template

The first step is to create the label template. You choose the Graphic behavior for the label and then duplicate it as needed for the other labels in your navigation bar.

To create a label template:

1. Choose Insert⇨New Symbol.

   The Create New Symbol dialog box appears.

2. Choose the Graphic behavior and enter a name for the symbol.

   Choose the same name that will appear on the navigation bar. This makes it easier to keep track of the symbol in a crowded document Library.

3. Click OK to enter symbol-editing mode.

4. Create the text for your label by choosing the desired font style, size, and color. After you create the text, check the W: field in the Property inspector to make sure the text is no wider than the button you'll be creating for it.

5. Click the Back button to exit symbol-editing mode.

After you create the button template, open the document Library, select the symbol you just created, and make enough duplicates for each button on the navigation bar. When you duplicate each button, name it as it will appear on the navigation bar. After you create the duplicates, edit each one, changing the text to read as it will appear on the navigation bar.

Creating a button template

After you have all of your labels created, you create a button and nest one label with the button. As a rule, a navigation bar uses a rectangular button. If you want a border around the button choose a stroke that is 1 pixel wide when creating the button shape. Be sure to choose a color that contrasts nicely with the button fill color.

To create the button template:

1. Choose Insert⇨New Symbol to access the Create New Symbol dialog box.

2. Choose the button behavior and enter a name for the button. Choose a name that matches the first button on your navigation bar, for example, *aboutButton*.

3. Create the basic shape for the button.

4. Create a new layer.

5. Select the first frame in the new layer, open the document Library, and drag an instance of the appropriate label on Stage.

6. Align the label to the center of the Stage.

7. Create additional frames for the other button states you want to use.

8. Modify the color and fill of the button shape for the other button states.

9. To modify the color of the label symbol, open the Property inspector, click the triangle to the right of the Color field and choose Tint. Click the color swatch and select a color from the pop-up palette.

Now that you have the first button created, you can quickly create the rest of the buttons for your navigation bar by doing the following:

1. Open the document Library.

2. Select the button symbol you just created.

3. Click the Options menu icon in the upper right corner of the Library panel and choose Duplicate. Alternately, you can right-click (Windows) or Ctrl+click (Macintosh) and choose Duplicate from the drop-down menu.

4. In the Duplicate Symbol dialog box, enter a name for the symbol. Choose a name that matches the button's title, for example, *servicesButton*.

5. Create one duplicate for each button on your navigation bar.

6. After you duplicate the buttons, double-click each button to enter symbol-editing mode.

7. Select the label symbol, open the Property inspector, and click the Swap button to open the Swap Symbol dialog box (see Figure 10-4).

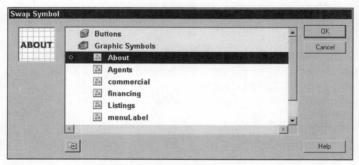

Figure 10-4: You can quickly swap the label symbol with another from the document Library.

8. Select the appropriate label symbol for this button and click OK to swap the symbol. If you created additional states for the button, select the keyframe, select the symbol, and swap it. When you swap a symbol, any effect you applied to the previous symbol is inherited by the new symbol.

9. Continue in this manner until you have swapped the label symbol for all duplicated buttons.

Swapping symbols is an easy way to quickly create several buttons. Instead of creating the shape for each button and then creating the text, you create the button shape one time, duplicate the button, and swap the label. If you need to use the label symbol in other parts of the movie, just drag an instance of it on Stage and modify it to suit.

Building the navigation bar

After you create the buttons, drag them onto the Stage, select them, and then align them with the Align panel. If the buttons are sized to fill the width of the movie, click the Distribute horizontal center button and the Stage button to align the buttons. A finished nav bar is shown in Figure 10-5.

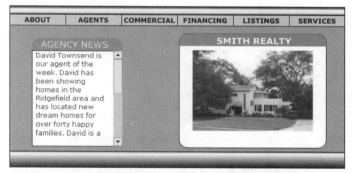

Figure 10-5: You can quickly create a navigation bar by duplicating a button symbol.

Creating an Animated Button

Buttons play a major art in many Flash designs. You can add variety to a basic button by changing the shape or changing the color of the shape in a different button state. Rollover buttons are rather commonplace in Flash work and are expected by the experienced Web surfer. You can take a rollover button a step further by nesting a movie clip in the button's Over state. The movie clip plays when users roll their mouse over the button. If you use motion tweening or frame by frame animation in the movie clip, the results are predictable after the button is rolled over a second or third time. You can create a more interesting effect by randomly changing one or more properties of an object with ActionScript.

On the CD-ROM

To learn how to create an animated button with ActionScript, copy to your hard drive the file Jittery.fla from this chapter's folder on the CD-ROM that accompanies this book. Use your operating system to disable the file's read-only attribute.

Creating the movie clip

When you decide to add a button with random animation to your design, the first step is to create the movie clip. Remember when you animate an object with ActionScript, you animate an instance of a movie clip. Therefore, if you are animating a symbol already in your movie, you must nest the symbol in a movie clip. You then create another movie clip and nest the previous movie clip in it and then use ActionScript to animate the nested movie clip.

To create an animated movie clip:

1. Launch Flash and open the Jittery.fla file.

2. Choose Insert⇨New Symbol to open the Create New Symbol dialog box.

3. Name the movie clip **jittery**, choose the Movie Clip behavior, and then click OK to enter symbol-editing mode.

4. Choose Window⇨Library to open the document Library.

5. Drag an instance of the aboutLabel symbol on Stage and then center it to Stage with the Align panel.

6. Click the Back button to exit symbol-editing mode.

7. Choose Insert⇨New Symbol to open the Create New Symbol dialog box.

8. Name the movie clip **jitteryClip**, choose the Movie Clip behavior, and click OK to enter symbol-editing mode.

9. Open the document Library and drag an instance of the jittery movie clip you created in Step 3 on Stage and then use the Align panel to center it to Stage.

10. Click the arrow to the left of the word Properties to open the Property inspector.

11. In the <Instance Name> field, type **Jitter**

12. Click the next frame on the timeline, drag right to select an additional frame, and press F6 to convert the selected frames to keyframes.

After you create the keyframes, it's time to change one or more properties of the movie clip. When you created the additional keyframes, you copied the instance of the movie clip and preserved the instance name. You'll be referring to the instance name in your ActionScript as shown in the following section.

Creating the ActionScript to animate the label

To animate the label, in the first frame, you set the properties of the object to their original states. In the second frame of the animation, you modify the property — for example, increase the object's _xscale property by a random percentage. In the third frame, you loop the animation back to the first frame and the cycle begins anew. When you use ActionScript to animate an object, the change is instantaneous, meaning that it happens as soon as the actions execute. You can add a few frames after the second frame to display the label with its changed properties, or you can pause the movie at the frame for a random amount of time. (You do the latter by adding a user-defined timer component to the second frame that pauses the movie for a random amount of time.)

To animate the label:

1. Select the first keyframe and then click the triangle to the left of the word Actions.

2. In the left pane of the actions panel, click Actions⇨Miscellaneous Actions and then double-click `evaluate`.

   The Expression field appears above the Script pane.

3. In the Expression field, type the following: **Jitter._xscale=100**

   This line of code sets the _xscale property of the movie clip Jitter to 100 percent. You don't have to specify a target path for the movie clip as it is nested within the movie clip you're creating the ActionScript in.

4. Repeat Step 3 to set additional properties as shown in Listing 10-3.

Listing 10-3: **Setting Other Properties of the Movie Clip**

```
Jitter._yscale=100;
Jitter._x=0;
Jitter._y=0;
Jitter._rotation=0;
```

5. Select the second keyframe.

6. In the left pane of the Actions panel, click Actions⇨Miscellaneous Actions and then double-click `evaluate`.

7. In the Expression field, type the following code: **Jitter._xscale+=Math. random()*75**. This line of code adds a random value between 0 and 75 to the _xscale property of the movie clip Jitter. As you may remember, the random method of the Math object generates a random number between 0 and 1. Multiplying the result of the random method by another number generates a random value between 0 and that number.

   Now that you've modified the _xscale, you can modify other properties to animate the movie clip.

8. Repeat Step 7 to modify the _yscale, _x, and _y properties of the movie clip, as shown in Listing 10-4.

Listing 10-4: Creating the Code to Change the Movie Clip's Properties

```
Jitter._yscale+=Math.random()*75;
Jitter._x+=Math.random()*3;
Jitter._y+=Math.random()*3;
```

The only property you haven't modified is the movie clip's rotation. You can modify the rotation property by a given number of degrees to make the movie clip rotate, but it will rotate in only one direction. To get the movie clip to rotate clockwise and counterclockwise, you create a conditional statement.

9. In the left pane of the Actions panel, click Actions⇨Conditions/Loops and then double-click if.

The Condition field appears above the Script pane.

10. In the Condition field, type the following: **Jitter._x<1.5**

11. In the left pane of the Actions panel, click Actions⇨Miscellaneous Actions and then double-click evaluate.

12. In the Expression field, type the following: **Jitter._rotation+=Math.random()*15**

13. In the left pane of the Actions panel, click Actions⇨Conditions/Loops and then double-click else.

14. In the left pane of the Actions panel click Actions⇨Miscellaneous Actions and then double-click evaluate.

15. In the Expression field, type the following: **Jitter._rotation-=Math.random()*15**

Your code for the conditional statement should look like Listing 10-5

The conditional statement you just created checks to see if the value of the movie clip's _x property is less than 1.5. When it is, the _rotation property of the movie clip is incremented by a random value between 0 and 15; in other words, the movie clip rotates in a clockwise direction. If the value is greater than 1.5, the _rotation property decrements by a random value between 0 and 15, rotating the movie clip in a counterclockwise direction.

Listing 10-5: Creating a Conditional Statement to Change Rotation

```
if (Jitter._x<2) {
  Jitter._rotation+=Math.random()*15;
} else {
  Jitter._rotation-=Math.random()*15;
}
```

16. Choose Window⇨Library to open the document Library.

17. Drag the timer component anywhere on Stage.

18. Click the arrow to the left of the word Properties to open the Property inspector.

19. In the Pause for: field, enter a value of **.3**

    The component you just added to the movie clip will pause the movie on the frame for a random amount of time equal to or less than the value entered in the Pause for: field.

20. Select the third keyframe.

21. In the left pane of the Actions panel, click Actions⇨Movie Control and then double-click goto. Accept the default parameters to go to and play frame 1.

22. Click the Back button to exit symbol-editing mode.

After you exit symbol-editing mode, the symbol is added to the document Library. To finish creating the animated button, you nest the movie clip in a button symbol.

Nesting the movie clip in a button symbol

To finish the project, you create a button. The movie clip will be added to the button's Over frame. When the document is published as a *.SWF movie, the movie clip will be playing in the background, but won't be visible until viewers roll their mouse over the button. Then the movie clip will randomly jitter away until the mouse is rolled off the button.

To nest the movie clip in a button:

1. Choose Insert⇨New Symbol to open the Create New Symbol dialog box.

2. Enter a name for the symbol, choose the Button behavior and then click OK to enter symbol-editing mode.

3. Click the Up frame to select it and then choose Window⇨Library.

4. Drag an instance of the aboutLabel symbol on Stage and use the Align panel to center the symbol to Stage.

5. Select the first layer, right-click (Windows) or Ctrl+click(Macintosh) and then choose Insert Layer from the context menu. Name the layer **Movie clip**.

6. Select the Over frame and press F7 to insert a blank keyframe.

7. Drag an instance of jitteryClip from the document Library on Stage and center it with the Align panel.

8. Click the Back button to exit symbol-editing mode.

9. Drag an instance of the button on Stage and then choose Control⇨Test movie.

After the movie is published, roll your mouse over the button. The label should start randomly moving around. When you roll off the button, the motion stops. If the motion wasn't frenetic enough for your tastes, edit the jitteryClip and change the value in the timer component's pause for field.

Note that the actual object being animated is a symbol. By duplicating the movie clips and button, and then swapping symbols, you can quickly create additional animated buttons.

Chapter Project: Creating a Flyout Menu

When you create a flyout menu, you combine the tried and true Flash animation staple known as motion tweening with ActionScript to create a menu that flies out when summoned, and tucks neatly back into the interface after a button has been clicked.

When you create a flyout menu, you first create a navigation bar as outlined previously in this chapter. Create the code for what you want each button to do when clicked. If you're creating the flyout menu for a large Flash movie, use the loadMovie action to load other content. You can also program the buttons to play movie clips. To learn how to convert a navigation bar to a flyout menu, follow the upcoming steps.

On the CD-ROM

To create the flyout menu project, copy to your hard drive the flyoutMenu.fla file from this chapter's folder on the CD-ROM that accompanies this book. Use your operating system to disable the file's read-only attribute.

1. Launch Flash and open the flyoutMenu.fla file.

The document contains a navigation bar and a Menu button, as shown in Figure 10-6. If you were creating your own flyout menu, at this stage you'd have each button programmed with the exception of the ActionScript needed to activate the flyout menu.

2. Click the arrow to the left of the word Actions. After the Actions panel opens, click the scroll bar to the right of the Stage and drag it so that both the Actions panel and the buttons are visible, as shown in Figure 10-7.

3. Select the Services button and in the left pane of the Actions panel, click Actions⇨Movie Control and then double-click play.

The default release event is added to the script.

4. Select the three lines of code and then right-click (Windows) or Ctrl+click (Macintosh) and select Copy from the context menu.

5. Click the Listings button and then in the Script pane, right-click (Windows) or Ctrl+click (Macintosh) and select Paste from the context menu.

6. Repeat Step 5 to paste the code to the other buttons.

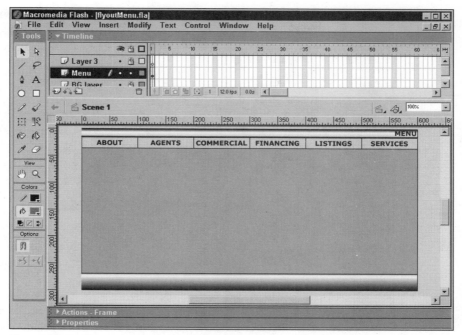

Figure 10-6: You can convert a navigation bar into a flyout menu.

The previous steps demonstrated how you can save time when you need to use the same code on several objects. Now that you've programmed the buttons, it's time to convert the navigation bar into a symbol.

To convert the navigation bar to a symbol, do the following.

1. Select the buttons on the navigation bar.

2. Choose Insert⇨Convert to Symbol. The Convert to Symbol dialog box opens.

3. Enter a name for the symbol, choose the Movie Clip behavior, and click the center left square for the registration point, as shown in Figure 10-8.

   This sets the symbol registration point equal the left side of the buttons, which makes it easier to manipulate the position of the buttons with the Property inspector because the x, y coordinates in symbol-editing mode are the same as the x, y coordinates of the Stage.

4. Click OK to convert the buttons into a symbol.

   At this stage the new symbol is added to the document Library. It should also be selected on Stage.

5. Choose Edit⇨Edit in Place.

   The workspace is converted to symbol-editing mode.

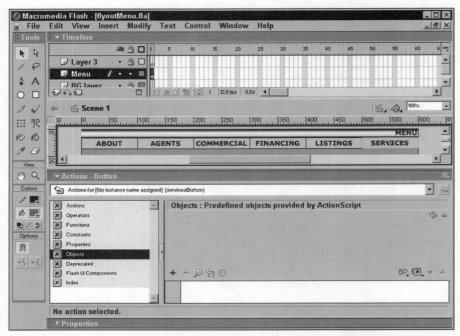

Figure 10-7: You can save time by copying code from one button and pasting it to another.

Symbol registration point

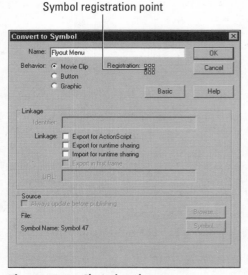

Figure 10-8: Choosing the proper registration point.

6. With the buttons still selected, choose Modify⇨Distribute to layers.

A separate layer is created for each button. Each layer has the same name as the button within the layer. Select Layer 1 and rename it to Actions.

7. Select the buttons, open the Property inspector, and type **600** in the X: Field.

This moves the buttons to the left of the Stage, exactly where you want them to appear when the movie begins playing.

8. Press Ctrl (Windows) or ⌘ (Macintosh), click frame 12 in the Actions layer, and drag down to select frame 12 in all layers.

9. Press F6 to convert the frames to keyframes.

10. Click the first frame in the service layer and then drag down to select all of the button layers.

11. Choose Insert⇨Create Motion Tween.

A motion tween arrow appears between the beginning and ending keyframes on each button layer.

12. Click the sixth frame in the Actions layer, press Ctrl (Windows) or ⌘ (Macintosh) and drag down to select all the frames.

13. Press F6 to convert the frames to keyframes. All the buttons will be selected.

14. Open the Property inspector, click the About button and change the value in the X: Field to **0**.

The buttons are moved to their flyout position, as shown in Figure 10-9. This sets up the basic animation for the buttons. When the movie initially begins, the buttons are not visible. When the flyout menu is activated, the buttons move to the left side of the movie.

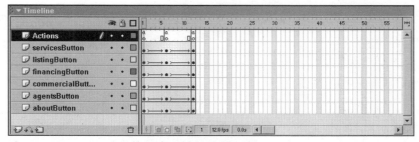

Figure 10-9: Your timeline should look like this.

15. Click the first keyframe in the Actions layer, and then click the arrow to the left of the word Actions.

16. In the left pane of the Actions panel, click Actions⇨Movie Control and then double-click stop.

17. Repeat Step 16 for the sixth frame in the Actions layer.

18. Select the 12th frame in the Actions layer and open the Actions panel.

19. In the left pane of the Actions panel, click Actions⇨Movie Control and then double-click `goto`.

20. Click the Go to and Stop radio button. Accept all the other parameters.

21. Click the Back button to exit symbol-editing mode.

22. Click the arrow to the left of the word Properties to open the Property inspector.

23. Type **menu** in the <Instance Name> field.

24. Click the Menu button in the upper-right corner of the document.

25. Click the arrow to the left of the word Actions. The Actions panel should read Actions-Button. If it doesn't, select the button again.

26. In the left pane of the Actions panel, click Actions⇨Variables and then double-click `with`.

27. Click the Insert a Target Path button to open the Insert Target Path dialog box.

28. Click the button labeled `menu` and then click OK to add the target path to the script.

29. In the left pane of the Actions panel, click Actions⇨Movie Control and then double-click `play`.

30. Choose Control⇨Test Movie.

    When you click the Menu button, the menu should fly in from the side of the interface. After the menu flies open, click any of the buttons to retract the menu.

In a nutshell, this is how the menu works: When the movie plays, the `stop` action on the first frame of the menu movie clip prevents the movie clip from playing. When the Menu button is clicked, the `play` action starts the movie clip, the motion tween moves the buttons into position, and the `stop` action in frame 6 halts the movie. When you click any button on the navigation bar, the `play` action starts the movie again and the buttons retract. When frame 12 is reached, the `goto` action sends the movie to frame 1 where it stops until the Menu button is clicked and the movie clip starts again.

Designer Notes

In this chapter, you learned to add some interactive navigation elements to your designs. You learned how to break a movie down into scenes as well as how to create named anchors for use as browser navigation devices. You learned how to quickly create a navigation bar by duplicating buttons and swapping symbols. The chapter project showed you how to create a flyout menu. In the next chapter you'll to use ActionScript with dynamic text.

✦   ✦   ✦

Composing Dynamic Text

✦   ✦   ✦   ✦

In This Chapter

Working with
dynamic text

Creating input text
boxes

Creating rich
formatted text

Creating text links

Loading text into a
movie

Chapter project:
Creating a scrolling
text box

Creating text fields

Chapter project:
Creating a ticker text
marquee

✦   ✦   ✦   ✦

In your previous Flash forays, you probably used text in
your designs, possibly even dynamic text. ActionScript and
dynamic text make it possible for you to display data that you
store in variables. When you combine variables with dynamic
text, it is possible for you to change the content of dynamic
text boxes. You can use dynamic text boxes to respond to
viewer inputs, display data from within a text array, or load
data from an external source.

Input text boxes, on the other hand, accept input from viewers of your designs. For example, you can use input text boxes
to accept information in an e-commerce design such as a
user's name and shipping address.

In this chapter, you learn how to create dynamic text and
input text. As for chapter projects, you create a scrolling text
box that is populated by data loaded from an external source
and also create a scrolling marquee.

Note   The Actions panel's got lots of books. And some of these
books have books within a book. To add some actions to
your scripts, you have to click this book icon, then click that
book icon, then click another book icon, and so on. Rather
than bore you with a lot of words, I'm going to show the
path to each action as shown in the following example:
Click Actions⇨Movie Control and then double-click goto.

Creating Flashy Text with the Property Inspector

If you're a Flash veteran, no doubt you've worked with the
Text tool. You may have even used input text or dynamic text
in your prior designs. When you add dynamic text to a design,
you can add scrolling text boxes to your designs or create
a text box where information is updated as the movie

progresses. (You were introduced to a dynamic text box when you worked through the project in Chapter 7.) You create text with the Text tool and then use the Property inspector to specify whether the text is dynamic text, input text, or static text.

Creating input text boxes

When you add an input text box to your design, you create an interface between the published Flash movie and the viewer. You use input text boxes whenever you need to receive information from the viewer. You assign a variable to an input text box and a variable on the timeline to receive the information from the input text box and pass it along to another function or ActionScript in your design. You can also use the data stored by the input text box variable to transfer data to a Web site. For example, if you create a customer response form for an e-commerce site, you can transfer the information directly to a Web server's CGI mailto script that passes the information on to the designated part.

To create an input text box, do the following:

1. Open the Property inspector, shown in Figure 11-1.

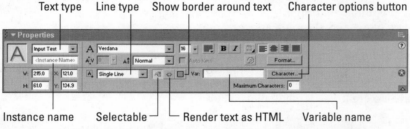

Figure 11-1: You specify text parameters with the Property inspector.

2. Click the triangle to the left of the Text type field and choose Input Text from the drop-down menu.

3. Specify the font size, font type, and font color.

4. Enter a name in the <Instance name> field.

Although you can't assign actions to a input text box, you can refer to it from ActionScript in other objects or keyframes.

5. Click the triangle to the right of the line type field and choose one of the following options:

- **Single Line:** Displays text as a single line.

- **Multiline:** Wraps text to the next line when it exceeds the boundary of the text box.

- **Multiline No Wrap:** Wraps text to the next line when the user presses Enter or Return; otherwise, the text exceeds the boundary of the box.

> • **Password:** Displays each letter entered as an asterisk to prevent the user's password from being intercepted by someone nearby.

6. Enter a name in the Var field.

   If you will be displaying this data in a dynamic text box, use the same name in the dynamic text box's Var field. Remember to adhere to the variable naming conventions discussed in Chapter 9.

7. Enter a value in the Maximum Characters field.

   This is the maximum amount of characters the input text box will accept. Users can enter as many characters as they want, but when the user clicks a button to submit the data, the variable assigned to the text box won't accept more data characters than the value you specify in this field.

8. Click the Show Border around Text button.

   When you choose this option, Flash displays a border around the text when the movie is published. Without a border, an input text box would never be seen by the users, even though their cursors would change to I-beams if they happened to click inside the box.

9. Select the Text tool and drag across to create a text box of the desired length.

   Drag across to create a text box that accepts a single line of text, or drag down and across to create a text box that accepts multiple lines of text, such as the comments field in an online form.

After you set the parameters for an input text box, it is ready to accept data from a user. As you can see by the options, you can use an input text box for quite a few things in your designs. They can be the basis for an online form, much like the one you'll work with in Chapter 15. Input text boxes can also be used to password-protect a site. The data entered by the user is evaluated using a conditional statement you create that determines whether the password entered is valid or not. You can limit the type of data entered by the user by changing character options, which is presented before the end of this chapter.

Creating dynamic text boxes

You create a dynamic text box to display data previously entered by a user in an input text box or to display data stored in one or more variables. You can also use a dynamic text box to display the contents of an array. When you use a dynamic text box to display the content of multiple variables, you create ActionScript that sets value of the dynamic text box variable equal to the value of the variable that contains the data you want displayed in the dynamic text box.

To create a dynamic text box:

1. Select the Text tool and then open the Property inspector.

2. Click the triangle to the right of the text type field and choose Dynamic Text from the drop-down menu.

3. Specify a font size, font color, font type, and other parameters you want assigned to the text box.

4. If the dynamic text box will be referenced in other ActionScript, enter a name in the <Instance Name> field.

5. Enter a name in the Var field.

   This is the variable name you'll be referring to when you want to display the contents of other variables, or data in this field.

6. Click the triangle to the right of the line type field and choose one of the following:

   • **Single Line:** Displays a single line of text in the field and does not wrap text when the boundary of the text box is exceeded.

   • **Multiline:** Displays text as multiple lines, wrapping to the next line when the text exceeds the border of the text box.

   • **Multiline No Wrap:** Displays text as multiple lines. The Flash Player wraps text to a new line when encountering a hard break character caused by pressing Enter or Return in a word processing program.

7. Click the Selectable button if you want users to be able to select the text displayed in this box.

8. Click the Render as HTML button to render text with HTML tags with rich text formatting options. (You learn how to create rich formatted text in an upcoming section.)

9. Select the Text tool and then drag a text box on Stage.

The dynamic text box is now ready to receive data. If you suspect the text you specify may not be available on computers used to view your design, you can embed the fonts with the movie by following the instructions in the next section.

Setting character options

When you create an input or dynamic text box, you can specify whether or not to embed fonts when the movie is published. You can choose to embed an entire font set or a partial font set. When you embed a partial font set, you limit the characters that will be accepted in an input text box or displayed in dynamic text box, therefore controlling the content of associated variables to values that work with your design. You do this by setting character options for the text box.

To set character options:

1. Create a dynamic or input text box following the steps in the previous sections.

2. In the Property inspector, click the Characters button to open the dialog box shown in Figure 11-2.

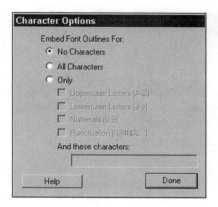

Figure 11-2: You can embed an entire font set or a partial font set by specifying character options.

3. Choose to embed the entire font set by clicking the All Characters radio button. To embed a partial font set, click the Only button and choose an option.

   When you choose to embed a partial font set with an input text box, only the embedded characters are passed on to the variable. This is handy when you're accepting numeric input. Limit the maximum number of characters to 5 and embed only numerals, and in the Include These Characters field, type a decimal point (.). By doing this, you limit the maximum value the users can input to 99999 with no decimal point, or 99.99 with a decimal point.

4. Click Done to close the dialog box.

Creating rich formatted text

You can display rich formatted text in a dynamic text box. When you create text with HTML tags to specify the font color, font size, and other attributes, you can configure a dynamic text box to properly read the HTML tags as instructions instead of string data. To do this, you click the Render As HTML button when specifying the parameters for the dynamic text box as outlined previously.

You can use HTML 1.0 tags when formatting the text in a word processing program. You must use beginning (<) and ending (>) symbols to reference the data between the tags as HTML. If you've ever manually coded HTML, you're familiar with these tags. If not, Table 11-1 will show you the proper formatting for HTML tags. You can use the tags in Table 11-1 to create rich formatted text.

You create the document with rich text formatting in a word processing program. You begin the document with the variable name (the Var field) of the dynamic text box the rich formatted text is to be displayed in, followed by the equals sign (=) and the rich formatted text. The finished document is saved as a .txt file. Figure 11-3 shows a document in a word processing program that will be saved for use in a Flash design.

Table 11-1
HTML Tags for Creating Rich Formatted Text

Tag	Description
<a href="http://www. mysite.com">text<a>	The text between the tags is hyperlinked to the referenced site. If the link is in the same directory on the host Web site, you need only enter the relative path.
Text	The text between the tags is boldfaced.
<I>Text<I>	The text between these tags is italicized.
<p>Text</p>	The text between the tags is displayed as a separate paragraph.
<u>Text</u>	The text encompassed by the tags is italicized.
<Font Size="x" >Text</Font>	The text between these tags is displayed at the specified font size.
<Font Face="Arial" >Text</Font Face>	The text between these tags is displayed using the specified font face. In this case, the text is displayed with the Arial font face.
<Font Color ="#FF0000" >Text</Font Color>	The text between these tags is displayed using the color between the quotation marks. In this example, the color would be bright red. The font color must be designated using a hexadecimal value.

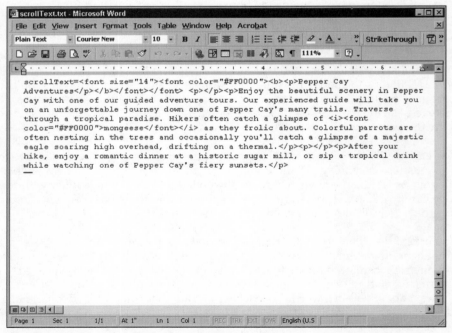

Figure 11-3: Creating rich formatted text for a design

To display rich formatted text in your design, you create a dynamic text box as outlined previously. Click the Render as HTML button and when the movie is published, the formatting specified by the tags is used to display the text. Figure 11-4 shows a published movie with a block of rich formatted text.

Dynamic text rendered as HTML

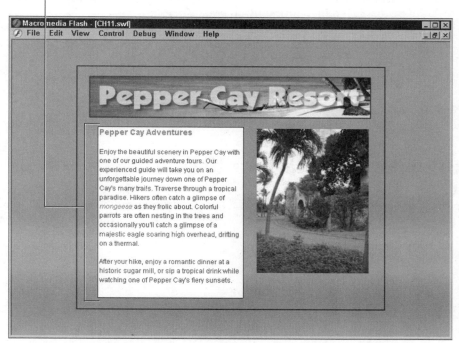

Figure 11-4: You can liven up a design by using rich formatted text.

Loading Text from External Sources

When you create a dynamic text box, you can display a great deal of information. However, creating copious amounts of text in the Action panel's Script pane can be a pain (pun intended). The Script pane is small, and there's no spell checker. You can save yourself a lot of time and headache by creating large amounts of text data in a word processing program, saving it as a text document, and then loading the document into a movie as variable data. Not only is the initial document easier to create, it's also easier to update. If your client wants you to update the text data in a movie, you edit the text file and upload it to your client's serve. The next time the movie is viewed, the dynamic text box displays the contents of the edited text file. You display the text data in a dynamic text box with the same name as specified in the text file.

Creating text data

When you need to pack a lot of data into a small dynamic text box, create the data in your word processing software as follows:

1. Create a new document.

2. Enter the name of the variable you assigned to the dynamic text box the text will be displayed in followed by an equals (=) sign.

3. Save the document as a *.txt file.

   You'll be using this name to load the document into your movie. Remember to use proper variable naming conventions for the variable name in Step 2 as well as the document name.

Naming variables is covered in Chapter 8.

Using the loadVariables action

After you create the text data, use the `loadVariables` action to bring it into your movie. You can use the `loadVariables` action at any time; however, it's good practice to declare all of your variables in the first frame of your movie, even the ones you load from external sources.

To load data into your movie:

1. Select the first frame of your movie.

2. Click the arrow to the left of the word Actions to open the Actions panel.

3. In the left pane of the Actions panel, click Actions⇨Browser/Network Control and then double-click `loadVariables`.

4. In the URL parameter text box, enter the name of the document that contains the variables. If the document is in the same directory or a different directory, enter the relative path to the document, for example: `myData.txt`. If the document is stored at another Web site, enter the absolute path to the document, for example: `http://www.mysite.com/documents/data.txt`.

That's all you need to do to get the data into your design. You can now load the text data in any dynamic text box that has the same variable name as you designated in the first line of the document.

Creating an E-Mail Link

You can add an e-mail link to your designs by taking advantage of the ability to use HTML tags in a dynamic text field. To create an e-mail link, add the proper tags to a text file and then use the `loadVariables` action to load the text data into the movie.

To create an e-mail link, do the following:

1. Create a document in a word processing program.

2. In the first line of the document, enter the variable name you will assign to the dynamic text box that will display the e-mail link.

3. At the spot where you want the e-mail link to appear in the document, type the following tag: **<a href="mailto:myEmail@myserver.com"> E-mail me</a>**.

4. Save the document as a text(*.txt) file.

5. In Flash, create a dynamic text box.

6. In the Var field, enter the same name you used when creating the text file.

7. Click the Render Text as HTML button.

8. Select the first frame of the document and use the `loadVariables` action to load the text file into the movie as outlined previously.

When the movie is published and played in a Web browser, the familiar hand icon appears when viewers roll their mouse over the text link. When the link is clicked, the Web browser's mail program opens a blank e-mail document addressed to recipient specified in the HTML tag.

Chapter Project: Creating a Scrolling Text Box

If you have a client who needs to display a large amount of text in a small area, a scrolling text box is the ticket. In Chapter 12, you'll learn to use one of the new Flash UI Components to create a scrolling text box. However, if you want to create a scrolling text box with buttons of your own design, follow the steps in this section.

On the CD-ROM To follow along with this tutorial, locate the scrollText.fla and scrollText.txt files located in this chapter's folder on the CD-ROM that accompanies this book. Copy the files to your computer and use your operating system to disable the file's read-only attributes.

To begin the creating scrolling text:

1. Launch Flash and open the scrollText.fla file.

   Most of the project is completed for you. The document, as shown in Figure 11-5, consists of a banner, two images, and a blank text field. The `loadVariables` action has already been assigned to the first frame. To the right of the text field is a multi-functional slider. The upper and lower arrows scroll the text. The white bar at the top of the slider can also be dragged to scroll the text. The up and down arrows are buttons nested in a movie clip. The white bar is in a movie clip nested with an invisible button that is coded so that the movie clip can be dragged vertically when the button is pressed.

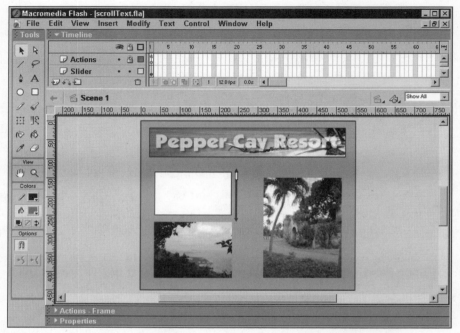

Figure 11-5: You have all the necessary elements to create scrolling text.

2. Choose Control⇨Test Movie.

    After Flash publishes the movie and opens it in another window, you see the result of the `loadVariables` action. The dynamic text field is filled with rich formatted text. Click the white bar and drag down. The text starts scrolling as shown in Figure 11-6. After you scroll to the end of the text, click the up arrow at the top of the slider and hold the mouse button. (This is the same type of button you learned to create in Chapter 10.) Click the down arrow at the bottom of the slider bar, and the text stays still because the button hasn't been programmed yet. You'll be programming this button to scroll the text in just a few minutes.

3. Close the window to return to movie-editing mode.

Programming the down arrow

Dynamic text fields are considered Text Field objects. While dynamic text blocks cannot have code assigned to them, they can be addressed with other ActionScript. The dynamic text box has been given an instance name of ScrollBox. The variable name scrollText has been assigned to the object, the same variable name in the first line of the document that is loaded into the movie when it starts.

The code used to load the text document into the movie is shown in Listing 11-1. The code is on the first frame of the Actions layer.

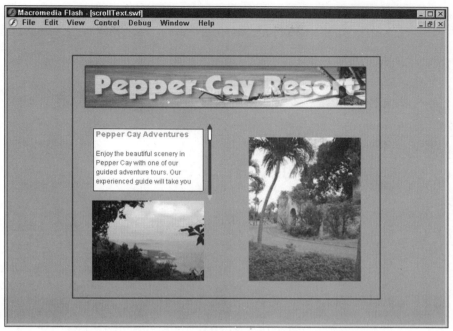

Figure 11-6: Rich formatted text makes a message stand out.

Listing 11-1: **Loading the Text Document into the Movie**

```
loadVariablesNum("scrollText.txt", 0);
```

To program the down arrow, follow these steps:

1. Select the Slider layer and then double-click the slider to the right of the text box.

   After you double-click the symbol, you enter symbol-editing mode. You may find it helpful to zoom in on the slider before continuing.

2. Click the down arrow.

   The down arrow is a movie clip nested within the symbol. The actual button is nested within the arrow movie clip. This button has two Boolean statements that set the value of the variable clicked to true when the button is pressed, false when the button is released. This is the same code you created when you learned to create a button that is on when pressed in Chapter 10.

3. Open the Actions panel.

Notice that most of the code is already written for you. Listing 11-2 shows the code already created for you.

```
onClipEvent (enterFrame) {
  if (clicked) {

    if (_root.CompSlider.slideBar._y>=100) {
      _root.CompSlider.slideBar._y=100;
    }
  }
}
```

The code in the previous listing is executed when the frame is entered. As you learned previously, when you use the enterFrame clip event, the actions that follow are constantly evaluated. You have two conditional statements to work with. You create the code for the first conditional statement, which advances the text one line at a time when the button is pressed while at the same time synchronizing the movement of the slider bar. The second conditional statement prevents the slider bar from moving beyond the boundary of the slider.

4. In the Actions panel, select the second line of code that reads: `if (clicked) {`.

5. In the left pane of the Actions panel, click Actions⇨Miscellaneous Actions and double-click `evaluate`. The Expression text parameter box opens above the Script pane.

6. Place your cursor inside the Expression field and click the Insert a Target Path icon. The Insert Target Path dialog box opens.

7. Click the ScrollBox icon as shown in Figure 11-7 and then click OK. This is the target path to the dynamic text box.

8. In the left pane of the Actions panel, click Objects⇨Movie⇨Text Field⇨ Properties and double-click `scroll`.

The scroll property of the Text Field object reads the current position of the text in the dynamic text box. When the movie loads, the scroll value of the text is 1. As the text scrolls to another line, the scroll value increases by 1. The expression you are creating will increment the value of the Text Field object ScrollBox by a value of 1 as long as the button is pressed.

9. In the Expression field, following the word *scroll,* type =+**1**.

Your finished line of code should read: `_root.ScrollBox.scroll+=1;`. This completes the code needed to scroll the text by an increment of 1.

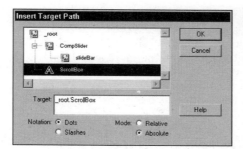

Figure 11-7: You insert the target path to the text box using this dialog box.

10. In the left pane of the Actions panel, click Actions➪Miscellaneous Actions and then double-click `evaluate`.

    The Expression parameter text box appears.

11. Enter the following code: `_root.CompSlider.slideBar._y+=5.5555555`

    This line of code synchronizes the movement of the white slider bar with the down button when clicked. You may recognize this as an incremental statement. As long as the button is pressed, the white slider bar (a movie clip with the instance name of sliderBar) advances 5.555555 pixels towards the bottom of the slider. The next section explains how the value was determined.

12. Choose Control➪Test Movie.

    Click the down arrow on the slider bar and the text should start scrolling nicely.

The Text Field object has several properties that you can use when adding text objects to your designs. For example, if you want to add an End of Page button to a text box, you use the maxscroll property. If you want to add an End of Page button to the project you just finished, the button code looks like Listing 11-3.

Listing 11-3: **Code for an End of Page Button**

```
on(release){
    _root.ScrollBox.scroll=maxscroll
}
```

To take the design one step further, you can add a Top of Page button. To do so, set the scroll property of the text box equal to 1, which returns the user to the first line of text when the button is clicked.

Deciphering the rest of the code

This section gives you an idea of what went into the code for creating the slider and coordinating the movement of the slider with the scrolling text. There's also the code for the slider bar to consider. An invisible button in the slideBar movie clip is programmed to execute the startDrag action when the button is pressed. The code constrains the movie clip's movement from 0 to 100 along the y axis. The slider movement had to be converted into equal increments to scroll the text. After determining the maxscroll property of the text is 18, that result is divided into 100 to return a value of 5.55555. Therefore, the value of the scroll property of the text box is set to the _y property of the slider divided by 5.5555, as shown in Listing 11-4.

Listing 11-4: **Scrolling Text with the Slider**

```
onClipEvent (enterFrame) {
  // Value determined by dividing 100 by maxscroll
  _root.ScrollBox.scroll = this._y/5.5555;
}
```

When the slider isn't being use to scroll the text, the slider must be set to move in synch with the scrolling text in case the user decides to switch from button scrolling to dragging the slider. Therefore, an expression needs to be set up to increment the slider when an arrow is clicked, as shown in Listing 11-5.

Listing 11-5: **Synching the Slider to the Scrolling Text**

```
onClipEvent (enterFrame) {
  if (clicked) {
    _root.ScrollBox.scroll+=1;
    _root.CompSlider.slideBar._y+=5.5555;
    if (_root.CompSlider.slideBar._y>=100) {
      _root.CompSlider.slideBar._y=100;
    }
  }
}
```

The third line of code shown in the previous listing moves the slideBar by 5.5555 (the result of dividing 100 by the maxscroll value of the text box) when the button is pressed. The next line of code has a conditional statement that prevents the _y property of the slider from exceeding 100. Without this line of code, the slider would continue past the down arrow if the arrow is pressed long enough. The code for the up arrow, shown in Listing 11-6, decrements moves the slider in the opposite direction and prevents it from going above the up arrow.

Listing 11-6: **The Code for the Up Arrow**

```
onClipEvent (enterFrame) {
  if (clicked) {
    _root.ScrollBox.scroll-=1;
    _root.CompSlider.slideBar._y-=5.5555555;
    if (_root.CompSlider.slideBar._y<=0) {
      _root.CompSlider.slideBar._y=0;
    }
  }
}
```

Tip

To determine the maxscroll value of a block of text, select the frame where the text box is displayed in your movie. Make sure it is a keyframe. Open the Actions panel and click Actions⇨Miscellaneous Actions and then double-click `trace`. In the Message field, type the name of the dynamic text box variable, followed by a dot (.) and the word **maxscroll**. Click the Expression check box and choose Control⇨Test Movie. The maxscroll value of the text box is displayed in the Output window. After you determine the maxscroll value, you can delete the `trace` action.

Creating a Text Hyperlink

When you need to create a text hyperlink for an HTML page, use either your HTML editor or enter hard code such as: `<a href="http://www.dasdesigns.net>DAS Designs Web Site</a>`. When you create a hyperlink in this manner, you're limited to certain fonts and the hyperlink is underlined. Of course, you can create a Cascading Style Sheet (CSS) to do away with the underline and specify a text font. In previous versions of Flash, you could not create a text hyperlink. Now you can easily create a text hyperlink using a text font, color, and size to match your design.

To create a text hyperlink:

1. Select the text tool and create a block of text on Stage.

2. With the Text tool, click inside the text box and drag backwards to select the block of text.

3. Open the Property inspector.

4. Click the triangle to the right of the text type field and choose Static Text.

5. In the URL target field, enter the path of the Web site to which you want to hyperlink the text. If the page resides at the same URL, enter the relative path; if the HTML document is at another Web site, enter the absolute path, for example: `htttp://www.dasdesigns.net/about.htm`.

6. Click the triangle to the right of the target field and choose one of the following:

   • **Self:** Opens the URL in the same window as the link.

   • **Blank:** Opens the specified URL in a new browser window. Choose this option and your Flash movie will play in the background.

   • **Parent:** Loads the URL in the window of the frame that called the link. If the frame isn't nested, the URL opens in the full browser window.

   • **Top:** Loads the URL in the full browser window, removing all frames.

That's all there is to it. When the movie is published, the user's cursor becomes the familiar pointing hand when moved over the text. When the text link is clicked, the linked page opens up in the browser window you specified.

Populating Dynamic Text with Array Elements

As you learned in Chapter 9, arrays are the perfect tool to store lots of data. When you create dynamic text and assign a variable name to the text box, you can easily display the content from an array in a text box. When you want to display an element from an array in a dynamic text box, you create a variable that's equal to the array element you want to display.

To create a dynamic text box that displays an array element:

1. Create a dynamic text box as outlined earlier.

2. Open the Property inspector.

3. In the Var field, enter a name for the text box variable. Remember to adhere to the variable naming conventions discussed in Chapter 9.

   Your next step is to create the variable and set it equal to the array element you want to display in the text box. You can create the variable on a keyframe, within a button, or within a movie clip, depending on your design requirements.

4. Select the keyframe, button, or object where the variable will reside.

5. Click Actions⇨Variables and then double-click `set variable`.

6. In the Variable field, enter the same name as the dynamic text box variable the array element will be displayed in.

7. In the Value field, enter the array name and then the element number you want to display.

   The element number is surrounded with square brackets. Remember the first element of an array is always 0.

8. Click the Expression checkbox.

   Listing 11-7 shows a variable with a value equal to the third element of an array.

Listing 11-7: **Creating a Variable to Display an Array Element in a Dynamic Text Box**

```
tickerText = tickerList[2];
```

Chapter Project: Creating a Ticker Text Marquee

In this project, you combine your knowledge of arrays and dynamic text boxes to create a ticker display. You also learn to display text one letter at a time by adding characters from an array element to the display in the dynamic text box.

On the CD-ROM

To follow along with this project, copy to your hard drive the scrollTick.fla file from this chapter's folder in the CD-ROM that accompanies this book. Use your operating system to disable the file's read-only attribute.

To begin the project:

1. Launch Flash and open the scrollTick.fla file. Notice that this project builds on the scrolling text project you completed earlier in this chapter. The elements have been rearranged slightly to accommodate the text box below the banner (see Figure 11-8).

   The text box is actually nested in a movie clip. If you'll remember the discussion about modular ActionScript, you can use this movie clip in any of your designs by choosing File⇨Open as Library and dragging an instance of the movie clip into the current document Library.

Scrolling ticker

Figure 11-8: The scrolling ticker is added to the previous project.

2. Click the text box movie clip and then right-click (Windows) or Ctrl+click (Macintosh) and choose Edit from the context menu.

After the movie clip is displayed in symbol-editing mode, notice you have six keyframes on the Actions layer. Select the first keyframe and open the Actions panel to display the code shown here:

```
// initialize labels and counter
k = 0;
tickText = "";
tickerList = new Array();
tickerList[0] = "Welcome to Pepper Cay... your vacation
paradise... ";
tickerList[1] = "White water rafting trips... ";
tickerList[2] = "Fishing for marlin and kingfish... ";
tickerList[3] = "Experienced guides available... ";
tickerList[4] = "Create your own adventure in paradise... ";
endLine = tickerList.length;
```

The code in this keyframe initializes the array and three variables. The variable *k* is used as a counter, the variable endLine returns the number of elements (length) of the array, which in this case is five. The value of endLine could have been set equal to 5, but that limits you to using this movie clip only with an array with five elements. If you modify this movie clip for use in another design, you can add as many array elements as needed, and the endLine variable will always return the number of elements in the array. The variable tickText is the same variable assigned to the dynamic text box that displays the elements of the array. Another thing to notice is the manner in which the array has been created; each element is created separately. You can accomplish the same thing by creating a variable named tickerList and then entering each array element in quotes and separating them with commas. This particular method was chosen for this project because it's easier to see each array element's offset. You'll be referring to each array element by its off-set to complete the project.

3. Select the second keyframe.

   In the Actions panel, you see that a single line of code has been created that initializes a variable named lineNum and sets its value equal to 0. This is the offset of the first element in the tickerList array. This frame has been labeled newLine.

4. Select the third keyframe, which has been labeled lineLoop.

   In the Actions panel, notice that two lines of code have been created. Two new variables have been declared, as shown below.

   ```
   len = tickerList[lineNum].length;
   i = 0;
   ```

   The variable len returns the length of an individual array element. When the code is first executed, the variable returns the length of the element in the tickerList array at offset 0, the initial value of the variable lineNum. The variable i is another counter.

5. Select the fourth keyframe that has been labeled msgLoop.

   In the Actions panel, notice a conditional statement has been started for you. You'll be creating the action that executes when the value of k is less than 65.

6. In the Actions panel Script pane, select the first line of code

7. In the left pane of the Actions panel, click Actions⇨Variables and then double-click set variable.

8. In the Variable field, type **tickText**

9. In the Value field, type **tickText+tickerList[lineNum].charAt (i)**

   Be sure to click the Expression checkbox.

   This line of code begins displaying text. It takes the initial value of tickText, a null string variable, and sets it equal to itself plus the first character of the first element in the array. The .charAt(i) part of the code returns the string value of character at this position in the string. When the code first executes, it returns the first character (i=0) of the first element (the initial value of lineNum is 0) from the tickerList array. The .charAt element of the code is a Property of the String object.

10. In the left pane of the Actions panel, click Actions⇨Conditions/Loops and then double-click else. You'll now create the code that executes when the value of k exceeds 65.

    When k reaches 65, the dynamic text box cannot accept any additional characters. In order for the ticker to display the next character, one character must be removed from the string in tickText. In other words, the number of characters in tickText must be reduced to 64 before the next character can be displayed. To achieve this, you use the substring method of the String object. You'll use this method to return the 1st through 65th characters of the string tickText, which in essence removes the first character.

11. In the left pane of the Actions panel click Actions⇨Variables, and then double-click set variable.

12. In the Variable field, type **tickText**

13. In the Value field, type **tickText.substring(1,65)+tickerList[lineNum].charAt (i)** and click the Expression checkbox.

    This line of code returns a substring of the 1st through 65th characters of tickText and adds the next character to the string. Remember, the first character of a string is position 0. The rest of the code has been written for you.

14. Select the fifth keyframe and open the Actions panel to view the following code.

```
i = ++i;
k = ++k;
if (i<len) {
   gotoAndPlay("msgLoop");
}
```

    This line of code increments the value of the variables i and k by a value of 1. The conditional statement evaluates the value of the variable len, which is the length of an array element. As long as the value of i is less than the length of the array element, the movie clip loops to the frame labeled msgLoop and another letter from the array element is added. When the value of i becomes greater than len, frame 6 plays.

15. Select the sixth keyframe and notice the following code in the Actions panel.

```
lineNum = ++lineNum;
if (lineNum==endLine) {
   gotoAndPlay("newLine");
} else {
   gotoAndPlay("lineLoop");
}
```

    The code in this keyframe increments the value of lineNum by 1. When the value of lineNum is equal to endLine, the movie goes to the frame labeled newLine, which sets the value of lineNum equal to 0 and begins displaying the characters from the first array element. Otherwise the movie loops to the frame labeled lineLoop, which sets the value of i equal to 0 to display the first character from the next array element.

16. Click the Back button to exit symbol-editing mode and then choose Control⇨Test Movie.

    The movie plays and the text advances one letter at a time across the marquee until the text box is filled, whereupon the next letters advance one at a time.

Several things happen in this movie. After the variables are declared and the array is set, the first element in the array is displayed one letter at a time by evaluating the charAt() property of the string data in the array. When the last letter of the string is displayed as determined by the conditional statement, the next element in the array is selected. The conditional statement in frame 4 evaluates the length of the variable stored the string data. When it exceeds the specified value, the substring property of the String object takes the first character away from the string. When the last element in the array is displayed, the code loops back to newLine, which resets to the first element in the array and letters from that element are added to continue the ticker.

You can use this movie clip in one of your own designs. All you need to do is change the size of the text box to suit your movie. You can also modify the color, size, and font by selecting the text box and modifying the parameters in the Property inspector. When you change the size of the text box, or any of the text parameters, you have to experiment to get the proper value for k and the ending value of the substring. If you choose a smaller font size, you have to increase the value of k; otherwise, the code will start dropping letters before the end of the text box is reached. Change both values in the fourth keyframe until the text advances properly, as shown in Listing 11-8.

Listing 11-8: **Modifying the Code for a Different Text Size**

```
if (k<85) {
  tickText = tickText+tickerList[lineNum].charAt(i);
} else {
  tickText = tickText.substring(1,85)+tickerList[lineNum].charAt(i);
}
```

The values you use vary depending upon the font size and size of the text box. Each font has different kerning characteristics, which enters into the value you end up using.

Copy the file marqueeComponent.fla to your hard drive. Launch Flash and open the file. In the document Library, you'll find a single component. Drag the component on Stage and center it to the top of the document. Open the Property inspector and then click the Parameter tab. Click the magnifying glass to open the Values panel. Three values have already been entered. Click a value and enter your own text. To add additional values, click the button that looks like a plus sign and enter some text. Click OK to apply the modifications and then test the movie. You now have a programmable marquee ticker.

The String object has many properties you can use to evaluate string data. In this chapter you've been exposed to the scroll, charAt(), and substring properties. A detailed discussion of each string property is beyond the scope of this book. You are urged to experiment with these properties. To understand what each property does, open the Actions panel, click the Reference icon and then click Objects⇨ Core⇨String⇨Properties; then click each property for a detailed explanation.

Designer Notes

In this chapter you were introduced to dynamic and input text. You learned how to create a scrolling text box for your designs and how to create a ticker marquee. You were shown how to manipulate string data as well as display string data from an array in a dynamic text box. In the next chapter, you'll create some interactive elements for your movies.

✦   ✦   ✦

Building Interactive Interfaces

◆ ◆ ◆ ◆

In This Chapter

Building tooltips

Creating drag-and-drop elements

Creating a user customizable interface

Using the Date object

Using the Scrollbar component

Chapter project: Creating a moving navigation bar

◆ ◆ ◆ ◆

In previous chapters, you learned to create elements such as animated buttons and navigation bars for your designs. In this chapter, the interactivity is cranked up a notch or two. In this chapter, you learn to design interactive interface elements such as tooltips. If you'd like to give your viewers the option of dragging interface elements to different areas, you'll learn how to create the code to do that in this chapter. You'll also learn how to create the ActionScript where the user can change the color and opacity of a background object by clicking a button and dragging a slider. You can also use ActionScript objects to display the date and time in your designs. In Chapter 11, you learned to create a scrolling text box using buttons of your own design. If time constraints don't allow you the luxury of creating a custom scrolling text box, you can use a Flash UI component to quickly create a scrolling text box. In the chapter project, you learn to create a moving navigation bar.

Note   The Actions panel's got lots of books. And some of these books have books within a book. To add some actions to your scripts, you have to click this book icon, then click that book icon, then click another book icon, and so on. Rather than bore you with a lot of words, I'm going to show the path to each action as shown in the following example: Click Actions⇨Movie Control and then double-click `goto`.

Building Tooltips

If you add enough bells and whistles to your designs, it may be difficult for some viewers to ascertain exactly what each element of your design does. You can alleviate some of the confusion by creating tooltips that appear when the users roll their mouse over certain elements in your designs. For example, you can add a tooltip that tells the viewer what they'll see when a button is clicked, as shown in Figure 12-1.

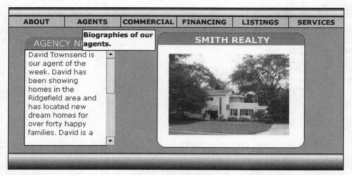

Figure 12-1: You can create a tooltip that displays information to the viewer.

Creating the tooltips

The actual tooltip itself is a movie clip. You can get as creative as you want when creating the graphics for the tooltip. For example, you can create a rounded rectangle with a triangle at the top that points to the object the user's mouse is over.

To create tooltips for a design:

1. Create the basic shape for the tooltip using any of the drawing tools or import an object.

   Do not create a new symbol. You want to create the shape and then convert it to a symbol so you can specify the registration point.

2. Choose Insert⇨Convert to Symbol.

   The Convert to Symbol dialog box appears, as shown in Figure 12-2.

3. Specify the registration point for the symbol.

   For most tooltips, you'll choose the upper-left corner. The symbol's registration point is the 0 coordinate for both the x and y axis.

4. Name the symbol, choose the Movie Clip behavior and click OK.

   The graphic is converted to a symbol.

5. Choose Edit⇨Edit Selected to work in symbol-editing mode.

6. Add the tooltip text and any other elements needed for your design.

7. Click the Back button to exit symbol-editing mode.

8. Delete the symbol instance.

    The master symbol is stored in the document Library. You'll duplicate it to create the other tooltips needed for your design.

9. Choose Window➪Library.

    The document Library opens.

10. Duplicate the basic tooltip symbol as needed to create the additional tooltips for your design. When you duplicate each symbol, give it a name that reflects the tooltip's function. After you create the duplicates, edit them to change the text. Remember, you can edit a symbol from the document Library by double-clicking its name.

After you create the tooltips, you're ready to add them to your design. When the movie loads, you don't want the tooltips to be visible so you place them off Stage. Then you create the necessary code to make the tooltip appear when the user's mouse hovers over a button.

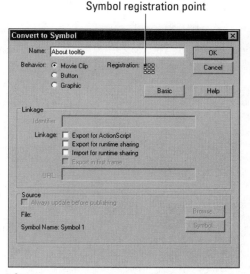

Figure 12-2: You can specify the registration point for the tooltip.

To position the tooltips, follow these steps:

1. Choose Window➪Library.

    The document Library opens.

2. Select all the tooltips.

To select all of them, select the first tooltip, and then click the additional tooltips while holding down the Shift key.

3. Drag the tooltips to a position off Stage.

4. Click the arrow to the left of the word Properties.

The Property inspector opens.

5. Record the values in the X: and Y: fields.

You'll need these values when you create the ActionScript to return the tooltips after the user's mouse rolls off the button.

6. Choose Modify⇨Distribute to Layers.

A new layer is created for each tooltip. The layer is labeled with the tooltip's name, as shown in Figure 12-3. By creating a separate layer for each tooltip, you can select each tooltip, even though they are in identical positions.

Tip   If you're creating a design that involves many objects, create a layer folder to store the tooltips in. After you create the tooltips, you can close the folder and it takes up only one position on the timeline. The tooltips in Figure 12-3 are stored in a folder.

7. Select a tooltip and then open the Property inspector.

To select an individual tooltip, lock and hide the other tooltip layers. Then you'll be able to select the tooltip by clicking it (see Figure 12-4).

8. Enter a name for the tooltip in the <Instance Name> field.

9. Repeat Steps 7 and 8 to name the other tooltips in your design.

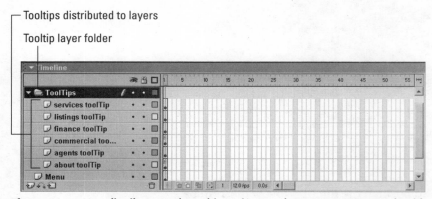

Figure 12-3: You distribute each tooltip to its own layer so you can work with them individually.

Selected tooltip layer   Locked and hidden tooltip layers

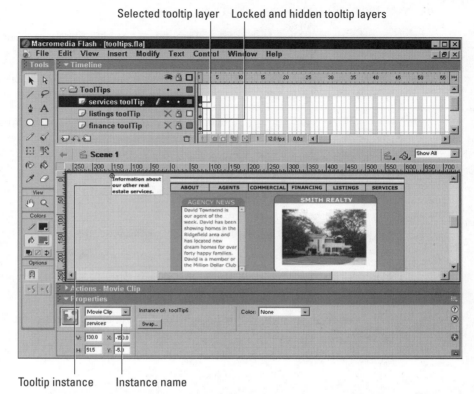

Tooltip instance   Instance name

Figure 12-4: Lock and hide the tooltip layers so you can edit an individual tooltip.

After you've named all of the tooltips, you're ready to create the ActionScript that makes the tooltips appear. You could create the same script for each object that uses a tooltip. However, that can get rather tedious if you have several tooltips. The easier solution is to create one function to display the tooltips and another to hide them.

Creating the tooltip functions

The functions you create to display and then hide the tooltips simplify your ActionScript work. The function that shows each tooltip changes the tooltip's _x and _y properties to the current x and y coordinates of the mouse, allowing for a bit of room if the user rolls over the top of the button. The function that hides each tooltip returns the tooltip to the _x and _y positions you recorded when you added the tooltips to your document.

To create the tooltip functions:

1. Select the top timeline layer and insert a layer. Label the layer **Actions**.

Tip   It's a good idea to get in the habit of creating a separate layer for actions you assign to keyframes on the timeline. All of your timeline ActionScript will be on one layer, making it easier for you to edit and debug the ActionScript.

2. Select the first frame on the Actions layer and then click the arrow to the left of the word Actions.

3. In the left pane of the Actions panel, click Actions⇨User-Defined Functions and then double-click `function`.

4. In the Name field, enter a name for the function.

5. In the Parameters field, type **mc**

   This designates that the function is applied to movie clips.

6. Click Actions⇨Miscellaneous Actions and then double-click `evaluate`.

   The Expression field appears above the Script pane.

7. In the Expression field, type **_root[mc]._x=_xmouse**

   This line of code sets the _x property of the movie clip called by the function equal to the current _x position of the mouse.

8. Click Actions⇨Miscellaneous Actions and then double-click `evaluate`.

9. In the Expression field, type **root[mc]._y=_ymouse**

The function you just created displays the tooltip. Now you need to create a function to hide the tooltip.

To create a function to hide the tooltips, follow these steps:

1. Select the last line of code (the solitary curly brace) you just created.

2. In the left pane of the Actions panel, click Actions⇨User-Defined Functions and then double-click `function`.

3. In the Name field, enter a name for the function.

4. In the Parameters field, type **mc**

5. In the left pane of the Actions panel, click Actions⇨Miscellaneous Actions and then double-click `evaluate`.

   The Expression field appears above the Script pane.

6. In the Expression field, type **_root[mc]._x=** followed by the value you recorded from the Property inspector when you added the tooltips to your design.

7. Repeat Steps 5 and 6 to create an expression for the _y property of the movie clip. Listing 12-1 shows two functions that show and hide tooltips.

Listing 12-1: Creating Functions to Show and Hide Tooltips

```
function showTip(mc) {
  _root[mc]._x=_xmouse+5;
  _root[mc]._y=_ymouse+5;
}
function hideTip(mc) {
  _root[mc]._x=-150;
  _root[mc]._y=-5;
}
```

Notice that a value of 5 was added to the _xmouse and _ymouse properties in the code shown in Listing 12-1. This was to allow a bit of space so the item the user's mouse hovers over is still visible.

After you create the functions, you create the code that displays or hides the movie clips depending on where the user's mouse is in relation to the button.

Programming the buttons

You've done most of the hard work by creating the functions. Now all you need to do is code each button to call the proper function when a user's mouse rolls over, or rolls out, of the button target area.

Note

> If you want a tooltip to appear when a user's mouse is over a graphic, you must nest the graphic in a movie clip with an invisible button.

To program the buttons:

1. Select a button and open the Actions panel.

2. In the left pane of the Actions panel, click Actions⇨User-Defined Functions and then double-click `call function`.

   Three parameter text boxes appear above the Script pane.

3. In the Object field, type **_root**

   This tells the Flash Player that the function will be applied to an object on the root timeline.

4. In the Method field, type the name of the function you created to display the tooltip.

5. In the Parameters field, type the instance name of the tooltip you want to appear. The instance name must be surrounded by quotation marks, as shown in Listing 12-2.

6. Click the first line of code and in the parameter text area, click the Roll Over checkbox, making sure you deselect the checkbox for the default Release event.

   The button is now programmed to call the tooltip when a user's mouse rolls over the button target area.

7. Click the last line of code (the curly brace) and repeat Steps 2 through 6 to call the function that hides the tooltip. For the event, choose Roll Out.

   Listing 12-2 shows a typical ActionScript to call and put a tooltip.

Listing 12-2: **Calling the Functions**

```
on (rollOver) {
  _root.showTip("about");
}
on (rollOut) {
  _root.hideTip("about");
}
```

To see an example of tooltips at work, copy to your hard drive the toolTips.fla file you'll find in this chapter's folder on the CD-ROM that accompanies this book. Disable the file's read-only attributes and then open the file in Flash. Choose Control➪Test Movie to publish the file and display it in another window. Roll your mouse over the buttons to display the tooltips. After you finish testing the movie, close the window. If you want to examine the ActionScript, open the Actions panel and then select the individual buttons.

If adding tooltips is cumbersome for your design, you can create a movie clip with a Help document and position it off Stage. Create a Help button that, when clicked, changes the position of the Help document so that it appears within the movie. Create a Close Window button that when clicked moves the document out of view.

Creating Drag-and-Drop Elements

Another way to add interactivity to your designs is to create drag-and-drop elements. You can create drag-and-drop menus or drag-and-drop windows. The easiest way to create a drag-and-drop element is to nest an invisible button in a movie clip and then use the startDrag action. You can either leave your viewers in the dark and let them discover the element can be dragged and dropped when they roll over it with their mouse, or you can create a small motion tween animation that shows the element moving when the movie begins.

Creating a drag-and-drop window

You can use the `startDrag` action to give you viewers the capability of dragging and dropping objects in your movie. When you create a window or object with the intention of using it as a drag-and-drop element in your design, create a tab for the viewer to grab onto. You make this area of the object active by placing an invisible button over the tab when you create the movie clip. By nesting the button inside a movie clip, you don't have to refer to a target path — you can use the `this` alias to refer to the movie clip the button is nested in.

To convert a movie clip into a drag-and-drop object:

1. Select the movie clip on Stage that you want to convert to a drag-and-drop object.

2. Choose Edit⇨Edit Selected.

    The object is now in symbol-editing mode.

3. Choose Window⇨Library.

4. Select an invisible button and drag it on Stage. Align the invisible button over the target area of the movie clip where the user will be able to click and drag.

5. Click the arrow to the left of the word Actions.

6. In the left pane of the Actions panel, click Actions⇨Movie Clip Control and then double-click `startDrag`.

7. In the Target field, type **this** and click the Expression checkbox.

8. Click the last line of code signified by the curly brace.

9. In the left pane of the Actions panel, click Actions⇨Movie Clip Control and then double-click `stopDrag`.

    The `stopDrag` action has no parameters. It stops the drag action currently in progress.

10. Select the first line of code that reads `on(release) {`.

11. In the parameter text area, select the Press event and deselect the Release event.

    Listing 12-3 shows a typical script for a drag-and-drop element.

Listing 12-3: **Creating the Code for a Drag-and-Drop Element**

```
on (press) {
  startDrag(this);
}
on (release) {
  stopDrag();
}
```

If you create target windows for loading movie clips, you can use the `startDrag` action to give the viewer the capability of dragging the window after the movie clip loads. If your target window is a movie clip with a blank first frame, add the invisible button to the second frame of the movie clip.

Closing a window

You can give viewers of your movies the option to close a window by creating a small movie clip with the letter X inside an unfilled rectangle. Nest an invisible button in the movie clip and then program the button to close the window.

The method you use to program the button depends on how the window was created. If the window is second frame of a target movie clip that another movie is loaded into, program the button to unload the movie and go to the first frame of the target movie clip, which is blank. Listing 12-4 shows typical ActionScript for closing a target movie clip window and unloading a movie from the target.

Listing 12-4: **Closing a Window**

```
on (release) {
  _root.art_clip_client.gotoAndStop(1);
  unloadMovie(_root.art_clip_client);
}
```

You can also close a window by changing its _visible property to false. The code for a button that hides a window from view is shown in Listing 12-5.

Listing 12-5: **Hiding a Window**

```
on (release) {
  this._visible=false;
}
```

To view a document with a few drag-and-drop elements, copy to your hard drive the dragNdrop.fla file found in this chapter's folder on the CD-ROM that accompanies this book. Use your operating system to disable the file's read-only attribute. Launch Flash, open the file and choose Control⇨Test Movie. You can drag-and-drop the windows and the menu. The menu is a derivate of the flyout menu you created in Chapter 10. Click Menu to expand the menu. Both windows can be closed by clicking the X. After you're finished testing the movie, close the window and open the Actions panel to examine the various scripts used in the movie.

Creating a User Customizable Interface

In addition to giving viewers the capability of dragging and dropping objects, you can also make if possible for them to modify the interface. You can do this by creating a movie that uses a background image and then using the Color object and a function to make it possible for the viewer to change the color of the background image by clicking a button.

On the CD-ROM To learn how you can create a background that the user can change, copy to your hard drive the interface.fla file found in this chapter's folder on the CD-ROM the accompanies this book. Disable the file's read-only attribute using your operating system utilities.

To create a user-customizable interface:

1. Launch Flash and open the interface.fla file.

2. Choose Control⇨Test Movie.

   The document is published and appears in a new window.

3. Click the Control Panel label.

   The control panel slides into the interface. The panel motion was created by using a motion tween.

4. Drag the slider bar.

   The opacity of the background movie clip changes, as shown in Figure 12-5.

   The slider used to change the opacity is constrained to a motion between 0 and 100 along the x axis. The _alpha property of the background image is set equal to the _X property of the slider. When the slider is all the way to the right, its _x property is 100 and the background is opaque; when the slider is at 0, the background movie clip is transparent.

Note The color swatches are not functional yet. You'll be programming them to change the color of the background when they are clicked. But instead of creating a long ActionScript for each button, you're going to create a function named setBGcolor that is called when each button is clicked.

5. Close the window to return the movie-editing mode.

The buttons are nested within a movie clip. You can edit items nested in a movie clip by double-clicking the movie clip and then double-clicking individual items nested in the movie clip. Every time you double-click, you open a nested symbol and make it available for editing.

Figure 12-5: The control panel is programmed to change the color characteristics of the background image.

To program the buttons:

1. Double-click the control panel on the left side of the Stage.

   You are now in symbol-editing mode and the workspace title bar reads Control Panel, the name of the symbol.

2. Click the arrow to the left of the word Properties.

   The Property inspector opens. Notice that the symbol has already been given an instance name of open panel. This is part of the path to the buttons.

3. Double-click the panel again.

   The title bar should now read Inner Panel.

4. Click the color swatch in the upper-right corner of the lower panel, directly below the word *color*.

   If you still have the Property inspector open, the description should read "instance of #FF6699." When the buttons were created, they were named after their hexadecimal value.

5. Click the arrow to the left of the word Actions.

   The panel title bar should read Actions-Button.

6. In the left pane of the Actions panel, click Actions⇨Variable and then double-click set variable.

7. In the Variable field, type **chip**

   You'll use the contents of this variable to change the color of the background when the button is clicked.

8. In the Value field, type **0xFF6699**

   That nomenclature may look familiar. This is the same formatting used to change an object's color characteristics using the Color object.

9. Click the Expression checkbox.

When you create code like this for your own designs, you'll already know the name of the function; therefore, you can create the code to call the function while coding the button. As mentioned in the previous section, the name of the function you'll be creating is called setBGcolor. The instance name of the background movie clip you'll be applying the function to has been labeled bg.

10. In the left pane of the Actions panel, click Actions⇨User-Defined Functions and then double-click call function.

11. In the Object field, type **_root**

12. In the Method field, type **setBGcolor**

13. In the Parameters field, type **"bg"**. Your finished code for the button should look exactly like Listing 12-6.

Listing 12-6: **Creating the Code for the Button**

```
on (release) {
  chip = 0xFF6699;
  _root.setBGcolor("bg");
}
```

14. Click the Scene 1 button to the right of the Back button to return to movie-editing mode.

The other buttons have already been programmed. In order to make the buttons active, you need to create a function that uses the setRGB method of the Color object to apply the transformation.

To create the function:

1. Click the first frame on the Actions layer.

2. Click the arrow to the left of the word Actions.

3. In the left pane of the Actions panel, click Actions⇨User Defined Functions and then double-click function.

4. In the Name field, type **setBGcolor**

5. In the Parameters field, type **mc**

This signifies the function is to be used on a movie clip.

6. In the left pane of the Actions panel, click Actions⇨Variables and then double-click set variable.

7. In the Variable field, type **myColorObject**

8. Place your cursor in the Value field and then in the left pane of the Actions panel, click Objects⇨Movie⇨Color and then double-click newColor.

   The object is added to the script and your cursor blinks between two parentheses.

9. Type **mc** and click the Expression checkbox.

10. In the left pane of the Actions panel, click Objects⇨Movie⇨Color⇨Methods and then double-click setRGB.

11. In the Object field, type **myColorObject** and then place your cursor inside the Parameters field.

    When you worked with the color object in Chapter 9, you specified a hexadecimal value in this field. However, you're using the function with more than one color value. The value changes whenever one of the color buttons in the control panel is clicked. You set the variable of the variable chip equal to the hexadecimal value of the button's color using the proper formatting for the Color object. You use the value of the variable in the parameters field by specifying the path to the variable and the name of the variable.

12. Click the Insert a Target Path button to open the Insert Target Path dialog box. Click the Absolute mode radio button if it's not already selected.

13. Click the plus sign (+) to the left of the fullPanel button and then click openPanel, as shown in Figure 12-6.

    This is the target path to the button where you set the value of the variable chip.

14. In the Value field, place your cursor to the right of the target path that was entered when you clicked the button and type **.chip**

    The code for your finished function should look exactly like Listing 12-7.

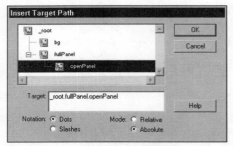

Figure 12-6: Adding the target path to the script.

Listing 12-7: **Creating the setBGcolor Function**

```
function setBGcolor(mc) {
  myColorObject = new Color(mc);
  myColorObject.setRGB(_root.fullPanel.openPanel.chip);
}
```

The other buttons are already programmed. The value of the variable chip is set equal to the hexadecimal value of the button's color, formatted for the setRGB method of the color object. To test your code choose Control⇨Test Movie. After the movie opens in another window, click the control panel button to open the panel. Click each color button and watch the color of the background movie clip change. Drag the slider to vary the look of the background even further by changing the value of background movie clip's _alpha property.

Telling Time with ActionScript

You can add the time and date to your designs using ActionScript. You can use the various methods of the Date object to retrieve the date and time from the user's computer. The information retrieved by the Date object is variable — it changes as the computer updates the time. In order to retrieve the time or date for the computer playing your Flash movie, you must first create a Date object.

Creating a Date object

Before you can retrieve the date or time from a computer using the Date object, you must first create an instance of the Date object. You can create an instance of the Date object on a keyframe or within a movie clip.

To create an instance of the Date object:

1. Click the arrow to the left of the word Actions.

2. In the left pane of the Actions panel, click Actions⇨Variables and then double-click set variable.

3. In the Variable field, type a name for the instance of the Date object, for example myDate.

4. Place your cursor inside the Value field, and in the left pane of the Actions panel, click Objects⇨Core⇨Date and then double-click new Date.

5. Click the Expression checkbox.

After you create an instance of the Date object, you can use the object's methods to retrieve date and time information from the host computer playing your Flash design.

Displaying the current date

When you use methods of the Date object to display the date, you display the date in a dynamic text box. You then create a variable with the same name as the dynamic text box variable and set the value of the variable equal to the various methods of the Date object. The following list shows some of the most commonly used Date object methods:

✦ **getDate:** Returns the current date of the month as a number.

✦ **getDay:** Returns the current day of the week as a number. The week begins with Sunday, which is designated by the number 0. In order to display the day's name, you create an array with each day of the week. The first element in the array is Sunday, which is array offset 0, the same number the getDay method returns when the day of the week is Sunday.

✦ **getMonth:** Returns the current month of the year as a number. January is returned as a 0, December as an 11. To display the month's name instead of a number, you create an array with each day of the month. If you display the month as a number, you have to create ActionScript to increase the value the getMonth method returns by 1.

✦ **getFullYear:** Returns the current year as a four-digit number; for example, 2002.

To retrieve the current date from the computer's operating system, you create an instance of the Date object as described in the previous section. After you create the object, you then create individual variables to retrieve the day, month, date, and year from the host computer's operating system. Listing 12-8 shows a typical script to retrieve the date.

Listing 12-8: Retrieving the Current Date Using Methods of the Date Object

```
mydate = new Date();
day = mydate.getDay();
month = mydate.getMonth();
currentdate = mydate.getDate();
year = mydate.getFullYear();
```

The code in Listing 12-8 returns the date. To display the date in a dynamic text box with a variable name of current date, you'd create the script in Listing 12-9.

Listing 12-9: **Displaying the Date**

```
// Set day array
myday = new Array("Sunday", "Monday", "Tuesday", "Wednesday", "Thursday",
"Friday", "Saturday");
// create date object and variables for day, month,date, and year
mymonth = new Array("January", "February", "March", "April", "May", "June",
"July", "August", "September", "October", "November", "December");
mydate = new Date();
day = mydate.getDay();
month = mydate.getMonth();
currentdate = mydate.getDate();
year = mydate.getFullYear();
current_date = myday[day]+", "+mymonth[month]+" "+currentdate+", "+year;
```

The two arrays contain the days and months as string objects. The first element of an array is 0. The getDay and getMonth methods of the Date object returns Sunday and January as a 0. The last lines of code combine the elements to display the date in a dynamic text box with the variable name of `current_date`. The first element of the `current_date variable`, myday[day] gets the current day for the week from the myday array. The `mymonth[month]` element of the variable gets the current month from the mymonth array. You retrieve an element from an array by specifying its offset surrounded by square brackets. The variable day and month return a number that retrieves the proper element from each array.

On the CD-ROM

In this chapter's folder on the CD-ROM that accompanies this book is a file named currentDate.fla. Copy the file to your hard drive and use your operating system utilities to disable the file's read-only attributes. Open the file in Flash for an example of a movie clip that displays the current date. Choose Control⇨Test Movie to see the date displayed. To use the movie clip in your own design, open the file using the Open as Library command and then drag the movie clip into the current document Library. You can then edit the movie clip to change the attributes in the dynamic text box to display a different font or different font color.

Displaying the current Time

To retrieve the current time from the host computer playing your Flash design, you create an instance of the Date object as outlined previously. After you create an instance of the Date object, you can use the object's methods to retrieve the current time. The following list shows the most commonly used methods to retrieve the time.

- ✦ **getHours:** Returns the current hour from the host computer as a whole number. The time returned is based on a 24-hour clock. Midnight is returned as a 0; 11:00 PM is returned as 23.

- ✦ **getMinutes:** Displays the current minute from the host computer's clock as a whole number.

- ✦ **getSeconds:** Displays the current second from the host computer's clock as a whole number.

After creating an instance of the Date object, you create a variable for each method you want to retrieve. Listing 12-10 shows a script that creates an instance of the Date object and three variables to store the information.

Listing 12-10: Retrieving the Current Time from the Host Computer

```
mydate = new Date();
hours = mydate.getHours();
minutes = mydate.getMinutes();
seconds = mydate.getSeconds();
```

To display the date in a dynamic text box, you have to convert the 24-hour clock to a 12-hour clock, unless of course your client is a military organization. Listing 12-11 shows a script that displays the time correctly in a dynamic text box.

Listing 12-11: Displaying the Time on a 12-Hour Clock

```
onClipEvent (enterFrame) {
  mydate = new Date();
  hours = mydate.getHours();
  minutes = mydate.getMinutes();
  seconds = mydate.getSeconds();
  // Calculate value of AMorPM variable before changing hours variable to
compensate for military time
  if (hours<12) {
    AMorPM = "AM";
  } else {
    AMorPM = "PM";
  }
  // At midnight military time =0
  if (hours<1) {
    hours = 12;
  }
  if (hours>12) {
    hours = hours-12;
  }
  if (minutes<10) {
    minutes = "0"+minutes;
  }
  if (seconds<10) {
    seconds = "0"+seconds;
  }
  current_time = hours+":"+minutes+":"+seconds+" "+AMorPM;
}
```

Notice that the code in the previous example specifies the enterFrame clip event. This code is in a movie clip. Choosing the enterFrame clip event continually updates the time as the host computer's clock ticks away. The lines of code below the seconds variable set the display time to AM or PM and modify the output to a 12-hour clock. These are all conditional statements. If the variable hours returns a value less than 1, it's midnight and the variable's value is reset to 12 — midnight on a 12-hour clock. If the value of hours exceeds 12, the value is reduced by 12 to display the proper time on a 12-hour clock; for example, 1300 hours is 1:00 PM on a 12-hour clock. The last two variables add the string "0" to seconds or minutes if they are less than 10. The current_time variable combines all the variables with the necessary punctuation to properly display the time in a dynamic text box.

On the CD-ROM

In this chapter's folder on the CD-ROM that accompanies this book is a file named currentTime.fla. Copy the file to your hard drive and use your operating system utilities to disable the file's read-only attributes. Open the file in Flash for an example of a movie clip that displays the current time. Choose Control⇨Test Movie to see the date displayed. To use the movie clip in your own design, open the file using the Open as Library command and then drag the movie clip into the document Library of your current project. You can then edit the dynamic text box in the movie clip to change the text attributes and choose a different font style or color. If you choose a larger font size, you may have to resize the dynamic text box with the Text tool.

Using the ScrollBar Component

In Chapter 11, you learned how to create a scrolling text box that displays dynamic text using a button and/or slider of your own design. If you're ever under the gun to get a project completed in a short period of time and you need to include a scrolling text box in the design, you can use the ScrollBar component to quickly get the job done.

To create a scrolling text box with the ScrollBar component:

1. Select the Text tool.

2. Drag a text box on Stage.

3. Click the arrow to the left of the word Properties.

   The Property inspector opens.

4. Choose the font style, color, and size.

5. Click the triangle to the right of the Text Type field and choose Dynamic Text from the drop-down menu.

6. Enter a name for the text box in the <Instance Name> field.

   Enter a name with no spaces. If you must have a separation between two words, use an underscore.

7. Click the triangle to the right of the Line Type field and choose Multiline from the drop-down menu.

8. Select the dynamic text box with the Arrow tool and then right-click (Windows) or Ctrl+click (Macintosh) and choose Scrollable from the context menu.

9. Double-click the text box to return to text-editing mode.

10. Enter the desired text in the box or paste the contents of a document you've copied from a word processing program. Make sure you enter enough text to exceed the boundary of the text box.

11. Choose Window⇨Components.

    The Components panel opens.

12. Drag an instance of the ScrollBar component and drop it inside the text box.

    The component resizes itself to the height of the text box (see Figure 12-7).

When the movie is published, the scrollbar becomes functional.

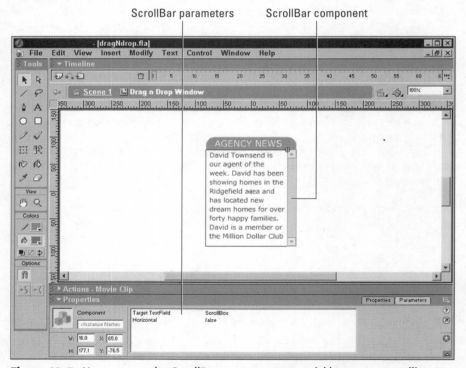

Figure 12-7: You can use the ScrollBar component to quickly create a scrolling text box.

Chapter Project: Creating a Moving Navigation Bar

If you've ever seen a Flash design with a navigation menu that is moving from left to right and the first item of the menu reappears after the last in a seemingly endless loop, you know what a compelling effect this is. The code to create this effect is relatively simple. You begin by creating a navigation bar as outlined previously in Chapter 10 and then use a bit of ActionScript trickery to pull off the effect.

On the CD-ROM

To learn how to create a moving navigation bar, copy to your hard drive the movingNavBar.fla file you'll find in this chapter's folder on the CD-ROM that accompanies this book. Disable the file's read-only attributes using your operating system utilities.

To create the moving navigation bar:

1. Launch Flash and open the movingNavBar.fla file.

The project is partially completed. You have a basic interface and a navigation bar, as shown in Figure 12-8.

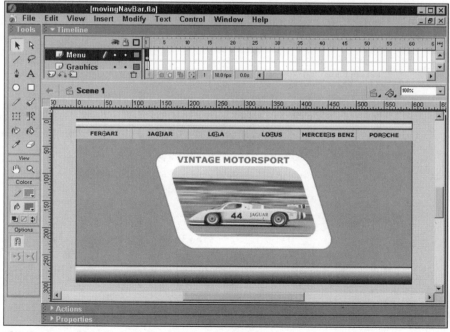

Figure 12-8: Your first step is to create a navigation bar.

2. Select all the buttons and then choose Insert⇨Convert to Symbol.

The Convert to Symbol dialog box appears.

3. Name the symbol, choose the movie clip behavior, and click the center left square in the Registration section (see Figure 12-9).

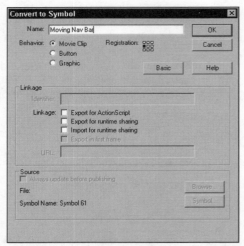

Figure 12-9: You convert the navigation bar to a movie clip symbol.

4. Click OK.

The buttons are converted to a movie clip symbol and the symbol is added to the document Library.

5. Select the symbol you just created and then choose Edit⇨Edit Selected.

You are now working in symbol-editing mode.

6. Select all the buttons and then choose Edit⇨Copy.

The buttons are copied to the clipboard.

7. Choose Edit⇨Paste in Place.

You now have a carbon copy of the buttons in the navigation bar. Your next task is to align the first button so that it appears after the last button on the navigation bar you copied. The document you are working with is 600 pixels wide, as is the navigation bar. To move the selected buttons, you change the x value in the Property inspector.

8. Click the arrow to the left of the word Properties to open the Property inspector.

9. In the X field, type **600**

The buttons are perfectly aligned.

10. Click the Back button to exit symbol-editing mode.

When you return to movie editing mode, the symbol is still selected.

11. Click the triangle to the left of the word Actions.

The Actions panel opens.

12. In the left pane of the Actions panel, click Actions⇨Conditions/Loops and then double-click `if`.

13. In the Condition field, type **this**

14. In the left pane of the Actions panel, click Objects⇨Movie⇨Movie Clip⇨Methods and then double-click `hitTest`.

Your cursor flashes between a pair of parentheses.

15. Type the following: **_root._xmouse, _root._ymouse,true**

The condition you just created tests to see if the mouse has hit the navigation bar.

16. In the left pane of the Actions panel, click Actions⇨Miscellaneous Actions and then double-click `evaluate`.

17. In the Expression field, type **this._x-=0**

You may recognize this as a decremental expression. If the mouse hits the navigation bar, the x position of the navigation bar decrements by a value of 0. In other words, there is no motion. To set the navigation bar in motion, you need to use the `else` action.

18. In the left pane of the Actions panel, click Actions⇨Conditions/Loops and then double-click `else`.

19. In the left pane of the Actions panel, click Actions⇨Miscellaneous Actions and then double-click `evaluate`.

20. In the Expression field, type **this._x-=5**

This expression decrements the x position of the navigation bar by a value of five pixels. But if the navigation bar continues to move, eventually it will scroll past the end of the movie. To prevent this, you create another conditional statement using the `if` action. The navigation bar is 600 pixels long, and you tacked a 600 pixel duplicate to the back end. The first button on the navigation bar is at x coordinate 0. When the navigation bar moves 600 pixels to the left, the navigation bar you copied to the back end is fully displayed. Therefore, you set the _x property of the navigation bar to 0 as soon as it exceeds –600. This is how the navigation bar appears to be continuous.

21. In the left pane of the Actions panel, click Actions⇨Conditions/Loops and then double-click if.

22. In the Condition field, type **this._x<=-600**

23. In the left pane of the Actions panel, click Actions⇨Miscellaneous Actions and then double-click evaluate.

24. In the Expression field, type **this._x=0**

    As soon the movie clips _x property is less than or equal to –600, the property is reset to 0 and the navigation bar appears as though it is never-ending.

25. Select the first line of code that reads onClipEvent (load) {.

26. In the parameter text area, select the Enter Frame clip event. Your code for the navigation bar should look like Listing 12-12.

Listing 12-12: Creating ActionScript for a Moving Navigation Bar

```
onClipEvent (enterFrame) {
  if (this.hitTest(_root._xmouse, _root._ymouse,true)) {
    this._x-=0;
  } else {
    this._x-=5;
  }
  if (this._x<=-600) {
    this._x=0;
  }
}
```

27. Choose Control⇨Test Movie.

    After the movie publishes, it displays in another window. If you followed the steps exactly, the navigation bar should begin moving to the left. Move your mouse over the navigation bar and it stops.

This technique can also be used when the navigation bar exceeds the width of the movie. For example, if you create a document that is 600 pixels wide, and you have eight buttons that are 100 pixels long, you change the values accordingly. When you duplicate the buttons and paste them onto the back end of the original navigation bar, you change the value in the X field of the Property inspector to 800. When the navigation bar's _x property is less than or equal to –800, you reset the property value to 0.

Tip For another interesting variation, you can create a vertical navigation bar and have it continuously scroll from top to bottom by decrementing the navigation bar's _y property.

Designer Notes

In this chapter, you learned to create interactive elements for your interfaces. You learned how to create tooltips as well as how to create an interface that the user can modify. You learned to use the Date object to display the time and date in your designs. The chapter project showed you how to create a navigation menu that moves from left to right and appears to have no end. In the next chapter, you learn to use the Sound object to modify the characteristics of sounds in your Flash designs.

✦   ✦   ✦

Creating ActionScript Sound Objects

✦ ✦ ✦ ✦

In This Chapter

Creating a soundtrack

Looping a soundtrack

Using streaming sound

Creating a Sound object

Using methods of the Sound object

Chapter project: Creating a sound controller

✦ ✦ ✦ ✦

When you design a movie, chances are sound will be included. The vast majority of Web surfers seem to expect sound as a given with any Flash design. However, not everyone likes sound when viewing a Web site. And not everyone likes the same type of music. Therefore, it is necessary to provide some type of control the viewer can use to control the sound. And that job is left to you, the designer of the movie.

Soundtracks can be incorporated in the document Library, or you can add a soundtrack at runtime. In this chapter, you'll learn to create a movie with nothing but a soundtrack that is loaded into another movie. You'll also learn to create an instance of the ActionScript Sound object. When you create an instance of the Sound object, you can use methods of the Sound object to control the volume of the sound, pan the sound between speakers, or start and stop the sound. When you complete the chapter project, you'll know how to create a working sound controller.

Note The Actions panel's got lots of books. And some of these books have books within a book. To add some actions to your scripts, you have to click this book icon, then click that book icon, then click another book icon, and so on. Rather than bore you with a lot of words, I'm going to show the path to each action as shown in the following example: Click Actions➪Movie Control and then double-click `goto`.

Creating a Soundtrack

There are two ways you can work a soundtrack into your designs. First, you can import the sound file into the document Library and add it to the timeline. When you use a soundtrack in this manner, the soundtrack must load at runtime before the first frame of the movie plays. If you have a relatively small sound file, this is generally not a problem.

However, a better solution for adding sound to your Flash production is to publish the soundtrack in a separate movie and then give the viewer the option to load the soundtrack or not. When you choose this option, your base movie loads more quickly because you don't have the overhead of the sound file to load in addition to your other content. Whichever method you choose, you must first import the sound into the document.

Importing a sound

When you decide to use a soundtrack in one of your designs, you can import any of the following file types:

✦ WAV (Windows only)

✦ AIFF (Macintosh only)

✦ MP3 (Windows and Macintosh)

If you have QuickTime 4 installed on your machine, you can also import the following sound format types:

✦ AIFF (Windows or Macintosh)

✦ Sound Designer II (Macintosh only)

✦ Sound only QuickTime Movies (Windows and Macintosh)

✦ Sun AU (Windows or Macintosh)

✦ System 7 Sounds (Macintosh only)

✦ WAV (Windows or Macintosh)

The format you import depends on the source material you have available. If you use sound sampling software to create your own loops, you can choose a format to render the file with. The AIFF and WAV formats create a good quality soundtrack at the expense of a large file size. If you choose the MP3 format, you can choose a compression setting to apply to the file. However, you can also apply MP3 compression to a sound file within Flash. When you apply MP3 compression using Flash export settings, you can choose a Bit Rate as high as 160 kbps. This setting gives you CD-quality sound, but it also generates the largest file size. Unless you need a Bit Rate setting higher than 160, it is recommended that you render a file in the native format for your operating system (WAV for Windows and AIFF for Macintosh) and apply MP3 compression within Flash.

To import a sound file into a Flash document:

1. Choose File⇨Import.

   The Import dialog box opens.

2. Locate the sound file you want to import and then click Open.

   The dialog box closes and the sound is stored in the document Library.

After you import a sound into Flash, you can then add it anywhere on the timeline. To add a sound to the timeline, you use the Property inspector. To add a sound to the timeline, do the following:

1. Select the keyframe where you want the sound to begin playing.

2. Click the arrow to the left of the word Properties.

   The Property inspector opens.

3. Click the triangle to the right of the Sound field.

   A menu appears with a list of all sounds stored in the document Library.

4. Select a sound from the menu.

5. Click the triangle to the right of the Effect field and choose one of the following:

   - **None:** The default setting applies no effect to the sound.
   - **Left Channel:** Plays sound in left channel only.
   - **Right Channel:** Plays sound in right channel only. You can use this effect in conjunction with the Left Channel effect applied to a different sound on a different timeline to play different sounds in each speaker.
   - **Fade Left to Right:** Fades sound from left speaker to the right.
   - **Fade Right to Left:** Fades sound from right speaker to the left.
   - **Fade In:** Gradually increases the amplitude of the sound to full volume during the duration of the sound.
   - **Fade Out:** Gradually decreases the amplitude of the sound to silence during the duration of the sound.
   - **Custom:** Lets you create your own effect by modifying the sound's characteristics. When you choose this option, a dialog box appears. Creating a custom effect will be covered in the next section.

6. Click the triangle to the right of the Sync field and choose one of the following options:

   - **Event:** An event sound is synched to the keyframe where you add the sound. The sound plays in its entirety, regardless of the length of the timeline and regardless of whether the movie is still playing. Choose Event when you are creating a background sound loop. Event sounds are mixed when the movie is published.

When you use the Event Sync option for a button sound, the sound starts when the button is clicked and plays for its duration. If the button is clicked again before the sound finishes playing, a second instance of the sound plays simultaneously.

- **Start:** Works the same as Event. However, if the sound is already playing, a new instance of the sound does not start. This setting is recommended for a button sound.

- **Stop:** Stops a sound.

Tip   If you create an introduction with sound for one of your designs, add a keyframe to the last frame of your introduction, open the Property inspector, and from the Sound field menu, choose your intro soundtrack and from the Sync field menu choose Stop. Open the Actions panel and create the code to go to and play the first frame of the main movie. Create a "skip intro" button and program the button to go to and play the last frame of the introduction. When the user clicks the button, the last frame of the introduction plays, stops the introduction sound, and transports the viewer to the first frame of the main scene of your design.

- **Stream:** Streams the sound into the viewer's browser. The Flash Player forces the animation to synchronize with the streaming sound, dropping frames if necessary to keep up. If the data can't download into the user's browser quickly enough, the sound will stop. If you do not have enough frames on the timeline, the sound will stop when the last frame is reached. Streaming sound is best used to synchronize a narration with a movie. Streaming sound is not recommended for background music as popping sounds and other artifacts may occur when Flash breaks the sound into packets for streaming.

7. In the Loop field, enter the number of times you want the sound to loop for.

When you're using a sound for background music, enter a high value so the sound plays continuously while the movie is being viewed. However, when you create background music that loops continuously, provide some way for the viewer to stop the sound. Either create a button and assign the stopAllSounds action to it or create a sound controller with volume control and an Off switch (as you will do in this chapter's project).

After you complete the previous steps, the sound is added to the timeline. If you have enough frames on the timeline, the sound's waveform is displayed, as shown in Figure 13-1. Otherwise, you see a truncated waveform, but if you choose Event or Start for the Sync method, the sound will still play in its entirety

Creating a custom effect

If you don't own sound-editing software, you can still do some basic sound editing within Flash. You can create a custom fade in or fade out, vary the volume of the sound as it plays, or change the duration of a sound. When you edit a sound, you create a *custom effect.*

Sound begins at this keyframe   Sound waveform

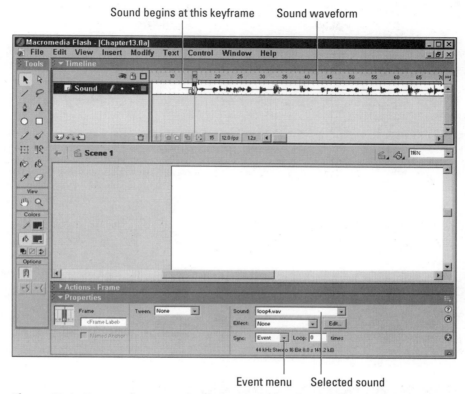

Event menu   Selected sound

Figure 13-1: You can insert a sound at any point on the timeline.

To create a custom effect:

1. Import a sound and add it to the timeline as discussed previously, or select a sound on the timeline you want to edit.

2. Click the arrow to the left of the word Properties.

   The Property inspector opens. If the sound is already on the timeline, the sound's name is displayed in the Sound field. Otherwise, follow the previous steps to set up the imported sound on the timeline.

3. Click the triangle to the right of the Effect field and choose Custom. Alternately, you can click the Edit button.

   The Edit Envelope dialog box opens (see Figure 13-2), and you can perform any of the following tasks:

   • To shorten the duration of the sound, drag the Time In and/or Time Out controls. With these controls, you change the duration of the sound and also the point where the sound begins or stops.

- To edit the sound, click anywhere inside one of the windows to create a handle. You have two windows, one for each channel. When you create a new handle, one appears in each window. You can drag each handle independently to apply different settings to each channel and create custom fade in or fade out effects. Drag a handle down to decrease the amplitude (volume) of the sound.
- To zoom in on the sound waveform, click the magnifying glass with a plus sign (+) in it.
- To zoom out and view more of the waveform, click the magnifying glass with a minus sign (–) in it.
- To toggle the unit of measure between seconds and frames, click the Seconds and Frames buttons.
- To preview the sound, click the Play button.
- To stop the sound, click the Stop button.

4. Click Done to apply the edits to the selected sound.

Tip

Select one of the preset effects as a starting point for a custom effect. Click the Edit button and then follow the previous steps to modify the effect to suit your design.

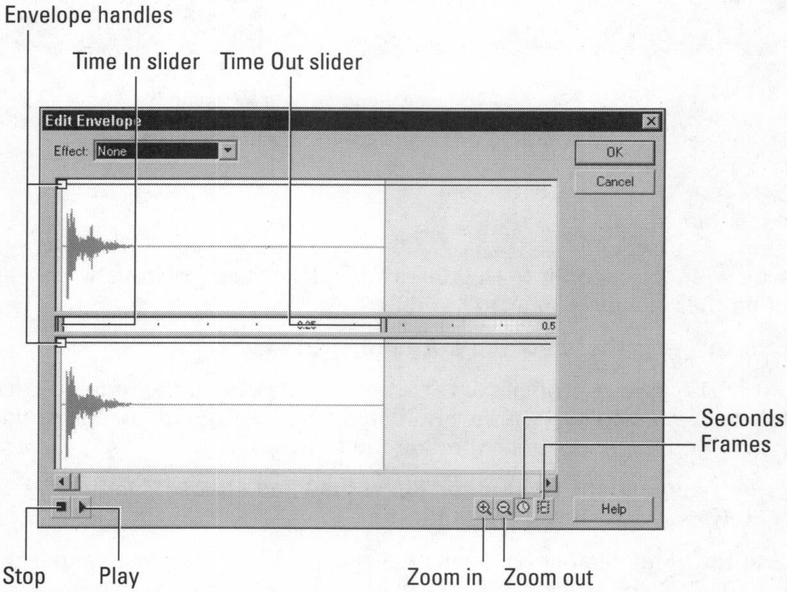
Envelope handles
Time In slider
Time Out slider
Edit Envelope
Effect: None
OK
Cancel
0.25
0.5
Seconds
Frames
Help
Stop
Play
Zoom in
Zoom out

Figure 13-2: You can edit a sound's characteristics within Flash.

Modifying export settings

When you import a sound into Flash, it is compressed to create a small file size. You can accept the default settings for the majority of the sounds you use for buttons and the like. However, when it comes to music or the spoken word, you can modify the compression settings to suit your design. In addition to the Default settings, you can choose ADPCM, MP3, Raw, and Speech. In the following sections, the MP3 and Speech export settings are covered in detail as they are used most frequently. You can use the ADPCM sound compression format for 8- and 16-bit sounds such as button clicks. Use the Raw option for sounds that have been optimized using other software as this option applies no compression to the sound when exported with a Flash movie.

Using the MP3 export option

When you have a soundtrack in your design, your best compression option is MP3. When you use MP3, you get a combination of the smallest possible file size and the highest fidelity. As mentioned earlier, if you use sound-editing software to create sound loops, export the file in your operating system's native format (WAV for Windows, AIFF for Macintosh), and then use this compression method for the best results.

To use MP3 compression:

1. Choose Window⇨Library.

   The document Library opens.

2. Double-click the sound whose export settings you want to modify. Alternately, you can choose Properties from the Library options menu.

   After you choose one of these options, the Sound Properties dialog box appears.

3. Click the triangle to the right of the Compression field and choose MP3.

4. Click the triangle to the right of the Bit Rate field and choose an option from the drop-down menu.

   Choose a higher setting for better sound fidelity or a lower setting for a smaller file size. If you choose a setting 20 kbps or higher, the option to Convert Stereo to Mono becomes available. This option is selected by default. As you modify the Bit Rate, Flash displays the Bit Rate and the file size of the sound at the bottom of the dialog box, as shown in Figure 13-3.

5. To play the sound in Stereo, click the Convert Stereo to Mono check box to deselect the option.

6. Click the triangle to the right of the Quality field and choose Fast, Medium, or Best.

This setting determines the amount of time Flash spends analyzing the sound as it is compressed. When you choose Best, Flash takes longer to analyze the sound while compressing it, resulting in a higher quality sound. If you have a slower machine and you are changing the settings on a large sound file, it will take longer to publish the movie or test the sound when you choose Best. If you have the time, choose Best for the highest sound quality.

7. To preview the sound with the new settings, click Test.

Flash applies the current compression settings to the sound and plays it. If the sound quality is acceptable, click OK to apply the settings; otherwise, select a different Bit Rate. Your objective is to get the smallest possible file size with acceptable sound quality. Of course, what is acceptable will be largely dependent on the client you are creating the site for. For example, if you're applying compression settings to sound files for a musician's Web site, you'll end up using a higher Bit Rate to showcase the subtle nuances of the music and best showcase the musician's talent.

Note   If you are compressing a sound for a multimedia application that plays from a CD-ROM, you can choose a higher Bit Rate as file size is not as important when you play a Flash movie from CD-ROM.

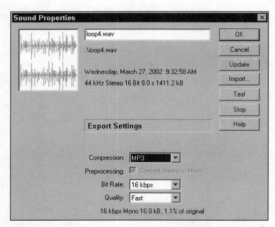

Figure 13-3: You can use MP3 compression when high quality music and a small file size are required.

Using the Speech compression option

When you have spoken narratives in your design, you can use the Speech compression option. Speech compression is ideally suited for optimizing sound files containing the spoken word.

To use the Speech compression option:

1. Choose Window⇨Library.

   The document Library opens.

2. Double-click the sound you want to compress with the Speech option.

   The Sound Properties dialog box appears.

3. Click the triangle to the right of the Compression field and choose Speech from the drop-down menu.

4. Click the triangle to the right of the Sample Rate field and choose one of the following:

   • **5 khz** is the lowest sample rate acceptable for human speech. This setting results in the smallest file size at the expense of quality.

   • **11 khz** is the best compromise between sound quality and file size.

   • **22 khz** is the setting to choose if there is background music with the spoken narrative.

   • **44 khz** is recommended if the narrative includes background music and is to be included in a CD-ROM multimedia application.

   When you choose a setting, the file size of the sound is displayed at the bottom of the dialog box, as shown in Figure 13-4.

5. Click the Test button to preview the sound.

   If the sound quality is acceptable, click OK to apply the new settings to the sound and close the dialog box. Otherwise, select a different sample rate and retest the sound.

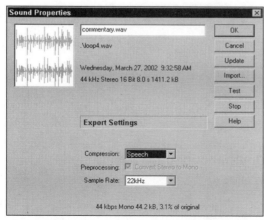

Figure 13-4: You can choose the Speech compression option for sound files with narration.

Creating a Movie with Interactive Sound

If you are creating an interactive design and giving the viewer the option to listen to sound or not, you create a button that loads the soundtrack when clicked. When you design a movie in this manner, the movie loads quicker because it is does not have to load the sound file in addition to the other content. You program the button using the `loadMovie` action to load the soundtrack. The movie that is loaded contains nothing but a soundtrack.

Creating a soundtrack movie

When you decide to give viewers the option of listening to music or not, the first step is to create a movie that contains the soundtrack for the site. As mentioned previously, the movie contains nothing but a sound file that loops continuously.

To create a soundtrack movie:

1. Create a new document.

2. Choose Modify⇨Document.

   The Document Properties dialog box opens.

3. Enter a value of 1 in the width and height fields.

   Entering these values creates a 1 pixel by 1 pixel document.

4. Import a soundtrack as outlined in the previous section.

5. Select the first frame and then click the arrow to the left of the word Properties.

   The Property inspector opens.

6. Click the triangle to the right of the Sound field and choose the sound loop you imported.

7. Click the triangle to the right of the Event field and choose Event. In the Loops field, enter a high value such as 1000.

8. Save the document as a .FLA file.

   When you save the document, choose a name that you'll use to load the soundtrack movie into your main design; *soundtrack* is a logical choice.

9. Choose File⇨Publish Settings and deselect the HTML option by clicking to remove the checkmark from the checkbox.

10. Publish the file as a .SWF movie.

After you publish the soundtrack movie, you need to create the ActionScript in your design that will load the soundtrack.

Loading the soundtrack into your design

When you create a soundtrack, you can use the loadMovie action to load the file when the first frame of your movie plays. If the soundtrack is a background sound, this is fine. However, depending on the size of your soundtrack movie, it may load and play before the main movie does. The better solution is to create a preloader to load your entire movie, and then load the soundtrack movie on the first frame of the main scene. Or if you want to give the viewer the choice of whether to listen to the soundtrack or not, create a button that loads the movie.

To load a soundtrack into your movie:

1. Select the keyframe where you want the soundtrack movie to load or the button that, when clicked, will load the soundtrack movie.

2. Click the arrow to the left of the word Actions.

3. Choose Actions⇨Browser/Network and then double-click loadMovie.

4. In the URL field, enter the name of the soundtrack movie.

   When you enter the name of the movie, enter the complete filename, for example, soundtrack.swf. If the movie is in a different directory at the same Web site, enter the relative path to the file. If the soundtrack movie is at a different Web site, enter the absolute path to the file, for example, http://www.mysite.com/soundtrack.swf.

5. Accept Level, the default Location option, and in the Text field, type **99**.

   This is the highest level in a Flash movie. Specifying level 99 for a soundtrack movie is always a safe bet. You can load content into the lower layers and not interfere with the soundtrack. Remember that when you load a movie into a level, it takes the place of any movie previously playing in that level.

If you want to give your viewers the option of turning off the soundtrack after it starts playing, create a button and assign the unLoad movie action to it. Be sure to specify the same level you loaded the movie into. This is another good reason for always using level 99 for your soundtrack movies — it's easy to remember.

Loading a soundtrack movie into a document and giving viewers the choice to listen or not listen is but one level of interactivity you can add to your designs. You can create multiple soundtrack movies and create a button for each music loop. As long as you use the same level for each button's loadMovie action, clicking a button will unload the previous soundtrack movie and load another. If you want to give viewer the ability to control the properties of a soundtrack, such as sound volume and balance between speakers, you can use methods of Sound object to accomplish this.

Using the Sound Object

The Sound object was introduced in Flash 5. You can use the methods of the Sound object to modify various properties of a sound, for example, to vary the volume of a sound, start a sound, or pan a sound from one speaker to another. When you use the Sound object in one of your designs, you create an instance of the Sound object and then attach a sound to the instance of the Sound object. You can then modify the properties of the attached sound with the Sound object's methods.

Creating an instance of the Sound object

You can use the Sound object to modify a soundtrack movie that is loaded into the base movie or to modify a sound in the document Library. After you create an instance of the Sound object, you attach the sound that you want to modify. You can create the instance on a keyframe, within a movie clip, or within a button.

To create an instance of the Sound object:

1. Select the object or keyframe where you want to create the instance.

2. Click Actions⇨Variables and then double-click `set variable`.

3. Enter a name in the Variable field.

    This is the name you will use to refer to the Sound object. Enter a logical name such as *mySound* or *globalSound*.

4. Place your cursor in the Value field, choose Objects⇨Movie⇨Sound, and then double-click `new Sound`.

That's all you need to do to create an instance of the Sound object. If you're going to use buttons to load movie soundtracks into a document, use the first keyframe in the movie to create the Sound object instance. Then you can create the ActionScript to load the sound and attach the sound when a button is clicked. If you're creating a movie clip that you'll use to control the soundtrack in a movie, create the Sound object instance on the first frame of the movie clip.

Working with sound from the document Library

If you're going to use the Sound object to modify sounds from within the document Library, you must create the linkage that you will use to refer to the sound when attaching it. If you have several sounds in the document Library, you can attach them and play them at keyframes within your movie or attach them when a button is clicked. After you attach a sound, you can then modify its properties with methods of the Sound object.

To create the linkage for ActionScript:

1. Choose Window⇨Library.

   The document Library opens.

2. Select a sound and then right-click (Windows) or Ctrl-click (Macintosh) and choose Linkage from the context menu. Alternately, choose Linkage from the Library options menu. Either method opens the Linkage Properties dialog box.

3. Click the Export for ActionScript check box (shown in Figure 13-5).

4. Enter a name in the text field.

   By default Flash uses the filename of the sound. You can choose to use the filename as an ActionScript identifier or enter a name such as sound1. Don't use any spaces when you create the name. If you must separate two words in a name, either capitalize the first letter of the second word or separate the words with an underscore.

5. Click OK to apply the linkage and close the dialog box.

After you create ActionScript linkage for a sound in the document Library, you can attach the sound to an instance of the Sound object.

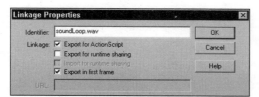

Figure 13-5: You create ActionScript linkage to modify a sound in the document Library.

Attaching a sound

You can attach a sound from the document Library that has ActionScript linkage to an instance of the Sound object. You can also attach an instance of the Sound object to a .SWF movie that you have loaded into the base movie. When you attach a sound, you refer to it by its linkage nomenclature or by the level that you load the sound into. You can attach the sound to a movie clip, a button, or to a keyframe on the timeline.

To attach a sound to an instance of the Sound object:

1. Select the object or keyframe where you want to create ActionScript to attach a sound.

2. Click the arrow to the left of the word Actions.

   The Actions panel opens.

3. Click Objects⇨Movie⇨Sound⇨Methods and then double-click `attachSound`.

Two parameter text boxes open above the Script pane.

4. In the Object field, enter the name of the Sound object instance you created.

5. In the Parameters field, enter either the linkage identifier of a sound from the document Library or the level into which you loaded a soundtrack movie.

If you enter an ActionScript identifier, place quotation marks around the name. Listing 13-1 shows the ActionScript to attach a sound from the document Library to a Sound object; Listing 13-2 shows the ActionScript to attach a sound loaded into level 99 to an instance of the Sound object.

Listing 13-1: Attaching a Document Library Sound

```
mysound.attachSound("sound1");
```

Listing 13-2: Attaching a Soundtrack Movie

```
mysound.attachSound(_level99);
```

After you attach a sound to your instance of the Sound object, you can use the various methods of the Sound object to manipulate the sound. If you load a soundtrack movie into a movie, it begins playing as soon as the keyframe or object in which you created the ActionScript to load the movie with loads. If you're affording your viewers the option of whether or not to listen to the soundtrack, you create a button that, when clicked, loads the soundtrack. However, if you attach a sound from the document Library, it won't begin playing until you invoke the Start method of the Sound object.

Starting a sound

You can start an attached sound from the document Library by using the `start` method of the Sound object when a keyframe is reached, a movie clip loads, or a button is clicked. When you use the `start` method, you can specify at which point in the duration of a sound it begins playing and you can specify the number of times the sound plays. After a sound starts, it plays in its entirety, even if ActionScript is executed to attach and play a different sound from the document Library.

To start a sound:

1. Select the object or keyframe that you want to trigger the sound.
2. Choose Objects⇨Movie⇨Sound⇨Methods and then double-click `start`.

   Two parameter text boxes appear above the Script pane.
3. In the Object field, enter the name of the Sound object you want to begin playing.
4. In the Parameters field, enter the parameters for the sound offset and number of loops.

   If you want the sound to play only once, you don't need to enter anything in the Parameters field. However, you can change the point at which the sound begins playing and the number of times the sound plays by entering values in the Parameters field. Below the field you see the message (`secondsOffset`, `loops`). This is the proper syntax for offsetting the start of the sound and specifying the number of loops. If you just want to loop the sound, enter 0 for the seconds offset followed by a comma and a value for the number of times you want the sound to play. If you want to offset the starting point of the sound, enter a value in the field followed by a comma and the number of times you want the sound to loop. Listing 13-3 shows ActionScript for a sound that starts playing the sound three seconds into its duration and loops the sound 16 times. Note that when you offset the start of a sound, the offset is applied to each loop.

Listing 13-3: **Starting a Sound**

```
mysound.start(3,16);
```

Stopping a sound

You use the `stop` method of the Sound object to stop playing the sound currently attached to the instance of the Sound object. This method is useful if you have several sounds in a document Library that are programmed to play when a button is clicked. If viewers click another button before the previous sound has finished playing, Flash mixes the sounds, which is an undesirable occurrence if the sound being playing is background music or is linked to another action such as the frames of a movie clip the sound is attached to. In order to prevent this, you create ActionScript for each button using the `stop` method to cease playing the currently attached sound.

Note   If you program several buttons to load different movie soundtracks, as long as all of the movie soundtracks are loaded into the same level, clicking a button will stop the current soundtrack from playing when the new soundtrack is loaded. To stop all sounds from playing, create a button and then create the ActionScript to unload the soundtrack movie from the level soundtracks are loaded into.

To stop a sound from playing:

1. Select the object or keyframe that will cause the sound to stop.
2. Click Objects⇨Movie⇨Sound⇨Methods and then double-click `stop`.

   The Object parameter text box appears above the script pane.
3. Enter the name you assigned to the instance of the Sound object.

   Listing 13-4 shows ActionScript to stop a Sound object named mysound from playing.

Listing 13-4: Stopping a sound

```
mysound.stop();
```

In addition to starting and stopping a sound, you can use methods of the Sound object to control the volume of the sound, pan the sound from one speaker to the other, and cause another action to execute when the sound stops playing.

Changing a sound's volume

You can control the volume of a sound using the `setVolume` method of the Sound object. You use this method to specify the percentage of amplitude (volume) of the sound. Enter a value between 0 (silence) and 100 (full volume).

To change a sound's volume:

1. Choose the keyframe or object that will trigger the volume change.
2. Click the arrow to the left of the word Actions. The Actions panel opens.
3. Choose Objects⇨Movie⇨Sound⇨Methods and then double-click `setVolume`.

   The Object and Parameters text boxes appear above the Script pane.
4. In the Object field, enter the name of your Sound object.
5. In the Parameters field, enter a value for volume percentage.

   Listing 13-5 shows ActionScript that will cause a sound to play at 75 percent of its original volume when a button is clicked.

Listing 13-5: **Modifying Sound Volume**

```
on (release) {
  mysound.setVolume(75);
}
```

 Note   It is possible to play a sound at a higher amplitude (volume) than original by specifying a value greater than 100. To a limited extent, you can do this to compensate
for a sound with low volume. However, when you exceed the original amplitude
of a sound by a large percentage, distortion occurs.

Panning a sound

Another useful sound method is the setPan method. You use the setPan method
to vary the balance of a sound between speakers. By default, a sound is distributed
evenly between the left and right speakers. You can use the setPan method and
enter a value between 0 and 100 to pan the sound towards the right speaker; a
value between 0 and –100 pans the sound to the left speaker.

To pan a sound:

1. Select the object or keyframe that will cause the balance of the sound to
change.

2. Choose Objects⇨Movie⇨Sound⇨Methods and then double-click setPan.

The Object and Parameters text fields appear above the Script pane.

3. In the object field, enter the name of the Sound object you are modifying.

4. In the Parameters field, enter a value.

Listing 13-6 shows ActionScript that when executed pans the sound towards
the left speaker.

Listing 13-6: **Panning a Sound**

```
on (release) {
  mysound.setPan(-75);
}
```

Triggering an event with the onSoundComplete event

If your design has sounds that are synchronized to other events in your design,
such as a movie clip playing, you can use the onSoundComplete event of the Sound

object to trigger another action when the sound finishes. For example, if you create a scene that displays images while a background narration plays, you can use the onSoundComplete event to play the next scene immediately after the sound finishes playing.

To trigger an event when a sound finishes playing:

1. Select the object or keyframe that will cause the onSoundComplete event to be invoked.

   For example, you can create ActionScript on a keyframe to start playing a sound at the beginning of a scene. You can add the onSoundComplete event on this frame to start playing the next scene when the sound stops.

2. Choose Objects➪Movie➪Sounds➪Events and then double-click onSoundComplete.

   Three parameter text boxes appear: Object, Method, and Parameters. The method field is already filled in with onSoundComplete.

3. In the Object field, enter the name of the Sound object.

4. In the Parameters field, you can enter the name of a user-defined function that you want the Flash Player to execute when the sound finishes playing. Alternately, you can select another action you want executed when the sound stops, such as the goto action.

   Listing 13-7 shows ActionScript that plays a frame labeled Slide1 in the History scene when the sound stops.

Listing 13-7: **Using the onSoundComplete Event**

```
gotoAndPlay("History", "Slide1");
```

Chapter Project: Creating a Sound Controller

Now that you're familiar with creating a soundtrack movie, creating an instance of the Sound object, and attaching and modifying a sound with methods of the Sound object, it's time to put your knowledge to work and create a working sound controller. The controller you're going to create uses a slider to control the volume and pan the sound between speakers. This controller gives the viewer the option to choose between two soundtracks.

On the CD-ROM

Copy to your hard drive the Soundcontroller folder from this chapter's folder on the CD-ROM that accompanies this book. Use your operating system to disable each file's read-only attribute.

To begin the project:

1. Launch Flash and open the soundbegin.fla file.
2. Choose Insert⇨New Symbol.

   The Insert New Symbol dialog box opens.
3. Choose the Movie Clip behavior, name the symbol *soundController,* and click OK to enter symbol-editing mode.
4. Select the first frame and then click the arrow to the left of the word Actions.

   The Actions panel opens.
5. Click Actions⇨Variables and then double-click `set variable`.

   Two parameter text boxes appear above the Script pane.
6. In the Variable field, type **mysound**
7. Click inside the Value field, and in the left pane of the Actions panel, click Objects⇨Movie⇨Sound and then double-click `newSound`.

   After creating an instance of the Sound object, you need to attach a sound to it. In this case, you'll use a button to load a soundtrack movie and also create the ActionScript to attach the sound. After you create an instance of the Sound object, you add the buttons to load additional soundtracks and sliders to control the sound to the movie clip.

Adding the sliders

Creating an instance of the Sound object is the first step in creating a controller. Now you need to add the sliders to control the sound and the buttons to load the sounds.

To add the buttons and sliders:

1. Choose Window⇨Library.

   The document Library opens.
2. Drag an instance of the Slider Control symbol on Stage.
3. Open the Property inspector and in the X field, type **0**. In the Y field, type **–25**.

   Before going on to the next step, right-click (Windows) or Ctrl-click (Macintosh) the symbol and choose Edit. Select the round button. Open the Property inspector and notice that this is a movie clip that has already been labeled *knob*. You'll be referring to this instance name when you program the slider.

   With the button movie clip still selected, right-click (Windows) or Ctrl-click (Macintosh) and choose Edit from the context menu. Click the arrow to the left of the word Actions and you see the ActionScript shown in Listing 13-8.

Listing 13-8: **Programming the Button for Drag and Drop**

```
on (press) {
  startDrag("", false, 0, 0, 100, 0);
  dragging = true;
  _root.dragging = true;
}
on (release) {
  stopDrag();
  dragging = false;
  _root.dragging = false;
}
```

This code gives the button drag-and-drop capability. The button's motion is constrained to 100 pixels on the x axis, which is perfect for creating a sound controller.

4. Click the soundController title above the workspace.

5. Click the arrow to the left of the word Properties.

   The Property inspector opens.

6. Type **volControl** in the <Instance Name> field.

7. Click the slider movie clip, and while holding down the Alt key (Windows) or Options key (Macintosh), drag the symbol to create a new instance of it.

8. In the Property inspector, type **0** in the X field and **25** in the Y field.

9. In the <Instance Name> field, type **panControl**

10. Choose Window⇨Library.

11. Drag an instance of the soundButton symbol on Stage and align it to the left of the two sliders.

12. Click the Arrow to the left of the work Actions.

    The Actions panel opens.

13. Choose Actions⇨Browser/Network and then double-click loadMovie.

14. In the URL field, type **sound1.swf**, accept the default Level option, and in the Text field, type **99**.

    This code loads the soundtrack movie into level99.

15. Choose Objects⇨Movie⇨Sound⇨Methods and then double-click attachSound.

    Two parameter text boxes appear above the Script pane.

16. In the Object field, type **mysound** and in the Parameters field, type **_level99**.

    Your code should look exactly like Listing 13-9.

17. Click the button labeled "Sound" to select it, and then press the Alt key (Windows) or Option key (Macintosh) to create another instance of the button.

18. With the button still selected, click the arrow to the left of the word Actions and modify the button's script by changing the second line of code to `loadMovieNum("sound2.swf", 99)`.

    There are two more soundtracks in the project folder. If you feel ambitious, create two more instances of the button and change the code so that the buttons load `sound3.swf` and `sound4.swf` respectively.

19. Click the Back button to exit symbol-editing mode.

Listing 13-9: **Loading and Attaching the Sound**

```
on (release) {
  loadMovieNum("sound1.swf", 99);
  mysound.attachSound(_level99);
}
```

Now that the movie clip components are programmed, it's time to put the symbol to work. To do this you drag an instance of the soundController symbol on Stage, create the initial states for each slider, and then use methods of the Sound object to manipulate the sounds when the sliders are dragged.

Programming the movie clip

When you program the movie clip, you'll use the `setVolume` and `setPan` methods of the Sound object to modify the sound. The `setVolume` and `setPan` methods parameters will be set equal to the _x property of each slider, which at 100 pixels long gives you a range of 0 to 100 to work with.

To program the movie clip:

1. Choose Window⇨Library.

   The document Library opens.

2. Drag an instance of the soundController movie clip on Stage.

3. Click the arrow to the left of the word Actions.

The Actions panel opens.

4. Choose Actions➪Miscellaneous Actions and then double-click evalutate.

The Expression parameter text box appears above the Script pane.

5. With your cursor inside the Expression field, click the Insert a Target Path button.

The Insert Target Path dialog box opens.

6. Click the Relative mode radio button, click the plus sign (+) to the left of panControl button, and then click knob (see Figure 13-6).

7. Click OK to add the target path and close the dialog box.

8. In the Expression field, type the following text after the target path: ._x=50

This code sets the _x position of the pan slider to 50, the halfway point of the scale, which is a perfect balance between the two speakers.

9. Repeat Steps 5 through 8 but insert the target path to the volControl knob and set the _x property to 75. Accept the default load clip event.

Your code should look like Listing 13-10.

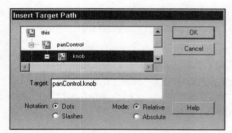

Figure 13-6: Adding the target path to the slider knob.

Listing 13-10: Setting the Initial Values for the Sliders

```
onClipEvent (load) {
  panControl.knob._x=50;
  volControl.knob._x=75;
}
```

The initial value for each slider sets the volume and balance when viewers click a button to load a sound. After setting the initial values for the sliders, you have to create the code that sets the volume and balance of the Sound object as the sliders are dragged. To constantly evaluate the position of each slider as the movie plays, you use the enterFrame clip event.

To create the code that evaluates the position of the sliders:

1. Click the arrow to the left of the word Actions.

   The Actions panel opens.

2. Select the last line of code (the solitary curly brace).

3. Choose Objects⇨Movie⇨Sound⇨Methods and then double-click setVolume.

   The Object and Parameters fields appear above the Script pane.

4. In the Object field, type **mysound**

5. Click inside the Parameters field and type **volControl.knob._x**

   You may recognize this as the target path to the volume control slider knob. This time instead of setting the value of the slider knob's _x property, the code evaluates and returns the value of the property. When the slider is dragged, the value of the knob's _x property changes and sets the volume of the sound.

6. Choose Objects⇨Movie⇨Sound⇨Methods and then double-click setPan.

7. In the Object field, type **mysound**

8. In the Parameters field, type **100-(panControl.knob._x*2)**

   To perfectly balance the sound between the speakers, the parameter of the setPan method must be 0. The initial position of the slider is 50. The expression in the Parameters field equates the position of the slider to a value that can be used by the setPan method. When the slider is dragged all the way to the right, the _x property of the slider is 50. The equation bumps it up to 100, the value needed to pan the sound to the right speaker. Using this equation makes it possible to use the same slider to set the volume and pan of the sound.

9. Click the line of code that contains the second clip event and change the clip event to enterFrame.

   Your finished code for the movie clip should look like Listing 13-11.

10. Choose Control➪Test Movie.

   Flash publishes the movie and plays it in another window. The slider knobs move to their initial positions.

11. Click either of the sound buttons to begin playing a soundtrack.

12. Drag the volume slider to vary the volume and then drag the pan slider to change the balance between speakers. After you're done experimenting with the sliders, close the window to return to movie-editing mode.

13. Add any needed labels to identify the sliders and sound buttons and then select all the objects on Stage that comprise the sound controller.

Tip   As a finishing touch, you can add a button to stop the sound. When you program this button, use the `unloadMovie` action and in the Parameter text box, specify the level you've loaded the soundtrack into.

14. Choose Insert➪Convert to Symbol.

   The Convert to Symbol dialog box opens.

15. Choose the Movie Clip behavior, name the symbol *Sound Controls*, and then click OK.

Listing 13-11: Programming the Movie Clip

```
onClipEvent (load) {
  panControl.knob._x=50;
  volControl.knob._x=75;
}
onClipEvent (enterFrame) {
  mysound.setVolume(volControl.knob._x);
  mysound.setPan(100-(panControl.knob._x*2));
}
```

After you convert the movie clip to a symbol, it becomes modular and you can use it in any movie. To use it in another movie, choose File➪Open as Library. Drag an instance of the Sound Controls movie clip into the current document Library and you can use it in your design. When you publish the movie and upload it to a Web site, upload files named sound1.swf and sound2.swf. Now the soundtracks will play when the buttons are clicked and viewers can control the volume and balance by dragging the sliders. Figure 13-7 shows the controller at work in a published Flash movie.

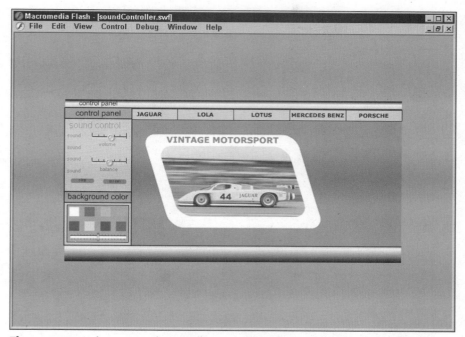

Figure 13-7: Using a sound controller to modify sound in a published Flash movie.

Designer Notes

In this chapter, you learned to work with sound in Flash. You learned to create a soundtrack within the movie and modify sounds by creating a custom effect. Also presented was creating a soundtrack movie and creating the necessary ActionScript to load the soundtrack on demand. You were also shown how to use methods of the Sound object to modify sounds in the document Library or modify soundtracks loaded into the movie. The chapter project showed you how to create a working sound controller. In the next chapter you'll learn to use the Flash MX diagnostic tools to debug faulty ActionScript.

✦   ✦   ✦

Debugging an ActionScript

✦ ✦ ✦ ✦

In This Chapter

Using the Debugger

Using the trace action

Tracking ActionScript
with comments

Tracing a variable

Using the Movie
Explorer

✦ ✦ ✦ ✦

When you add ActionScript to a design, your take your production to the next level. The ability to add interactivity to a design with ActionScript is what gets you the big jobs from high-paying clients.

At the same time, adding interactivity to a design can also increase the level of difficulty for you as a designer. ActionScript by its very nature is created on different keyframes, within different objects, and assigned to different buttons. When something goes awry with a complex ActionScript design, you can't just look at a written script and figure out the error is on line such and such. True, the error will be in one or more specific lines of code, but on which frame is the faulty code; in which movie clip? There are so many places to look, tracking down faulty code can be a time-consuming process.

Fortunately you have two indispensable tools you can use to debug a movie: the Debugger and the Movie Explorer. You can also add elements to your ActionScript to trace variables. You can also stop a movie at selected places to see what is happening when a line of code executes, or if there is an error in your ActionScript, doesn't execute. In this chapter you'll learn to use the Debugger to trace your ActionScript designs as well as add actions to your scripts that enable you to keep track of what's happening as the movie plays.

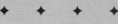

Note The Actions panel's got lots of books. And some of these books have books within a book. To add some actions to your scripts, you have to click this book icon, then click that book icon, then click another book icon, and so on. Rather than bore you with a lot of words, I'm going to show the path to each action as shown in the following example: Click Actions⇨Movie Control and then double-click goto.

Testing Your Design

Your first clue to a potential ActionScript problem generally occurs when you preview the production. There are two ways you can test your design: in a separate window within the Flash environment or within your Web browser.

To test the movie in the Flash environment, choose Control⇨Test Movie. After you choose the command, the movie is published and plays in another window, as shown in Figure 14-1. Test all the components of your design to make sure everything is up to snuff.

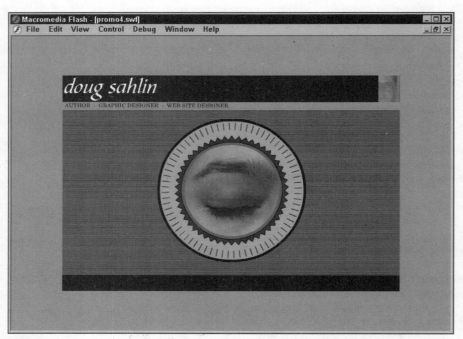

Figure 14-1: You can test the movie within the authoring environment.

Notice the graph across the top of the workspace in Figure 14-1. This is the Bandwidth Profiler. (You'll use the Bandwidth Profiler in Chapter 15 when you create an animated preloader.) Across the top of the workspace, you see a timeline. As the movie plays, the small arrow moves from frame to frame. If the multi-frame movie stops due to faulty ActionScript, you know exactly which frame the problem occurs on by viewing this timeline. If your design is a single-frame production and your ActionScript is embedded in movie clips, your task of tracking down the faulty script isn't quite as easy.

You can also preview your design in a Web browser. When you use a Web browser to preview your productions, you see exactly what the end user sees. If you use ActionScript to achieve visual effects, you should preview your production in a Web browser as well as in the authoring environment. To preview your design in a Web browser, choose File⇨Publish Preview⇨HTML. After choosing this command, the movie is published and plays in your system's default Web browser, as shown in Figure 14-2.

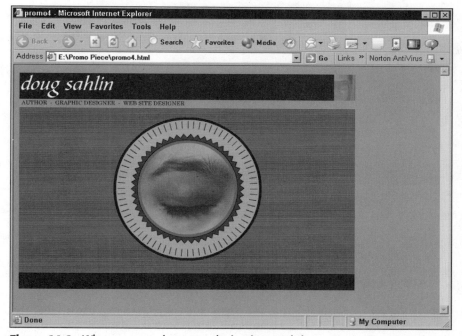

Figure 14-2: When you preview your design in a Web browser, you see exactly what your audience will see.

If you notice an error when testing the movie, you'll probably have a pretty good idea what part of your code went awry. But sometimes it can get a bit trickier, especially when you have arrays and variables scattered throughout your movie. The easiest way to track a problem with variables is by using the Debugger.

Using the Debugger

You use the Debugger to track objects and their properties as well as the value of variables. Often you use variables to record one or more of an object's properties and then transfer the value to a different variable (as you did in the scrolling text project in Chapter 11when the _y property of the slider determined when the text scrolled).

To launch the Debugger, choose Control⇨Debug Movie. After choosing the command, the movie is published and displays in another window. The movie is halted on the first frame and the Debugger is displayed (see Figure 14-3).

Movie clip instance   Variables

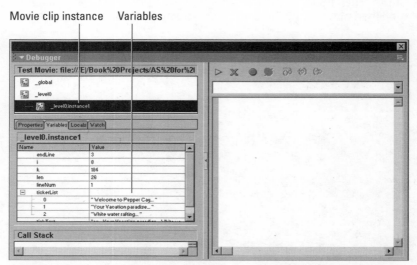

Figure 14-3: You can use the Debugger to trace elements in your movie.

To begin debugging the movie, click the Continue button. In Figure 14-3, the Continue button has already been clicked. Notice that in the left window of the upper window, there are several icons similar to the ones you see in the Insert Target Path dialog box. These icons represent all the objects in your design that can have ActionScript assigned to them. If you don't assign an instance name to a movie clip, a default name is assigned to it; for example, _level0.instance1. Named instances are referred to by the level they reside in followed by their label. Now you can see how important labeling movie clips is.

To find out something about a movie clip, click its icon. After selecting a named instance, you can find out what the properties of the instance are by clicking the Properties tab. You can trace variables by clicking the Variable tab. If a movie clip has local variables, you can trace their values by clicking the Locals tab. You can also target one or more variable and trace their values by clicking the Watch tab.

Watching a variable

You can trace the value of several variables and watch their values change as the movie plays. This is the course of action to take if you suspect the problem with your ActionScript is due to a variable.

To watch a variable:

1. In the left pane of the Debugger, click any named instance icon you know contains the variable you want to watch.

2. Click the Variables tab.

3. Select the variable you want to watch.

4. Right-click (Windows) or Ctrl+click (Macintosh) and choose Watch from the context menu.

5. Select any additional variable you want to watch and repeat Step 4.

6. Click the Watch tab to watch the values change as the movie plays.

If you're not sure which objects or which variables are in your movie, you can view a list of them while you're debugging the movie.

Displaying a list of movie objects

When you create a complex movie, it's often hard to remember exactly which items you created for the production. You can view a list of movie objects in the Output window shown in Figure 14-4 by choosing Debug⇨List Objects.

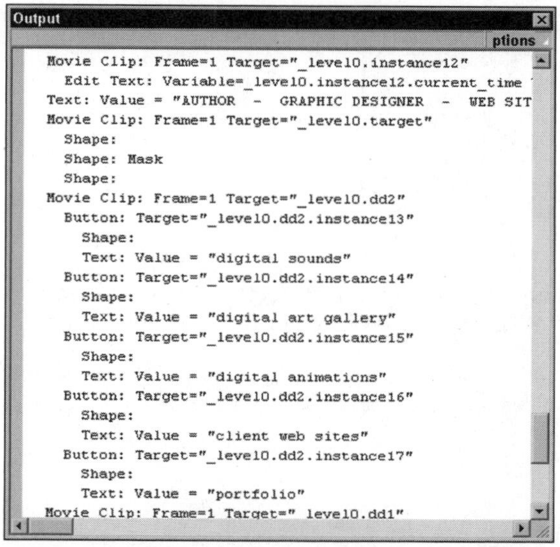

Figure 14-4: You can display a list of movie objects while debugging your design.

After you view the objects in your movie, you may remember a variable value that should be displayed in the variables window but isn't.

Displaying a list of variables in the movie

Viewing a list of variables can jog your memory and help you ascertain which variables should have a certain value as the movie plays. For example, if you're debugging a movie that records information submitted in an input text box, after an entry is made and a button is clicked, the variable's value should display in the Variables window. To display a list of the variables in your movie, choose Debug⇨List Variables to open the Output window with a list of your variables, as shown in Figure 14-5.

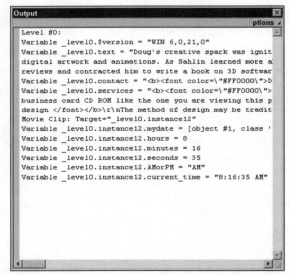

```
Output                                                    X
                                                 ptions ◢
Level #0:
Variable _level0.$version = "WIN 6,0,21,0"
Variable _level0.text = "Doug's creative spark was ignit
digital artwork and animations. As Sahlin learned more a
reviews and contracted him to write a book on 3D softwar
Variable _level0.contact = "<b><font color=\"#FF0000\">D
Variable _level0.services = "<b><font color=\"#FF0000\">
business card CD ROM like the one you are viewing this p
design </font></b>\r\nThe method of design may be tradit
Movie Clip: Target="_level0.instance12"
Variable _level0.instance12.mydate = [object #1, class '
Variable _level0.instance12.hours = 8
Variable _level0.instance12.minutes = 16
Variable _level0.instance12.seconds = 35
Variable _level0.instance12.AMorPM = "AM"
Variable _level0.instance12.current_time = "8:16:35 AM"
```

Figure 14-5: You can display a list of all the variables in your movie.

After viewing a list of variables and watching the Debugger, you may decide you need to trace a variable's value at one or more points in the movie.

Tip   You can print a hard copy of the variables in your movie by right-clicking (Windows) or Ctrl+clicking (Macintosh) inside the Output window and then choosing Print from the context menu.

Using the Trace Action

You use the `trace` action to trace the value of a variable at a certain point in the movie or to display a message at a certain point in the movie. For example, you can use the `trace` action to display a message when a certain frame plays. If the message is never displayed when you test or debug the movie, you know the frame is not playing and the ActionScript you created to play the frame is in error. When you use the `trace` action, the results of the trace are displayed in the Output window.

To keep track of a variable or object with the `trace` action:

1. Select the keyframe or object you want to trace.

2. Open the Actions panel and choose Actions⇨Miscellaneous Actions and then double-click `trace`.

    The Message field appears above the Script pane.

3. Enter the message you want displayed when this point in the movie occurs. To trace the value of a variable at this juncture in the movie, enter the variable's name and click the Expression checkbox.

4. Repeat Steps 1 through 3 for any additional objects you want to trace.

After you trace one or more objects, the message or value of the variable is displayed in the Output window when you test or debug the movie. If you trace several objects, you may not know which value relates to a particular variable. In order to know what variable value is displaying, you can combine a text message with the value of the variable by enclosing the message in quotes, typing a plus sign (+) and then the name of the variable.

Figure 14-6 shows the ActionScript for displaying a message in the Output window along with the variable's value.

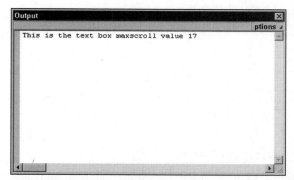

Figure 14-6: You can combine a message with the value of a variable.

When you trace several objects in a movie, the message in the Output window updates quickly, sometimes so quickly you can't read the message as it scrolls past. When you trace several objects, you can momentarily stop the movie by setting breakpoints.

Stopping the Movie with Breakpoints

When you debug a complex movie with code in several different places, you can stop the movie after a line of code executes. When the movie stops at a breakpoint, the line of code is displayed in the right pane of the Debugger. If you use the breakpoint in conjunction with the `trace` action, you can compare the line of code to what is happening in the movie and to the message in the Output window. This three-pronged approach to debugging a movie can help narrow down the source of a bug. You can set breakpoints in the Actions panel or in the Debugger itself.

Setting a breakpoint

When you set a breakpoint in the Actions panel, the breakpoint is stored with the saved *.FLA file. When you set a breakpoint in the Debugger, it is in effect only for the current debugging session. When you close the window and return to movie-editing mode, the breakpoints you set in the Debugger are lost.

To set a breakpoint in the Actions panel:

1. Select the object or keyframe that contains the code where you want to set a breakpoint.

2. Open the Actions panel and select the line of code where you want the movie to pause.

3. Click the Viewing options icon and choose View Line Numbers.

    When you set breakpoints and line numbers are visible, a red dot appears alongside all line numbers where breakpoints are set.

4. Click the Debugger Options icon that looks like a stethoscope and choose Set Breakpoint from the menu.

5. Continue adding breakpoints as needed.

After you set breakpoints and add `trace` actions, you're ready to flush out the source of your bug.

Debugging a movie with breakpoints

When you debug a movie with breakpoints, the debugging session begins with the movie paused. After you click the Continue button, the movie begins and then halts when it encounters the first breakpoint. As you pause and restart the movie, you can view each line of code where a breakpoint is set and compare it with what is happening in the movie.

To debug a movie with breakpoints:

1. Choose Control⇨Debug Movie.

   The movie is published and opens in another window. The Debugger appears and is paused on the first frame of the movie.

2. Click the Continue button.

   The movie begins playing and halts at the first breakpoint, as shown in Figure 14-7.

   After the movie pauses at a breakpoint, a yellow arrow appears to the left of the breakpoint line number. While the movie is paused at a breakpoint, you can exercise different options by clicking one of the buttons shown in Figure 14-7. The buttons and their functions are:

   • **Continue:** Restarts the movie and stops it at the next breakpoint.

   • **Stop Debugging:** Resumes the movie but does not stop the movie at breakpoints.

   • **Step Over:** Advances the movie to the next line of code after the breakpoint.

   • **Step In:** If the line of code where the breakpoint is set calls a function, clicking this button displays the first line of code in the function. Click the button again to advance to the next line of code in the function.

   • **Step Out:** Steps out of the function and restarts the movie.

Note When you're in a debugging session, you modify breakpoints from within the Debugger, as the next section discusses.

Setting breakpoints while debugging

If while debugging a movie you see a suspicious line of code, you can set an additional breakpoint without exiting the Debugger. Breakpoints you add during a debugging session are only in effect during the session. You can set a breakpoint when the movie is paused by selecting a line of code and then clicking the Toggle Breakpoint button (refer to Figure 14-6).

After you run through a few cycles in a debugging session and determine that the line of code where you set a breakpoint is not the source of your problem, you can remove the breakpoint by clicking the Toggle Breakpoint button. To remove all breakpoints and continue testing the movie, click the Remove All Breakpoints button.

Removing breakpoints after a debugging session

After you track down the source of your bug, you can remove breakpoints and publish the movie. If you were not able to track down the source of the bug, you can save the document as a *.FLA file. Breakpoints that were set in the Actions panel are saved with the file so you can debug the document at a later date. You can remove a single breakpoint or all breakpoints using the Actions panel.

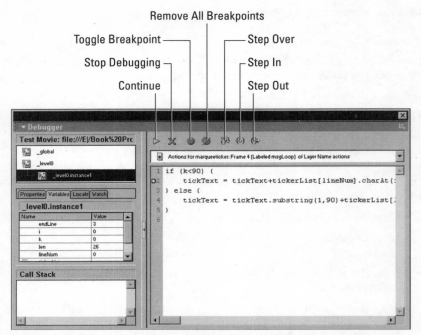

Figure 14-7: The Debugger pauses the movie at each breakpoint.

To remove a single breakpoint:

1. Select the keyframe or object that contains the code where the breakpoint is set.

2. Open the Actions panel.

3. Select the line of code with the breakpoint. A red dot is displayed to the left of each line number where you set a breakpoint. If breakpoints are not visible, choose the View Line Numbers option from the View Options menu.

4. Click the Debugger Options button and choose Remove Breakpoint.

To remove all breakpoints from a document, open the Actions panel, click the Debugger Options button that looks like a stethoscope, and choose Remove All Breakpoints.

Tracking ActionScript with Comments

Another useful tool you can use when creating complex ActionScript for your designs is the comment. You can add a comment before any line of code in a document.

A *comment* is a note you can add to describe what a line of ActionScript does. Comments are useful when debugging a movie. They are also useful when you modify the movie after a period of time and may not remember exactly what a line of code is meant to accomplish. You add comments to a script in the Actions panel.

To add a comment to your ActionScript:

1. Select the object or keyframe that contains the code you want to add a comment to.

2. Open the Actions panel.

3. Select the line of code prior to where you want the comment to appear.

4. Choose Actions➪Miscellaneous Actions and then double-click `comment`.

    The Comment field appears above the Script pane.

5. Enter any descriptive text and close the Actions panel.

When you see a comment in the Actions panel or Debugger, it is preceded by two forward slashes (//). The default syntax color for a comment is light gray.

Using the Movie Explorer

If you prefer to work with a visual outline of objects and ActionScript in a document, you can use the Movie Explorer. The Movie Explorer, shown in Figure 14-8, displays an icon to represent each item in your movie followed by a text description of the item.

By default, the Movie Explorer displays text objects, symbols, and ActionScript. You can also choose to display sounds, video and bitmaps or frames and layers or to customize the items to display by clicking the appropriate button, as shown in Figure 14-8. Notice at the top of the panel, there is a search field. Enter text in the field and the explorer locates the item. After you locate an item, you can double-click it to launch the appropriate editor. For example, if you double-click an action, the Actions panel opens with the action selected.

In Figure 14-8, you see a plus sign (+) to the left of several items. This designates that there are symbols nested within the object or actions associated with the object. Click the plus sign (+) to expand the group.

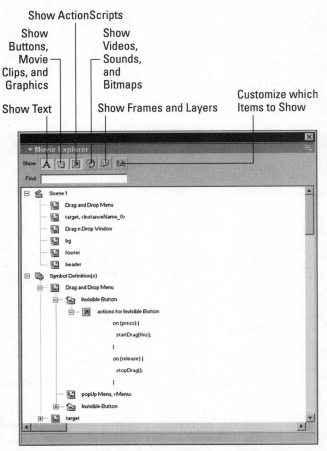

Figure 14-8: The Movie Explorer is a visual outline of your document.

Designer Notes

In this chapter you learned to use the Debugger to track down faulty ActionScript. You also learned to trace variables and add comments to your ActionScript to clarify what a line of code is designed to do. You were shown how to add breakpoints within your ActionScript to pause the movie so you could compare what is happening when a line of code is reached. You also learned to use the Movie Explorer to track down items and code in your documents. In the next chapter, you learn to create ActionScript objects for your movies.

✦   ✦   ✦

Building Additional Design Elements for Your Movie

P A R T

IV

◆ ◆ ◆ ◆

In This Part

Chapter 15
Building Web Site
Elements with
ActionScript

Chapter 16
Creating Flash
Eye Candy

Chapter 17
Integrating Flash
with HTML

◆ ◆ ◆ ◆

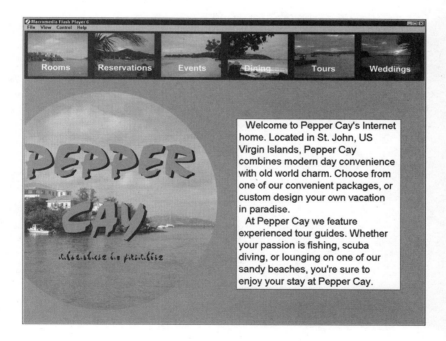

Welcome to Pepper Cay's Internet home. Located in St. John, US Virgin Islands, Pepper Cay combines modern day convenience with old world charm. Choose from one of our convenient packages, or custom design your own vacation in paradise.

At Pepper Cay we feature experienced tour guides. Whether your passion is fishing, scuba diving, or lounging on one of our sandy beaches, you're sure to enjoy your stay at Pepper Cay.

Building Web Site Elements with ActionScript

✦ ✦ ✦ ✦

In This Chapter

Creating a Flash form

Creating an
animated preloader

Creating a printable
frame

Chapter project:
Creating an
e-commerce catalog

✦ ✦ ✦ ✦

When you are approached by a client to design a Web site using Flash, you can use ActionScript to add interactivity to a design. When you use ActionScript, the resulting file size of the published movie is generally much smaller than designs where extensive frame by frame or tweening animation is used. However, there are still times when you have enough data or images in a design that prevent it from loading quickly. In this chapter, you'll learn to analyze your finished design to make sure it doesn't exceed the bandwidth of your intended audience. If it does, you'll learn how to create an animated preloader to keep your visitors entertained and informed on the amount of data that has loaded until your design is fully loaded.

When you create an HTML design, you can use the built-in form elements to create a user response form. However, the HTML form elements are not very aesthetically pleasing. In this chapter, you'll learn to create a Flash form and transmit the results of the form to a Web server's mail forwarding script. Additionally, you'll learn to create a page that can be printed on demand. The chapter project shows you how to create an e-commerce catalog.

Note   The Actions panel's got lots of books. And some of these books have books within a book. To add some actions to your scripts, you have to click this book icon, then click that book icon, then click another book icon, and so on. Rather than bore you with a lot of words, I'm going to show the path to each action as shown in the following example: Click Actions⇨Movie Control and then double-click goto.

Creating an Animated Preloader

If you've ever visited a Web site created using Flash and the movie halted and then started again, the designer exceeded the available bandwidth of your connection. *Bandwidth* is the number of kilobytes that can be downloaded in one second at a given connection speed. When a Flash movie is downloaded from the Internet, the information streams into the viewer's browser. When enough information has loaded, the first frame of the movie plays. When a frame is reached that exceeds the available bandwidth of a connection, the Flash Player halts the movie until enough additional data has downloaded to resume playing. When a movie stops, the result is jarring. Consider the case of a Flash introduction with a soundtrack. If the soundtrack has already downloaded and begun playing, and the movie halts on a frame and the soundtrack finishes playing before the intro does.

Your job as a designer is to create a compelling movie that downloads quickly into the user's browser. However, there may be times when your client requests a design that's too large to play without interruption. When this occurs, you have no alternative but to create a preloader. A *preloader* is a small animation that informs viewers that the data for a movie is loading. You create the ActionScript to continue playing the preloader until enough data has loaded to play the movie without interruption. Figure 15-1 shows a preloader that informs viewers how much of the movie has downloaded and keeps them entertained with a field of stars that follows their mouse.

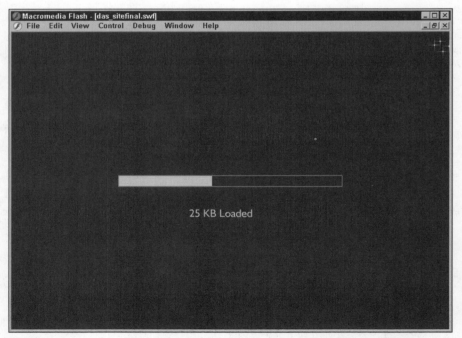

Figure 15-1: You create a preloader to keep the viewer entertained while the main movie loads.

Analyzing your movie

Before you upload any Flash design to a client's Web site, always test it to make sure that it downloads without hesitation into the viewer's browser. Fortunately, this is a test you can easily complete within Flash using the Test Movie command in conjunction with the Bandwidth Profiler. After you've analyzed the movie with the Bandwidth Profiler, you can use the Show Streaming command to view the movie as if it were streaming into a browser from an Internet site.

Using the Bandwidth Profiler

As you create a movie, you use the Test Movie command from time to time to make sure the ActionScript and other elements of your movie are performing as intended. After you finish the movie, test it again before publishing it. When you do the final test, use the Bandwidth Profiler to analyze the movie frame by frame to spot a potential bottleneck when the amount of information needed for a given frame exceeds the bandwidth of your intended audience.

To test a movie with the Bandwidth Profiler:

1. Choose Control⇨Test Movie.

    Flash publishes the movie and plays it in another window.

2. Choose View⇨Bandwidth Profiler.

    The Bandwidth Profiler appears, as shown in Figure 15-2.

The Bandwidth Profiler in Figure 15-2 is displayed as a Frame by Frame graph. The window at the left of the Bandwidth Profiler is divided into three sections: Movie, Settings, and State.

✦ The Movie section displays pertinent information about your design, the size of the document in pixels, the frame rate, the size of the published movie in kilobytes, the duration of the movie, and the preload time.

✦ The Settings section displays the currently selected bandwidth setting.

✦ The State section tells you how large the frame data is in kilobytes.

You can also view the Bandwidth Profiler as a streaming graph by choosing View⇨Streaming Graph. When you view the Bandwidth Profiler as a streaming graph, the profiler gives you a representation of how the information streams into the user's browser. Figure 15-3 shows the Bandwidth Profiler as a streaming graph. If you compare this graph with Figure 15-2, you see there are some frames where no information is streaming into the browser. Choose whichever view you prefer. Your goal is to identify the frames where the frame's data exceeds the bandwidth setting of your intended audience.

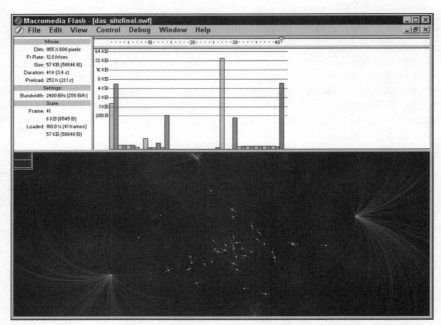

Figure 15-2: You use the Bandwidth Profiler to analyze your movie.

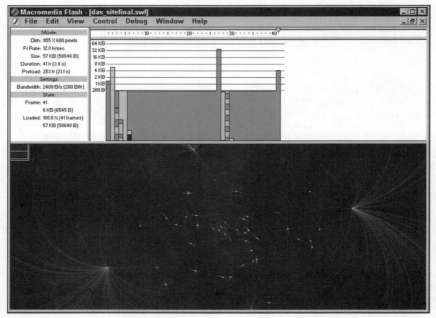

Figure 15-3: If you prefer, you can view the Bandwidth Profiler as a streaming graph.

You can modify the bandwidth setting by choosing Debug and then choosing one of the menu settings (14.4K, 28.8K, or 56K), or you can choose one of the User Settings. You can modify a user setting to suit a specific bandwidth (such as a user's intranet) by doing the following:

1. Choose Debug⇨Customize to open the Custom Modem Settings dialog box shown in Figure 15-4.

2. Decide which menu setting you are going to modify, and in the Menu Text field, select the current menu text and enter your own description for the custom setting.

3. Inside the Bit Rate field, enter a bandwidth setting.

   If you are modifying a setting for a client's intranet, contact the client's system administrator for the proper value.

4. Click OK to close the dialog box.

   The custom setting is added as a menu command.

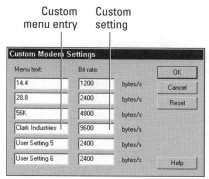

Figure 15-4: You can create a custom modem setting to suit a particular need.

After you select a bandwidth setting, a red line appears at the bottom of the Bandwidth Profiler. If any frame appears above the red line, it contains more information than the selected modem setting can download and may cause the movie to pause while additional data streams into the user's browser. Click the frame to select it, and the amount of data contained in the frame is displayed in the State section in the Bandwidth Profiler's left pane. After you identify one or more frames as a potential bottleneck, you can test the movie in streaming mode as your viewers will see it.

Using the Show Streaming command

When you are analyzing your movie for a potential bandwidth problem, your last step is to view the movie in streaming mode. When you view your design in streaming mode, you can compare the progress of the streaming data to the current frame playing. By comparing the streaming data to the progress of the movie, you'll know whether or not you need to create a preloader.

To view the movie in streaming mode:

1. Choose Control⇨Test Movie.

    Flash publishes the movie and plays it in another window.

2. Choose View⇨Bandwidth Profiler.

3. Choose Debug and then choose a modem connection setting.

    Choose the setting that comes closest to the connection speed your viewers will access the Internet with. It's always best to err on the lower side of the scale and choose the next lowest setting.

4. Choose View⇨Show Streaming.

    Flash starts playing the movie again, only this time it loads at the selected connection speed. As the movie loads, a green bar appears at the top of the timeline indicating the amount of data that has been loaded. Flash begins playing the movie when enough data has streamed to play the first few frames. As the movie starts playing, a playhead in the form of a small inverted triangle begins moving across the timeline. This indicates the current frame being played. If the playhead catches up with the green bar and stops, this indicates that Flash does not have enough data to play the frame. The Flash Player plays the next frame when it has received enough additional data.

5. If the playhead stops before the movie loads completely, record the number of the frame the movie stops on. When the movie begins playing again, watch the playhead's progress in reference to the streaming indicator bar. If it stops again, record the position. If not, the previous frame where the playhead stopped is the source of the bottleneck.

After you determine which frame is causing your movie to halt, your next task is to create a preloader that plays until enough data has loaded to play the movie without interruption.

Creating the preloader

After you determine that your design doesn't download completely without pausing, your next task is to create a preloader. A *preloader* is a series of frames that loops while enough data is loaded for the movie to play without interruption. As a rule, a preloader has a small animation or greeting that asks the viewer to please wait while the movie loads. Some designers create preloaders that are animated with an impressive display of graphic images. However, if you put too much animation into a preloader, your preloader will pause while waiting for enough data to stream in to play the preloader in its entirety. Talk about your double-whammy.

The best preloader is one that's short, sweet, and to the point. Follow the steps below to create a preloader with a small bar that gets larger as the movie loads, giving the viewer a visual representation of the download progress. To create a preloader:

1. Choose Window⇨Scene.

   The Scene panel opens.

2. Click the Add Scene button that looks like a plus sign (+).

3. Name the scene Preloader, drag it to the top of the hierarchy, and then close the Scene panel.

4. Choose Insert⇨New Symbol.

   The New Symbol dialog box appears.

5. Choose the Graphic behavior, name the symbol *bezel,* and click OK to enter symbol-editing mode.

6. Create a wide and short rectangle with a stroke and no fill.

   This will be the outline for your preload progress bar.

7. After you create the symbol, click the Back button to exit symbol-editing mode.

8. Create a new symbol, only this time choose the Movie Clip behavior, name the symbol *preloadBar,* and click OK to enter symbol-editing mode.

9. Create a rectangle with a fill and no stroke the same width and height as the bezel symbol you just created. Choose a color that is harmonious to your design. Align the rectangle so that its left edge is at the registration point. You can do this by selecting the rectangle, opening the Property inspector, and then entering a value in the X field that is half the rectangle's width.

10. After you create the rectangle, click the Back button to exit symbol-editing mode.

11. Select the first frame of your preloader and drag an instance of the preloadBar movie clip on Stage. Use the Align panel to center it to Stage.

12. Create a second layer and drag an instance of the bezel symbol on Stage. Use the Align panel to center it to the Stage.

13. Select the preloadBar movie clip and click the arrow to the left of the word Properties.

    The Property inspector opens.

14. Type **bar** in the <Instance Name> field and close the Property inspector.

After you create the symbols for your preload bar and align them to Stage, you create the ActionScript that loops the animation while the movie data loads. To animate the preloadBar symbol, you change its _xscale to 0, rendering the movie clip invisible. You'll create an expression that increases the _xscale property of the preloadBar movie clip as more data loads. Then you'll create the actual loop that plays the preload animation. In one frame of the loop, you'll create a conditional statement that evaluates how many frames have loaded. When the number of frames loaded is greater than the frame that caused the movie to stop playing when you tested the movie, the preload loop stops and the first frame of the movie plays.

To create the ActionScript for the preload loop:

1. Create a new layer and label it *Actions*.

2. Select the first frame of the Actions layer, and then click the arrow to the left of the word Actions.

3. Choose Actions⇨Variables and then double-click `set variable`.

4. In the Variable field enter `siteLoaded` and in the Value field enter `0`.

5. Choose Actions⇨Variable and then double-click `set variable`.

6. In the Variable field, type **_root.bar._xscale** and in the Value field, type **siteLoaded**

   This sets the initial size of the preloadBar movie clip to 0 pixels wide.

7. Select the second frame on the Actions layer and then press F6 to convert it to a keyframe.

8. Click the arrow to the left of the word Actions to open the Actions panel.

9. Choose Actions⇨Variables and then double-click `set variable`.

10. In the Variable field, type **siteLoaded**

11. Place your cursor in the Value field and type **(_root**

12. In the left pane of the Actions panel, choose Objects⇨Movie⇨Movie Clip⇨Methods and then double-click `getBytesLoaded`.

    This method of the Movie Clip object measures the number of bytes that have loaded. The fact that you've specified the _root timeline instructs the Flash Player to measure the number of bytes that have loaded.

13. Place your cursor to the right of the parentheses in the value field and type **_root**

14. In the left pane of the Actions panel, choose Objects⇨Movie⇨Movie Clip⇨ Methods and then double-click `getBytesTotal`.

    This method of the Movie Clip object measures the total number of bytes in the movie.

15. Place your cursor to the right of the word *Total* and type the following: **)*100**

    Dividing the bytes loaded by the total bytes gives you a value that when multiplied by 100 gives you a value you can use to increase the _xscale of the preloadBar, which gives the viewer a visual representation of the loading progress. Your finished code for the second frame of the preloader should look like Listing 15-1.

Listing 15-1: **Creating the Code to Animate the Preloader Bar**

```
_root.bar._xscale = siteLoaded;
siteLoaded = (_root.getBytesLoaded()/_root.getBytesTotal())*100;
```

To complete the preloader, you need to create two more keyframes: a conditional statement and ActionScript to recycle the preload loop if the conditional statement evaluates as false. To finish creating the preload loop:

1. Select the ninth frame and convert it to a keyframe by pressing F6.

2. Click the arrow to the left of the word Actions to open the Actions panel.

3. Choose Actions⇨Conditions/Loops and then double-click if.

   The Condition parameter text box appears above the Script pane.

4. In the left pane of the Actions panel, click Properties and then double-click framesLoaded.

5. Enter > followed by the frame number you determined caused the movie to pause plus 10. (You add 10 to compensate for the number of frames in the preload loop.)

   For example, if the frame number is 30, you would enter >40.

6. In the left pane of the Actions panel, choose Actions⇨Movie Control and then double-click goto.

   After you add the goto action to your script, the action's parameters appear above the Script pane. You'll have to specify the frame number and the scene to go to when the proper frame has loaded.

7. In the Scene parameter text box, choose Next Scene, or if you've named the main scene, choose the scene name from the drop-down menu. Choose 1 for the frame number. Listing 15-2 shows the code for a conditional statement that breaks the preload loop after the seventeenth frame has loaded.

8. Select the tenth frame and convert it to a keyframe by pressing F6.

9. In the left pane of the Actions panel, choose Actions⇨Movie Control and double-click goto.

10. Type **2** in the Frame field.

11. Choose Control⇨Test Movie.

    Flash publishes the movie and plays it in another window.

12. After the movie begins playing, choose View⇨Show Streaming.

    Flash begins playing the movie again, streaming the data with the current connection setting. The preload bar slowly advances as the data loads. When the bar is fully extended, the first frame of the main movie begins playing.

Listing 15-2: Creating the Conditional Statement

```
if (_framesloaded>17) {
  gotoAndPlay("Scene 1", 1);
}
```

That's the basic formula for creating a preloader. You can make the preloader more interesting by creating a simple animation where the message "Loading, Please Wait" appears letter by letter. You can also create an expression similar to the one used to increase the scale of the preload bar to display the number of bytes in the movie and the total number of bytes loaded. You display the results of this expression in a dynamic text box with the same variable name you use to create the expression. In order to give the viewer a whole number to look at, use the round method of the Math object. Listing 15-3 shows the code required to create a preloader that displays the number of bytes loaded. Notice the string expression "KB Loaded" that's added to the result.

Listing 15-3: Code That Displays the Number of Bytes Loaded

```
bytesLoaded = Math.round((_root.getBytesLoaded())/1000)+" KB Loaded";
```

Creating a Flash Form

Standard HTML forms are not very artistic. In fact, they're downright boring. In Flash, you can use your design talent to create an interesting form for a client. When you create a form, you create input text boxes. Each input text box is assigned a variable name. When the user is finished filling out the form and clicks the Submit button, the information is transmitted to the Web site's mail forwarding scripts. Each Web hosting service uses a different script to forward mail. Check with the site that will host your design for specific information. In the sections that follow, you'll learn to transmit the results to a Web server's mail forwarding CGI script.

Note CGI is being used for this example. The process is similar for a server that uses ASP, PHP, or ColdFusion. Check with the support personnel of the server hosting the site where your Flash form will be displayed for specific instructions.

Creating the form elements

To create the form elements, you use the Text tool. Create a separate input text box for each form element. Each input text box has a variable assigned to it. When the user inputs information into the text box, Flash stores the data until the user clicks the Submit button. Figure 15-5 shows input text box parameters being modified in the Property inspector.

Figure 15-5: You create the form elements using the text tool.

 Cross-Reference

Remember that when you create input text boxes, you can specify the type of information that will be accepted by the variable. You can also limit the number of characters that will be stored by the variable. For more information on creating input text boxes, refer to Chapter 11.

Figure 15-6 shows a finished Flash form complete with a Submit and Reset button.

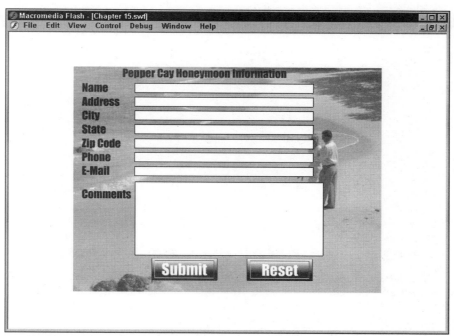

Figure 15-6: You can use input text boxes and other elements to create an aesthetically pleasing form for your designs.

Creating ActionScript for the Reset button

When you create a form for a Flash movie and users input information into the form, you can give them the option to erase all the information in the form and start over. This option comes in handy if more than one user is viewing your design from the same computer. After one user fills in the form and submits the information, a different user can click the Reset button to clear the form and then submit his information. When you create the code for a Reset button, you are resetting the variable for each input text box to null. In other words, you are resetting the variable for each input text box to a variable with no data.

To reset a variable:

1. Click the arrow to the left of the word Actions to open the Actions panel.
2. Choose Actions⇨Variables and then double-click set variable.
3. In the Variable field, enter the name of the variable you want to reset.
4. Leave the Value field blank.

   Listing 15-4 shows ActionScript to reset several variables when a button is clicked.

Listing 15-4: **Code for a Reset Button**

```
on (release) {
  name = "";
  address = "";
  city = "";
  state = "";
  zip = "";
  phone = "";
  e_mail = "";
}
```

Creating ActionScript for the Submit button

Creating the input text boxes and buttons are the easy parts of creating a Flash form. The difficult part comes when you need to submit the information to the designated recipient at a Web site. Each Web server uses different scripts to forward form results. Check with the support staff of the Web hosting service where your design will be uploaded for specific information. In the section that follows, you'll learn how to interpret an HTML mail forwarding script and use that information to transmit the data from your Flash form to the intended recipient. Listing 15-5 shows a typical CGI mail forwarding script.

Listing 15-5: **An HTML Mail Forwarding Script**

```
<form action="http://scripts.myserver.com/cgi-bin/mailto.exe"
method="POST" onSubmit="return
FrontPage_Form1_Validator(this)"name="FrontPage_Form1">
<input type="hidden" name="sendto" value="webmaster↓sdesigns.net">
  <input type="hidden" name="server" value="smtp.myserver.com">
<input type="hidden" name="subject" value="Form Processed Email Response">
<input type="hidden" name="resulturl"
value="http://www.dasdesigns.net/thanks.htm">
<input type="hidden" name="VTI-GROUP" value="0">
```

The code may look a little daunting. When you analyze a script like this, you're looking for the information that is required to forward the information to a recipient. When you create a variable, you need to enter a value and a name for the variable. If you analyze the script, you notice several instances where the script asks for a value. With each value is also a name. This is the information you need to create the ActionScript to submit the form results to the intended recipient. The script in Listing 15-5 requires values for four items: sendto, server, subject, and resulturl. When you create the ActionScript for the Submit button, you create a variable for each required item in the CGI script and set the variable value equal to the value in the script.

To code a Submit button for the above CGI script, follow these steps:

1. Select the button that will submit the information.
2. Click the arrow to the left of the word Actions to open the Actions panel.
3. Choose Actions⇨Variables and then double-click set variable.

   Two parameter text boxes appear above the Script pane.

4. In the Variable field, enter the first name from the CGI mail forwarding script. If you are coding a Submit button for the example in Listing 15-5, type **sendto**

   This is the recipient. All mail forwarding scripts require a recipient.

5. In the Value field, enter the value for the name. Following the scenario for Listing 15-5, you would enter **das001@earthlink.net**

6. Repeat Steps 3 through 5 for the other required names in the CGI script.

7. Click Actions⇨Browser Network and then double-click getURL.

   Three parameter text boxes appear above the Script pane.

8. In the URL field, enter the path to the Web hosting service's CGI bin. For example: **http://scripts.digitalchainsaw.com/cgi-bin/mailto.exe**

9. Click the triangle to the right of the Variables field and choose Send Using GET.

This instructs the Flash Player to get the data from the variables in the movie and send them to the specified URL.

After the document is published as a Flash movie and you upload it to the Internet, when a user fills out the form and clicks the Submit button, the information is forwarded to the specified recipient. Listing 15-6 shows the ActionScript for the example in Listing 15-5.

Listing 15-6: Creating ActionScript for a Submit Button

```
on (release) {
  sendto = "das001@earthlink.net";
  server = "smtp.tignet.com";
  subject = "Form Processed Email Response";
  resulturl = "http://www.dasdesigns.net/thanks.htm";
  getURL("http://scripts.digitalchainsaw.com/cgi-bin/mailto.exe", "", "GET");
}
```

Creating a Printable Frame

If you create an e-commerce design for a client, you can create a printable frame. The contents of the frame can be a spec sheet, a catalog product, or a form that the user can fill out and mail in. When you create a printable frame, you can specify the print area and then create the code for a button that, when clicked, prints the page on the user's default printer.

If you create the page using vector graphics, it will print out just fine, even when increased to the size of the printer paper. However, if you use bitmap graphics on the page, the image may be pixilated when increased to the size of the printer paper. If you're creating a frame with bitmap graphics and intend for it be a printable frame, import a bitmap image into the document with a resolution of 150 ppi (or dpi depending on which image-editing software you use) or better. The resulting Flash file size will be slightly larger, but your viewers will get a more faithful rendition of the image when they print it.

When you create a printable frame, put it in a two-frame movie clip and a button that, when clicked by a viewer, summons the movie clip with the image the viewer wants a hard copy of.

To create a printable frame:

1. Choose Insert⇨New Symbol.

   The Create New Symbol dialog box appears.

2. Name the symbol and choose the Movie Clip behavior.

3. Select the first frame and either import the artwork you want to give viewers the capability of printing or open the document Library and drag an instance of it into the movie clip.

4. Add a print button to the frame.

   You can use a button from one of the Common Libraries or create one of your own.

5. Select the keyframe and then click the arrow to the left of the word Properties.

   The Property inspector opens.

6. Type **#p** in the <Frame Label> field.

   This syntax tells the Flash Player that the frame is printable. If you create the ActionScript to print the frame as is, Flash prints everything, including the button.

   To restrict printing to a given area, follow the next steps.

7. Select the next frame in the movie and convert it to a keyframe by pressing F6.

8. Open the Property inspector and in the <Frame Label> field, type **b#**

   This nomenclature tells Flash that the contents of the frame act as a bounding box, restricting the print area.

9. Click the Onion Skin button near the bottom of the timeline. By enabling Onion Skins, you can see the content of the printable frame.

10. Select the Rectangle tool and create a rectangle with no fill that surrounds the area you want to give viewers the capability of printing.

11. Click the printable frame and then click the arrow to the left of the word Actions to open the Actions panel.

    If you don't add the stop action to the printable frame, the movie clip will advance to the second frame and all viewers see is the bounding box you created in Step 10.

12. Choose Actions⇨Movie Control and then double-click stop.

13. Select the button and in the left pane of the Actions panel, choose Actions⇨Printing and then double-click Print.

That's all you need to do to create a printable frame. When the movie is published and the button is clicked, the frame prints on the viewer's default printer.

Chapter Project: Create an E-Commerce Catalog

If you need to design a movie for a client that sells merchandise online, you can create a very effective display by creating a movie clip for each product in your customer's catalog. Instead of setting up an extensive timeline that advances to a different frame each time a button is clicked, you can store the movie clips in the document Library, create ActionScript linkage for each product movie clip, and then use the `attachMovie` method of the Movie Clip object to attach the movie clip to a target window.

On the CD-ROM   To follow along with this exercise, copy the eCommerce.fla file to your hard drive from this chapter's folder on the CD-ROM that accompanies this book. Use your operating system utilities to disable the file's read-only attributes.

To create an e-commerce catalog:

1. Launch Flash and open the eCommerce.fla file.

   You already have several buttons set up on the Stage and a target window. The movie clips for each product are already in the document Library. You'll create ActionScript linkage for the Hat movie clip.

2. Choose Window⇨Library.

   The document Library opens.

3. Right-click (Windows) or Ctrl+click (Macintosh) the movie clip symbol named Hat and then choose Linkage from the context menu.

   The Linkage Properties dialog box opens.

4. Click Export for ActionScript.

   Flash automatically assigns the name Hat as an ActionScript identifier, as shown in Figure 15-7.

5. Click OK to close the dialog box and assign the identifier to the movie clip.

6. Click the button on Stage with the hat icon and then double-click the arrow to the left of the word Actions to open the Actions panel.

7. Choose Objects⇨Movie⇨Movie Clip⇨Methods and then double-click `attachMovie`.

   Two parameter text boxes appear above the Script pane.

8. Place your cursor in the Object field and then click the Insert A Target Path button.

   The Insert Target Path dialog box appears. Make sure you're in Absolute mode.

9. Click the button labeled Product.

   This is the instance name of the target window on the right side of the movie that was already labeled for your convenience.

10. Click OK to add the target path to the script and close the dialog box.

    Now that you've assigned the target path, you need to fill in the parameters. The `attachMovie` method has four parameters, three of which you'll be using to attach the Hat movie clip to the target window. The first parameter is the linkage identifier, the second parameter is the new name of the attached movie clip, and the third parameter is the depth. The depth is the level you attach the movie clip to. The base movie is _level0. You'll be attaching the movie clip to _level1, so the depth is 1 as well.

11. In the Parameters field, type **"Hat","Product",1**

    Make sure to place quotation marks around the linkage identifier and the new name.

12. Choose Control⇨Test Movie.

    Flash publishes the movie and plays it in another window.

13. Click any of the buttons to display a different product in the target window.

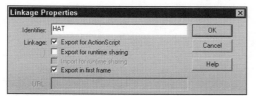

Figure 15-7: You can create ActionScript linkage for a movie clip.

By using the same methods presented in this exercise, you can create a one-frame movie and display many different products. If you're using other ActionScript to modify the object, when you attach each movie clip, use the same New Name for each movie clip to simplify the task of creating other code. If your client has an extensive product catalog, break the catalog into categories and create a separate movie for each catalog. Create a product category menu using one of the techniques presented earlier in this book and then use the `loadMovie` action to load a category movie on demand.

Designer Notes

You covered quite a bit of ground in this chapter. You learned to analyze a finished design to make sure it loads quickly into a user's browser. Expanding on this knowledge, you learned to create a preloader to prevent a movie from halting before enough data streamed to the user's browser. You learned to create elements for a Flash form and create the ActionScript to forward the results to a recipient via a CGI forwarding script. Also covered was creating ActionScript to print out a frame. By completing the chapter project, you learned how to use the `attachMovie` method of the Movie Clip object to load a movie clip from the document Library into a target window. In the next chapter, you'll learn to use ActionScript to create appealing eye candy for your designs.

✦   ✦   ✦

Creating Flash Eye Candy

In This Chapter

Using the Mouse object

Creating a mouse chaser

Creating a dynamic background

Creating a mask with ActionScript

Creating a custom cursor

Creating motion trails

Creating a starburst backdrop

Chapter project: Creating a Flash slide show

If you create movies for clients who demand all the eye candy that the available bandwidth will allow and then some, you've got a tough task if you rely on standard Flash animation methods. In order to get effects like starburst backgrounds, animated mouse trails, and the like, you've got to create lots of movie clips. However, if you use ActionScript, you can create one movie clip and have hundreds of clones darting across the screen with just a few lines of code.

In this chapter, you'll learn to create some Flash eye candy. If your clients insist on doing away with the hum-drum arrow cursor, you can do it by hiding the mouse with ActionScript and then replacing the cursor with one of your own designs or perhaps your client's logo. Another effect you'll learn to create in this chapter is the mouse chaser. They seem to be everywhere, but a mouse chaser is still a desirable effect, especially when you put your own twist on it. If your client demands something special, you can create a backdrop of twinkling stars that refreshes and changes every few seconds. Finally, you'll learn to create a slide show that moves across the screen to display images. This is the ideal answer if you need to design a site for a photographer.

Note The Actions panel's got lots of books. And some of these books have books within a book. To add some actions to your scripts, you have to click this book icon, then click that book icon, then click another book icon, and so on. Rather than bore you with a lot of words, I'm going to show the path to each action as shown in the following example: Click Actions⇨Movie Control and then double-click `goto`.

Creating a Mouse Chaser

There are as many ways to create a mouse chaser as there are to animate objects. Each designer has a favorite method. In this section, you'll learn how to create a basic mouse chaser. The mouse chaser you'll be creating is a movie clip nested in a movie clip. The nested movie clip uses the `duplicateMovieClip` action and the `setProperty` action to create random clones of a star shape. You'll be programming the parent movie clip to follow the mouse.

On the CD-ROM

To follow along with this exercise, copy to your hard drive the mouseChaserBegin.fla that you'll find in this chapter's folder on the CD-ROM that accompanies this book. Use your operating system utilities to disable the file's read-only attributes.

To create a mouse chaser:

1. Launch Flash and open the mouseChaserBegin.fla file.

   In the center of the scene, you see one solitary movie clip.

2. Double-click the movie clip.

   Flash enters symbol-editing mode and the dark_star movie clip is available for editing. This is the movie clip that creates the clones of the star. The ActionScript has already been written for you. Before you program the main movie clip, examine the ActionScript for this movie clip.

3. Click the arrow to the left of the word Actions.

   The Actions panel opens and the code shown in Listing 16-1 is displayed.

Listing 16-1: **Duplicating the Star**

```
onClipEvent (enterFrame) {
  for (i=0; i<10; ++i) {
    duplicateMovieClip(this, chase+i, i);
    setProperty(eval("chase"+i), _x, this_.x+Math.random()*i*3);
    setProperty(eval("chase"+i), _y, this_.y+Math.random()*i*3);
    setProperty(eval("chase"+i), _alpha,Math.random()*100);
  }
}
```

The actions for this movie clip are executed every time the frame is entered; therefore, the code is continually creating ten copies of the original star. The second line of code creates a for loop with ten iterations. The next line of code duplicates the original movie clip, giving it a new name of *chase* appended by the current iteration of the loop. The third through fifth lines of code set the _x, _y, and _alpha (opacity)properties of the duplicate movie clips. The target part of the `setProperty` action uses the `eval` action to evaluate each duplicate as it is created. The value of each property is generated using the random method of the Math object. When the movie clip chases the mouse, you'll see a field of twinkling stars lagging slightly behind the mouse.

To finish creating the ActionScript for the mouse chaser:

1. Click the Back button to exit symbol-editing mode.

2. Select the movie clip and then click the arrow to the left of the word Actions to open the Actions panel.

3. Choose Actions⇨Variables and then double-click set variable.

   Two parameter text boxes appear above the Script pane.

4. In the Variable field, type **diff_x**

5. In the Value field, type **_x-_root._xmouse** and click the Expression checkbox.

   This line of code figures the distance between the current _x position of the mouse chaser and the current _x position of the mouse.

6. Repeat Steps 3 through 5 to create a variable named diff_y and set its value equal to _y_root._ymouse.

   This line of code records the distance between the _y position of the mouse chaser and the _y position of the mouse. Again, make sure to click the Expression checkbox.

7. In the left pane of the Actions panel, choose Actions⇨Miscellaneous Actions and then double-click evaluate.

8. In the Expression field, type **_x=_root._xmouse+(diff_x/2)**

   This line of code sets the _x position of the mouse chaser equal to the x position of the mouse plus the variable diff_x divided by 2. In a nutshell, this line of code creates a slight lag behind the mouse. The faster the mouse is moved, the larger the value of diff_x. The variable is divided by 2 so the mouse chaser doesn't lag too far behind when the mouse is moved rapidly.

9. Repeat Steps 7 and 8 to create a new expression that reads **_y=_root._ymouse+(diff_y/2)**

   This expression sets the _y position of the mouse chaser, again creating a lag between the mouse chaser clip and the mouse.

10. Select the first line of code that reads onClipEvent (load) { and in the parameter text area, click the Mouse move radio button.

    When you choose the Mouse move clip event, the code will be executed when viewers move their mouse across the scene.

11. Choose Control⇨Test Movie.

    Flash publishes the movie and plays it in another window. Drag your mouse around the screen and watch the sparkling field of stars follow it, similar to what is shown in Figure 16-1.

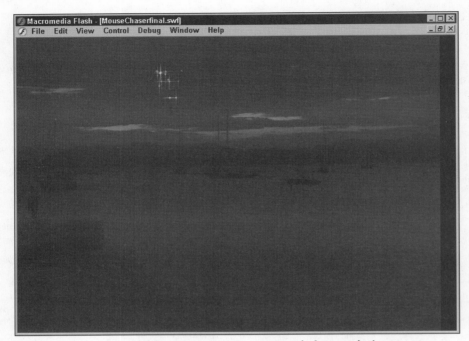

Figure 16-1: A mouse chaser is entertaining eye candy for any design.

Creating an ActionScript Mouse Chaser

In this section, you'll use one of the new Flash MX objects to create a mouse chaser. Flash MX has a new method of the Movie Clip object that enables you to create an empty movie clip. When you create an empty movie clip, you can use the drawing methods of the Movie Clip object to create shapes. The mouse chaser you'll be creating uses an empty movie clip to create a line that curves toward the cursor.

To follow along with this exercise, copy to your hard drive the simpleChaserBegin.fla file. Use your operating system's utility to disable the file's read-only attribute.

To create an ActionScript mouse chaser:

1. Launch Flash and open the simpleChaserBegin.fla file.

   All you have to work with is a solitary movie clip, which is designated by the white registration point in the center of the Stage.

2. Click the movie clip to select it and then click the arrow to the left of the word Actions.

The Actions panel opens. Notice that a considerable amount of ActionScript has already been created for you. The code (shown in Listing 16-2) generates a random color for the mouse chaser.

Listing 16-2: **Creating a Random Color**

```
onClipEvent (load) {
HexDec = new Array("0", "1", "2", "3", "4", "5", "6", "7", "8", "9", "A", "B",
"C", "D", "E", "F");
}
onClipEvent (enterFrame) {
  colorArray = new Array();
  for (i=0; i<6; ++i) {
    k = Math.round(Math.random()*15);
    colorArray[i] = HexDec[k];
  }
  rndColor =
"0x"+colorArray[0]+colorArray[1]+colorArray[2]+colorArray[3]+colorArray[4]+color
Array[5];
}
```

Before creating the empty movie clip, take a moment or two to examine the ActionScript in Listing 16-1. You can modify this script to suit other movies where you need to generate a random color. When the movie clip initially loads, a new array is created. The elements of the array are the same numbers and letters that are used to designate the hexadecimal format of a color. The code to generate the color appears after the enterFrame clip event. The first order of business is a new array called colorArray. Notice there are no elements specified for the array. This is an *associative* array. It will be storing the data generated by the next few lines of code. The for loop runs for six iterations, which is the exact number of characters used to designate a hexadecimal color. Each iteration of the loop generates a random number between 0 and 15. Remember that the first element of an array is always 0. The next line of code starts filling the colorArray. Each element of the colorArray is set equal to the [k] (the random number between 1 and 15 generated by the last line of code) element number of the HexDec array. Finally, a variable called rndColor is created by plucking the elements from the colorArray.

Now that you know how to create ActionScript to generate a random color, it's time to create the empty movie clip.

To create the empty movie clip:

1. Select the last line of code that reads `rndColor = "0x"+colorArray[0]+colorArray[1]+colorArray[2]+colorArray[3]+colorArray[4]+colorArray[5];`.

2. In the left pane of the Actions panel, choose Objects⇨Movie⇨Movie Clip⇨Methods and then double-click `createEmptyMovieClip`.

   Two parameter text boxes appear: Object and Parameters.

3. In the Object field, type **_root**

   The empty movie clip will reside on the root timeline.

4. In the Parameters field, type **"line", 1**

   The first parameter (line) is the ActionScript identifier for the empty movie clip. ActionScript identifiers are always specified with quotation marks. The second parameter is the depth, or level, that the object will be displayed on. In this case, the line will be displayed on _level1. Remember this code follows an enterFrame clip event. Therefore, the code is evaluated every time the Flash Player enters the frame.

5. In the left pane of the Actions panel, choose Actions⇨Variables and then double-click `with`.

6. In the Object field, type **_root.line**

7. In the left pane of the Actions panel, choose Objects⇨Movie⇨Movie Clip⇨ Drawing Methods and then double-click `lineStyle`.

   Two parameter text boxes appear above the Script pane: Object and Parameter.

8. In the Object field, type **_root.line**

   This is the path to the empty movie clip. In the Parameters field, you'll be specifying the actual style of the line. The lineStyle has three parameters: thickness, RGB value, and alpha. The ActionScript has already been generated to create a random color value. You'll also be creating code to generate a random thickness and alpha properties.

9. Place your cursor inside the Parameter field and type **Math.random()*6, rndColor, Math.random()*100**

   The completed code does three things:

   - The first section generates a random value between 0 and 6, which creates a line thickness between 0 (hairline thickness) and 6 pixels.

   - The second part of the code plugs in the value of the random color to designate the rgb (color) parameter.

- The third part of the code generates a random value for the line's _alpha property, which varies the opacity of the line. When the line bends towards the cursor, the opacity of the line varies between transparent and solid depending on the value generated by the random method of the Math object.

10. In the left pane of the Actions panel, choose Objects⇨Movie⇨Movie Clip⇨Drawing Methods and then double-click moveTo.

    The moveTo Drawing method specifies the starting point for the object being drawn. You can enter specific x and y coordinates. In this case, you'll be entering code to generate a random position.

11. In the Object field, type **_root.line**

12. In the Parameters field, type **Math.random()*500, Math.random()*100**

    This code generates a random starting point for the line within an area of 500 pixels by 100 pixels from the center of the empty movie clip.

13. In the left pane of the Actions panel, click Objects⇨Movie⇨Movie Clip⇨Drawing Methods and then double-click curveTo.

    This Drawing method curves a line to a designated point. In this case, you want the line to curve to the mouse from a randomly generated point in the movie.

14. In the Object field, type **_root.line**

15. In the Parameters field, type **Math.random()*500,Math.random()*100, _xmouse, _ymouse**

    This line of code curves the line from a random point within the specified coordinates directly to the mouse's x and y coordinates.

16. Choose Control⇨Test Movie.

    Flash publishes the movie and plays it in another window. As you move your mouse around the Stage, a line curves towards the mouse from different starting points. The line will be of random width, color, and thickness. It kind of looks like a fireworks sparkler on the 4th of July.

This type of mouse chaser is way too frenetic for the main part of a movie but is an excellent device to add to a preloader. The curving line will keep your visitors entertained and occupied while the main site loads.

Creating a Mask with ActionScript

In previous versions of Flash, you can create a mask layer. The shape you put on the mask layer reveals objects on masked layers beneath it. You could add a degree of interest to the mask by creating a rudimentary motion tween animation. With Flash MX, you can create a movie clip with animation and then use it to mask another movie clip. If you create a random animation in the movie clip that masks another other movie clip, you can create Flash eye candy that will interest even the most jaundiced Web surfer.

To create an ActionScript mask:

1. Create a movie clip symbol that you want to use as a mask. You can animate the movie clip if desired using motion tweening, frame-by-frame animation, or by using ActionScript to generate random motion.

2. Create a movie clip for the object that will be masked. This movie clip can be animated as well. However, you'll get your best results if you mask a static image such as a vector graphic or a bitmap.

3. Open the document Library and drag an instance of the movie clip you want to mask onto the Stage.

4. Drag an instance of the movie clip that will serve as the mask onto the Stage.

5. With the mask movie clip still selected, click the arrow to the left of the word Properties to open the Property inspector.

6. Enter a name for the movie clip in the <Instance Name> field and close the Property inspector.

7. Select the movie clip that will be masked.

8. Click the arrow to the left of the word Actions to open the Actions panel.

9. Choose Objects⇨Movie⇨Movie Clip⇨Methods and then double-click `setMask`.

   Two parameter text boxes appear above the Script pane.

10. In the Object field, type **this**

   The object is what is being masked. Because the ActionScript is being applied to the object being masked, the this alias can be used. If the ActionScript is assigned to a button, the absolute path to the movie clip needs to be entered in this field.

11. Place your cursor in the Parameters field and click the Insert a Target Path button to open the Insert Target Path dialog box.

12. Click the button that represents the movie clip you are using as a mask and then click OK to close the dialog box.

When the movie is published, the animated movie clip mask will reveal the mask object. Figure 16-2 shows four frames of a movie clip mask in action.

You can also create an ActionScript mask within a movie clip symbol. You do this by nesting the movie clip and the movie clip that will serve as a mask within a movie clip. Then it's a simple matter of applying the ActionScript and choosing the right path, as shown in the following steps:

1. Create the movie clip that will serve as the mask as outlined previously.

2. Create a movie clip symbol for the object you want to mask as outlined previously.

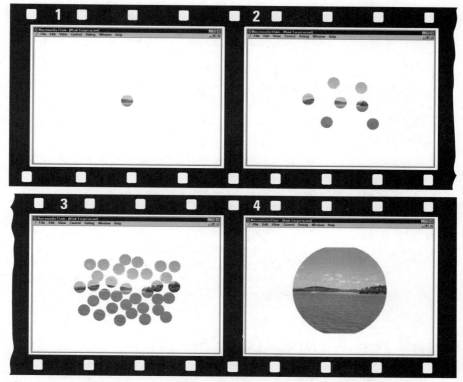

Figure 16-2: You can create dazzling eye candy using the setMask action.

3. Choose Insert⇨New Symbol.

   The Create New Symbol dialog box appears.

4. Name the symbol, choose the Movie Clip behavior, and then click OK to enter symbol-editing mode.

5. Choose Window⇨Library to open the document Library.

6. Drag an instance of the movie clip symbol you want to mask onto the Stage. Use the Align panel to center the movie clip to Stage.

7. Drag an instance of the movie clip that you'll use as a mask from the document Library to the Stage and align it to the center of the Stage.

8. With the movie clip still selected, click the arrow to the left of the word Properties to open the Property inspector.

9. Type **mask** in the <Instance Name> field and then close the Property inspector.

10. Select the movie clip that will be masked and then click the arrow to the left of the word Actions to open the Actions panel.

11. Choose Objects⇨Movie⇨Movie Clip⇨Methods and then double-click `setMask`.

    Two parameter text boxes appear above the Script pane.

12. In the Object field, type **this**

    The object you are masking is the selected object; therefore, you can refer to it by the this alias.

13. Place your cursor inside the Parameters field and then click the Insert a Target Path button. The Insert Target Path dialog box opens.

14. Click the Relative radio button and then click the button that reads `mask`. Click OK to close the dialog box.

15. Click the Back button to exit symbol-editing mode.

When you create an ActionScript mask in a movie clip symbol, you can use it anywhere in the document. You can have two or three instances of the ActionScript mask playing at one time, or you can create several movie clips where you use ActionScript to mask different objects. You can resize the movie clips to a different size as needed. Consider the effect you can achieve by having multiple instances of an animated mask movie clip on Stage, each clip a different size.

Using the Mouse Object

When you want to create a custom cursor, you use the Mouse object. The most common methods of the Mouse object are Show and Hide. When you create a custom cursor, you use the `hide` method of the Mouse object. After you hide the mouse, you can make it visible at any time by choosing the `show` method of the Mouse object. When you hide or show the Mouse object, you usually assign the action to a keyframe, although you can use the action in conjunction with a button click when beginning a game. When you hide the mouse, make sure you use the `startDrag` action to attach a movie clip in place of the mouse as outlined in the upcoming section; otherwise, your viewers will have no idea of where their cursor is — unless, of course, that's the effect you're after.

To hide the mouse:

1. Select the keyframe or object where you want to create the ActionScript to hide the mouse.

2. Click the arrow to the left of the word Actions to open the Actions panel.

3. Choose Objects⇨Movie⇨Mouse⇨Methods and then double-click `hide`.

To display the mouse after it has been hidden:

1. Select the keyframe or object where you want to create the ActionScript to reveal the mouse.

2. Click the arrow to the left of the word Actions to open the Actions panel.

3. Click Objects⇨Movie⇨Mouse⇨Methods and then double-click show.

Creating a Custom Cursor

If you have a client who wants something different, consider creating a custom cursor using either the client's logo or a tool of the client's trade. For example, if your client is an artist, create a paint brush cursor. If your client is a rock guitarist, create a cursor that looks like the musician's guitar.

To create a custom cursor:

1. Choose Insert⇨New Symbol.

    The Create New Symbol dialog box opens.

2. Name the symbol *cursor*, choose the Movie Clip behavior, and then click OK to enter symbol-editing mode.

3. Create the object you want to use as a cursor for your design or import a vector graphic or bitmap.

4. Click the Back button to exit symbol-editing mode.

5. Choose Window⇨Library.

    The document Library opens.

6. Drag an instance of your cursor movie clip onto the Stage.

7. Click the arrow to the left of the word Properties.

    The Property inspector opens.

8. In the <Instance Name> field, type **cursor**

9. Select the first frame in your document.

10. Click the arrow to the left of the word Actions.

    The Actions panel opens.

11. Choose Objects⇨Movie⇨Mouse⇨Methods and then double-click hide.

12. In the left pane of the Actions panel, choose Actions⇨Movie Clip Control and then double-click startDrag.

13. Place your cursor inside the Target field and click the Insert a Target Path button to open the Insert Target Path dialog box.

14. Click the button labeled cursor to add the target path of your cursor movie clip to the code and then click OK to close the dialog box.

15. Click the Lock Mouse to Center check box. Your finished ActionScript should look like Listing 16-3.

Listing 16-3: Creating ActionScript for a Custom Cursor

```
Mouse.hide();
startDrag("_root.cursor", true);
```

Figure 16-3 shows an example of a custom cursor.

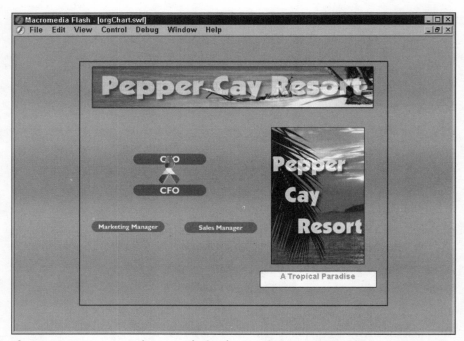

Figure 16-3: You can spice up a design by creating a custom cursor.

Creating Motion Trails

Another bit of eye candy you can use to spice up your designs is a motion trail. When you create a motion trail, an object moves across the movie and leaves a trail of images in its wake, each image being a little fainter as it disappears into the background. The motion trails finally catch up with the object and disappear. To create this effect, you first create a movie clip with a motion tween animation in it. Then you use the `duplicateMovieClip` action to create the trails and modify each duplicated movie clip's alpha property to create the fading effect.

To create a motion trail:

1. Choose Insert⇨New Symbol.

   The Create New Symbol dialog box appears.

2. Choose the Graphic behavior and then click OK to enter symbol-editing mode.

3. Use the drawing tools to create an object or import a vector or bitmap image.

4. Click OK to exit symbol-editing mode.

5. Create another new symbol, this time choosing the Movie Clip behavior.

6. Choose Window⇨Library.

   The document Library opens.

7. Drag an instance of the graphic symbol into the movie clip symbol.

8. Create a motion tween animation. Vary the size of the object between keyframes.

   Motion paths also make good motion tween animations.

9. Click the Back button to exit symbol-editing mode.

   Figure 16-4 shows a motion tween animation created for a motion trail movie clip.

After you create the motion tween animation, you nest it in another movie clip and the fun begins. The ActionScript to finish the motion trail effect uses three frames. The first frame initializes the variables, the second frame uses the `duplicateMovieClip` action to create the trails, and the third frame loops the animation.

To complete the motion trail effect

1. Create a new movie clip symbol.

2. Choose Window⇨Library.

   The document Library opens.

3. Drag an instance of the motion tween animation you just created on Stage.

4. Open the Property inspector and in the <Instance Name> field, type **clip**

5. Create a new layer and label it *actions*.

6. Select the second and third frames and press F6 to convert them to keyframes.

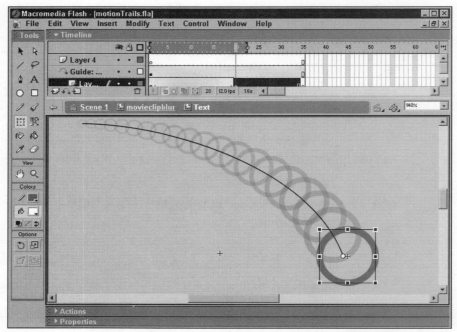

Figure 16-4: A motion tween animation is the first step in creating a motion trail effect.

7. Select the third frame on the first layer and press F5 to create additional frames.

8. Select the first keyframe on the Actions layer and then click the arrow to the left of the word Actions.

9. In the left pane of the Actions panel, choose Actions➪Variables and then double-click set variable.

10. In the Variable field, type **loops** and in the Value field, type **0**

11. In the Value field, click the Expression check box.

12. Repeat Steps 8 thorough 10 to create a new variable. Name the variable **trails** and set its value equal to **12**. Be sure to check the Expression check box in the Value field.

   The actual value you choose for trails is largely a matter of personal taste. The sample file in this chapter's CD-ROM uses a value of 15. Experiment with different values to suit the design you are creating.

13. Select the second keyframe and in the left pane of the Actions panel, choose Actions➪Conditions/Loops and then double-click if.

   The Condition parameter text box appears above the Script pane.

14. In the Condition field, type **loops<trails+1**

15. In the left pane of the Actions panel, choose Actions⇨Movie Clip Control and then double-click `duplicateMovieClip`.

   The parameter text boxes appear above the Script pane.

16. In the Target field, type **clip**

   This is the instance name of the motion tween animation that will be duplicated to create the motion trails.

17. In the New Name field, type **"clip" + loops**

   Be sure to click the Expression check box. This line of code names the duplicated movie clips.

18. In the Depth field, type **loops**

19. Click Actions⇨Movie Clip Control and then double-click `setProperty`.

20. Click the triangle to the right of the Property field and choose _alpha(Alpha).

   The line of code will vary the opacity of the duplicate clips.

21. In the Target field, type **"clip" + loops** and click the Expression check box.

22. In the Value field, type **70-(loops*(50/trails))**

   This may look a little complex, but actually it isn't. Each duplicated movie clip becomes more transparent as the loop continues. The next line of code increases the value of loops by 1.

23. In the left pane of the Actions panel, choose Actions⇨Variables and then double-click `set variable`.

24. In the Variable field, type **loops** and in the Value field, type **loops + 1**

   Your finished code should look like Listing 16-4.

25. Select the third frame and click the arrow to the left of the word Actions.

   The Actions panel opens.

26. In the left pane of the Actions panel, click Actions⇨Movie Control and then double-click `goto`.

27. Accept the default parameters and in the Frame field enter 2.

   Your ActionScript should read `gotoAndPlay(2)`.

Listing 16-4: **Creating the Code to Create the Motion Trails**

```
if (loops<trails+1) {
  duplicateMovieClip("clip", "clip"+loops, loops);
  setProperty("clip"+loops, _alpha, 70-(loops*(50/trails)));
  loops = loops+1;
}
```

The heart of this effect is in the code you create on the second keyframe. This duplicates the motion tween animation movie clip and decreases the opacity of each duplicate. When you create this effect for your own designs, remember that you can swap the motion tween animation symbol with another to create a different effect. Just remember to name the instance of the new symbol, "clip" and the effect plays without a hitch. You can also vary the effect by changing the number of trails and the beginning alpha value. Instead of using 70 as the base alpha for the effect, try a lower or higher value. Figure 16-5 shows a movie that uses the motion trail effect to good effect.

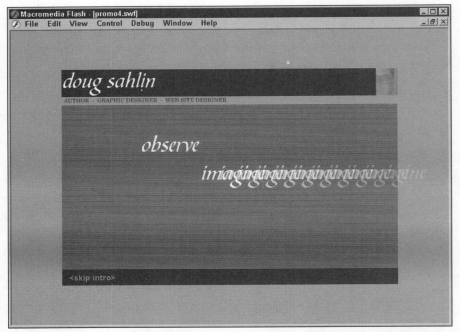

Figure 16-5: You can add excitement to your designs with the motion trail effect.

To view an example of a motion trail movie, copy to your hard drive the motionTrails.fla file that you find in this chapter's folder on the CD-ROM that accompanies this book. Use your computer operating system utilities to disable the file's read-only attributes and launch the file in Flash. Choose Control⇨Test Movie to see the effect.

Creating a Starburst Backdrop

Another scintillating effect you can add to your designs is a starburst backdrop. This effect creates random duplicates of a small sphere to simulate a starfield.

Unfortunately, the number of steps involved in creating this effect are quite numerous. Rather than have you read a lengthy tutorial, the steps that follow dissect the ActionScript used to create the effect.

On the CD-ROM To learn how to create a starburst backdrop, copy to your hard drive the randomStars.fla file found in this chapter's folder on the CD-ROM that accompanies this book. Use your operating system utilities to disable the file's read-only attributes.

To learn how the starburst backdrop effect is created:

1. Launch Flash and open the randomStars.fla file.
2. Choose Control⇨Test Movie.

Flash publishes the file and plays it in another window (see Figure 16-6).

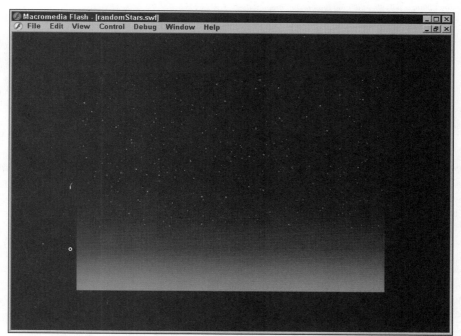

Figure 16-6: You can use ActionScript to create a starburst background like this.

As the movie plays, you see what appears to be an ever changing field of stars. In reality, it's only one movie clip duplicated over a hundred times. The entire file is only 155 KB, dainty by any designer's standards. You can use this file or a similar one of your own creation for an interesting backdrop. To see how the effect is created, close the window and follow the upcoming steps.

1. Click the small white dot in the upper-left corner of the movie and choose Edit⇨Edit Selected.

   Flash enters symbol-editing mode. The entire movie clip is only two keyframes long.

2. Click the arrow to the left of the word Actions to open the Actions panel.

3. Click the small white dot just above the center of the Stage. This is a small circle nested in the movie clip.

   Listing 16-5 shows the ActionScript that is used to set the initial position of the movie clip.

Listing 16-5: **Initializing the Movie Clip**

```
onClipEvent (load) {
  this._x=Math.random()*540;
  this._y=Math.random()*280;
  this._xscale=Math.random()*100;
  this._yscale=this._xscale;
  this._alpha=Math.random() * 100;
  if (this._alpha<50) {
    this._alpha=50;
  }
}
```

When the movie clip first loads, the _x and _y properties of the movie clip are set to random positions. The value of 540 for the _x was chosen to keep the movie clip within the boundary of the movie. The value of 280 for the _y property was chosen to keep the stars above the orange part of the background, which is a gradient blend created with the Color Mixer. The fourth line of code generates a random value for the _xscale of the movie clip, and the fifth line of code sets the _yscale equal to the _xscale so the movie clip resizes proportionately. The next line of code varies the opacity of the movie clip. The conditional statement sets the _alpha property equal to 50 if the random value generated drops below 50. This statement was entered to prevent the movie clip from blending into the background. The desired effect was to simulate twinkling stars; an alpha value less than 50 would cause the stars to all but disappear.

To see the code used to create the rest of the effect, click the first keyframe. If you still have the Actions panel open, you see the code in Listing 16-6.

Listing 16-6: **Creating the Stars**

```
k = 0;
i = Math.random()*200;
while (k<i) {
  duplicateMovieClip("circle", "circle"+k, k);
  k = ++k;
}
```

The first line of code declares a variable named *k* and sets it equal to 0. The second line of code initializes a variable named *i* and sets its value equal to a random number between 1 and 200. The third line of code initializes a while loop. While the value of *k* is less than *i,* the movie clip is duplicated. The movie clip is duplicated each time it loads and new random values are generated, which simulates the appearance of a star on another part of the Stage. The next line of code increments the value of *k* by 1. The loop continues creating duplicate stars until the value of *k* exceeds *i.* After the loop finishes, the movie clip plays frame 2 which has a goto action that returns it to frame 1, whereupon the whole process repeats itself and a new field of stars is generated. However, there's one additional item on the second frame that pauses the movie so the viewer can see the stars.

Click the small white dot below the center of the Stage. This is a user-defined component that contains nothing but ActionScript. The component pauses the movie. You could pause the movie by adding a few frames between the keyframes. However, if you ever needed to change the effect, you'd have to add or delete frames. Also, with a given number of frames, the effect would be too predictable. The user-defined component is a timer that pauses the movie for a different amount of time every time the frame plays. With the component still selected, click the arrow to the left of the word Properties to open the Property inspector. The component has only one parameter: Seconds (shown in Figure 16-6). The ActionScript in the component pauses the movie for a random amount of time up to the value entered in the Seconds field. To see how the component works, click the number (.6) to the right of seconds and enter a higher value. Choose Control⬎ Test Movie. After Flash publishes the file, you'll see that the stars don't change as quickly. Enter a smaller value in the seconds field, and a new star field is generated more quickly.

You can create a similar effect by recreating the code in your own movie, or you can modify this movie to suit your needs by creating a different background or by creating a new movie clip symbol with a different graphic than a circle. Edit the starfield movie clip and swap the circle movie clip for your own symbol.

Chapter Project: Creating a Flash Slide Show

For the chapter project, you'll be examining the code used to create a slide show. The slide show is a moving strip of images. The speed of the strip varies depending on the position of the user's mouse. To examine any of the images in greater detail, viewers move their mouse towards the image and the strip stops moving.

 To follow along with this exercise, copy to your hard drive the slideShow.fla file you find in this chapter's folder on the CD-ROM that accompanies this book. Use your computer operating system utilities to disable the file's read-only attributes.

To dissect the code used to create the slide show movie:

1. Launch Flash and open the slideShow.fla file.

2. Choose Control⇨Test Movie.

   Flash publishes the movie and plays it in another window. When the movie begins, all you see are instructions for the user.

3. Move your mouse over the scroll left control and the images begin moving (see Figure 16-7).

4. Move your mouse farther to the left and the images move faster. Move your mouse toward the images and they stop moving so you can get a better look. Move your mouse over the scroll right control and the images move to the right, picking up speed as you move farther away from the center of the movie.

   After you've finished playing the movie, close the window.

Now that you've seen the effect in action, it's time to examine the code and see what makes this effect work. As shown in Figure 16-7, the actual movie consists of three keyframes and several layers. There's a mask layer with an image the same size as the movie. By adding the mask, you can load this movie into a target window in a larger movie. The mask prevents the other images from being seen as they scroll past the edge of the movie. The actual image was created in an image editing program. Several individual images were combined to create the strip. The image was given an instance name of *strip*.

To examine the code used to create this effect:

1. Click the arrow next to the word Actions to open the Actions panel.

2. Click the first keyframe on the Actions layer and you see the code shown in Listing 16-7.

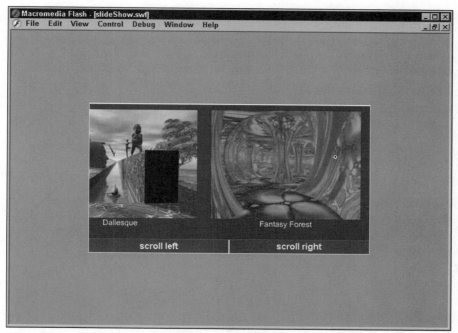

Figure 16-7: The images in the slide show scroll across the screen.

Listing 16-7: **Initializing the Variables**

```
center = 250;
rightBorder = -3496;
leftBorder = 0;
stripPos = strip._x;
```

The ActionScript in Listing 16-7 initializes the variables for the movie. The variable named center defines the center of the movie; rightBorder defines the end of the image strip. The leftBorder variable is equal to 0. The registration point is set to x=0 instead of the center of the film strip. The last variable, stripPos, is set equal to the _x property of *strip*, the instance name of the movie clip with the image. Figure 16-8 shows the movie clip with the image. Notice that the left side of the image is aligned to the center of the Stage. The image is 3496 pixels long, making its right border –3496.

Registration point

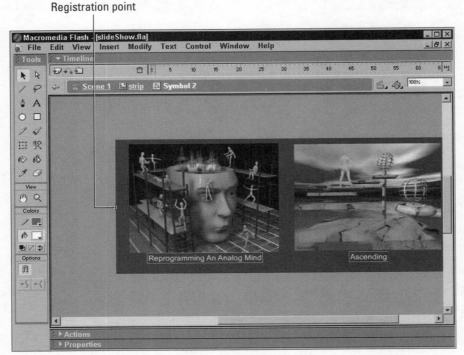

Figure 16-8: The image is nested in a movie clip symbol.

When the movie begins playing, the first frame sets up all the variables and then the second keyframe plays. The code for the second keyframe is shown in Listing 16-8.

Listing 16-8: **ActionScript to Move the Image**

```
if (_ymouse>250) {
  stripSpeed = (_xmouse-center)/8;
  stripPos = (stripPos+stripSpeed );
  if (stripPos>leftBorder) {
    stripPos = leftBorder;
  }
  if (stripPos<rightBorder) {
    stripPos = rightBorder;
  }
  strip._x = stripPos;
}
```

Notice that the ActionScript consists of three conditional statements. The first conditional statement evaluates the _y property of the mouse. When the _y property of the mouse is greater than 250 (the top border of the scroll controls), the variable stripSpeed is set equal to the _x property of the mouse minus the value of center divided by 8. If you experiment with this effect, you can speed up the scrolling by choosing a value less than 8, or slow it down by choosing a value higher than 8. The variable center defines the center of the movie. This defines the speed and direction of the strip. The result was divided by 8 to slow the speed down. The next line of code sets the value for the variable stripPos. The first frame initialized the value of stripPos and set it equal to the _x property of the image strip. As the user moves the mouse to the left, the value of stripSpeed decreases. When this value is added to stripPos, it causes the strip to move to the left. When the user moves the mouse to the right, the value of stripSpeed increases and when added to stripPos, causes the image strip to move to the right. As the user moves the mouse farther in either direction, the speed increases.

The next two conditional statements reset the value of stripPos in order to keep the film strip from scrolling out of the movie. The final line of code sets the _x property of the strip movie clip equal to stripPos.

The third keyframe loops the movie back to the second frame so that the Flash Player can continually evaluate the position of the user's mouse and move the film strip.

When you need to create an effect like this for a client, all you need to do is change the value of the variable center to equal the center of your document (width/2) and change the value of rightBorder to the negative of the width of the image you are displaying. When you create the movie clip for the image, remember to align the left edge of the image to x=0. Alternately, you can import the image into the document, select it, and then click F8 to convert the image into a symbol. Choose the movie clip behavior and the middle left registration point and you're good to go.

Designer Notes

In this chapter, you learned to create some of the fun frilly things that make a Flash design a success. You learned to create a custom cursor and a mouse chaser, two items sure to keep your viewers entertained. You also learned to create the motion trail effect and create a custom background of twinkling stars. In the chapter project, you learned how to create the ActionScript needed to create a moving slide show. In the next chapter, you'll learn to integrate Flash movies with your HTML designs.

✦   ✦   ✦

Integrating Flash with HTML

In This Chapter

Creating a pop-up window

Creating banner ads

Detecting the Flash Player

Creating a Flash introduction

Chapter project: Creating an animated Flash banner

Flash MX is a complete solution for Web publishing. You can create designs with video, audio, complex navigation systems, and much more. However, as powerful as Flash is, the content is still embedded in an HTML document. When you publish a Flash movie and choose the HTML option, the *.swf file is automatically embedded in an HTML document using the browser's default alignment, which places the Flash movie in the upper-left corner of the document — not the most desirable place. You can change the location by modifying the alignment in an HTML editor.

In this chapter, you'll learn to integrate Flash with HTML. You'll learn to create a pop-up window from within Flash to display an HTML page in another window. You'll also learn to detect the version of the Flash Player your movie is being viewed with. In addition, you'll learn to create a compelling Flash introduction, as well as create banner ads to integrate with your HTML designs.

 Note
The Actions panel's got lots of books. And some of these books have books within a book. To add some actions to your scripts, you have to click this book icon, then click that book icon, then click another book icon, and so on. Rather than bore you with a lot of words, I'm going to show the path to each action as shown in the following example: Click Actions⇨Movie Control and then double-click goto.

Creating a Pop-Up Window with JavaScript

If you create a design for a client that needs to include links to external Web sites, you can use a bit of JavaScript in conjunction with the getURL action to display the link in another browser window. Displaying a URL link in another window gives you control over the parameters of the pop-up window. You can specify the size of the window and whether the new window has scrollbars or not.

To display a link in a pop-up window:

1. Select the button or keyframe that will cause the new window to pop up.
2. Click the arrow to the left of the word Actions to open the Actions panel.
3. Choose Actions⇨Browser/Network and then double-click `getURL`.
4. In the URL field, type **Javascript:newwin1 ()**

   This bit of code tells the Flash Player that the URL for the link is located within JavaScript in the HTML document the movie is embedded in.
5. To create additional links that open in another window, repeat Steps 3 and 4, and in the URL field, type **Javascript:newwin2**, **()Javascript:newwin3 ()**, and so on.

After you publish the document as a Flash movie, you have to modify the HTML document the movie is embedded in to include the JavaScript that will open the link in a new window.

To modify the HTML document:

1. In your HTML editor, open the HTML document the Flash movie is embedded in. Alternately, you can open the document in a text editor.
2. In the head of the HTML document, enter the JavaScript shown in Listing 17-1.

Listing 17-1: **JavaScript to Open a Link in Another Window**

```
<script language="Javascript"> function newwin1() {
window.open('http://www.dasdesigns.net/about.htm', 'links'
,'scrollbars=yes,width=640,height=480') }
</script>
```

The JavaScript in the previous listing opens the link in a browser window 640 pixels wide by 480 pixels high. The window has scrollbars. When you create the JavaScript to open the new window, it's always a good idea to size it smaller than the parent window. A desktop size of 800 pixels by 600 pixels seems to be the most popular these days. Therefore, if you size the pop-up window to 640 x 480, the HTML page with your Flash design is visible in the background.

You can also use this technique to play your Flash design in an HTML document the exact size of the movie. To do this, you create two movies. The first movie has nothing but the `getURL` action with the `Javascript newwin 1()` code. In the

HTML page, you create the JavaScript to open the main movie in a new window called flashMovie.html that is sized to the movie. Listing 17-2 shows the code that will open the main movie in a sized window.

Listing 17-2: **JavaScript to Open a Flash File in a Sized Window**

```
<HTML>
<HEAD>
<meta http-equiv=Content-Type content="text/html; charset=ISO-8859-1">
<TITLE>Untitled-1</TITLE>
<script language="Javascript"> function newwin1() {
window.open('flashMovie.html', 'links' ,'scrollbars=yes, menu=yes,
width=550,height=400') } </script>
</HEAD>
<BODY bgcolor="#FFFFFF">
<!-- URL's used in the movie-->
<!-- text used in the movie-->
<OBJECT classid="clsid:D27CDB6E-AE6D-11cf-96B8-444553540000"

codebase="http://download.macromedia.com/pub/shockwave/cabs/flash/swflash.cab#ve
rsion=6,0,0,0"
 WIDTH="1" HEIGHT="1" id="Untitled-1" ALIGN="">
 <PARAM NAME=movie VALUE="mainMovie.swf"> <PARAM NAME=quality VALUE=high> <PARAM
NAME=bgcolor VALUE=#FFFFFF> <EMBED src="browserSize.swf" quality=high
bgcolor=#FFFFFF WIDTH="1" HEIGHT="1" NAME="Untitled-1" ALIGN=""
 TYPE="application/x-shockwave-flash"
PLUGINSPAGE="http://www.macromedia.com/go/getflashplayer"></EMBED>
</OBJECT>
</BODY>
</HTML>
```

In the preceding code, you notice the HTML page with the Flash movie is referred to by its relative path. When the HTML document the movie is embedded in is in the same root directory, you can refer to it by name and extension. Also notice that the size of the Flash movie embedded in the HTML document that opens the main movie is only 1 pixel by 1 pixel.

Creating Banner Ads

Banner ads seem to be everywhere on the Internet these days. Before Flash became a popular Web development tool, designers resorted to the old tried-and-true Animated GIF to get the job done. However, Animated GIFs with any degree of advanced animation are comprised of several frames and the file size may be too large to download quickly. This is where Flash has come into favor with Web designers. Using Flash, you can quickly create an impressive banner ad that downloads quickly into the user's browser.

But before you rush headlong into Flash and create the banner, consider where the banner will appear in your HTML design. Many Web designers display a single banner across the top of a page; other designers prefer to display one or more banner ads on the side of the page. Figure 17-1 shows a Flash banner across the top of a Web page.

Figure 17-1: You can display a banner ad across the top of an HTML page.

When you do decide on a position for the banner ad, keep the elements in your HTML design in mind. Stick with similar colors or the same colors that appear in your HTML design. You don't want your finished product looking like some of the cut and paste HTML designs that run rampant in the backwaters of the Internet. Figure 17-2 shows a Web page displaying ad banners on the side of the page.

Another popular alternative is the pop-up ad that appears when a page loads or a button is clicked. Whether you decide to place your banner ad at the top or side of the page, there's no need to reinvent the wheel when you create the ad in Flash. Most of the popular layouts and sizes for banner ads are available as templates.

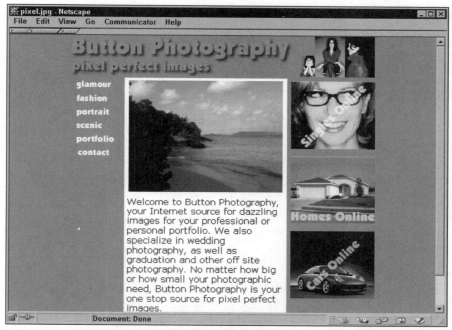

Figure 17-2: Many Web designers display banner ads on the side of a design.

To create a banner ad:

1. Launch Flash and choose File⇨New from Template.

Flash opens the New Document dialog box.

2. In the Category column, click Ads to display the Flash ad templates (see Figure 17-3).

3. Choose one of the presets.

Flash opens the template, as shown in Figure 17-4.

Notice the text in Figure 17-4. These are instructions and guidelines the designers of Flash have thoughtfully included with the template. They offer some good advice, such as keeping the file size of the initial load below 15K. The information is all on a guide layer. After you finish reading the information, delete the guide layer and you're ready to go to work.

At the end of this chapter, you'll be creating a small banner ad.

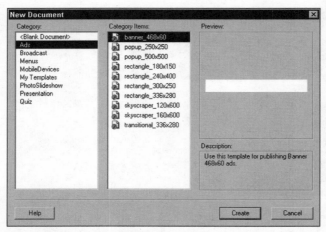

Figure 17-3: You can create banner ads from a preset template.

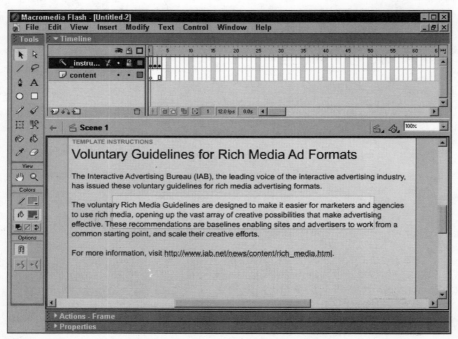

Figure 17-4: You can quickly create an ad using a template.

Detecting the Flash Player

Most popular Web browsers include a version of the Flash Player as standard equipment. But when a new version of Flash is released, the general population may not have the latest version of the Flash Player for a few months. If you anticipate this occurrence, you can create a small movie with ActionScript to detect the version of the Flash Player the movie is being viewed with. After the version is detected, you can create a conditional statement that either loads the main movie or loads an alternate version of the movie published for the detected version of the Flash Player. Or you can direct viewers to the Macromedia Web site where they can download the latest version of the Flash Player.

When you debug a movie, one of the first variables displayed is the version of the Flash Player. The version of the Flash Player is designated by the OS and then the version of the Flash Player. The nomenclature for the latest Windows version of the Flash Player as this is written is WIN 6,0,21,0. This information is string data. The fifth character in the string designates which version of the Player is being used. All you have to do is create a variable that records the version of the Flash Player and a conditional statement to evaluate which version of the Player is being used to view your design.

To create a movie that detects the Flash Player, do the following:

1. Create a new document.

2. Select the first frame and then click the arrow to the left of the word Actions.

   The Actions panel opens.

3. Choose Actions⇨Variables and then double-click `set variable`.

4. In the Variable field, type **Version**

5. Place your cursor in the Value field and then in the left pane of the Actions panel, choose Functions⇨Conversion Functions and then double-click `getVersion`.

   This line of code gets the version of the Flash Player being used and stores it in the variable named Version. Now you have to create a conditional statement that detects which version of the player is being used.

6. In the left pane of the Actions panel, choose Actions⇨Conditions/Loops and then double-click `if`.

7. In the Condition field, type **_root.Version** and then in the left pane of the Actions panel, choose Objects⇨Core⇨String⇨Methods and double-click `charAt`.

   Flash adds the action to your script and highlights the word *Index*.

8. Type **4**

This evaluates the fifth character in the version string. Remember that the first index of a string is 0.

9. Place your cursor the right of the last parentheses in the field and type **==6**

How you finish the ActionScript depends on how you have structured your movie. Listing 17-3 shows ActionScript that loads one movie if Flash Player 6 is detected, another if Flash Player 5 is detected, and directs the viewer to an HTML version of the site if neither Player is detected.

Listing 17-3: **Detecting the Flash Player Version**

```
Version = getVersion();
if (_root.Version.charAt(4)==6) {
  loadMovieNum("Flash6.swf", 0);
} else if (_root.Version.charAt(4)==5) {
  loadMovieNum("Flash5.swf", 0);
} else {
  getURL("nonFlash.html");
}
```

Another option you may want to consider is creating an HTML page that welcomes viewers to the site and lists the Flash Player required to view the site and other necessary hardware. The page has two buttons, one that links viewers to the Flash version of the site and another that directs viewers to the HTML version of the site.

Tip   If you prefer, you can use some ready made Macromedia detection tools. Log on to the Internet and point your Web browser to: http://dynamic. macromedia.com/bin/MM/software/trial/hwswrec.jsp?product= flash_deployment_kit to download the Flash Deployment Kit.

Creating a Flash Introduction

If despite your best efforts, a prospective client will not foot the bill for a full-fledged Flash site, revise your proposal to include a Flash introduction (intro) that leads into a standard HTML design. When you create a Flash intro, you create a Flash movie with animation to whet the viewer's appetites for the HTML page. Your Flash intro should be like a commercial with lots of movement, sound, and other eye candy to draw the viewer into the site. However, you can create too much interactivity, which bloats the file size and causes a lengthy download. Use just enough eye candy and other bells and whistles to pique the viewer's interest. Figure 17-5 shows an example of a Flash intro.

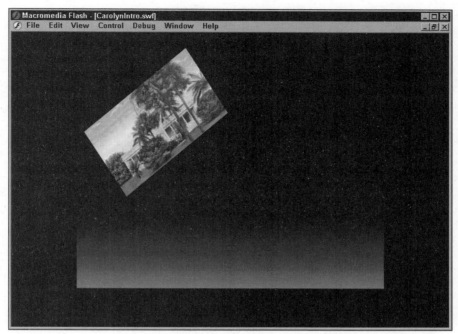

Figure 17-5: You create an intro to whet the viewer's appetite for an HTML site.

If your client runs television commercials, request copies of the images used in the commercial for use in the intro. You can then use some of the techniques presented in this book to add motion. If you have image-editing software at your disposal, create a strip of images and then have them move across the screen. Add another layer with highly transparent text moving in the opposite direction, and you've got a compelling intro.

If you add music to your intro, use an interesting four-second music loop, play it four times, and you've got a 16-second intro. Alternately, you can loop the sound three times and then position another instance of the sound on the timeline four seconds before the intro ends. If you have a 16-second intro playing at 12 fps (frames per second), your timeline is 192 frames long. Place an instance of the sound on frame 144, open the Property inspector, click the arrow to the right of the Effect field, and choose Fade Out. When you publish the movie, the sound will fade out at the end of the intro.

You should always include a Skip Intro button so viewers who have been to the site before have the choice of viewing the intro again or not. If you do your job correctly, new viewers to the site won't use the Skip Intro button. If you have no sound with your intro, program the Skip Intro button with the getURL action to launch the first page in the HTML site. However, if you have sound with your intro, the sound continues playing even though the intro is no longer playing. If you have a soundtrack on your intro, program the Skip Intro button as follows:

1. Create a symbol button symbol with text that reads something like "*<Skip Intro>*" and then place an instance of the button on Stage.

2. Select the Skip Intro button, click the arrow to the left of the word Actions.

3. Choose Actions⇨Movie Control and double-click `goto`.

   Code the ActionScript to go to and play the last frame of the intro.

4. Select the last frame of the intro and press F6 to convert it to a keyframe.

5. Click the arrow to the left of the word Properties to open the Property inspector.

6. Click the triangle to the right of the Sound field and choose your intro sound from the drop-down menu.

7. Click the arrow to the right of the Event field and then choose Stop.

8. Click the arrow to the left of the word Actions to open the Actions panel.

9. Choose Actions⇨Browser/Network and then double-click `getURL`.

10. In the URL field, enter the path to your main HTML page. If the page is in the same directory as the movie, you need only enter the relative path, for example: homePage.html.

11. Choose Control⇨Test Movie.

When your intro starts playing, click the Skip Intro button. The movie advances to the last frame and the sound stops playing. When you create a Skip Intro button for a movie with no soundtrack, you don't have to worry about advancing the movie to the last frame and then stopping the soundtrack. Therefore, all you have to do is create the button and then use the `getURL` action to load the main HTML page. When the button is clicked, the specified URL loads.

Tip

If you meet face-to-face with your clients and you have a small laptop, consider adding a directory to the laptop and storing some examples of your best Flash work in the directory. Create an HTML document with links to play the movies. Create a desktop shortcut to the HTML page, and you can demonstrate your work to the client. If a picture is worth a thousand words, a great Flash intro must be worth at least a million. A quick demonstration of your work can be the difference between getting a job on the spot or having your potential customer shop your quote with other designers.

Integrating Flash with Dreamweaver

When you publish a Flash movie and choose the Flash and HTML publishing options, Flash embeds the .SWF file in the document. However, the movie plays in the brower's default location. Unless your movie is sized to a specific maximized browser size, the movie plays in the upper left-hand corner of the browser. To center the movie to the browser, open the HTML file in an HTML editing program such as Dreamweaver and center the movie. Each software program uses slightly different tools to achieve this. In Dreamweaver, you can place your cursor before the Flash movie, open the Property inspector, and click the Center alignment button. If you edit the document in software where you can work directly with the code, type the following tag before the Flash object: **<div align="center">**. Then type the following tag after the object: **</div>**. Listing 17-4 shows the HTML code for a Flash object that has been centered in an HTML page.

Listing 17-4: **Centering the Flash Object in the HTML Page**

```
<HTML>
<HEAD>
<meta http-equiv=Content-Type content="text/html; charset=ISO-8859-1">
<TITLE>test</TITLE>
</HEAD>
<BODY bgcolor="#E6E6FF">
<!-- URL's used in the movie-->
<!-- text used in the movie-->
<!--button photographypixel perfect-->
<div align="center"><OBJECT classid="clsid:D27CDB6E-AE6D-11cf-96B8-444553540000"

codebase="http://download.macromedia.com/pub/shockwave/cabs/flash/swflash.cab#ve
rsion=6,0,0,0"
 WIDTH="800" HEIGHT="600" id="test" ALIGN="">
  <PARAM NAME=movie VALUE="homePage.swf">
  <PARAM NAME=quality VALUE=high>
  <PARAM NAME=bgcolor VALUE=#E6E6FF>
  <EMBED src="test.swf" quality=high bgcolor=#E6E6FF WIDTH="800" HEIGHT="600"
NAME="test" ALIGN=""
 TYPE="application/x-shockwave-flash"
PLUGINSPAGE="http://www.macromedia.com/go/getflashplayer">
  </EMBED>
 </OBJECT> </div>
</BODY>
</HTML>
```

Notice the PLUGINSPAGE line in the previous listing. If the viewer doesn't have the Flash plug in and the user's browser supports redirecting, the browser displays the warning that the Flash plug in is required to view the page and offers an option to redirect the viewer to the listed URL.

If you integrate items such as banners and menus you create in Flash with your HTML pages, you can import them directly into an HTML document in Dreamweaver. Many designers find it convenient to nest a Flash banner or menu in an HTML table.

This gives you the most flexibility as you can size your table rows and columns around the Flash documents. From within Dreamweaver, you can select a table row or column and then choose Insert⇨Media⇨Flash. Figure 17-6 shows a Flash movie in an HTML document being edited in Dreamweaver.

When you select a Flash file within Dreamweaver and then open the Dreamweaver Property inspector, you can preview the file by clicking the Play button (refer to Figure 17-6).

Dreamweaver Property inspector   Flash banner ads

Figure 17-6: You can insert your Flash work directly into an HTML document.

Dreamweaver also has built-in Flash objects. If you're working on an HTML document in Dreamweaver, you can add Flash buttons and Flash text on the fly. To add a Flash button to an HTML document from within Dreamweaver, choose Insert⇨Interactive Images⇨Flash Buttons to open the dialog box, as shown in Figure 17-7.

To insert Flash text, choose Insert⇨Interactive Images⇨Flash Text. When you insert Flash text in a document, you can specify different font parameters than the rest of the document, select a background color, select a rollover color, and specify a link and target browser window. Figure 17-8 shows several examples of Flash buttons and text created in Dreamweaver.

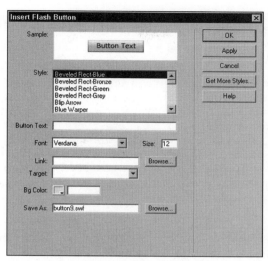

Figure 17-7: You can insert a Flash button from within Dreamweaver.

Figure 17-8: You can add Flash interactivity to an HTML page from within Dreamweaver.

Chapter Project: Creating an Animated Flash Banner

One way you can dress up a static HTML design is to add an animated Flash banner to the site. An animated Flash banner is yet another weapon in your arsenal against hum-drum Web pages. If you're competing for a Web design job against a designer who proposes an Animated GIF banner, you'll win hands-down every time if you can show your prospective client an example of an animated Flash banner. You can add more action and still come in at a fraction of the file size of an Animated GIF. In this project, you'll be using ActionScript to creating a steady stream of moving stars on a banner. You'll also be adding a small movie clip that's already been prepared for you and a banner image of a hypothetical company.

On the CD-ROM   To follow along with this project, copy to your hard drive the animatedBannerBegin. fla file that you'll find in this chapter's folder on the CD-ROM that accompanies this book. Use your computer operating system utilities to disable the file's read-only attributes.

To create an animated banner:

1. Launch Flash and open the animatedBannerBegin.fla file.

   Notice that the document has already been sized to 550 x 100, a typical size for a Web site splash banner. The banner is long enough and wide enough to attract attention and showcase your talent. You can incorporate the banner within a table that displays text and images below the banner.

2. Choose Window⇨Library.

   The document Library opens.

3. Open the Movie Clips folder and drag an instance of the corporateOfficers movie clip onto the Stage.

4. Using the Align panel, align the movie clip to the left corner of the Stage.

5. Drag an instance of the corpLogo symbol from the document Library onto the Stage.

6. Align the symbol to the center of the document.

7. Choose Control⇨Test Movie.

   Flash publishes the movie and displays it in another window.

What you've just created is interesting enough. There's a nice little animation playing in the corner along with a good-looking logo in the center of the banner. However, you can add so much more with just a bit of ActionScript. When you've finished looking at the movie, close the window to exit symbol-editing mode.

To add a bit of excitement to the banner, you're going to add three fields of animated stars to the banner that move from left to right.

To finish the animated banner:

1. Choose Window⇨Library to open the document Library.

2. Drag an instance of the dark_star movie clip onto the Stage.

   If this looks somewhat familiar, it should. This is the same movie clip you used to create the mouse chaser in Chapter 15.

3. With the dark_star movie clip still selected, click the arrow to the left of the word Actions to open the Actions panel.

4. Choose Actions⇨Miscellaneous Actions and then double-click `evaluate`.

   The Expression field appears above the Script pane.

5. In the Expression field, type **this._x-=5**

   This expression moves the movie clip to the left in increments of five pixels. However, when it reaches the end of the movie clip, it keeps on going unless you add a conditional statement.

6. In the left pane of the Actions panel, choose Actions⇨Conditions/Loops and then double-click `if`.

   The action is added to the script, and the Condition field appears above the Script pane.

7. In the Condition field, type **this._x<0**

   As soon as the movie clip moves beyond the left border of the movie, the next action is executed.

8. In the left pane of the Actions panel, choose Actions⇨Miscellaneous Actions and then double-click `evaluate`.

   The Expression field appears above the Script pane.

9. In the Expression field, type **this._x=550**

   As soon as the movie clip moves beyond the left boundary of the Stage, this expression moves it back to the right side and it begins moving again.

10. Click the first line of code and in the parameter text box area, change the Clip Event to EnterFrame.

    Your finished code should resemble Listing 17-5. But wait, there's more.

Listing 17-5: **Adding Motion to the Banner**

```
onClipEvent (enterFrame) {
  this._x-=5;
  if (this._x<0) {
    this._x=550;
  }
}
```

11. Select the dark_star movie clip, and while holding down the Alt key (Windows) or Option key (Macintosh), drag down and to the left to create a duplicate instance of the symbol. Do this once more, this time dragging down and to the right.

    You should now have three instances of the movie clip on the Stage.

12. Select one of the duplicates and then click the arrow to the left of the word Actions to open the Actions panel.

13. Modify the existing code for the movie clip so the second line of code reads **this._x-=7**

14. Select the last duplicate and in the Actions panel, modify the second line of code to read **this._x-=12**

15. Choose Control⇨Test Movie.

    You should see three star fields moving across the banner at different speeds. As the star fields reach the end of the movie and reappear a time or two, eventually one starfield passes the other. If the motion is too frenetic for your taste, you can modify the ActionScript by choosing smaller values to make the star fields move more slowly. Figure 17-9 shows the banner tucked into a static HTML Page.

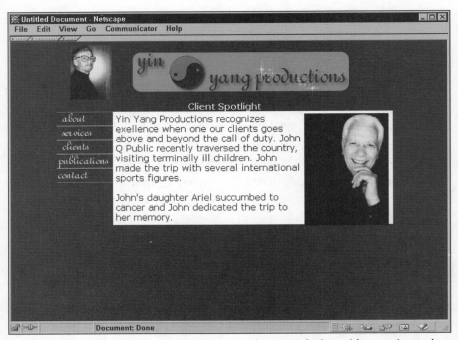

Figure 17-9: You can add excitement to a static HTML design with an animated banner.

Designer Notes

In this chapter, you were shown how easy it is to integrate Flash elements into your HTML designs. You learned how to open up a Web page in a different browser window from within a Flash movie. You learned to detect which version of the Flash Player your design is viewed with. And you also learned to create an intro for a static HTML page. Animated Flash banners were also presented, and the chapter project showed you how to spice up an HTML design with an animated splash banner.

Where to Go from Here

Now that you've worked your way through this book and the tutorials, you're beginning to see the awesome diversity ActionScript can add to your designs. The topics presented here are only the tip of the ActionScript iceberg. Literally, you could dabble full-time in ActionScript for the next year and still not master the language. However, that's what makes ActionScript so user friendly. You don't have to know it all — you need to know only enough for the project you are working on. As you venture forth with Flash ActionScript, make it a point to experiment. Make it a point to learn how to implement one new action into your work each week. Keep that up and by the end of the year, you'll have mastered 52 new actions.

To expand your knowledge of ActionScript, modify the projects you created while working through this book. View the work of other designers and ask yourself how a certain effect was created. Ask yourself if you can duplicate the effect and perhaps better it. ActionScript may seem daunting for a designer, someone whose first love is images and colors. However, the more you work with it, the more comfortable ActionScript becomes. Strive to make ActionScript as familiar as an old pair of bedroom slippers, your favorite song, or the faded old pair of jeans you refuse to toss out because they just feel so good. Do this, and you'll create some truly wonderful designs.

✦   ✦   ✦

What's on the CD-ROM

This appendix provides you with information on the contents of the CD that accompanies this book. (For the latest and greatest information, please refer to the ReadMe file located at the root of the CD.) Here is what you will find:

✦ System Requirements

✦ Using the CD with Windows, and Macintosh

✦ What's on the CD

✦ Troubleshooting

System Requirements

Make sure that your computer meets the minimum system requirements listed in this section. If your computer doesn't match up to most of these requirements, you may have a problem using the contents of the CD.

For Windows 9x, Windows 2000, Windows NT4 (with SP 4 or later), Windows Me, or Windows XP:

✦ Intel Pentium processor (Pentium II or better)

✦ 64 MB of available RAM, 128 MB recommended

✦ 800 x 600, 256-color display (1024 x 768, millions colors recommended)

✦ 100 MB of free hard disk space

✦ Adobe Type Manager Version 4 or later with Type 1 fonts

For Macintosh:

✦ Power Macintosh Processor (G3 or higher recommended)

✦ Mac OS 9.1 or later, MacOS X.1 or later

+ 64 MB of available RAM

+ 800 x 600, 256-color display (1024 x 768, millions of colors recommended)

+ 100 MB of free hard disk space

+ Adobe Type Manager Version 4 or later with Type 1 fonts

Using the CD with Windows

To install the items from the CD to your hard drive, follow these steps:

1. Insert the CD into your computer's CD-ROM drive.

2. A window will appear with the following options. Install, Explore eBook, Links, and Exit.

   Install: This will give you the option to install the supplied software and/or the author-created samples on the CD-ROM.

   Explore: Allows you to view the contents of the CD-ROM in its directory structure.

   eBook: Allows you to view an electronic version of the book.

   Links: Opens a hyperlinked page of the Web sites.

   Exit: Closes the autorun window.

Note: If you do not have autorun enabled or if the autorun window does not appear, follow the steps below to access the CD.

1. Click Start ⇨ Run.

2. In the dialog box that appears, type **d:\setup.exe**, where *d* is the letter of your CD-ROM drive. This will bring up the autorun window described above.

3. Choose the Install, Explore eBook, Links, or Exit option from the menu. (See Step 2 in the preceding list for a description of these options.)

Using the CD with the Mac OS

To install the items from the CD to your hard drive, follow these steps:

1. Insert the CD into your CD-ROM drive.

2. Double-click the icon for the CD after it appears on the Desktop.

3. Most programs come with installers; with those, you simply open the program's folder on the CD and double-click the Install or Installer icon. Note: To install some programs, just drag the program's folder from the CD window and drop it on your hard drive icon.

What's on the CD

The following sections provide a summary of the software and other materials you'll find on the CD.

Shareware programs are fully functional, trial versions of copyrighted programs. If you like particular programs register with their authors for a nominal fee and receive licenses, enhanced versions, and technical support. *Freeware programs* are free, copyrighted games, applications, and utilities. Unlike shareware, these programs do not require a fee or provide technical support. *GNU software* is governed by its own license, which is included inside the folder of the GNU product. See the GNU license for more details.

Trial, demo, or evaluation versions are usually limited either by time or functionality (such as being unable to save projects). Some trial versions are very sensitive to system date changes. If you alter your computer's date, the programs will "time out" and will no longer be functional.

Author-created materials

All author-created material from the book including code listings and samples are on the CD in the folder named "Author". In this folder you'll find all of the raw materials for each chapter project, as well as the finished project. You'll also find other goodies such as user-defined components that you can drag and drop into your designs. Where applicable, you'll also find a file that contains the finished project. These files are appended by _final.

Applications

The following applications are on the CD:

Acrobat Reader

Freeware Version. This program lets you view and print the Portable Document Format (PDF) files like the files on this CD. To find out more about using Adobe Acrobat Reader, choose the Reader Online Guide from the Help menu, or view the Acrobat.pdf file installed in the same folder as the program. You can also get more information by visiting the Adobe Systems Web site at www.adobe.com.

Macromedia Dreamweaver

If you want an idea of the magic you can include in your Web designs, check out this trial software. You can include sophisticated behaviors in your designs without having to cloud your mind with the first bit of JavaScript. You can also easily incorporate your Flash work in Dreamweaver.

Macromedia Fireworks

If you have the need for sophisticated image editing software that allows you to optimize graphics for the Web, Fireworks is the tool for you. You can combine vector graphics and bitmaps to create a sophisticated design that you can export as HTML and images, complete with all the JavaScript needed to pull off the effects you use.

Macromedia FreeHand

If you like to create sophisticated vector graphics, and find that the Flash tools — as good as they are — fall a bit short, give FreeHand a try. FreeHand makes it possible for you to create complex vector graphics and export them in Flash's native *.SWF format.

Swift 3D

Swift 3D is the solution you're looking for to add three-dimensional vector objects to your Flash movies. Swift 3D is a Windows®/Macintosh® application that you use to create and convert 3D images and animations to 3D vector graphics. Swift 3D exports the completed file in the Flash SWF format. Please visit Electric Rain's Web site at www.electricrain.org for the latest updates on this product.

WildForm SWfx

SWfx is an easy-to-use text animation tool. You can choose from over 200 different effects to create swirling text, swooping text, and fading text, to name a few. The animation you create is exported in Flash's native SWF format. Use animated text to spice up your Flash designs.

Electronic version of *Flash MX ActionScript For Designers*

The complete text of this book is on the CD in Adobe's Portable Document Format (PDF). You can read and search through the file with the Adobe Acrobat Reader (also included on the CD).

Troubleshooting

If you have difficulty installing or using any of the materials on the companion CD, try the following solutions:

+ **Turn off any anti-virus software that you may have running.** Installers sometimes mimic virus activity and can make your computer incorrectly believe that it is being infected by a virus. (Be sure to turn the anti-virus software back on later.)

✦ **Close all running programs.** The more programs you're running, the less memory is available to other programs. Installers also typically update files and programs; if you keep other programs running installation may not work properly.

✦ **Reference the ReadMe.txt:** Please refer to the ReadMe file located at the root of the CD-ROM for the latest product information at the time of publication.

If you still have trouble with the CD, please call the Wiley Publishing Customer Care phone number: (800) 762-2974. Outside the United States, call 1 (317) 572-3993. You can also contact Wiley Publishing Customer Service by e-mail at techsupdum@ wiley.com. Wiley Publishing will provide technical support only for installation and other general quality control items; for technical support on the applications themselves, consult the program's vendor or author.

✦   ✦   ✦

Flash Resources

Flash is extremely popular software. There is a plethora of information on the Internet about Flash. You can download tutorials, completed *.FLA documents, and music loops for your designs. There are also several ancillary, third-party plug-in manufacturers that feature interesting software you can use to enhance your designs. This software ranges from 2D animation programs to software that produces 3D animations in the *.SWF format. In this appendix, you'll find the URLs for these sites and a brief description of what you can expect to find at the site. This appendix is divided into three sections: resources, sounds, and third-party applications.

Resources

The Internet seems to have as many resources for Flash as it does Flash Web sites. This is a good thing. You can never get enough information. The sites in this section begin with the Macromedia resource sites followed by additional resources, which are listed in alphabetical order.

Macromedia resources

When you need to find out about an application, what better source than the maker? In this section you'll find Macromedia resources for Flash.

Macromedia Flash Designer and Developer Center

Here's a Macromedia site (www.macromedia.com/desdev/mx/flash) devoted exclusively to Flash MX. Download sample files and sample applications as well as view tutorials. This section of the Macromedia Web site is in its infancy as of this writing and is sure to grow as MX gains in popularity.

Macromedia Support

Macromedia offers extensive support for their flagship product at www.macromedia.com/support/flash. Here you'll find in-depth support in the form of technical notes, as well as tutorials prepared by Macromedia technicians. If you've run into a snag using ActionScript, chances are you can find a solution here.

Other Flash resources

In this section, you'll find Internet sites that are devoted to Flash. Many of the sites are treasure troves, jam-packed with Flash information and tutorials. Others are devoted to a specific aspect of Flash.

ActionScript.org

If you want to know all about ActionScript, ActionScript.org (`www.actionscript.org`) is the site to visit. At this site you'll find tutorials and other useful information about ActionScript.

Brendan Dawes-Digital Creative

At Brendan's site (`www.brendandawes.com/headshop/#`) you can view his experimental Flash work and download source files. Currently all of the source files are Flash 5, but that's sure to change in the near future.

Crazy Raven Productions

The portal to this site (`www.crazyraven.com`) lets you choose between two different interfaces. Once you've made a choice, check out the tutorial of the day or one of the other resources featured at this site.

Extreme Flash

At Extreme Flash (`www.extremeflash.com`), you'll find tutorials in the beginning, intermediate, and advanced categories. You can also download source files to analyze the files of other Flash designers.

Flahoo

Flahoo (`www.flahoo.com`) has links to sites designed with Flash. The links are divided by category. When you're between assignments, check out some of the sites featured here to get your creative juices flowing.

Flash Academy

At Flash Academy (`www.enetserve.com/tutorials`), you'll find another source for Flash tutorials. The site has three sections: tutorials, examples, and experiments.

Flash 5 ActionScript

Even though the current version of Flash is MX, you can still find some useful information at Flash5ActionScript (`www.flash5actionscript.com`). At this site, you can download source files and view examples of code.

Flash Kit

If you're looking for tutorials, sample *.FLA files, and a host of other information about Flash, you're sure to find a lot to pique your interest at this site (www. flashkit.com). In addition to tutorials, you can also download free music loops from this site. Sources files can also be found in abundance. Download them and dissect them at your convenience. If you download a source file from a previous version of Flash, Flash MX updates the ActionScript where needed.

Flash Magazine

For the latest information about Flash, point your Web browser to www. flashmagazine.com. The site features noteworthy news flashes about Flash plus other valuable information and resources about the software.

ProFlasher

ProFlasher (www.proflasher.com) features several forums where you can gain valuable information about Flash from other designers and developers. There is a link where you can request tutorials, a link where you can request a review of a site you are creating, a link devoted to ActionScript, and much more.

TurtleShell.com

At turtleshell.com (www.turtleshell.com/2000), you'll find resources and inspiration. The graphics are vector-based, and the author of the site uses them to good effect. When you click on a link, the vector shapes move and resize. This is the 2000 version of the site, which is still at the server. After you finish marveling the construction of the site, check out the Creation section, which features tutorials and other goodies. The main site (www.turtleshell.com) is undergoing a revision as this is being written. By the time you have this book in your hands, it may be up and running.

Virtual FX

The Internet seems to be a never-ending source of Flash information. Virtual FX (www.virtual-fx.net) features a tutorial search engine, source files, sample movies, and more. The source files and tutorials are currently in Flash 5 or earlier format. However, in a short matter of time, there's bound to be Flash MX source files and tutorials at this site. There is also a message board where you can communicate with other Flash designers.

Web Monkey

Web Monkey has a section of their site devoted to Flash. The URL is hotwired. lycos.com/webmonkey/multimedia/shockwave_flash. Here you'll find tutorials and information about the application. You can subscribe to Web Monkey and have this valuable resource delivered to your via e-mail on a regular basis.

We're Here Forums

Here's another site where you'll find a boatload of useful information for your Flash work. The site even features a forum for Flash MX ActionScript, even though the software has only been out for three days as this is written. You'll also find a wide variety of tutorials and downloads at this site.

Sounds

Sound has become a very important element in Flash designs. You can add background music to your Flash designs and use sound effects for buttons or timeline events. The sites in this section feature loops you can purchase or download for free and software applications you can use to create your own sounds.

Free Sound Effects

At this site (`www.stonewashed.net/sfx.html`), you'll find links to sites that offer free sound effects for use in your productions. Sound effects can be used as an interesting variations for button sounds, or you can mix them on the timeline with background music to emphasize a visual effect in your design.

GrooveMaker

Here's another site (`www.groovemaker.com`) that offers impressive sound mixing software. Available for both Windows and Macintosh platforms, this software can be controlled with an external midi-controller or keyboard. You can render the sounds you mix in the popular MP3 format.

Killer Sound

At this site (`www.killersound.com`), you can purchase royalty-free music for use in your Flash designs. Choose from a number of musical genres from classical to jazz and then preview the music while online.

Sonic Foundry.com

If your clients require sophisticated background music and other sounds, you can create your own background music with the software available at this site (`www.sonicfoundry.com`). Sonic Foundry's Acid Music is resampling software. The software features a timeline similar to that found in Flash. You can arrange sound samples on the timeline to create unique music loops. You can also purchase libraries of sound samples at this site in a wide variety of genres from hip-hop to classical. You can render your creation in a wide variety of sound formats. This software is only available for the PC.

Sonic Foundry also features a program called Sound Forge. You can use Sound Forge to record sounds or modify sounds with sophisticated effects like echo and reverb. This software is only available for the PC.

Sound Shopper.com

If you need royalty-free music loops, buttons sounds, or other sounds for your designs, you'll find a wide variety at this site (www.soundshopper.com). You can preview the sounds while online. The sounds are sold in bundles and priced quite reasonably.

Sound Strike

Soundstrike.com (www.soundstrike.com) offers free sound loops for download and other loop packs you can purchase. You can also purchase a bundle of button sounds.

Third-Party Applications

Flash is such a popular application, everyone seems to want a piece of the pie. There are several very useful applications you can use to enhance your designs. In this section, you'll find a brief description of the type of software offered by the vendor, plus the URL to the Web site where you can purchase the software, download a demo version, or find out more information about the application.

Electric Rain

At this Web site (www.electricrain.org), you'll find several solutions for including 3D artwork in your designs. Their main product, Swift 3D2.0, is used to create animations of 3D objects. The completed projects can be exported as .SWF movies. They also produce plug-ins for popular 3D software, that are used to generate *.SWF Movies from 3D animations and scenes created in the 3D application.

FlashJester

FlashJester (www.flashjester.com) features interesting products that you can use to augment your work. At this writing, all of their software is being updated to support Flash MX.

Flax

Flax (www.flaxfx.com) is another third-party program you can use to add text effects to your Flash work. You can choose from 31 effects that you can tweak using sliders and buttons. When the effect is the way you want it, you can export the file as a *.SWF file for inclusion in your design.

Sorenson

At Sorenson (www.sorenson.com), you can download a copy of Squeeze, which is software for compressing video files into the *.FLX format for importing into Flash or as an *.SWF movie. The software has settings for different connection speeds and does an admirable job of producing a small file size with the least amount of image degradation possible for the intended connection speed.

Swish

If you like text effects, Swish (www.swishzone.com) offers a relatively inexpensive program that you can use to add animated text to your designs. The site offers tutorials and support for Swish users.

Toon Boom Studio

Toon Boom Studio is a sophisticated 2D animation program that features lip synching. You can use the program to create 2D animations that can be imported directly into Flash MX. You can download an evaluation copy from their Web site (www.toonboomstudio.com) to see if the software is beneficial for your designs.

Wildform.com

At this Web site (www.wildform.com), you can purchase a standalone program called SWfX that you can use to create some interesting text effects for your productions. The site also features a useful resources section with informative tutorials and source files for download.

✦   ✦   ✦

Flash Inspiration

◆ ◆ ◆ ◆

Some days the creative juices flow like the headwaters of a clear mountain stream; other days, they're stagnant like a slow river in the heat of summer. When you find your creativity is at a low ebb, you can find inspiration at many of the sites listed in this section. Each site uses Flash in a unique or artistic way to create a compelling site that keeps visitors returning.

When you're at a loss for what to do or you simply want to explore a site that's visually exciting, visit one of the sites listed in this appendix. Begin your journey at Macromedia's site of the day and branch out from there. If the site lists the URL or a link to the designer's Web site, visit that site for more inspiration. You can also find Flash sites by typing Flash into your favorite search engine. The sites in this appendix begin with Macromedia's site. The sites that follow are listed in no particular order, which is probably the way you look find inspiration on the net — in no particular order.

Macromedia Site of the Day

Macromedia's Site of the Day (www.macromedia.com/showcase) is generally created with Flash. You'll find excellent examples of the latest innovations created by avant garde Flash designers. You'll find the feature sites get you thinking and push your own design envelope to come up with new and interesting uses for Flash.

While you're at the site of the day, check out the Archive section for previous sites of the day. The site's designer is listed along with information about the site.

Eva Hesse

This site (www.sfmoma.org/hesse) uses Flash to explore the work of Eva Hesse. During the '60s, this artist created sculptures and paintings. The site is informative and features an interesting navigation system.

Madonna

This popular singer's Web site (www.madonna.com) features an innovative navigation system. Move your cursor over one of the moving images and then drag down. When the three images line up, a different song is loaded.

John Frieda

At John Frieda's site (www.johnfrieda.com/flash.htm), you'll find links to two excellent Flash productions: Sheer Blonde and Relax. Both movies promote hair products and combine an excellent use of text drop-down menus with bitmap images. The Sheer Blonde side of the site features an intro song and the models used to promote the products are easy on the eyes.

n.fuse.gfx

This site (www.nfusegfx.com) gives the viewer the option of choosing a low-bandwidth or high-bandwidth site. Both options provide excellent eye candy, intriguing background music, and an interesting navigation system.

Pickled the Movie

This branch of Billabong's site (www.billabong-usa.com) was created by Juxt Interactive. You'll find an excellent example of animated buttons here and an artful balance of vector and bitmap images. Like most Juxt Interactive sites, there's an element of fun involved. Enjoy.

Rob Allen Photography

This photographer's Web site (www.roballen.ca) features a moving navigation bar like the one you created in the Chapter 12 chapter project and a tasteful balance of black and white bitmap images to showcase the photographer's images.

Pepworks.com

This title bar for Pepworks.com (www.pepworks.com) advertises designs, games, and fun. The site has a compelling introduction. Click the Leo's Great Day button for an example of an excellent Flash game.

Juxt Interactive

Juxt Interactive (www.juxtinteractive.com) has designed some of the more innovative Flash sites in existence today. Their own site is a perfect example of this. They provide an excellent balance of stationary and animated graphics along with an interesting drag-and-drop navigation system in their portfolio section. You can launch some of their impressive designs right from the portfolio section.

Dox Thrash Revealed

The former Macromedia site of the day (http://www.philamuseum.org/ exhibitions/exhibits/thrash/flash.html) is devoted to the work of an artist whose career spanned five decades. The navigation menu is set up on a timeline of key years in the artist's career. Move your mouse over a button and a tooltip appears with thumbnail images. Click the button and the images load in a target window.

Lenny Kravitz.com

Lenny Kravitz's Web site (www.lennykravitz.com) has an animated preloader, a pop-up navigation menu, and a jukebox that fans can use to preview the musician's latest work. The movie loads quickly despite a heavy use of bitmap images.

Jaguar X Type

Jaguar.com (www.jaguar.com.au), an Australian Web site, uses Flash to introduce the manufacturer's new model. After the movie loads, move your mouse around the screen and a movie clip with an animation follows. The animation changes size as you move it around the screen, an effect no doubt achieved by altering the properties of the movie clip that houses the animation.

Velocity Studio

At Velocity Studio (www.velocitystudio.com), you'll find a unique preloader. The site features a stunning use of bitmap images and a unique navigation menu that seems to actively defy your attempts to choose a button and then click it.

Milla and Partner

Go to `www.milla.de` and click the Flash link. The site is in German, but offers an example of a unique navigation menu and some very interesting visual effects.

Andy Foulds

Photographer's Web sites always seem to be the epitome of good taste and this one (`www.foulds2000.freeserve.co.uk`) is no exception. Entertain yourself with one of the amusements while the main site loads. After the main site loads, click a link to view examples of Andy's photography or Web designs.

Tweened.com

After this site (`www.tweened.com`) loads, use your arrow keys to navigate the site. A cute little animated cartoon figure jumps up and down when you press the Up arrow key and crouches when you press the Down arrow key. When you roll your mouse over the character, a bubble pops up with a saying. Do it once too often and the saying in the bubble informs you that the character is ignoring you and ceases to recognize your existence.

Simian Volume 6 Revolt

Simian Volume 6 Revolt (`www.simian.nu/#`)is listed as an experimental online Flash narrative. You can view the site in a pop-up window or full screen (Internet Explorer only). After the movie loads, click the small dot to launch various parts of the site. At one part of the site, a background bitmap images assembles itself block by block as you move your mouse over the screen. Some of the content takes a while to load, but the visual effects are worth the wait.

Pray Station

At praystation.com (`www.praystation.com`), you can view the online Flash explorations of Joshua Davis. Click a link in the left window to experience some very compelling visual effects. The effects in this site feature some very sophisticated ActionScript. Take a look at the animations and see if you can figure out how they were created.

Audi A4 Avant

Audi uses Flash to introduce the Audi A4 Avant (`www.audi-a4.com/avant/a4_avant.html`). The site's preloader features bitmap images. Tasteful background music and an intriguing navigation menu are a few of the features you'll find here.

John Coltrane

The life of legendary musician John Coltrane (`www.johncoltrane.com`) is portrayed through the use of Flash. The quick loading site features another example of an innovative navigation device, similar to the flyout menu project in Chapter 10, yet done entirely with text.

✦ ✦ ✦

Index

SYMBOLS

* (asterisk) with `random` method, 109
, (comma) separating array elements, 153
{} (curly braces) for statements in code, 38
. (dot) as separator in code, 38, 39
// (forward slashes) for comments, 38–39, 70
() (parentheses) for parameters in code, 38, 39
" (quotation marks) for string literal data, 143
; (semi-colon) as end of line identifier, 38, 39

A

absolute mode for target path, 130, 131
Acrobat Reader (on CD-ROM), 359
action books. *See also specific books*
    expanding to display actions, 22, 23
    path to actions, 19–20
actions. *See also specific actions and books*
    adding to your script, 29
    assigning to buttons, 7, 74–75, 91–96
    assigning to keyframes, 7, 29, 70–71
    assigning to objects, 29, 87–91
    compatibility issues, 26
    deleting from your script, 31
    deprecated, 26
    designation for frames with actions assigned, 69
    displaying information about, 34–35
    drop-down menu, 29
    expanding books to display, 22, 23
    finding using Index book, 4, 26
    for Flash Player, 30
    hierarchy, rearranging, 31
    learning as you need them, 21
    looking up in Reference panel, 34
    for navigating, 76–80
    overview, 10
    parameter text boxes for, 30
    path to, 19–20, 51
    Reference panel for, 17
    reserved keywords, 40–41

Actions book. *See also specific books and actions*
    Browser/Network book, 23
    Conditions/Loops book, 24
    Miscellaneous book, 24
    Movie Clip Control book, 23–24
    Movie Control book, 22
    overview, 21–24
    Printing book, 24
    User Defined Functions book, 24
    Variables book, 24
Actions command (Window menu), 27
Actions layer, creating, 69–70
Actions panel
    action books in, 19–20
    adding actions to your script, 29
    context menu, 37
    deleting actions from your script, 31
    Designer panel layout and, 27
    expert mode, 28, 35, 36
    Find and Replace button, 33
    Find button, 33
    Insert a Target Path button, 130
    modes, 28, 35
    Move the Selected Actions Down button, 31
    Move the Selected Actions Up button, 31
    normal mode, 28, 35
    opening, 27
    Options menu, 35–36
    overview, 20–21
    Pin Current Script button, 32
    Reference panel, 4, 17
    Scene button, 191
    Script pane, 21
    setting breakpoints in, 289
    switching modes, 35
    using with other panels, 28
    viewing options, 35
ActionScript. *See also code; debugging; scripts*
    as design element, 12–14
    HTML design versus, 52
    JavaScript versus, 8–9
    overview, 8–12
    questions to consider, 16–17
    uses for designers, 4–7
ActionScript loops. *See loops*
ActionScript objects. *See objects*
ActionScript.org site, 364
AIFF sound format, 258

alias for target path, 132
Allen, Rob, 370
`_alpha` property, 44, 48, 169
anchors, named, 189, 193–194
AND operator, 158–159
Andy Foulds Web site, 372
animated buttons
    animating the label, 200–203
    creating movie clip for, 200
    nesting the movie clip in a button symbol, 203–204
    uses for, 199
animated Flash banner project
    adding motion to the banner, 353–354
    creating the banner, 352
    overview, 352
animated preloader. *See preloaders*
animatedBannerBegin.fla file, 352
animation
    animated buttons, 199–204
    animated Flash banner project, 352–354
    animated preloader, 298–306
    for drag-and-drop elements, 238
    interactive animation project, 183–187
    uses for, 14
applications on CD-ROM, 359–360
arithmetic operators, 145, 147
Arithmetic Operators book, 24
Array user-defined component type, 132
arrays
    accessing, 161–163
    associative, 154–155
    combining elements in a variable, 152
    comparing multiple values to, 151–152
    creating, 152–153
    creating elements for, 153–154
    overview, 6, 151
    for populating dynamic text boxes, 224–225
    for random quote generation, 160
    ticker text marquee project, 225–230
    uses for, 6
    using word processor to create data, 154, 160
    variables versus, 151–152

artwork. *See* graphics; movie clips
AS-02Start.fla file, 45
.asf files, 84
Assets folder, 58–59
assigning actions
  to buttons, 7, 74–75, 91–96
  to keyframes, 7, 29, 70–71
  to objects, 29, 87–91
associative arrays, 154–155
asterisk (*) with random method, 109
attaching a sound, 269–270, 276, 277
attachSound method of Sound
  object, 270, 276
Audi A4 Avant Web site, 373
audio. *See* Sound object; soundtracks
.avi files, 84

B
bandwidth. *See also* preloaders
  analyzing movies with Bandwidth
    Profiler, 299–301
  analyzing movies with Show
    Streaming command,
    301–302
  defined, 298
  playing movies and, 298
  preloader for large movies, 298
Bandwidth Profiler, 299–301
Bandwidth Profiler command (View
  menu), 299
banner ads
  animated Flash banner project,
    352–354
  creating, 343–344
  overview, 341–342
  planning, 342
banner.swf file, 136
base movie
  contents of, 120
  creating, 121
  for hiding your designs or
    techniques, 138
  level of, 121
  loading movies into, 121, 123–125
  unloading movies, 123, 124–125
Billabong Web site, 370
bitmaps
  nesting in movie clips, 100
  swapping nested bitmaps, 100,
    101–102
black (syntax coloring), 39
Blank Keyframe command
  (Insert menu), 68
blank keyframes. *See also* keyframes
  converting standard frames to, 68
  creating, 68
  for movie clips, 83

removing content from
    keyframes, 68
  timeline designation for, 66
  uses for, 68
blue (syntax coloring), 39
BODMAS acronym for operator
  precedence, 146
books. *See* action books;
    specific books
Boolean data variables, 142
Boolean expressions
  defined, 53
  for down arrow, 219–221
  for On When Pressed button, 196
  for password evaluation, 53, 159
  using, 159
Boolean user-defined component
  type, 133
breaking movies into segments.
    See also scenes
  base movie, 120, 121
  dimensions for segment movies,
    121, 125
  levels for movies, 121
  naming section movies, 123
  planning, 120
  template for section movies,
    121–123
  uses for, 119–120
breakpoints
  buttons for, 291
  debugging a movie with, 290–292
  deleting, 291–292
  setting in Actions panel, 289
  setting in Debugger, 291
  storing, 290, 291
  with trace action, 290
Brendan Dawes-Digital Creative
  Web site, 364
Browser/Network Control book.
    See also specific actions
  getURL action, 77–80, 339, 340,
    347, 348
  loadMovie action, 123–124, 125,
    127–129, 138, 267
  loadVariables action, 216, 217,
    218–219
  overview, 23
  unloadMovie action, 123,
    124–125, 267
browsers. *See* Web browsers
button.fla file, 96
buttonPhotography.fla file, 114
buttons
  ActionScript uses for, 7, 12
  animated, 199–204
  assigning actions to, 7, 74–75,
    91–96

CEO button, 138
  to change size and opacity of
    movie clip, 44–49
  copying code between, 204, 206
  creating, 72–73
  End of Page button, 221
  Event Sync option for sounds, 260
  frames for, 72
  invisible, 74, 75
  Key Press event for, 93–94
  layers for, 72, 73
  mouse events, 9, 42, 75, 92–94
  multiple events for, 92–93
  for navigation, 95
  nesting movie clips in, 203–204
  On When Press button, 194–196
  play action with, 76
  Reset button for Flash forms, 308
  rndFrame action with, 116–117
  rollOver and rollOut events
    for, 93
  Skip Intro button, 260, 347–348
  for sound controller project,
    275–276
  states, 73–74
  Submit button for Flash forms,
    308–310
  swapping labels for, 198–199
  symbol, 42
  for tooltips, programming,
    237–238
  for user-customizable interface,
    programming, 242–243
  uses for, 81

C
call function action, 112–113,
  237, 243
calling functions, 112–113, 116–117
CD-ROM
  animatedBannerBegin.fla file
    on, 352
  AS-02Start.fla file on, 45
  button.fla file on, 96
  buttonPhotography.fla file on, 114
  colorComponents.fla file on, 179
  contents, 359–360
  currentDate.fla file on, 247
  currentTime.fla file on, 249
  dragNdrop.fla file on, 240
  drawOutside.fla file on, 60
  eCommerce.fla file on, 312
  flyoutMenu.fla file on, 204
  interface.fla file on, 241
  Jittery.fla file on, 199
  marqueeComponent.fla file on, 230
  mouseChaserBegin.fla file on, 316

movingNavBar.fla file on, 251
Orgchart folder on, 136
orgChart.fla file on, 136
randomStars.fla file on, 331
rndQuote.fla file on, 160
scrollText.fla file on, 217
scrollText.txt files on, 217
scrollTick.fla file on, 225
simpleChaserBegin.fla file on, 318
slideShow.fla file on, 334
Soundcontroller folder on, 274
submarine.fla file on, 183
system requirements, 357–358
technical support, 361
toolTips.fla file on, 238
troubleshooting, 360–361
centering Flash objects on HTML
    page, 349
CEO button, programming, 138
ceo.jpg tile, 137, 138
CGI script for HTML mail forwarding,
    308–309
character options, setting, 212–213
child movie clips, 131
Clear Keyframe command (Insert
    menu), 68
clients, knowing expectations of, 55
clip events. *See also* events
    available events, 88–89
    defined, 9
    overview, 87–88
code. *See also* debugging; scripts
    copying between buttons, 204, 206
    editing in expert mode, 36
    formatting, 38–39
    hints in expert mode, 40
    identifiers in, 38–39
    process of creating, 19
    reserved keywords, 40–41
    syntax coloring, 37, 39
code handlers, 9. *See also* events
code hints in expert mode, 40
Color object
    creating, 175
    methods of, 175
    setRGB method, 175–176, 244
    setTransform method, 174–180
Color user-defined component
    type, 133
colorComponents.fla file, 179
colors
    Color object, 175–180
    random, for mouse chaser, 319
    reserved keywords warning, 40
    syntax coloring, 37, 39
    user-customizable interface,
        241–245

Coltrane, John, 373
combining
    array elements in a variable, 152
    contents of variables, 143–144, 150
comma (,) separating array
    elements, 153
comment action, 293
comments
    adding to ActionScripts, 293
    for debugging ActionScripts,
        292–293
    forward slashes for, 38–39, 70
    for keyframes, 70
Common Libraries command
    (Window menu), 113
Common Libraries menu, adding
    effects Libraries to, 113
communicating between timelines,
    129–130
Comparison Operators book, 24–25
compatibility
    deprecated actions and, 26
    detecting Flash Player version,
        345–346
    Flash Player versions and, 26
competitor URLs, researching, 55
Component Definition dialog box,
    132–134
components
    in colorComponents.fla file, 179
    Flash UI Components book, 26
    in marqueeComponent.fla file, 230
    overview, 43
    ScrollBar component, 249–250
    symbol, 43
    user-defined, 132–135
concatenating variables, 143–144, 150
conditional statements. *See also*
        if action
    for animated button label, 202
    Boolean expressions in, 53, 159
    to change rotation, 202
    controlling the flow of a movie, 53
    creating, 156
    defined, 11
    for detecting Flash Player version,
        344, 345
    example, 11
    for Flash slide show project,
        336–337
    for Key objects, 181–182
    logical operators with, 158–159
    multiple outcomes for, 156–157
    overview, 24, 155–156
    for password evaluation, 53
    for preloaders, 305, 306

Conditions/Loops book. *See also*
        conditional statements;
        if action; loops
    else action, 47, 156–157, 253
    elseif action, 156–157
    for action, 105
    overview, 24
constants, 25
Constants book
    Down constant, 184
    overview, 25
    Up constant, 184
context menu of Actions panel, 37
Control menu
    Debug Movie command, 286, 291
    Test Movie command, 49, 163
controlling the flow of Flash movies,
    53–54
Convert to Blank Keyframes command
    (Modify menu), 68
Convert to Keyframes command
    (Modify menu), 68
Convert to Symbol command
    (Insert menu), 98, 205,
    232, 252, 280
Convert to Symbol dialog box
    for graphics, 98, 99
    for movie clips, 280
    for navigation bar, 205, 252
    for tooltip shapes, 232
converting
    buttons to movie clips, 252
    graphics to a symbol, 98, 99
    movie clip to symbol, 280
    movie clips to masks, 60–62
    navigation bar to a symbol, 205
    navigation bar to flyout menu,
        205–208
    standard frames to keyframes, 68
    timeline animation to movie clip,
        98–99
    tooltip shapes to symbols, 232
Copy Frames command
    (Edit menu), 98
copying. *See* duplicating
Crazy Raven Productions Web site, 364
Create New Symbol dialog box
    for button templates, 197–198
    for buttons, 72, 194–195, 203–204
    for label templates, 197
    for movie clips, 82, 99, 200, 311,
        323, 327
createEmptyMovieClip method, 320
curly braces ({}) for statements in
        code, 38
currentDate.fla file, 247

_currentframe property, 169
currentTime.fla file, 249
curveTo Drawing method, 321
Custom Modem Settings dialog
         box, 301
Customize command
         (Debug menu), 201

D

dark_star movie clip, 316, 353, 354
Data event, 89
Date object
   creating, 245
   displaying current date using,
         246–247
   displaying current time using,
         247–249
   example files on CD-ROM, 247, 249
   methods for dates, 246
   methods for times, 247–248
   retrieving date from host
         computer, 246
   uses for, 14
Davis, Joshua, 372
Debug menu
   Customize command, 201
   List Objects command, 287
   List Variables command, 288
Debug Movie command (Control
         menu), 286, 291
Debugger
   breakpoints with, 290–292
   displaying list of movie objects, 287
   launching, 286
   overview, 285–286
   watching a variable, 286–287
debugging ActionScripts
   breakpoints for, 290–292
   comments for, 292–293
   Debugger for, 285–287
   Movie Explorer for, 293, 294
   need for, 283
   testing your design, 284–285
   trace action for, 288–289
decision making. See conditional
         statements
declaring variables
   basic process, 148–149
   local variables, 149–150
Default user-defined component
         type, 132
deleting
   actions from your script, 31
   breakpoints, 291–292
   content from keyframes, 68
   frames, 68
   parts of code in expert mode, 36
   scenes, 191–192
   undoing, 42

demo versions of programs, 359
deprecated actions, 26
Deprecated book, 26
Designer panel layout, 27
detecting
   Flash Player version, 345–346
   ready-made Macromedia tools
         for, 346
DirectX, video files supported by, 84
displaying. See also hiding and
         showing
   actions information, 34–35
   current date, 246–247
   current time, 247–249
   expanding action books to
         display actions, 22, 23
   line numbers in scripts, 35, 290
   link in pop-up window, 340
   list of movie objects with
         Debugger, 287
   list of variables with Debugger, 288
   number of bytes loaded, 306
Distribute to Layers command
         (Modify menu), 234
do while loops, 103, 106–107
Document command
         (Modify menu), 266
document Library
   creating button templates using,
         198–199
   creating movie clip instances
         from, 86
   gathering assets from, 59
   opening .FLA files as, 59
   overview, 43–44
   storing effects embedded in
         movie clips in, 113
   storing user-defined components
         in, 134–135
   using symbols from, 43, 100
   working with sound from, 268–269
Document Properties dialog box, 266
dot (.) as separator in code, 38, 39
down arrow for scrolling, 219–221
Down button state, 74
Down constant, in interactive
         animation project, 184
downloading
   extensions, 59, 135
   user-defined components, 135
Dox Thrash Revealed Web site, 371
drafting your design, 56
Drag Out event, 92
Drag Over event, 92
drag-and-drop elements
   closing a window, 240
   creating a drag-and-drop window,
         239–240
   example file on CD-ROM, 240

motion tween animation for, 238
   startDrag action, 238, 239, 240
dragNdrop.fla file, 240
drawOutside.fla file, 60
Dreamweaver (Macromedia)
   on CD-ROM, 359
   integrating Flash with, 348–351
drop-down menus of action
         groups, 29
_droptarget property, 169
duplicateMovieClip action
   cloning movie clips using, 87
   duplicating objects using, 182–183
   motion trails using, 326–330
duplicating
   cloning movie clips, 87
   code between buttons, 204, 206
   frames, 98–99
   objects with
         duplicateMovieClip
         action, 182–183
   rollOut and rollOver events, 93
   scenes, 192
.dv files, 84
dynamic text boxes
   creating, 211–212
   displaying current date in, 246–247
   displaying current time in, 248–249
   options, 212
   in organizational chart project,
         135, 138
   populating with array elements,
         224–225
   rich formatted text for, 213–215
   scrolling text box project, 217–223
   scrolling text box using ScrollBar
         component, 249–250
   setting character options,
         212–213
   ticker text marquee project,
         225–230
   uses for, 209–210

E

e-commerce catalog project, 312–313
eCommerce.fla file, 312
Edit Envelope dialog box, 261–262
Edit menu
   Copy Frames command, 98
   Edit Selected command, 239
   Paste Frames command, 99
   Paste in Place command, 252
   Undo command, 42
Edit Selected command
         (Edit menu), 239
editing
   code in expert mode, 36
   sound characteristics, 261–262
   symbols, 42

effects
  custom effects for sounds,
    260–262
  free sound effects, 366
  movie clips as effects modules, 113
  for soundtracks, 259, 260–262
  storing in document Library, 113
Electric Rain Web site, 367
else action
  adding to script, 47
  in conditional statements with
    multiple outcomes,
    156–157
  in moving navigation bar
    project, 253
elseif action, 156–157
e-mail forwarding, CGI script for,
    308–309
e-mail links, creating, 216–217
embedding fonts, 213
embedding video files in movie clips,
    84, 85
empty movie clip, creating, 320
End of Page button, 221
EnterFrame event, 89
erasing. See deleting
error messages and warnings. See also
    debugging ActionScripts
  for incorrect variable names,
    40, 148
  for loops unable to execute in
    single frame, 103
  <not set yet>, 47, 90
eval action, 155
evaluate action
  for animating banner ad, 353
  for animating button label, 201–202
  for down arrow, 220–221
  expressions using, 172
  in interactive animation project,
    184–185
  in moving navigation bar project,
    253–254
evaluation versions of programs, 359
event handlers. See also on
    (Release) event handler
  for button symbol, 42
  for movie clips, 89
Event Sync option, 260
events
  clip events, 9, 87–89
  defined, 81
  mouse events, 9, 42, 75, 92–94
  for objects, 88–89
  overview, 9
  plain English for planning, 57
  sound events, 259–260
  triggering at sound completion,
    273–274

evolution of an ActionScript, 52–54
expanding books to display actions,
    22, 23
expert mode
  code hints in, 40
  creating ActionScripts in, 36
  described, 29
  formatting code in, 38–39
  identifiers, 38–39
  switching from normal mode, 35
  syntax coloring in, 37, 39
Export as File command
    (Options menu), 41
exporting
  scripts, 41
  sounds, settings for, 263–265
expressions
  Boolean, 53, 159, 196, 219–221
  for changing properties by given
    value, 172
  creating mathematical
    expressions, 145–146
  defined, 143
  in moving navigation bar project,
    253–254
  operator precedence for, 146
  overview, 144
extensions, 59
Extensions Manager, 59
Extreme Flash Web site, 364
eye candy
  custom mouse cursor, 325–326
  Flash slide show project, 334–337
  hiding and showing the mouse
    cursor, 324–325
  motion trails, 326–330
  mouse chaser using Flash MX
    object, 318–321
  mouse chaser using movie clip,
    315–318
  movie clip as mask, 321–324
  overview, 13
  starburst backdrop, 330–333

F
file formats
  supported sound formats, 258
  supported video formats, 84
File menu
  Import command, 58, 84, 259
  New from Template command, 343
  Open as Library command, 59,
    113, 134
  Publish Settings command,
    193, 266
  Save As command, 123
Find and Replace button (Actions
    panel), 33

Find button (Actions panel), 33
Find command (Options menu), 33
Find dialog box, using, 33
finding
  actions using Index book, 4, 26
  and replacing text in a script, 33
  text in a script, 33
Fireworks (Macromedia), on
    CD-ROM, 360
.FLA files, opening as libraries, 59
Flahoo Web site, 364
Flash 5 ActionScript Web site, 364
Flash Academy Web site, 364
Flash animations. See animation
Flash Deployment Kit, 346
Flash forms
  creating elements for, 306–307
  example, 14
  HTML forms versus, 297, 306
  Reset button, 308
  Submit button, 308–310
Flash introduction, creating, 346–348
Flash Kit Web site, 365
Flash Magazine Web site, 365
Flash movies. See also movie clips;
    planning your ActionScript
    movie; timelines
  analyzing for bandwidth
    problems, 299–302
  base movie, 120, 121
  breaking into segments, 119–123
  controlling flow of, 53–54
  creating target movie clip, 125–127
  dimensions for segment movies,
    121, 125
  hiding your designs or
    techniques, 138
  introduction movie, 346–348
  loading into base movie,
    123–124, 125
  loading into target movie clip,
    127–129
  navigating with ActionScript,
    76–80
  organizational chart example,
    135–139
  passwords for access to
    parts of, 53
  planning, 51–62
  preloaders for, 6, 102, 103,
    298–306
  size of, 119, 120
  slide show project, 334–337
  testing, 128, 284–285
  unloading, 123, 124–125
  user-defined components for,
    132–135

Flash MX ActionScript For Designers,
   electronic version on
   CD-ROM, 360
Flash objects. *See* objects
Flash Player
   actions for, 30
   compatibility for older
      versions, 26
   detecting version of, 345–346
   Flash movie creation and, 53
Flash slide show project
   ActionScript to move the image,
      336–337
   customizing for a client, 337
   examining code for, 334
   example file for, 334
   initializing the variables, 335
Flash UI Components book, 26.
      See also components
FlashJester Web site, 367
Flax Web site, 367
flow, controlling for Flash movies,
      53–54
flyout menu project
   beginning the project, 204
   converting navigation bar to a
      symbol, 205
   converting navigation bar to
      flyout menu, 205–208
   overview, 204, 208
flyoutMenu.fla file, 204
_focuserect property, 169
Font user-defined component
      type, 133
fonts, embedding, 213
for loops, 103, 104–106
formatting code, 38–39
forms. *See* Flash forms
forward slashes (//) for comments,
      38–39, 70
Foulds, Andy, 372
Frame command (Insert menu), 67
frame-based loops, 102, 103.
      See also loops
frames. *See also* keyframes
   adding, 67
   for buttons, 72
   converting standard frames
      to keyframes, 68
   copying and pasting, 98–99
   creating, 66–67
   deleting, 68
   designation on timeline, 66
   first frame of movie clips, 82
   frame-based loops, 102, 103
   goto action for, 77
   last frame of movie clips, 83, 86
   navigating to random frame, 97,
      114–117

   printable, 310–311
   types of, 66
   uses for, 66
_framesloaded property, 169
FreeHand (Macromedia)
   on CD-ROM, 360
   as planning tool, 56
Frieda, John, 370
function action, 110–111, 236, 243
functions
   calling, 112–113, 116–117
   creating, 110–111
   generating random frame number,
      14–16
   getting properties of objects,
      173–174
   getting property values, 174
   overview, 110
   reserved keywords, 40–41
   for tooltips, 235–237
   for user-customizable interface,
      243–245
Functions book, 25

G

getDate method of Date object, 246
getDay method of Date object, 246
getFullYear method of Date
      object, 246
getHours method of Date object, 247
getMinutes method of Date
      object, 247
getMonth method of Date object, 246
getProperty function
   getting properties for objects,
      173–174
   getting property values, 174
getRGB method of Color object, 175
getSeconds method of Date
      object, 248
getTransform method of Color
      object, 175
getURL action
   opening URL in different size
      window, 79–80
   parameters, 78
   for pop-up window, 339, 340
   for Skip Intro button, 347, 348
   using, 77–79
Go To command (View menu), 191
goto action
   adding to script, 47, 77
   for frame-based loops, 103
   parameters, 77
   for returning movie clips to first
      frame, 83, 86
   using, 77

graphics
   converting to a symbol, 98, 99
   nesting bitmaps in movie
      clips, 100
   swapping nested bitmaps,
      100, 101–102
graphics symbol
   converting graphics to, 98, 99
   interactivity for, 42, 81
   overview, 42
green (syntax coloring), 39
GrooveMaker Web site, 366

H

_height property, 169
Hesse, Eva, 369
hide method of Mouse object,
      324, 325
hiding and showing. *See also*
      displaying
   mouse cursor, 324–325
   tooltips, 236–237
   windows, 240
   your designs or techniques, 138
hierarchy of actions, rearranging, 31
hints for code, 40
Hit button state, 74
HTML. *See also* integrating Flash
      with HTML
   ActionScript versus, 52
   centering Flash objects on HTML
      page, 349
   CGI script for HTML mail
      forwarding, 308–309
   Flash forms versus HTML forms,
      297, 306
   JavaScript to open Flash file in
      sized window, 341
   JavaScript to open link in another
      window, 340
   tags for rich formatted text,
      213, 214
hyperlinks
   creating a text hyperlink, 223–224
   creating an e-mail link, 216–217

I

identifiers in ActionScript code, 38–39
if action. *See also* conditional
      statements
   adding to script, 46–47
   for animated button label, 202
   in conditional statements with
      multiple outcomes, 157
   creating conditional statements
      using, 156
   for detecting Flash Player version,
      344, 345

for Flash slide show project, 336–337
in interactive animation project, 184, 185, 186–187
for Key objects, 181–182
in moving navigation bar project, 253–254
for On When Pressed button, 195–196
in scrolling text box project, 219–220, 222, 223
images. *See* graphics; movie clips
Import command (File menu), 58, 84, 259
Import dialog box, 259
Import from File command (Options menu), 41
Import Video dialog box, 84–85
Import Video Settings dialog box, 85–86
importing. *See also* loading
audio for video files, 85
items to Assets folder, 58–59
scripts, 41–42
video files into movie clips, 84–86
Index book, finding actions using, 4, 26
input text boxes
creating, 210–211
options, 210–211
setting character options, 212–213
Insert a Target Path button (Actions panel), 130
Insert menu. *See also* New Symbol command (Insert menu)
Blank Keyframe command, 68
Clear Keyframe command, 68
Convert to Symbol command, 98, 205, 232, 252, 280
Frame command, 67
Keyframe command, 68
Layer command, 70
Remove Frames command, 68
Scene command, 190
Insert Target Path dialog box, 48, 90, 128
installing items from CD
on Macintosh computers, 358
troubleshooting, 360–361
on Windows computers, 358
integrating Flash with HTML
animated Flash banner project, 352–354
banner ads, 341–344
detecting the Flash Player version, 345–346
Flash introduction, 346–348

integrating Flash with Dreamweaver, 348–351
pop-up window with JavaScript, 339–341
interactive interfaces
displaying date and time, 245–249
drag-and-drop elements, 238–240
moving navigation bar project, 251–255
ScrollBar component for, 249–250
tooltips, 231–238
user-customizable interface, 241–245
interactivity. *See also* interactive interfaces; navigating
buttons for, 95–96
for graphics symbol, 42, 81
interactive animation project, 183–187
movie clips for, 82–83
interface.fla file, 241
introduction movie clip
overview, 346–347
Skip Intro button, 347–348
invisible buttons, 74, 75. *See also* buttons
isdown action, in interactive animation project, 184

J
Jaguar X Type Web site, 371
JavaScript
ActionScript versus, 8–9
creating a pop-up window with, 339–341
to open Flash file in sized window, 341
to open link in another window, 340
for opening URL in different size window, 79–80
Jittery.fla file, 199
John Coltrane Web site, 373
John Frieda Web site, 370
Juxt Interactive Web site, 371

K
Key down event, 89
Key object
uses for, 180–181
using, 181–182
Key Press event, 92, 93–94
Key up event, 89
Keyframe command (Insert menu), 68
keyframes. *See also* frames
Actions layer for, 69–70
assigning actions to, 7, 29, 70–71
blank, 66, 68, 83
comments for, 70

converting standard frames to, 68
creating, 68
designation for frames with actions assigned, 69
designation on timeline, 66
labeling, 68–69
removing content from, 68
stop action for, 76
ticker text marquee project, 226–229
uses for, 66, 67
keywords, reserved, 40–41
Killer Sound Web site, 366
KISS acronym for variable names, 147
Kravitz, Lenny, 371

L
labels
animating button labels, 200–203
for keyframes, 68–69
for movie clips, 86–87
reserved keywords, 40–41
swapping for buttons, 198–199
template for navigation bar, 197
Layer command (Insert menu), 70
layers
Actions layer, 69–70
for buttons, 72, 73
Distribute to Layers command (Modify menu), 234
for movie clips, 83
for section movie template, 122
for tooltips, 234, 235
Lenny Kravitz.com site, 371
levels for movies, 121
Library. *See* document Library
Library command (Window menu), 43
light gray (syntax coloring), 39
line numbers in scripts
setting breakpoints using, 290
viewing, 35
Linkage Properties dialog box, 312, 313
linking
creating a text hyperlink, 223–224
creating an e-mail link, 216–217
displaying link in pop-up window, 340
JavaScript to open link in another window, 340
to sounds in document Library, 268–269
to video files from movie clips, 85
List Objects command (Debug menu), 287
List user-defined component type, 133
List Variables command (Debug menu), 288

Load event, 88
loading
    data into movie, 216, 217, 218–219
    movies into base movie,
        123–124, 125
    movies into target movie clip,
        127–129
    movies to hide your design, 138
    soundtracks, 267, 277
    text from external sources,
        215–216
loadMovie action
    hiding your design and, 138
    loading movies into base movie,
        123–124, 125
    loading movies into target movie
        clip, 127–129
    for soundtracks, 267
loadVariables action
    in scrolling text box project, 217,
        218–219
    using, 216
locking a script in the Script
        window, 32
logical operators, 158–159
Logical operators book, 24, 25
loops
    controlling the flow of a movie, 54
    creating ActionScript loops,
        103–107
    creating frame-based loops, 103
    do while loops, 103, 106–107
    execution in single frame required
        for, 103
    frame-based versus
        ActionScript, 102
    for loops, 103, 104–106
    overview, 24
    for preloaders, 304–305
    for sounds, 260
    uses for, 11
    while loops, 103, 106

M

Macintosh computers
    installing items from CD, 358
    requirements for CD-ROM,
        357–358
Macromedia
    Dreamweaver, 348–351, 359
    Fireworks, 360
    Flash Designer and Developer
        Center Web site, 363
    FreeHand, 56, 360
    Showcase Web site, 12, 15, 369
    support Web site, 363–364
    Web site, 12
Madonna Web site, 370

managing movie content, 4–5
mapping your ActionScript, 57–58
marquee, ticker text, 225–230
marqueeComponent.fla file, 230
masks
    converting movie clips to, 60–62
    creating movie clip for, 322
    creating within movie clips,
        322–324
Math object
    random method, 107–109,
        115–116, 161
    round method, 109–110, 115, 161
mathematical operators, 145, 147
menus
    ActionScript for, 12
    context menu of Actions panel, 37
    drop-down menus of action
        groups, 29
    flyout menu project, 204–208
Milla and Partner Web site, 372
Miscellaneous book. See also
        evaluate action
    comment action, 293
    overview, 24
    trace action, 105, 288–289, 290
modem settings for testing
        movies, 301
Modify menu
    Convert to Blank Keyframes
        command, 68
    Convert to Keyframes
        command, 68
    Distribute to Layers
        command, 234
    Document command, 266
    Swap Bitmap command, 102
    Swap Symbol command, 101
modular ActionScript
    for interfaces, 13
    uses for, 14
    using movie clips for, 113
motion trails
    completing the effect, 327–329
    motion tween animation for, 327,
        328, 330
    overview, 326–327, 330
motion tween animation
    for drag-and-drop elements, 238
    for motion trails, 327, 328, 330
mouse chasers
    basic, 315–318
    Flash MX object for, 318–321
    random color for, 319
mouse cursor
    custom, 325–326
    showing and hiding, 324–325
Mouse down event, 89

mouse events. See also events
    available events, 92
    for button symbol, 42
    defined, 9
    Key Press, 93–94
    multiple events for buttons, 92–93
    on action for, 94
    overview, 92–93
    Release, 75
    rollOut, 93
    rollOver, 93
Mouse move event, 89
Mouse object
    custom cursor using, 325–326
    hide method, 324, 325
    overview, 324
    show method, 324, 325
Mouse up event, 89
mouseChaserBegin.fla file, 316
.mov files, 84
Move the Selected Actions Down
        button (Actions panel), 31
Move the Selected Actions Up button
        (Actions panel), 31
moveTo Drawing method, 321
Movie Clip Control book
    onClipEvent action, 87, 88, 89
    overview, 23–24
    setProperty action, 170
    startDrag action, 238, 239, 240
movie clips. See also Flash movies;
        target movie clip
    ActionScript options for, 7–8
    animated clips, creating, 200
    assigning actions to objects,
        87–91
    assigning event handler to, 89
    button to change size and
        opacity, 44–49
    buttons for interactivity, 95–96
    buttons for navigation, 95
    clip events, 9, 87–89
    cloning, 87
    for closing a window, 240
    communicating between
        timelines, 129–130
    converting timeline animation to,
        98–99
    converting to a mask, 60–62
    creating new clips, 82
    custom cursor using, 325–326
    detecting the Flash Player
        version, 345–346
    down arrow, 219–221
    for drag-and-drop windows,
        239–240
    duplicating with
        duplicateMovieClip
        action, 182–183

as effects modules, 113
empty, creating, 320
first frame, 82
importing video files, 84–86
instances, creating, 86
for interactivity, 82–83
introduction clip, creating,
    346–348
labeling, 86–87
last frame, 83, 86
layers for, 83
loading movies into target clip,
    127–129
for mask, 322
mask within, creating, 322–324
mouse chasers using, 315–321
naming, 45
navigating to random frame, 97
nesting symbols in, 74, 97, 99–100
On When Pressed button with,
    195–196
overview, 43, 81–82
preloaders for, 6, 102, 103,
    298–306
returning to first frame, 83, 86
for sound controller project,
    277–280
for starburst backdrop, 330–333
stop action, 46, 76, 82
symbol, 43
target clips, creating, 125–127
target path for, 48, 89–91
testing, 49
ticker text marquee project,
    225–230
with action for target path, 89–91
Movie Control book
    goto action, 47, 77, 83, 86, 103
    on action, 94, 238
    overview, 22
    play action, 76
    stop action, 46, 76, 82
Movie Explorer, debugging
    ActionScripts using,
    293, 294
movies. See Flash movies; movie clips
moving around. See navigating
moving navigation bar project,
    251–255
moving objects
    actions, changing order of, 31
    aligning navigation bar
        buttons, 199
    code in expert mode, 36
    positioning target movie clip, 126
    positioning tooltips, 233–234
    scenes, changing order of, 192
movingNavBar.fla file, 251

MP3 compression for soundtracks,
    258, 263–264
.mpg or .mpeg files, 84
multimedia, ActionScript uses for, 7

N
_name property, 169
named anchors, 189, 193–194
names. See also labels
    for movie clips, 45
    for scenes, 190
    for section movies, 123
    for tooltips, 234
    for variables, 147–148
navigating. See also interactive
        interfaces
    buttons for, 95
    getURL action for, 77–79
    goto action for, 77
    moving navigation bar project,
        251–255
    named anchors for, 189, 193–194
    navigation bar for, 196–199
    On When Press button for,
        194–196
    play action for, 76
    to random frame, 97, 114–117
    to scenes, 189–192
    to scripts in Script window, 31–32
    stop action for, 76
navigation bar
    building, 199
    button template for, 197–199
    converting to flyout menu, 205–208
    label template for, 197
    moving navigation bar project,
        251–255
    suiting document to, 196
    uses for, 196
    vertical, 255
    wider than movie, 254
nesting symbols
    animated movie clip in button
        symbol, 203–204
    bitmaps in movie clips, 100
    child versus parent movie clips,
        131
    defined, 97
    invisible buttons within another
        symbol, 74
    mouse chaser using movie clip,
        315–318
    in movie clips, 74, 97, 99–100
    overview, 97, 99–100
    swapping nested symbols, 101
New Document dialog box, 343, 344
New from Template command (File
        menu), 343

New Symbol command (Insert menu)
    for button templates, 197
    for buttons, 72, 74, 194, 203
    for label templates, 197
    for movie clips, 82, 99, 200, 311,
        323, 327
    for target movie clip, 125
newArray method, 153, 154
n.fuse.gfx Web site, 370
normal mode
    described, 28
    switching to expert mode, 35
NOT operator, 158–159
<not set yet> warning, 47, 90
Number user-defined component
        type, 133
numbers in variable names, 148
numeric data variables
    combining contents of, 144
    defined, 142
numeric literal data variables
    combining contents of, 144
    defined, 142
    string literals versus numeric
        literals, 143

O
Object user-defined component
        type, 132
object-oriented scripting, 7–8
objects. See also properties; specific
        objects
    assigning actions to, 29, 87–91
    centering on HTML page, 349
    displaying list of movie objects
        with Debugger, 287
    duplicating with
        duplicateMovieClip
        action, 182–183
    events for actions, 88–89
    Flash objects and variable
        names, 147
    getting properties, 172–173
    getting property value, 174
    methods in, 25–26
    overview, 7–8, 25–26
    passing variable value to, 150–151
    placing invisible buttons behind,
        74, 75
    properties of, 169
    setting properties, 108, 168–172
    tracking using trace action, 289
on (Release) event handler
    for closing a window, 240
    as default for buttons, 42, 91
    for drag-and-drop window, 239
    for hiding a window, 240
    overview, 75
    for single action, 49

on action
    for tooltips, 238
    using, 94
On When Pressed button
    creating, 194–195
    programming movie clip for,
        195–196
    uses for, 194
onClipEvent action, 87, 88, 89
online merchants, ActionScript uses
        for, 14
onSoundComplete event, 273–274
opacity. *See* _alpha property
Open as Library command (File
        menu), 59, 113, 134
Open dialog box, 41
opening
    action books, 22, 23
    Actions panel, 27
    Bandwidth Profiler, 299
    context menu of Actions panel, 37
    Debugger, 286
    document Library, 59
    Reference panel, 34
    Scene panel, 190
    URLs with getURL action, 77–80
operators
    arithmetic, 145, 147
    logical, 158–159
    post-increment form of
        operand, 146
    precedence for expressions, 146
    pre-increment syntax of
        operand, 145
Operators book
    Arithmetic Operators book, 24
    Comparison Operators book,
        24–25
    Logical operators book, 24, 25
Options menu
    Export as File command, 41
    Find command, 33
    Import from File command, 41
    overview, 35–36
    Preferences command, 39
OR operator, 158–159
order
    changing for actions, 31
    changing for scenes, 192
    precedence of operators for
        expressions, 146
organizational chart project
    beginning the design, 136–137
    creating, 135–139
    creating the ActionScript, 137–139
    described, 135
Orgchart folder on CD-ROM, 136
orgChart.fla file, 136

Over button state, 73

P
Panel Sets, adding panel layout to, 28
Panel Sets command
        (Window menu), 27
panels. *See also* Actions panel
    Designer panel layout, 27
    docking, 28
    Reference panel, 4, 17, 33–35
    saving layout for, 28
    Scene panel, 190
panning a sound, 273
parameter text boxes, using, 30
parent movie clips, 131
parentheses for parameters in code,
        38, 39
passing variable value to other
        objects, 150–151
passwords
    Boolean expression for
        evaluating, 53, 159
    input text box option, 211
    for limiting access to parts of
        movies, 53
    for sites, 53
Paste Frames command
        (Edit menu), 99
Paste in Place command
        (Edit menu), 252
path, target. *See* target path
Pepworks.com site, 370
Pickled the Movie Web site, 370
pictures. *See* graphics; movie clips
Pin Current Script button
        (Actions panel), 32
pinning a script, 32
plain English for planning, 57
planning your ActionScript movie
    controlling the flow, 53–54
    drafting your design, 56
    evolution of an
        ActionScript, 52–54
    example project, 60–62
    extensions, 59
    fleshing out your idea, 58–59
    gathering assets, 58–59
    importance of, 51
    mapping your ActionScript, 57–58
    planning your design, 55–58
    research, 55
    size of movies, 120
    storyboards, 56, 57, 126
play action, 76
PLUGINSPAGE line, 349
pop-up window, creating with
        JavaScript, 339–341

positioning. *See also* moving objects;
        order
    aligning navigation bar
        buttons, 199
    target movie clip, 126
    tooltips, 233–234
Pray Station Web site, 372
precedence of operators for
        expressions, 146
Preferences command (Options
        menu), 39
preferences for syntax coloring, 39
preloaders
    ActionScript for preload loop,
        304–305
    ActionScript for recycling the
        loop, 305
    analyzing movies for bandwidth
        problems, 299–302
    animated, 298–306
    conditional statement for,
        305, 306
    creating, 302–306
    defined, 298, 302
    displaying number of bytes
        loaded, 306
    frame-based loops in, 102, 103
    need for, 298
    progress bar for, 303
    visual effects for, 6
Press event, 92
previewing. *See also* testing
    designs in Flash
        environment, 284
    designs in Web browsers, 285
    sounds, 264, 265
printable frames, 310–311
Printing book, 24
ProFlasher Web site, 365
progress bar for preloader, 303
projects
    animated Flash banner, 352–354
    drawing outside the lines, 60–62
    e-commerce catalog, 312–313
    first ActionScript, 44–49
    Flash slide show, 334–337
    flyout menu, 204–208
    generating random quotes,
        160–164
    interactive animation, 183–187
    moving navigation bar, 251–255
    navigating to random frame,
        114–117
    organizational chart, 135–139
    scrolling text box, 217–223
    sound controller, 274–281
    ticker text marquee, 225–230

properties. *See also* Property
        inspector; setting
        properties
    available properties, 169
    changing by a given value, 172
    experimenting with, 62
    getting for objects, 172–173
    getting value of, 174
    overview, 25
    setting, 46, 108, 168–172
Properties book
    _alpha property, 48
    available properties, 169
    overview, 25
    _xscale property, 49
    _yscale property, 49
Property inspector
    for character options, 212–213
    for custom cursor, 325
    for dynamic text boxes, 211–212
    for input text boxes, 210–211
    for keyframe labels, 69
    for movie clip labels, 86–87
    in moving navigation bar
        project, 253
    for named anchors, 193
    for printable frames, 311
    for rich formatted text, 213–215
    Swap button, 101, 102
    for text hyperlinks, 223–224
Protect from Import option, 138
Publish Settings command (File
        menu), 193, 266
Publish Settings dialog box, 193–194
punctuation, variable names and, 147

Q
_quality property, 169
QuickTime
    linking from movie clips to
        external files, 85
    sound files supported by, 258
    video files supported by, 84
quotation marks (") for string literal
        data, 143

R
random frames, navigating to,
        97, 114–117
random numbers
    creating a variable with value
        equal to, 108–109
    generating with random method
        of Math object,
        107–109, 161
    navigating to random frame,
        114–117
    in random quote generation
        project, 160–164

rounding random values,
        109–110, 161
    setting highest number for, 109
    uses for, 107, 108
Random quote project
    adding a time and accessing the
        array, 161–163
    beginning the project, 160
    finishing the project, 163–164
    generating the random
        number, 161
randomStars.fla file, 331
ReadMe.txt file, 361
red
    flag for labeled keyframes, 69
    for warnings, 40, 47, 89
Reference panel, 4, 17, 33–35
registration point for symbols,
        205, 206
relative mode for target path, 130, 131
Release event, 75, 92. *See also* on
        (Release) event handler
Release Outside event, 92
Remove Frames command (Insert
        menu), 68
removing. *See* deleting
Replace dialog box, 33
replacing text in a script, 33
research, 55
reserved keywords
    list of, 40–41
    variable names and, 147
Reset button for Flash forms, 308
rich formatted text
    creating, 213–215
    HTML tags for, 214
rndFrame function
    calling, 112–113
    creating, 114–116
    using with a button, 116–117
rndQuote.fla file, 160
Rob Allen Photography Web site, 370
rollOut event, 92, 93, 238
rollOver event, 92, 93, 238
rotation, changing direction of, 202
_rotation property, 169
rounding random values, 109–110,
        115, 161

S
Save As command (File menu), 123
Save As dialog box, exporting scripts,
        41
Save Panel Layout command
        (Window menu), 28
saving breakpoints, 291
Scene command
    Insert menu, 190
    Window menu, 190, 191, 192

Scene panel, opening, 190
scenes. *See also* preloaders;
        segments
    adding to a movie, 190
    deleting, 191–192
    duplicating, 192
    naming, 190
    navigating to, 191
    opening Scene panel, 190
    for preloaders, 303
    rearranging order of, 192
    uses for, 189–190
Script pane. *See also* scripts
    described, 21, 32
    expert mode and, 36
    loading text from external
        sources, 215–216
Script window of Actions panel
    navigating to scripts with, 31–32
    pinning a script, 32
scripts. *See also* code; debugging;
        specific actions
    adding actions to, 29
    for animating button labels,
        200–203
    creating in expert mode, 36
    debugging, 283–294
    deleting actions from, 31
    experimenting with, 62
    exporting, 41
    finding and replacing text in, 33
    finding text in, 33
    importing, 41–42
    modular, using movie clips
        for, 113
    navigating to, with Script window,
        31–32
    pinning, 32
    programming a button to change
        size and opacity of image,
        44–49
    viewing line numbers in, 35
ScrollBar component, 249–250
scrolling text box project
    beginning the project, 217–218
    End of Page button, 221
    loading the text document into
        the movie, 218–219
    programming the down arrow,
        219–221
    slider code, 221–222
    up arrow, 223
scrollText.fla file, 217
scrollText.txt files, 217
scrollTick.fla file, 225
searching. *See* finding
sections of movies. *See* scenes;
        segments

security, hiding your designs or techniques, 138
segments. *See also* scenes
    base movie for, 120, 121
    dimensions of, 121, 125
    labels for, 190
    naming, 123
    planning, 120
    template for, 121–123
    uses for, 119–120
semi-colon (;) as end of line identifier, 38, 39
set variable action
    accessing arrays using, 162
    adding to script, 48
    for Color objects, 175
    for color transformation objects, 178
    creating variable equal to random number, 108–109, 114–116
    for Date objects, 245
    for detecting Flash Player version, 345
    resetting a variable, 308
setBGcolor function, 243–245
setMask method, 324
setPan method of Sound object, 273
setProperty action, adding to script, 170
setRGB method of Color object
    described, 175
    for user-customizable interface, 244
    using, 176
setting properties
    by addressing target path, 171–172
    directly, 168–170
    initial state, 46
    to random value, 108
    setProperty action for, 170
    with action for, 168–170
setTransform method of Color object
    described, 175–176
    offset values for, 177
    parameters, 176–177
    percentage values for, 177
    tinting a multi-colored object using, 178–180
setVariable action
    creating arrays, 153
    creating variables, 148–149
setVolume method of Sound object, 272–273
shareware programs, 359
show method of Mouse object, 324, 325
Show Streaming command (View menu), 302

showing. *See* displaying; hiding and showing
Simian Volume 6 Revolt Web site, 372
simpleChaserBegin.fla file, 318
Skip Intro button, 260, 347–348
slide show. *See* Flash slide show project
Slider Control symbol, 275–276
sliders
    for scrolling, 221–222
    for sound controller project, 275–276, 278–279
slideShow.fla file, 334
Sonic Foundry.com site, 366
Sorenson Web site, 368
sound controller project
    adding buttons and sliders, 275–277
    beginning the project, 275
    evaluating slider position, 279
    initial values for sliders, 278–279
    overview, 274
    programming the movie clip, 277–280
Sound Designer II format, 258
sound file formats, 258
Sound object
    attaching a sound, 269–270, 276, 277
    changing volume for sound, 272–273
    creating an instance, 268
    in document Library, attaching, 269–270
    in document Library, linkage for, 268–269
    panning a sound, 273
    sound controller project, 274–281
    starting a sound, 270–271
    stopping a sound, 271–272
    triggering an event at sound completion, 273–274
    uses for, 6, 268
Sound only QuickTime Movie format, 258
Sound Properties dialog box, 263–264, 265
Sound Shopper.com site, 367
Sound Strike Web site, 367
_soundbuftime property, 169
Soundcontroller folder on CD-ROM, 274
soundtracks
    adding to timeline, 257–258
    attaching, 269–270, 276, 277
    custom effects, 260–262
    effects, 259
    export settings, 263–265
    file formats supported, 258

importing for video files, 85
importing sounds, 258–260
loading into your design, 267, 277
MP3 compression for, 258, 263–264
in separate movie, 258, 266–267
size of file for, 258
sound controller project, 274–281
Speech compression for, 264–265
streaming sound, 260
Web sites, 366–367
spaces, variable names and, 148
Speech compression for soundtracks, 264–265
starburst backdrop
    creating the stars, 332–333
    example file for, 331
    initializing the movie clip, 332
    modifying the movie, 333
    overview, 330–331
start method of Sound object, 270–271
startDrag action, 238, 239, 240
sticky notes, for planning your ActionScript, 58
stop action, 46, 76, 82
stop method of Sound object, 271–272
storyboards
    creating, 56, 57
    usefulness of, 126
Streaming Graph command (View menu), 299
streaming sound, 260
string data variables, 142, 143
String user-defined component type, 133
strings, 25. *See also* text
submarine animation project, 183–187
submarine.fla file, 183
Submit button for Flash forms
    CGI script for HTML mail forwarding, 308–309
    programming the button, 309–310
Sun AU sound format, 258
Swap Bitmap command (Modify menu), 102
Swap Bitmap dialog box, 102
Swap Symbol command (Modify menu), 101
Swap Symbol dialog box, 101
swapping nested bitmaps, 100, 101–102
SWF (Small Web File)
    exporting from FreeHand, 56
    size of, 4, 119
SWfx (WildForm), on CD-ROM, 360
Swift 3D, on CD-ROM, 360

Swish Web site, 368
symbols. *See also* converting; Create
    New Symbol dialog box;
    nesting symbols; *specific
    types*
    in document Library, 43–44
    registration point for, 205, 206
    types of, 42–43
syntax coloring, 37, 39
syntax of actions, finding in Reference
    panel, 4
System 7 Sounds format, 258
system requirements for CD-ROM,
    357–358

T

target movie clip
    aligning for proper loading, 126
    communicating between
        timelines, 129–130
    creating, 125–127
    loading movies into, 127–129
    for organizational chart, 136, 137
    positioning, 126
target path
    absolute mode, 130, 131
    alias, 132
    defined, 9
    overview, 9–10
    relative mode, 130, 131
    setting properties by addressing,
        171–172
    specifying for movie clips, 48,
        89–91, 128
Target Path dialog box, 131
_target property, 169
technical support for CD-ROM, 361
templates
    for banner ads, 343, 344
    button templates, 197–198
    for documents with named
        anchors, 193–194
    label template for navigation
        bar, 197
    for section movies, 121–123
Test Movie command (Control menu),
    49, 163
testing
    after completing milestones, 128
    analyzing movies for bandwidth
        problems, 299–302
    designs in Flash environment, 284
    designs in Web browsers, 285
    modem settings for testing
        movies, 301
    movie clips, 49, 163
    sounds, 264, 265

text. *See also* dynamic text boxes
    creating data in word
        processor, 216
    dynamic text boxes, creating,
        211–212
    e-mail links, creating, 216–217
    finding and replacing in a
        script, 33
    finding in a script, 33
    hyperlinks, 223–224
    hyperlinks, creating, 223–224
    input text boxes, creating,
        210–211
    loading from external sources,
        215–216
    populating dynamic text boxes
        with array elements,
        224–225
    rich formatted text, creating,
        213–215
    scrolling text box project, 217–223
    setting character options,
        212–213
    ticker text marquee project,
        225–230
text boxes. *See* dynamic text boxes;
        input text boxes
text data variables. *See* string data
        variables
text objects, 25. *See also* text
TextField object, 6
Thrash, Dox, 371
ticker text marquee project, 225–230
time
    displaying current time, 247–249
    retrieving from host
        computer, 248
timelines
    adding comments to
        keyframes, 70
    assigning actions to keyframes,
        70–71
    communicating between, 129–130
    controlling, 66–70
    converting animation to movie
        clip, 98–99
    creating Actions layer for, 69–70
    creating buttons, 72–75
    navigating with ActionScript,
        76–80
    need for, 65
    overview, 9
    soundtrack in, 257–258
    typical timeline, 67
    working with frames, 66–69
timer component, 162, 203

tooltips
    creating, 232–233
    creating functions for, 235–237
    example file on CD-ROM, 238
    layers for, 234, 235
    naming, 234
    positioning, 233–234
    programming buttons for, 237–238
    showing and hiding, 236–237
    uses for, 231–232
toolTips.fla file, 238
Toon Boom Studio Web site, 368
_totalFrames property, 169
trace action
    breakpoints with, 290
    for loops with, 105
    tracking variables or objects
        using, 289
    uses for, 288–289
trial versions of programs, 359
troubleshooting the CD-ROM,
    360–361
TurtleShell.com site, 365
Tweened.com site, 372

U

UI components. *See* components
Undo command (Edit menu), 42
undoing, 42
Unload event, 89
unloading movies, 123, 124–125, 267
unloadMovie action,
    123, 124–125, 267
up arrow for scrolling, 223
Up button state, 73
Up constant, 184
_url property, 169
URLs. *See also* Web sites
    creating a text hyperlink, 223–224
    creating an e-mail link, 216–217
    getURL action, 77–80, 339, 340,
        347, 348
    for loadVariables action, 216
    researching competitor URLs, 55
User Defined Functions book
    call function action, 112–113,
        116, 237, 243
    function action,
        110–111, 236, 243
    overview, 24
    rndFrame action, 114–117
user-customizable interface
    creating, 241
    creating the function for,
        243–245
    programming the buttons,
        242–243

user-defined components
  creating instances of, 134
  creating new components,
    132–134
  defined, 132
  downloading, 135
  storing in document Library,
    134–135
  types of, 132–133
  using, 134–135

V

`var` action, 149
`The variable name you have
  entered...` message,
    40, 148
variables
  arrays versus, 151–152
  Boolean data, 142
  combining array elements in, 152
  combining contents of,
    143–144, 150
  comparing multiple values to an
    array, 151–152
  declaring, 148–150
  displaying list using
    Debugger, 288
  expressions in, 144–146
  local, creating, 149–150
  naming, 147–148
  numeric data, 142
  numeric literal data, 142
  passing value to other objects,
    150–151
  reserved keywords and
    commands, 40–41, 147
  resetting, 308
  setting value equal to two other
    variables, 151
  string data, 142, 143–144
  tracking using `trace` action, 289
  types of, 142
  uses for, 5, 141
  with value equal to random
    number, 108–109, 114
  watching with Debugger, 286–287
Variables book. *See also* `set
      variable` action
  overview, 24
  `setVariable` action, 148–149, 153
  `var` action, 149
  `with` action, 89–91, 129–130, 168

Velocity Studio Web site, 371
vertical navigation bar, 255
video files
  embedding, 84, 85
  importing into movie clips, 84–86
  linking from movie clips, 85
  types of, 84
View menu
  Bandwidth Profiler command, 299
  Go To command, 191
  Show Streaming command, 302
  Streaming Graph command, 299
viewing. *See* displaying; hiding and
    showing
Virtual FX Web site, 365
`_visible` property, 169
visual effects, for preloaders, 6
visual mind map, 58
volume for sound, changing, 272–273

W

warnings. *See* error messages and
    warnings
WAV sound format, 258
Web browsers
  JavaScript to open link in another
    window, 340
  previewing designs in, 285
Web Monkey Web site, 365
Web site designers
  orientation of, 3
  uses for ActionScript, 4–7
Web site elements
  animated preloader, 298–306
  e-commerce catalog project,
    312–313
  Flash forms, 206–210
  printable frames, 310–311
Web sites
  for extensions, 59, 135
  Flash Deployment Kit, 346
  Flash resources, 363–366
  Flash tutorial sites, 59
  for inspiration, 369–373
  Macromedia, 12
  Macromedia Showcase,
    12, 15, 369
  researching, 55
  for sounds and music, 366–367
  for third-party applications,
    367–368
  for user-defined components, 135

We're Here Forums Web site, 366
while loops, 103, 106
`_width` property, 169
WildForm SWfx
  on CD-ROM, 360
  Web site, 368
Wiley Publishing Customer Care, 361
Wiley Publishing Customer
    Service, 361
Window menu
  Actions command, 27
  Common Libraries command, 113
  Library command, 43
  Panel Sets command, 27
  Save Panel Layout command, 28
  Scene command, 190, 191, 192
windows
  creating a pop-up window with
    JavaScript, 339–341
  drag-and-drop, 239–240
  JavaScript to open Flash file in
    sized window, 341
  JavaScript to open link in another
    window, 340
  movie clip for closing, 240
Windows computers
  installing items from CD, 358
  requirements for CD-ROM, 357
`with` action
  for changing object
    properties, 168
  for communicating between
    timelines, 129–130
  for target path of movie clips,
    89–91
.wmv files, 84
word processor
  creating array data in, 154, 160
  creating text data in, 216

X

`_x` property, 169
`_xmouse` property, 169
`_xscale` property, 49, 169

Y

`_y` property, 169
`_ymouse` property, 169
`_yscale` property, 49, 169

Wiley Publishing, Inc.
End-User License Agreement